A Predictable Tragedy

A Predictable Tragedy

Robert Mugabe and the Collapse of Zimbabwe

Daniel Compagnon

PENN

UNIVERSITY OF PENNSYLVANIA PRESS

PHILADELPHIA

Published by
University of Pennsylvania Press
Philadelphia, Pennsylvania 19104-4112

Printed in the United States of America on acid-free paper
10 9 8 7 6 5 4 3 2 1

Library of Congress Cataloging-in-Publication Data

Compagnon, Daniel.
  A Predictable Tragedy: Robert Mugabe and the collapse of Zimbabwe / Daniel Compagnon.
    p.   cm.
  Includes bibliographical references and index.
  ISBN 978-0-8122-4267-6 (hardcover : alk. paper)
    1. Zimbabwe—Politics and government—1980–   2. Zimbabwe—Social conditions—1980–
3. Zimbabwe—Economic conditions—1980–   4. Mugabe, Robert, 1924–   I. Title.
DT2996.C66   2010
968.9105'1092—dc   2010004561

Contents

Introduction

When the Zimbabwean flag was raised officially in the early hours of 18 April 1980, symbolizing the dawn of a new era and the end of a bitter liberation war, who could have imagined then that the crowds cheering their hero—Robert Mugabe—would come to hate him some thirty years later after he led them to starvation, ruin, and anarchy? Who would have expected Zimbabwe to become the "sick man" of southern Africa, a security concern for its neighbors, and an irritant in the mind of progressive opinion leaders such as former anti-apartheid lead activist and Nobel Peace Prize winner archbishop Desmond Tutu, who would, in 2008, call for Mugabe's forced removal from power? As we shall see, this disaster should not have come as a complete surprise since there were, from the beginning, many worrying signs of Mugabe's thirst for power, his recklessness, and his lack of concern for the well-being of his fellow countrymen and women, as well as the greed and brutality of his lieutenants in his party, the Zimbabwe African National Union-Patriotic Front (ZANU-PF).[1]

Behind the suffering of Zimbabweans today are a series of political myths forged by the new regime and outsiders who, until recently, supported Mugabe's government unconditionally. One of the most enduring was the myth of a democratic multiracial Zimbabwe led by an urbane, educated politician—the mirror image of the bloodthirsty guerrilla leader portrayed in the Western press in the 1970s. Everyone marveled how this bright and magnanimous statesman extended political pardons not only to his rivals in the Zimbabwe African People's Union (ZAPU) but also to former Rhodesian foes. Even the cynical massacre of thousands of civilians in the early 1980s in Matabeleland in western and southwestern Zimbabwe—awareness of which the Zimbabwean government was able to suppress—did not break the charm.[2] Rhodesian leader Ian Smith's illegal white minority regime was despicable on many counts, but many ordinary black people in Zimbabwe realized years ago that Mugabe was no lesser evil, especially as the memories of racial discrimination withered away and social conditions worsened dramatically.[3] However, activists and intellectuals who had opposed Smith's regime and risked death or prison wanted desperately to believe that Mugabe was nothing but good news. Peace and salvation were coming at last and "majority rule" was to set Zimbabwe on the road to prosperity. Openly criticizing the ruling party was perceived for long as siding with the enemy—that is, with imperialism and the apartheid regime in South Africa. Even political opponents failed to analyze the nature of ZANU-PF domination and were repeatedly outmaneuvered by Mugabe.

Many Western journalists, diplomats, political analysts, and researchers familiar with the situation on the ground chose to disregard some inconvenient facts and picked the stories they wanted to believe in. Academics either remained silent or took for granted the Zimbabwean government's stance, for reasons best known to them.[4] The belief that ZANU's liberation war in the 1970s was a legitimate and noble cause somehow blunted the analytical edge of scholarship when it came to Mugabe's power techniques. Issues of widespread corruption and political murder remained taboo and many continued to hail Mugabe as Africa's liberation icon—although there were a few exceptions.[5] Hence, reports produced by human rights nongovernmental organizations (NGOs) over the years (in particular the Catholic Commission for Justice and Peace (CCJP)/Legal Resources Foundation (LRF) report on the Matabeleland massacres, which was met with a deafening silence by the same academics when first released in 1997) serve better to understand the nature of the ZANU-PF regime than most academic journals and books. It would require an entirely different book to fully explore the root causes and the extent of self-deception in Western academic and political circles on the nature of Mugabe's regime. Obviously, such bias prevented a sound understanding of the situation in Zimbabwe for more than two decades.

In the creation of this ideological smokescreen, the political mythology underlying the liberation war's official history played a pivotal role. Mugabe and other ZANU-PF leaders portrayed themselves as liberators who had given birth to modern Zimbabwe. Being entrusted with the task of nation building and eliminating the remnants of the settler state suffices to legitimize the ruling party's never-ending grip on state power.[6] Consequently, black Zimbabweans have to feel indebted forever to ruling party leaders for the "freedom" the nation has enjoyed since 1980. In this thoroughly reconstructed history, the contribution of ZAPU and other forces is minimized or blatantly ignored, and the role of the British government in sponsoring the Lancaster House agreement is downplayed. The ruling party ZANU-PF propagated the fiction that the Zimbabwe African National Liberation Army (ZANLA), its military arm, won the war on the battlefield and therefore the right to rule.

The war hero cult played an important part in this discourse. Former guerrillas—and many less genuine freedom fighters but true ZANU "big men"—were granted the official status of national and provincial heroes, and burial ceremonies provided recurrent occasions to rehearse the ruling party's contribution.[7] However, through the years, the granting of this status—with the pension accruing to the family—was increasingly perceived as tainted by political favoritism. Known nationalist leaders outside the ruling party, such as the late Ndabaningi Sithole (the first ZANU president) and the late Enoch Dumbutshena—repeatedly labeled "traitors" by government propaganda—were denied a burial in the national Heroes' Acre. On the contrary, Mugabe's henchmen in the first decade of the twenty-first century (such as Border Gezi or Hitler Hunzvi), who had a limited or nonexistent liberation war record, were buried there, ostensibly rewarded for their contribution to the "Third Chimurenga" (the regime's code name for violent farm invasions and subsequent political repression since 2000).

Beyond reward and retribution, this policy betrays a self-serving appropriation and political manipulation of the country's history. The nationalist posture remained to this date a powerful political resource for Mugabe and ZANU-PF, both locally and on the international scene, and the vindictive nationalist discourse on stolen land, fallen heroes, and the party's outstanding contribution to "liberation" was recycled at every election after 1980. Not only was this militant discourse a means to mobilize supporters and silence critics but it provided a convenient excuse to sideline embarrassing issues such as poverty alleviation and bad governance. To a large extent, the political developments unraveling since February 2000 constitute the culmination of this exhausted strategy.

Admittedly there were good enough reasons in the early 1980s for most observers to disregard ZANU-PF's autocratic tendencies. The regime boasted some early successes in the economic and social realm: growth in education and health services, and an initial increase of workers' wages—a gain already offset by inflation as early as 1983.[8] However, these policies were obviously not financially sustainable without a constant inflow of foreign aid, and the initial trend toward poverty alleviation and economic restructuring was reversed in the mid-1980s. While the Western and African Left hailed the so-called Zimbabwean "revolution" in the 1980s and passionately debated its socialist identity and level of achievements, it paid little attention to the true nature of the regime:

the retrogressive and authoritarian nature of the one-party state project and the selfish accumulation drive hidden behind the state's control of the economy.[9] The Marxist-Leninist rhetoric of the early years served handily to deceive the radical intellectuals, and many rallied behind ZANU-PF in want of better options.

However, rhetoric aside, the government's economic policy did not depart significantly from the interventionist policies of the Unilateral Declaration of Independence (UDI) period.[10] Mugabe and many of his associates saw Marxist-Leninist discourse as an idiom of power: they used it initially as a weapon in the guerrilla movement's "struggle within the struggle," and they retained it as a useful political tool when in control of the state. Therefore, Mugabe probably did not believe more in socialism than in democracy or human rights—or black empowerment for that matter.[11] These discourses had essentially a legitimization purpose.

Mugabe's agenda of monopolizing power and controlling resources was partly derailed by adverse circumstances, internal squabbles, and more decisively by the resilience of the people in keeping some democratic spaces open: at the university, in the media, in the trade union movement, in the judiciary, and by the Movement for Democratic Change (MDC), which formed a frontal challenge to ZANU-PF rule. The deep nature of Mugabe's regime pointed at the surface at least a decade earlier when the police violently quelled students and workers' protests.[12] The extensive use of repressive legal instruments originally created by the white settler state, such as the Law and Order Maintenance Act and the state of emergency, revealed the remarkable continuity in the security sector from the Rhodesian Front (RF) to ZANU-PF. Nevertheless, it took another ten years for most observers to understand the authoritarian nature of Mugabe's regime and its contempt for the rule of law. The one-party state mentality prevailed in daily politics and ZANU-PF showed no hesitation to use violence against its opponents when it felt threatened. The relative pluralism of the press in the 1990s—after an era of tight government control in the 1980s—and the seemingly independent and effective court system gave civil society at large, and political activists more specifically, a false sense of strength and security until mid-2000. Almost all opponents and media—reading from columns in the local press between 1994 and late 1999—underestimated Mugabe's recklessness and cynicism. According to the dominant view, in the mid-1990s—at least in domestic media and the diplomatic milieu—democratization was under way, and a "younger," "technocratic," "reformist" ZANU was willing to promote this agenda when conditions became more conducive—meaning when Mugabe retired. This was more wishful thinking than insightful vision, as later years demonstrated. With the food riots, the mass strikes, and the war in the Democratic Republic of the Congo (DRC), 1998 was certainly a turning point. However, for most observers only the violence associated with the farm invasions and the 2000 parliamentary elections was a true eye-opener. Many former ZANU-PF sympathizers then began to criticize Mugabe openly and asked the obvious question: What went wrong?

For analysts on the radical left, Mugabe had sold his soul to international capital when the government adopted the Economic Structural Adjustment Program (ESAP) in the early 1990s;[13] thus, the land reform was only a political gimmick to divert the workers' attention from the main struggle.[14] For some others, the nationalist project was derailed by Mugabe's transformation into a mad autocrat.[15] Further research will perhaps support the view that a selfish ruling class hijacked the nationalist project. Brian Raftopoulos, a veteran social scientist and a committed civil society activist, produced some promising material toward this end.[16] However, most of the literature published on the Zimbabwean crisis to date—with a strong contingent of books authored by foreign journalists formerly posted in Harare[17]—consists in chronological accounts of the major developments since February 2000. In these works there is little in-depth analysis offered of the processes leading to the current disaster. The reckless survival politics that plunged the country into ruin and desperation cannot be comprehended without a better understanding of Mugabe's political trajectory and that of his party since independence. Instead of betraying their original project—purportedly the liberation of the country and empowerment of the masses, as is often alleged, the ruling party's leaders remained faithful to their true albeit hidden ambition.

Their behavior since 2000 sheds a crude light on the nature of their domination, which is in essence autocratic and neopatrimonial. Derived from Max Weber's typology of the forms of political domination, the concept of neopatrimonialism describes political systems with a certain degree of institutional development, yet with personalized power relations and a trend toward systematic private appropriation of public money by the rulers.[18] Corruption, contempt for the rule of law, and abuse of state power are syndromes of neopatrimonial rule. Among African states, Zimbabwe was in 1980 one of the least patrimonialized—thanks to the relative sophistication of the Rhodesian state—but it changed radically through twenty-five years of ZANU-PF rule. An entire elite connected to ZANU-PF benefited from Mugabe's tenure in power and accumulated personal wealth at the expense of the nation and its economy, and still today a subtle blend of intimidation and patronage ensures its loyalty. However, the ruling party has long ceased to function as a collective decision-making body, if it ever did, and Mugabe's ultimate authority cannot be challenged with impunity—a complex situation best captured by the notion of personal rule.[19]

Zimbabwe's top leader's career therefore deserves close attention, starting with his rise to political prominence in the guerrilla war and culminating in his dominance of state politics for more than twenty years. Although this book's ambition is not to offer a biography of the Zimbabwean president, his personality and personal history deserve some scrutiny. Since 2000, Mugabe has stubbornly opposed any suggestion of political reform or resignation and is likely to do so to his death. He is a man of consuming ambition who worked very hard to reach his top position. He entertains a superiority complex and belittles other contenders for power—especially those without higher education—including aspiring successors from his own party. People who have met him in private acknowledge his brilliant mind, his sober and even Spartan way of life, and his intellectual sophistication backed by several university degrees. But behind this posture of the modest and seemingly competent statesman there is another Mugabe and a more sinister character: reckless, extremely cunning, and tactically patient, a born political animal. A former guerrilla commander who contributed to Mugabe's ascent to ZANU's leadership in the camps admitted having nurtured a political monster: "He was arrogant, paranoid, secretive and only interested in power."[20] A tormented psyche could explain his strange antics and any amateur psychiatrist would be tempted to speculate on possible childhood traumas.[21] This psychosis of power commonly plagues African political systems.[22] However, a psychological line of explanation would not lead us very far in understanding Mugabe's thirst for power and his cunning ability to remain in control of the state. Mugabe's mind is clearly behind the social and economic devastation in today's Zimbabwe, but this is the work of a cold-blooded, rational, political entrepreneur. Resorting to violence, for instance, is part of a shrewd calculation and the focus is always on specific targets: it is not the product of his emotions. For example, he is not known for taking pleasure in witnessing torture and killings, rather the opposite. He is no Idi Amin Dada or Macias Nguema.

In many ways the eventual subjugation of the Zimbabwean society, the violent suppression of any dissenting voice, and the complete collapse of the economy were virtually contained in Mugabe's political enterprise from the beginning. What needs to be clarified is not "What went wrong?" but rather "Why did it take so long to go obviously wrong?" In other words, we need to analyze Zimbabwe's society and social institutions' resistance to authoritarian incorporation, and the national economy's ability to countenance the predatory tendencies of the benefactors of state patronage for nearly two decades.

This book, therefore, is neither a detailed history of Zimbabwe since independence nor a theoretical essay on African politics, although we do use a few political science concepts. Nor is it a detailed chronology of political developments in Zimbabwe since 2000, and we make no pretense of addressing all dimensions of a complex crisis that has engulfed the whole Zimbabwean society. Our aim is to contribute to a better understanding of the process of institutional decay and growing authoritarianism generated by Mugabe's long tenure of power, in a country that had high potential in 1980. There was no curse, no Western plot against Black nationalism and Mugabe himself as alleged by the regime's propaganda, no fatal destiny that took Zimbabwe into the league of derelict, bankrupt, postcolonial African autocracies. For those having hope in Africa's future it is important to find out how and why this man-made disaster became reality. It is important also to set the record straight about the responsibilities of fellow African and non-African leaders who let Mugabe have his ways and taint the image of the continent through his actions.

Chapter 1

Authoritarian Control of the Political Arena

Contrary to a view commonly held in the media and by some observers—that there was a sudden turn of events in 2000, supposedly reversing a previous trend toward democratization—the political system set in place at independence and throughout the 1980s was authoritarian in essence. For ZANU-PF leaders, the institutions, values, and procedures of parliamentary democracy were alien and a potential impediment to their objective of fully controlling the postcolonial state—something hardly disguised by the claim to adhere to "socialism." Adopting an Eastern European Communist-style one-party state guaranteed absolute control over both state and society by those entitled to it—so they thought—by right of conquest. Power was theirs because they had won the "struggle" and the "struggle within the struggle." In spite of profound changes on the international scene since 1989, and unlike many other authoritarian regimes in Africa, ZANU-PF has retained the abusive vocabulary and the power techniques of former Communist parties and upheld the one-party-state mentality. The state capture of the economy and the bullying tactics used against the media, civic organizations, and judiciary are addressed in subsequent chapters. We will focus first on the political arena, and more precisely on the party system and the electoral process.

This drive for control has been the real political project of ZANU-PF's leaders, and within the ruling party Mugabe has always assumed prominence. His relations with his lieutenants bear similarities to those between a Mafia supreme boss and members of his crime syndicate. The boss has to quell dissent without mercy—including from "family" members—because the moment the president's authority is directly challenged he becomes vulnerable, exposed to an insider coup. For the sake of survival in power, control is a round-the-clock business. From the outset there were two arenas that Mugabe and his close associates needed to dominate: first, the ruling party (where power contenders could emerge from within the nationalist ranks), and, second, interparty politics (to prevent a credible opposition from disputing ZANU-PF's claim of an "inherent right" to rule). Although this was achieved in part using calculated violence, which is assessed in Chapter 2, the manipulation of the electoral process was the main conduit of ZANU-PF's monopolization of power.

Controlling ZANU-PF

To establish himself securely at the top of the power structure, Mugabe needed to maintain a constant grip on the ruling party. He transformed a liberation front riddled with tribal factionalism in the mid-1970s into an efficient political machine that took over power in 1980. Furthermore, Mugabe's personal drive for absolute power required the careful monitoring of party dynamics. As in other African autocracies, the personal ruler did not suppress factionalism but used the faction leaders' ambitions to his benefit. At one time posing as a benevolent referee above opposite camps, at another leading one coalition against would-be dissidents, Mugabe consolidated his authority over the years, effectively preventing an anti-Mugabe coalition from forming within the party. Free speech and open debate became increasingly rare in spite of the pretense of collective decision-making; although ZANU-PF Politburo and Central Committee meetings and party congresses and conferences continue to receive extensive coverage in the government press, the real decisions on important issues have always been Mugabe's preserve. When troublemakers appeared to be a potential threat, they were ruthlessly eliminated and punished—and some murdered. Mugabe's control over the party apparatus has endured in spite of the scale of the current national crisis, which is largely of the president's own making and is used as a power management tool. From this perspective, the so-called "succession" debate that has been going on since the mid-1990s, and with more intensity since 2002, is largely futile. Recurrent outsider speculations that a "reformist wing" within ZANU-PF could force Mugabe into retirement was not only wishful thinking but demonstrated a lack of understanding of his lifelong enterprise.

"Struggles Within the Struggle"

Factionalism was always the curse of African nationalism in Southern Rhodesia. There has been much debate about the nature of this "struggle within the struggle,"[1] especially among scholars of various neo-Marxist schools, many of whom assumed that ZANU was a genuine revolutionary movement. Thus they read the factional struggle as a confrontation between "radicals" and "reformists." David Moore, for example, identifies ideological cleavages within the nationalist camp that led to the elimination of the radical elements by the more conservative leadership of both ZANU and ZAPU.[2] Others, such as André Astrow, maintain that it was instead a classic nationalist movement fighting for genuine decolonization and equal rights for native Zimbabweans. In his view, the entire leadership of these movements being petit bourgeois by nature, factional struggle had a generational dimension, with younger leaders aspiring to a faster promotion.[3] Non-Marxist analysts such as Masipula Sithole take into account the tribal dimension of the successive purges that marred liberation-front politics during the liberation war. It is still taboo among Western academics to mention the influence of tribal affiliations in Zimbabwean politics. They usually point out (1) that regional/tribal identities are fabrications of Christian missionaries and colonial power, hence a relatively recent social construct;[4] (2) that there have always been minority elements of Shona speakers in Ndebele-led ZAPU and Ndebele speakers in Shona-led ZANU, while ZAPU leader Joshua Nkomo was from the Kalanga, a minority group; and (3) that often other motives could explain what was portrayed as tribal hostility.[5] However, the Shona/Ndebele antagonism was a major factor in the wartime rivalry between ZANU and ZAPU and contributed to the collapse of the Zimbabwe People's Army (ZIPA).[6] Ethnic hatred was also a component in the early 1980s annihilation of ZAPU, if not the principal motive (when state security minister Emmerson Mnangagwa called the Ndebele "cockroaches," it did not sound like a very sophisticated Marxist concept, even taking into account Lenin's own propensity for abusing his opponents).

In today's Zimbabwean politics, the respective share of the main Shona groupings (Manyika, Karanga, Zezuru) in government appointments is widely commented on among the people. As elsewhere in Africa, Zimbabwean tribalism is a modern phenomenon rather than a "tradition," a set of "fabricated" identities marshaled by politicians to advance their careers. The rift within the opposition MDC in 2004–5 that led to its breaking into two rival parties had a component of Shona/Ndebele antagonism (see Chapter 3). However, the "struggle within the struggle" in the 1970s was primarily a cutthroat fight for power between political entrepreneurs whose ideological differences were often very thin. The tactical use of ideological discourse to support one's personal ambitions, and, conversely, ritual claims that one's opponent is a tribalist, has remained typical of African politics in Zimbabwe. Obviously, Mugabe did not create factionalism in the liberation struggle, but he learned how to make good use of it to gain control of ZANU.

There had been a series of murders of ZAPU and ZANU leaders, some of which were undoubtedly the work of Rhodesian government intelligence. However, in most cases factional strife was to blame. ZAPU in exile also was weakened by severe infighting in 1970–71,[7] and the assassinations of Jason Z. Moyo in early 1977 and that of Alfred Mangena in mid-1978 are commonly attributed to ZAPU insiders.[8] When Herbert Wiltshire Chitepo, national chairman and leader of ZANU's external supreme council (Dare re Chimurenga) and its then rising political star, was killed in a bomb blast on 18 March 1975, many in Zambia suspected an inside job by a group of Karanga guerrilla commanders led by Josiah Tongogara, who resented the Manyikas' alleged domination of the front's civilian leadership.[9] In November–December 1974, a group of Manyika guerrillas led by Thomas Nhari had rebelled and attempted to abduct Tongogara (they kidnapped his wife instead). Factionalism had degenerated into feuding. Although Chitepo had approved Tongogara's crushing of the rebels and chaired the hurried treason trials and summary executions (including those of the other two Manyikas in the executive),[10] the Karanga elements in Dare re Chimurenga still believed he was behind the Nhari group.[11] The Zambian president, Kenneth Kaunda, set up an international commission of inquiry sanctioned by the Organization of African Unity (OAU), the report of which, published in March 1976, established that the ZANU high command under Tongogara's chairmanship had authorized Chitepo's murder two days before he was killed.[12] All members of the ZANU leadership in Zambia were detained—allegedly tortured—and the guerrilla camps closed down. Of course, the current ruling party's official line to date is very different. ZANU-PF fellow traveler David Martin, who befriended Tongogara and later benefited widely from Mugabe's patronage, wrote a book to explain that Chitepo was killed because Rhodesia's Ian Smith, South Africa's John Vorster, and Zambia's Kenneth Kaunda saw him as an obstacle to their exercise in détente.[13]

An active member of the nationalist movement since the inception of the National Democratic Party (NDP) in 1960, Mugabe had displayed some oratory skills, but until 1974 he was still only one among others in the group of nationalist leaders. When ZANU split from ZAPU in August 1963, Mugabe became secretary general of the new organization and was a potential contender for the top position at the ZANU congress in

1964 (he dropped his candidacy knowing he would not win against the more senior and better known Ndabaningi Sithole).[14] Mugabe and other ZANU leaders claimed in November 1974 that Sithole had been deposed,[15] while most of the party Central Committee was still in detention in Rhodesia, and as the new ZANU president he led a delegation to Lusaka. However, the leaders of the Front-Line States refused to condone the coup and demanded that Sithole be reinstated. In Salisbury in the first quarter of 1975, Mugabe had perhaps nothing to do directly with the plot against Chitepo. Yet Masipula Sithole labeled the Dare re Chimurenga members imprisoned in Lusaka "Mugabe's faction,"[16] alluding to possible complicity. Chitepo had refused to condone the Mugabe prison coup and was clearly an obstacle to the latter's ambitions. Before escaping to Mozambique, Mugabe released a statement supporting the imprisoned Dare re Chimurenga members and blaming Kaunda for complicity—that is, with Smith's agents—in Chitepo's assassination. One possibility is that Chitepo's elimination and Mugabe's subsequent exfiltration were part of the same plot to take over ZANU. Alternatively, there could be no plot: such factional strife effectively created a power vacuum in ZANU that Mugabe skillfully exploited.

When Mugabe made his escape to the Mozambican border in April 1975, he intended to build a following in the refugee camps. However, Mozambique's president Samora Machel, who believed that a genuine leader should emerge from the guerrilla ranks—as he himself had done within FRELIMO (the Mozambique Liberation Front)—did not trust Mugabe and let him sit at the border for three months. When Mugabe secretly entered the country, he was put under house arrest for several months in Quelimane, away from the camps. In October 1975, guerrillas in Tanzania, who vehemently denounced African National Council leader Abel Muzorewa, Sithole, and ZAPU breakaway faction leader James Chikerema's "insatiable lust for power," endorsed Mugabe as a compromise leader for a united nationalist movement. Apparently the young commanders were induced to choose him by the then imprisoned Dare re Chimurenga members (including Tongogara),[17] in the context of ZIPA's formation—the policy imposed by the Front-Line States leaders to quell the ZANU/ZAPU rivalry and the feuding among nationalists. Military operations in Rhodesia did resume in January 1976, and Samora Machel encouraged the guerrilla commanders in Mozambique to "pick" a new political head for ZANU to balance the ZAPU leadership within ZIPA (the latter being closer to Kaunda). Although Machel preferred Tongogara, still in the custody of the Zambian police, guerrilla commanders posing as leftists chose to support Mugabe, the last member of the old ZANU leadership who sounded committed to their radical line.[18] Then Mugabe negotiated with the Front-Line States

leaders the release of the jailed Dare re Chimurenga members in October 1976 as a condition for attending a peace conference.[19] Mugabe had
been forced to form a loose alliance with Joshua Nkomo—the Patriotic
Front—in order to negotiate with the Rhodesian delegation at the
Geneva conference.[20] However, and whatever he had to concede,
Mugabe remained opposed to "unity" and he was confident that in spite
of ZIPRA's being better trained and more disciplined he could take the
advantage in the field through political mobilization (see Chapter 2 on
ZANLA techniques).[21] He did not want to come second to Nkomo—or
anybody else for that matter—in a liberated Zimbabwe. When the Soviet
Union demanded that he recognize Nkomo as the leader as a condition
for the delivery of modern weaponry, Mugabe refused bluntly and
turned to the Chinese instead.

Mugabe came back from Geneva with a new international aura and
full backing from the Front-Line States to stir up the war. In order to
strengthen his grip on the organization, he persuaded Machel to neu-
tralize a group of Chinese-trained guerrilla cadres called *vashandi*
("workers"), led by Wilfred Mhanda (who used the name Dzinashe
Machingura in the war), a former ZANLA commander and political
commissar and formally third in the united ZIPA command.[22] They had
opposed the Geneva conference and criticized Mugabe for selling out
to the imperialist forces; they hoped to challenge Mugabe from a radical
perspective informed by Marxism.[23] Several hundred ZANLA guerrillas
were arrested (some in Tanzania) or murdered, and fifty top camp commanders were detained in Mozambican jails until 1979.[24] Another purge
took place in January 1978 in a context of mounting criticism of Mugabe
in the camps after the November 1977 debacle in Chimoi (the destruction of the main ZANU base by the Rhodesian forces). A group of cadres, led by Central Committee members Henry Hamadziripi and Rugare
Gumbo, were arrested, summarily convicted by a kangaroo court presided over by Mugabe, and detained in pit cells for months.[25] On both
occasions Tongogara and Rex Nhongo used brutal force to regain control of ZANLA and establish Mugabe as the undisputed leader of ZANU.

All the ZANLA dissidents jailed in Mozambique were released after
the Lancaster House agreement, when Lord Soames made it one of the
conditions allowing Mugabe back in Salisbury (now Harare).[26] Most of
them were never readmitted into ZANU. For the 1980 elections,
Mhanda and twenty-six of his colleagues aligned with ZAPU (others
went with Sithole or Muzorewa), only to be arrested again when Mugabe
assumed power. The protection of Joshua Nkomo saved them from further harassment,[27] but Mhanda was marked as an enemy of the regime
and had to go into exile in West Germany, where he eventually gradua-
ted with a degree in chemistry. When he returned in 1988, after the

Central Intelligence Organisation (CIO), the state intelligence agency, plotted to have his work permit in West Germany revoked, he found himself blacklisted for all jobs in the public sector and had a difficult time finding a job even in private companies because the CIO interfered with potential employers. Thanks to an intervention by army commander general Constantine Chiwenga, Mhanda managed to have the interdict lifted, provided he would never get involved in politics again.[28] Rugare Gumbo crept back into ZANU-PF after two decades of political oblivion (when he was a board member in a parastatal), received a commercial farm, and was elected to Parliament in 2000. He was made a deputy minister in 2002 and full minister after the 2005 elections.

The death of Josiah Magama Tongogara remains to this day clouded in mystery. However, it is very likely that he was killed because he was far too popular among the guerrillas and Mugabe feared the competition from a charismatic and ruthless army chief.[29] Further, the OAU Commission on the Assassination of Herbert Chitepo had noted that the ZANLA chief was a man "of inordinate ambitions" who once claimed he would be Zimbabwe's first president.[30] Many observers believed the military commander to be ZANU's real boss, and Mugabe a political figurehead. Tongogara astonished the British negotiators in Lancaster House with his nonpartisan views and moderating influence, and he emerged from the negotiations with a new national aura. In addition, at Central Committee meetings in London and Maputo, he had openly supported unity between ZANU and ZAPU and argued in favor of a joint election campaign under the Patriotic Front.[31] He affected being an admirer of Joshua Nkomo and backed the latter's aspirations to become Zimbabwe's first prime minister (possibly with a view to quickly succeeding a more pliant Nkomo).[32] An alliance between Tongogara and Nkomo would have looked attractive to the strong Karanga element in ZANLA. That was a mortal sin to Mugabe, and indeed the threat of such a "south-south" alliance—that is, Masvingo and Matabeleland Provinces—became Mugabe's obsession well into the 1990s. Tongogara was likely to gather support from Front-Line States leaders such as Tanzania's Julius Nyerere and Mozambique's Samora Machel, who had leaned on Mugabe to adhere to the peace agreement or lose their support but never trusted him. Machel was in tears when he heard the news of the "accident" in which Tongogara died. Thus there were good reasons for the paranoid power freak that Mugabe had become to order Tongogara's murder. It removed a potential hazard on his road to power, dissuaded others tempted to breach party discipline on the eve of the crucial electoral battle, and taught Front-Line States leaders a lesson: Mugabe ought not be treated like a schoolboy again, and he would no longer tolerate any interference in ZANU's internal affairs.

The highly suspect "car accident"[33] took place after Tongogara failed to win the vote in the Central Committee, and just before he was due to fly to Salisbury to oversee the assembling of ZANLA guerrillas (Mugabe had dispatched him away from Maputo to the guerrilla camps near the border, purportedly to explain the contents of the peace agreement). Although Mugabe insisted that there was no split between Tongogara and the rest of ZANU-PF's leadership, Samora Machel suggested the contrary at the ZANLA chief's burial when he urged the Central Committee to revise its position and work for unity, if only to honor Tongogara's memory. Although showing ostensible grief at the time and in spite of the official cult status rendered to the war "hero" after independence, Mugabe stuck to his electoral strategy. Tongogara's death also benefited others: the late Simon Muzenda, who had been promoted to the Central Committee to fill the gap left in 1978 by the arrest of prominent Karangas (Gumbo and Hamadziripi), was to be a lifelong vice president "representing" the Karangas; Rex Nhongo (Solomon Mujuru), a Zezuru close to Mugabe (himself a Zezuru), became ZANU's top military man and subsequently the head of the new Zimbabwean army. Nhongo had been ZIPA's chief when Tongogara was jailed in Zambia, and again his deputy upon his return as the supreme military commander at the time of the Geneva conference. He had been close to the ZIPA camp commanders from March 1975 until October 1976, when he changed sides (according to Wilfred Mhanda) after Mugabe offered to appoint him head of the army. From then on he took part in Mugabe's brutal suppression of all dissenters. If indeed he were the one carrying the bomb that killed Chitepo, as alleged by the OAU report, he probably would not have balked at organizing Tongogara's murder. Whatever the details, the alleged crime was likely to cement solidarity bonds between members of the ZANU leadership for the following decade. It set the rules of the game in Zimbabwean politics: be on Mugabe's side or pay the price.

Factionalism and Purges in ZANU Since 1980

Given the legacy of the 1970s, there was no room for dissent within the ruling party, even after the war was over and the Independence elections duly won. Mugabe had retained control of the liberation front in 1975–78 by violent means, both directly and indirectly and elections for the Central Committee, Politburo, and presidency were not competitive ballots. He was wary of losing control and would crush dissenting voices before any structured opposition could take hold. It was, in practice, almost impossible to oppose Mugabe from within. ZANU-PF internal proceedings were derived from Lenin's concept of "democratic centralism" and its congresses and national conferences followed a ritual similar to the proceedings of former Communist parties in Eastern Europe. The Politburo controlled both the agenda and the nominations, and party leaders would not hesitate to flout the party constitution to silence critical backbenchers. Before primary elections to select the party candidates for the local councils and Parliament were introduced in 1989, the people were given the names of their MP from a Politburo-vetted list in line with the one-party-state philosophy. Therefore, primaries really but temporarily opened a democratic space at a grassroots level, and several unpopular Cabinet ministers were trounced in the 1989 and 1994 primaries.

However, the selection of ZANU-PF candidates at the constituency level became heavily corrupt and manipulated, and the primaries were used by provincial and national barons as a conduit for the elimination of vocal outgoing MPs.[34] Such was the fate of Margaret Dongo, who was barred from standing for the ruling party in the 1995 parliamentary elections.[35] The party local apparatus was officially "restructured" in 1994 in order to manipulate the primary election in Harare South. Some fictitious branches were created to pack the voting assembly with supporters for her rival, CIO operative Vivian Mwashita. Violence was directed at Dongo's supporters and the full propaganda machinery put to use. Dongo did not waver and stood eventually as an independent candidate and won the election. Most outspoken backbenchers in the second, third, and fourth legislatures were sidelined at the following primary elections. Even the reform-minded Speaker of Parliament from 1995 to 2000, Cyril Ndebele, who infuriated the leadership when he refused to censure Dzikamayi Mavhaire in February 1998, after the Masvingo MP had said in Parliament "Mugabe must go." Ndebele invoked the Privileges, Immunities and Powers of Parliament Act that guarantees freedom of speech in the House of Assembly. Besides, Ndebele, who was the driving force behind the work of the Parliamentary Reform Committee, was a known supporter of the empowerment of Parliament to counterbalance the Office of the President. Political purges had been a recurrent process within the ruling party, as Politburo "big men" perceived any critical voice as a threat—to themselves let alone to Mugabe.

Prior to the 2000 parliamentary elections, Border Gezi, ZANU-PF's secretary for the commissariat and Mashonaland central governor, was tasked to discipline the party provincial executives who had supported the "reformers" since 1998. During the first quarter of 2000, he toured the provinces and "restructured" (in fact, purged) the provincial executives by promoting Mugabe's loyalists, many of whom had a CIO background and/or belonged to the "War Vets"—members of guerrilla forces during the liberation war. The same exercise was repeated or continued in the first quarter of 2001, especially in provinces where the party had not performed well in the parliamentary elections—such as Harare and all of Matabeleland. Predictably, all outspoken MPs were sidelined before or during the party primaries ahead of the June 2000 elections, especially those who had supported true constitutional reform, such as Mike Mataure (see Chapter 3). A few managed to secure another position, like Rita Makarau, who was appointed a High Court judge, but most of the others fell into oblivion. The ZANU-PF caucus has, since 2000, been dominated by hard-liners who would rubberstamp any repressive legislation presented to them by the government. Prior to the parliamentary elections in March 2005, heavily manipulated primaries again sidelined supporters of the Mnangagwa faction and promoted supporters of the Mujuru faction, including an inordinately large number of Zezuru candidates and Mugabe's family members.[36] The fact that a number of constituencies were reserved for some women candidates (in most cases unknown entities) helped the Politburo to further control candidacies. The same process was repeated for the November 2005 Senate elections and the March 2008 general elections.

To criticize Mugabe's decisions or his style of government was always taking a risk, not only of being excluded from the party, but also of losing your job and sometimes your life. There is a litany of alleged car crashes and other rather suspect "accidents" that conveniently helped Mugabe rid himself of annoying people, although it is difficult to understand why some were not touched and others died. It was probably linked to the actual threat they represented in Mugabe's view. Hence, when Edgar Tekere formed an opposition party in 1989 he was lambasted and harassed but not killed—perhaps he could be bought back. But the respected Bulawayo ZANU-PF member of Parliament and former ZAPU leader Sydney Malunga, who was a strong critic of the corruption in government, died in 1994 in a very suspect car accident; the driver having lost control after swerving to avoid a so-called "black dog" crossing the road. His death prevented him from standing for Parliament in 1995,[37] and from them on, when Dongo suspected possible attempts on her life, she would allude to "meeting a black dog." It was later used as a veiled threat by ZANU-PF thugs. Another prominent minister, Chris Ushewokunze, was killed in a car accident allegedly caused by abuse of alcohol in January 1994, but many suspected foul play. He was intellectually brilliant and bold enough to confront Mugabe in Cabinet meetings.[38]

Kinship ties were no protection once you incurred Mugabe's wrath. For example, Philip Chiyangwa, the outspoken indigenous businessman and ZANU-PF provincial chairman, although a relative of the president and long-time protégé, was jailed and tortured when suspected of plotting Mugabe's demise with South African spies.

Fearing for their lives and convinced that there was no political life outside ZANU-PF, none of the dissenting backbenchers have crossed the floor to join the opposition parties—Margaret Dongo chose to create her own party. The first to do so were Simba Makoni (when he stood as an independent for the presidential election in 2008) and former minister Dumiso Dabengwa, who supported him publicly. Admittedly, ruling party MPs and ministers were also blackmailed into staying quiet when they were indebted to the state financial institutions. Loans solicited for personal enrichment or to finance primary election campaigns (where gifts in various forms played a pivotal role in rallying the party rank and file) could be called back at any time, and most politicians were not in a position to repay them. This fate befell the Eddison Zvobgo in April 2001, after he progressively lost political control over the province of Masvingo: most Zvobgo's faction candidates lost in rigged party primaries prior to the parliamentary elections in June 2000. Subsequently, the veteran Cabinet minister was booted out of government and his trusted ally, ZANU-PF provincial chairman, Dzikamayi Mavhaire, was suspended and later replaced by Samuel Mumbengegwi of the rival faction of the late Simon Muzenda and Josiah Hungwe. Eventually Zvobgo lost his seat in the Politburo and was reduced to a mere backbencher's status. His close ally Mavhaire had survived the party primaries, but in a constituency eventually won by the MDC, which also won the mayoral election in 2001. This prompted the pro-Mugabe faction to hold Zvobgo responsible for the MDC foray in a province that had been a so-called "one-party-state area" since independence. In 2002, Zvobgo opposed a bill to rein in the media in a parliamentary committee but voted with the rest of the party when it was passed, and although he refused to campaign for Mugabe in the presidential election, he did not support MDC leader Morgan Tsvangirai either. Like Zvobgo, many ZANU-PF politicians had accumulated wealth and properties they feared losing if they defected to the opposition.

Although dissent was not allowed to develop, ZANU-PF was never a monolithic organization. Since the early 1990s the ruling party has been deeply divided by factional struggles in most provinces.[39] It took the form of petty quarrels rather than genuine debates over ideological differences or policy issues, but some of them ended in suspect deaths. In Masvingo the Zvobgo/Mavhaire faction clashed for most of the 1990s against another faction led by Muzenda and Hungwe. Mugabe always supported the latter (hence his appointment of Hungwe as a provincial governor) to prevent Karangas from rallying unanimously behind Zvobgo. As previously mentioned, Muzenda and Hungwe were able to seize control of the province in full only in 2001. Confrontation was also very tense in Manicaland in 1994–99, between the Didymus Mutasa–backed faction and the one aligned with Kumbirai Kangai, until the latter was arrested and then remanded for a corruption scandal at the Grain Marketing Board in 2000.[40] Mutasa was promoted as party secretary for administration, and subsequently as a powerful minister of state for national security, lands, land reform, and resettlement in 2005. As a senior figure personally loyal to Mugabe, he counterbalanced the Mujuru faction without serving Mnangagwa's ambitions.

The fight was over the spoils (economic rewards or positions of power), but ultimately the party "big men" were trying to position themselves for the future succession struggle. However, Mugabe played on these rivalries in a Machiavellian fashion. By allowing the party factions to settle scores at regional level in the selection of party executives and delegates to the ZANU-PF congresses and national conferences and in the parliamentary primaries, Mugabe managed to "provincialize" the other Politburo members and to remain the only national figure. They gave him a hand when relying on the regional/ethnic identities to advance their narrow-minded agendas and create a clientele. Although not a neutral referee, he was the only one who could blow the whistle when factionalism threatened to turn into a violent feud. Playing one faction against another and keeping approximate balances between cross-province factional alliances, Mugabe would alternate promotions and demotions and in the process give all provincial leaders a share of the spoils. Not directly affected by the defeat of a particular candidate, Mugabe emerged after every national election in full control of the ruling party.

Mugabe is not a tribal chauvinist, and he relied at various points in time—for example, in 1996—on politicians from Matabeleland to rein in the ambitions of his fellow Shona. He was always keen on using Karanga (Muzenda and Mnangagwa) or Manyika (Mutasa) trusted lieutenants in top structures of ZANU-PF, and he is more interested by his political survival than by building up Zezuru power. What was called the "Mashonaland East faction" in the mid-1990s, led by Solomon Mujuru and Sydney Sekeramayi, minister of defense at a time when Mujuru's successor at the helm of the armed forces, General Vitalis Zvinavashe, was a Karanga, could have spearheaded this Zezuru power. Yet, Mugabe made sure that they fought for the spoils with another Zezuru gang from Mashonaland West, where his own home village Zvimba is. However, a number of Zezurus have been promoted through the years to key positions in the state, such as his former secretary in the presidency, Charles Utete (a behind-the-scenes de facto prime minister in the 1990s), the police commissioner Augustine Chihuri, Generals Constantine Chiwenga and Perence Shiri at the head of the army and air force, and judge Godfrey Chidyausiku at the helm of the Supreme Court. Mugabe uses family ties and kinship bonds alongside other forms of loyalty. Chihuri, Chiwenga, and Shiri above all owe their careers and wealth to the president,[41] and their personal loyalty is more important than tribal solidarity. This is not to say that ordinary people do not read it otherwise and that tribal politics will not become prominent in the future.

A good example of Mugabe's manipulation of factionalism is the hidden succession struggle. When Joshua Nkomo passed away, Mugabe promoted the late Joseph Msika (next in command in the former ZAPU) to the vice presidency, but the real fight was the election of the party national chairman in December 1999. John Nkomo, supported by the Mashonaland East (Zezuru) faction led by Mujuru and Sekeramayi defeated Mnangagwa, and subsequently the former minister of justice lost his Midlands seat during the June 2000 parliamentary elections (to an MDC candidate). However, Mugabe immediately appointed him speaker of Parliament and in December 2000 ZANU-PF's secretary for administration—number five in the party hierarchy. His supporters in the party were also promoted to the Politburo, when his former rival Zvobgo was kicked out and Mnangagwa's controversial Midlands lieutenant Frederick Shava[42] became director of the ruling party's administration. Mnangagwa made further gains in August 2002, when John Nkomo lost Home Affairs in exchange for a powerless ministry.

However, Mnangagwa became too assertive when in late 2002 he and retired army chief of staff Zvinavashe secretly approached the opposition leader, Morgan Tsvangirai, to negotiate a settlement including an exit package and security guarantees for Mugabe. This move was supported by South African president Thabo Mbeki but had not received Mugabe's nod. In any case, Tsvangirai, who feared a trap, revealed the plot to the press in January 2003. When Muzenda died in October 2003, Mnangagwa, being the most prominent Karanga in government, demanded the post of vice president left vacant. However, Mugabe had not forgiven Mnangagwa's attempt to strike a deal with the MDC behind his back. In early 2004, the anticorruption campaign conveniently targeted Mnangagwa's close business associate Mutumva Mawere, who had to flee surreptitiously to South Africa while his properties were impounded.[43] Mnangagwa was accused also of shady deals in gold and foreign currencies, and a special committee was appointed to investigate his management of ZANU-PF's business empire when he had been party treasurer.

In the meantime Mnangagwa had secured the support of a majority of provincial party chairmen who could nominate him at the party congress and enrolled "Young Turks" opposed to the Mujuru/Sekeramayi

faction, such as Jonathan Moyo and Patrick Chinamasa or Philip Chiyangwa. To placate this threat, Mugabe appointed Joyce Mujuru as vice president in September 2004, purportedly for the sake of gender balance,
and in spite of her relative junior position in the original ZANU hierarchy. This choice satisfied the Mujuru faction while filling the position
with somebody lacking the stature and abilities to threaten Mugabe.[44] A
secret meeting organized by Moyo in Tsholotsho (Matabeleland) on 18
November 2004 to plan a strike back at the Mujuru faction was infiltrated by the CIO and exposed, and all the plotters (except Chinamasa)
were subsequently punished. Jonathan Moyo, who had a long-standing
feud with General Mujuru, lost his Cabinet and Politburo positions and
was expelled from the party in February 2005 when he vowed to contest
the seat in Tsholotsho as an independent (which he won).[45] The five
provincial chairmen involved in the plot were suspended and later
expelled from the party.[46] Chiyangwa was implicated in an alleged spying network and jailed from mid-December 2004 to late February 2005.
Mnangagwa himself was demoted in the party hierarchy and lost his
position as speaker of parliament to John Nkomo.

However, following the parliamentary elections in which Mnangagwa
failed once again to secure a seat, Mugabe reappointed him a noncon-
stituency MP and granted him a low-ranking position in Cabinet, if only
to prevent Solomon Mujuru's faction from feeling too powerful. The
latter had control over the ZANU-PF candidacies in most constituencies
in the subsequent 2005 elections and therefore strong influence over
the two houses of Parliament, and the former army chief enjoyed large
support in the national security agencies. This could have meant a threat
to Mugabe, and once again in late 2005 and early 2006 the purported
anticorruption drive was used to clip the wings of the Mujuru faction
this time. When Mugabe's attempt to have his presidential mandate
extended until 2010 was resisted by some of the ZANU-PF cadres at the
December 2006 party conference, the Mujuru faction was deemed
responsible. Throughout 2007 and 2008—especially after the first presidential election turn and the ensuing violence—Mnangagwa was
returned to his previous status of the right-hand man and potential successor. However, Mugabe despises his lieutenants' abilities, and he trusts
none of them to shield him from prosecution for human rights violations and guarantee his personal security. This is in part—besides his
ingrained arrogance—why he postpones his retirement forever. At least
until the fateful elections of 2008, he saw himself dying in office and
suggested it by joking publicly, in July 2006, about his lieutenants' having to resort to witchcraft to hasten the succession. When his henchman
Elliot Manyika announced at a Central Committee meeting on 30 March
2007 that Mugabe would be ZANU-PF's candidate in the 2008 presiden-

tial election, Mujuru had to go along with it, while Mnangagwa fully supported the idea, in order to gain time and fully redeem himself in Mugabe's eyes—hence his role in the run-off campaign. Ahead of the party congress in December 2009, the province executives competed to endorse Mugabe once again—even calling him "Supreme Leader"—while the death of Vice President Msika on 12 August gave a new impetus to the endless struggle between the main two factions over the appointment of his successor and the leadership of the women and youth leagues.

Annihilating the Opposition Parties

At independence, ZANU-PF emerged as the dominant political force from the 1980 elections. However, Mugabe formed a government of national unity with ZAPU and a few whites, a decision widely perceived as gesture of goodwill. The rhetoric of "national unity" certainly appealed to a majority of black Zimbabweans longing for peace at last, even though a distorted record of the liberation struggle backed it.[47] Mugabe also made his famous broadcast speech calling for reconciliation of all races in order to build a nonracial society and pledging to guarantee the white minority rights in future Zimbabwe, an undertaking reiterated at the independence ceremony.[48] Two Rhodesian Front politicians—in addition to Denis Norman, a farmer unionist who had lobbied for a negotiated settlement, at the agriculture ministry—were included in the Cabinet and Mugabe went as far as consulting Ian Smith—leader of the opposition in Parliament—on policy issues until March 1981.[49] However, there were perfectly rational motives behind this "Mr. Nice Guy" attitude. There was a strong economic rationale for the "reconciliation" with the whites, but it was primarily a political ploy preparing the ground for ZAPU's forced incorporation into ZANU. The two main methods for getting rid of a political opposition are incorporation—voluntary or forced—and suppression, used alternately to guarantee highest efficiency.

Abel Muzorewa's United African National Council (UANC),[50] which had seemed so potent in 1978, was reduced to a subregional party, with only three seats in 1980, and was no longer a threat.[51] Naturally, the political influence of the former white settlers was more of a concern. For the major part of the 1980s the experienced MPs of the former Rhodesian Front regrouped in the Conservative Alliance of Zimbabwe (CAZ) and offered indeed some counterweight to the ruling party's dominance in Parliament. However, a formal alliance between ZAPU and the Ian Smith-led CAZ was difficult to contemplate for the black nationalists, although Smith and Nkomo consulted each other frequently. Besides, the abolition of the separate voters roll and the reserved seats in 1987[52] technically put an end to white party politics in Zimbabwe. That removed an irritant (the government castigated the white electorate for returning 15 CAZ MPs out of 20 contested seats in the 1985 elections, and Norman then lost his Cabinet job), rather than suppressing a real threat to ZANU-PF power. In the meantime, Mugabe had confronted and subdued a more serious rival, and so complete was his triumph that the forced incorporation of ZAPU set a precedent—"no life outside ZANU-PF"—and certainly hampered the development of any serious opposition from 1987 to 1999.

Subjugating ZAPU

Mugabe decided that ZANU would fight the 1980 elections alone, instead of running for Parliament under the common banner of the Patriotic Front with ZAPU. Whatever the political arguments set forth, the truth of the matter was that Mugabe was not prepared to come second to Joshua Nkomo, his senior in the nationalist struggle, and let him become the first prime minister of an independent Zimbabwe. Once ZAPU was defeated in the founding elections and ZANU successfully established itself as the dominant partner in the coalition, it was perfectly logical to invite ZAPU leaders to join the Cabinet, not only for the sake of national unity but also to keep an eye on them. However, their subsequent elimination as an independent political force was from the outset Mugabe's utmost priority. The one-party-state objective required their forced incorporation. Besides, he could not accept the risk—however remote—of an alliance between ZAPU, the whites, and UANC to challenge his still fragile grip on state power. The rival liberation front would be brought into subservience and the sooner the better.

Therefore, everything was done in the first two years to push ZAPU leaders to err and give Mugabe the excuse to strike mercilessly. The coalition government was an astutely deceptive maneuver to prepare the final annihilation of ZAPU. Joshua Nkomo, having called before the elections for a united front that he too hoped to dominate, was not in a position to decline the offer. Nkomo was first offered the ceremonial presidency—a golden cage—and refused it, only to land in Home Affairs in a Cabinet where his party was blatantly underrepresented. He was further humiliated at the Independence ceremony, where Mugabe was in the spotlight while the "father of the Nation" was left in the anonymity of a back seat. These were the first steps of the strategy of tension, with repeated inflammatory statements and clashes between ZIPRA and

ZANLA elements. In the same vein, Nkomo was demoted to a junior Cabinet position of minister for the public service in January 1981. This was the first cycle of a pattern of inclusion-subjugation that Mugabe has consistently practiced with his opponents.

ZANU strategists (in particular Emmerson Mnangagwa, security minister and former head of ZANLA's intelligence, Enos Nkala, who had a long-standing score to settle with Nkomo, and Edgar Tekere, then a ZANU firebrand) found favorable ground in the outbreaks of armed violence in the assembly camps, where guerrillas were cantoned after the ceasefire.[53] These incidents were linked to the conditions of the protracted process of demobilization and integration in the new national army (ZNA).[54] In fact, the government favored its own guerrillas from ZANLA, and numerous military personnel affiliated with ZAPU were humiliated, beaten, or even murdered by their ZANLA colleagues. Many of these ZIPRA elements later defected from the ZNA and became "dissidents" to protect their own lives and out of desperation.[55] Mugabe later alleged with his usual cynicism that their behavior proved that ZAPU had plotted an insurgency.

In February 1982, the government claimed to have uncovered arms caches on ZAPU properties in Matabeleland and former ZIPRA assembly points and used it against ZAPU leaders as evidence of a plot in preparation. This was a weak excuse since government heads had prior knowledge of these arms caches and an ad hoc committee, including Mugabe and Mnangagwa on ZANU's side, met in early 1982 to discuss the matter.[56] Besides, the discovery of arms caches belonging to former guerrilla armies—or to the South African ANC with which ZAPU had strong ties—was routine in the years following the end of the war and ZAPU alone was not to be blamed. Both guerrilla armies had concealed weapons near the assembly points in the eventuality of their party losing the 1980 elections—to resume war if need be. Nevertheless the two most senior former ZIPRA commanders (Dumiso Dabengwa and Lookout Masuku) were arrested in March and detained until the end of 1986.[57] Most ZAPU Cabinet members then dramatically resigned. Mugabe called the ZAPU ministers in the government, especially Joshua Nkomo, "a cobra in the house."[58] The party's farms and properties were seized by the state—most of them never to be returned, even after the 1987 Unity Accord, which sanctioned ZAPU's defeat. Fearing for his life after a raid on his home, Joshua Nkomo left for exile in March 1983, to return only in 1985.

ZAPU leaders were apparently caught by surprise by the crisis unraveling. They refused to endorse the activities of the "dissidents" and the government never established that a direct connection existed between the unrest in Matabeleland and ZAPU's leadership. Nkomo himself did not believe that these "dissidents" had anything to do with his party. ZAPU leaders knew too well what the balance of forces in the country was; launching a new guerrilla insurgency once the ZIPRA forces had been disarmed and largely demobilized—hence the timing of Mugabe's attack—was nonsensical. In any case, verbal attacks and threats by ZANU-PF leaders against ZAPU began long before February 1982. A unit called the Fifth Brigade was tasked to perform scorched earth tactics in Matabeleland (see Chapter 2); it was in reality a political army operating outside the normal chain of command, led by a ZANU cadre, Perence Shiri, who owed his fast promotion not to his abilities but to his personal allegiance to Mugabe to whom he reported directly. The Fifth Brigade began training as early as August 1981, purportedly to deal with the then nonexistent "dissidents." An agreement with North Korea to train the brigade was signed as early as October 1980 and kept secret: Mugabe made his preparations for the brawl long before any "dissident" problem arose.

One of the benefits of "reconciliation" for Mugabe was the crucial role played by white civil servants in ZANU-PF's takeover of the state apparatus in all sectors, including security. Although General Peter Walls (former head of the Rhodesian army) took early retirement in July 1980 and was sent into exile in September the same year—after he revealed his distrust of Mugabe—some white commanding officers in the army, the police, and even the CIO were retained for a while. Thus, when fighting broke out among rival guerrilla armies, former Rhodesian army units under white officers' command dutifully moved into the camps at Mugabe's request and assaulted the ZIPRA forces—whom the government blamed for the violence. Later on, military operations against the alleged ZAPU "dissidents" in Matabeleland began with some units of the integrated national army under the command of white officers willing to demonstrate their loyalty, such as Lt. Colonel Lionel Dyke,[59] until the partisan Fifth Brigade was ready for deployment in January 1983. As Mugabe hinted to Smith once, professional soldiers led by Rhodesian officers loyal to the new constitutional government played a central role in his security.

By late 1982, several hundred former ZAPU guerrillas had taken refuge in the bush, thus giving the government the excuse it was looking for to violently attack Matabeleland. State violence targeted not only the former ZAPU guerrillas but the whole Ndebele community, which was accused without proof of helping and supporting the "dissidents"—and this was made painfully clear by numerous statements from top government officials. In the ensuing military operations, the Fifth Brigade terrorized civilians by committing countless war crimes but made no serious effort to chase and capture the "dissidents,"[60] in spite of the disproportion of forces: only 122 "dissidents" turned themselves in countrywide to benefit from the 1988 amnesty. At the peak of the phenomenon, there must have been no more than a few hundred in all of Matabeleland. What government propaganda presented as banditry, and many observers analyzed as an undeclared civil war, was in fact a premeditated mass political purge intended to uproot ZAPU and isolate its leaders from their popular support base. The modus operandi of the killings suggests that they were not excesses perpetrated by some unruly soldiers, but a planned policy of terror.[61] ZAPU's representation in Parliament was to be severely reduced if not totally annihilated. Prior to the 1985 elections, party branches were dismantled, party officials arrested, and ZAPU supporters intimidated both in Matabeleland and in areas outside Matabeleland where the party had received a significant share of the vote in the 1980 elections: north of Mashonaland West, southern Midlands, and some Harare townships. It worked there, but not in Matabeleland, where massive violence was counterproductive as the people voted nevertheless for Nkomo's party.[62]

The regime brushed aside criticisms of its brutal treatment of innocent civilians and alleged the existence of threats to its national security, pointing to South Africa's destabilization activities. As always in effective propaganda there was an element of truth. Small South African army units perpetrated raids on Zimbabwean territory. Saboteurs sent by the apartheid regime bombed an arsenal at Inkomo Barracks near Harare in August 1981, attempted to kill Mugabe in December the same year, and managed to destroy several aircrafts of the Zimbabwe Air Force in July 1982 at Thornhill Air Base in Gweru.[63] However, there was no link whatsoever between pro-ANC ZAPU and the then South African government. The South African Special Forces recruited among Matabeleland refugees in Botswana and trained them in Transvaal as a guerrilla unit called "Super-ZAPU," which operated intermittently in Matabeleland South and North.[64] However, Super-ZAPU was not recognized as genuine by other "dissidents" and ceased to operate in mid-1984. In any case, government security agency atrocities were by far the most compelling factor for people taking refuge in Botswana and later joining Super-ZAPU.[65] The apartheid regime did not miss the opportunity to weaken an avowed enemy, but the impact of its destabilization is overstated (especially in comparison with similar South African operations in Angola and Mozambique). The international context also facilitated the cover-up by Mugabe's regime of the state-sponsored atrocities: not only did Harare enjoy support from the Eastern bloc and China, but conservative Western governments in the United Kingdom and the United States did not want to antagonize Mugabe for fear of opening another battlefront for the besieged Apartheid regime. The ZANU-PF government imposed an efficient information blackout, supported by the sealing off of the affected area.[66] Smoke-screen field trips were organized by the Ministry of Information to deceive foreign press correspondents in Harare.[67]

Violence resumed in the fifteen constituencies that returned a ZAPU MP, and it did not stop completely until the Unity Accord was signed on 22 December 1987, becoming totally effective with the ruling party's 1989 congress, when ZAPU and ZANU structures were amalgamated. After the 1985 elections, Mugabe knew that he could not eradicate ZAPU so easily and that he would have to co-opt ZAPU leaders into the ruling party, but he wanted them as submissive junior partners not as equals. There are interesting similarities between his attitude toward ZAPU at the time and his tactics toward the MDC after the 2002 presidential election, and even more so in the 2008 power-sharing negotiations. Mugabe has never been willing to negotiate with his opposition and share power on a fair basis—as demonstrated again throughout 2009 by his biased implementation of the September 2008 agreement on the inclusive government. In 1986 pressure was put on ZAPU through the detention of MPs and Bulawayo city councillors and scores of supporters, while negotiations were brokered between the two parties by church and civic leaders. The breakdown of the unity talks announced by Mugabe in his 1987 New Year's message, the subsequent banning of all ZAPU meetings, and the closure of their offices clearly signaled that no less than a political surrender was demanded. ZAPU leaders had no other option given the amount of suffering in the Ndebele populated provinces.[68] Besides, they had no contingency plans to resume fighting and could expect no support from abroad, especially from the neighboring states. Zimbabwe had by then emerged forcefully as a new leader of the Front-Line States fighting apartheid. In addition, most of the ZAPU leaders were tired of war as much as the people and wanted to enjoy the spoils of state power. The Accord secured their co-option into Cabinet, Politburo, and Central Committee.

Therefore, Mugabe's war of attrition in Matabeleland was intended to force a merger on ZANU's terms, which is precisely what the "Unity Accord"—a misnomer emphasizing the propaganda line that served to delegitimize any emerging opposition afterward—amounted to.[69] Although the Unity Accord brought the state violence to an end, it also silenced voices from Matabeleland: the need to foster unity became an excuse for not acknowledging the past. Until the publication of the CCJP/LRF report in 1997, the subject was taboo even for Ndebele intellectuals.[70] As a result of such "unity" ZAPU leaders were politically emasculated and they never again enjoyed significant influence within ZANU-PF. Joshua Nkomo's elevation to the vice presidency was purely ceremonial and counterbalanced by the appointment of Simon

Muzenda, Mugabe's dedicated lieutenant, to the same position. Although Politburo and Central Committee members coming from ZAPU have sometimes been credited for a moderate influence in the ruling party politics (especially Dumiso Dabengwa or John Nkomo), they never confronted Mugabe and were easily whipped into line. Joseph Msika's and John Nkomo's official endorsement of the violent farm occupations since they began in 2000—in contradiction to their alleged inner feelings—underlines their political weakness. So by the late 1980s, Zimbabwe was a de facto one-party state and the situation remained similar until June 2000, when the MDC emerged as an effective contender for power.

Subverting Emerging Opposition Parties in the 1990s

From 1987 to 2000 opposition parties never obtained more than three seats at a given time in Parliament. There were more than twenty such organizations in Zimbabwe on the eve of the 1995 parliamentary elections. Yet, most of them were little more than a one-man party. Opposition MP contributions to parliamentary debates were minimal, while some outspoken ZANU-PF backbenchers, such as Margaret Dongo or the late Sydney Malunga (formerly a ZAPU member), exposed the ruling party's poor governance record. In the 1995–2000 legislature, the two opposition survivors were largely lackluster absentee MPs.[71] In fact, opposition parties did not have any significant impact on the political scene at all and issues of governance were raised more effectively by segments of civil society. Yet there have been several attempts to build a credible alternative to the ruling party prior to 1999. It is worth recalling these unsuccessful experiments, to understand the daunting task the MDC was facing and its own partly inherited shortcomings.

The first significant opposition to emerge was the Zimbabwe Unity Movement (ZUM), created in April 1989 by Edgar Tekere, a former ZANU-PF firebrand expelled from the Politburo for criticizing the widespread corruption in government ranks. Born in the midst of 1988–89 students' and workers' protests against corruption, censorship, and the one-party state project, ZUM got a significant share of the vote during the 1990 parliamentary and presidential elections, but it failed to break ZANU-PF's hegemony. Veteran nationalist leader Ndabaningi Sithole returned in 1992 from his self-imposed exile in the United States to revive the "original" ZANU, however his ZANU (Ndonga) only achieved a gain of two seats in Parliament in 1995 (like ZUM in the previous legislature), in the district of Chipinge populated by Ndau, Sithole's fellow tribesmen. Formed in March 1993, from the merger between the

Harare-based Forum for Democratic Reform Trust, and the Bulawayo-based Open Forum, the Forum Party of Zimbabwe (FORUM) emanated from civil society organizations with a substantial element of white liberals[72] and former junior ZAPU cadres, many of whom later found their way into the MDC. Led by the veteran nationalist and retired chief justice Enoch Dumbutshena, the FORUM failed to gain any seat in 1995, although it received a significant backing in several middle-class suburbs in Harare, Bulawayo, and Gweru. In September 1994, the United Parties (UP) attempted to melt together the old UANC with a splinter group from FORUM and some defectors from the collapsing ZUM. UP was Abel Muzorewa's second attempt to unite the opposition, after a failed merger with ZUM in January 1994.[73] However, the party's popularity was never tested, since it boycotted both the parliamentary elections in 1995 and the presidential election in 1996, and it fizzled away in the late 1990s.

After Margaret Dongo won her court case and the subsequent by-election in Harare South, she created the Movement of Independent Candidates in 1996, with a view toward attracting ZANU-PF dissenters, and she sponsored candidates for the Harare council elections. Because she was a former guerrilla and a founding member of the Zimbabwe National Liberation War Veterans Association (ZNLWVA), the vocal independent MP could lay credible claims on the nationalist legacy. However, she failed to attract a significant following outside her Harare South constituency. Being a gifted grassroots politician, she lacked the sophistication—and the resources—necessary to weave a nationwide network. She hurriedly launched the Zimbabwe Union of Democrats (ZUD) in December 1998, in part to preempt the creation of an opposition party backed by the Zimbabwe Congress of Trade Unions (ZCTU). After a promising beginning, ZUD was riddled by factionalism and was soon supplanted by a fast-expanding MDC. In 2000 Dongo responded to MDC overtures with unrealistic demands—17 constituencies reserved for her party—and she lost her parliamentary seat in the process. By then, most ZUD members had joined the newly formed MDC.

A combination of factors explain these successive failures: lack of funding;[74] poor organization, especially the absence of permanent party structures at a grassroots level (Dongo confessed in interview how difficult it was to set up local cells and branches); inability to penetrate the rural areas where the ruling party patronage structures were paramount; sometimes the low political caliber of their candidates; and finally repeated leadership squabbles—though not more than within ZANU-PF—that damaged their reputation in the electorate. Many opposition party leaders lacked credibility, either because they were aging politicians or because they were perceived as opportunists settling scores with

Mugabe. For example, Patrick Kombayi, who successively defected from ZANU-PF and ZUM, was an embarrassing and unreliable recruit for the FORUM: at one time he would stand in a ZANU-PF primary election for Gweru's executive mayor, and at another he would castigate Mugabe's regime and call for international sanctions. He had taken an active part in the Matabeleland massacres during the 1980s and shared ZANU-PF's intolerant political culture. Abel Muzorewa and Ndabaningi Sithole were tainted by their involvement in the "internal settlement" in 1978–79.[75] Some leaders, like Tekere, had autocratic tendencies and antagonized their own followers. Needless to say, ZANU-PF capitalized on these quarrels and would give maximum publicity to opposition "renegades" ostensibly (re)joining the ruling party. Most opposition parties at best enjoyed region-based support—or urban middle-class support in the case of the FORUM—and never succeeded to expand it (although ZUM in 1990 and FORUM in 1995 got a real share of the vote bigger than what the official results acknowledged; see below). In addition, they have never been able to put aside their differences and form a united front against ZANU-PF. They wasted money and energy competing with each other in supposedly winnable—mainly urban—constituencies while scores of rural ones were left to ZANU-PF candidates, who were elected unopposed. There was no electoral alliance again in 2000—except with ZANU (Ndonga) for the Chipinge South constituency—but the MDC succeeded in marginalizing every other opposition party.

Another weakness was the lack of credible manifestos and policy proposals. For instance, ZUM initially articulated the people's opposition to rampant corruption in the government and the one-party-state project, but it did not go beyond this populist stance to offer meaningful alternatives to government policies.[76] However, the FORUM and ZUD had more elaborate manifestos but limited means to disseminate them to the electorate. More important, perhaps, the opposition before 1999 lacked a clear political strategy as the episode of the partial boycott of the 1995 elections demonstrated.[77] Although the boycotting party grievances about the unfair electoral framework were valid and largely supported by civil society, their late decision to boycott was perceived as a petty maneuver. The fact that they did not actively campaign for the boycott and concentrated their attacks on political parties still contesting did nothing to dissipate this impression. Although the FORUM's attitude—contesting against all the odds—appeared more consistent with the raison d'être of a political party, its leaders had no post-election strategy. In particular, they had no contingency plans (or money) to systematically challenge the election results in court, like Margaret Dongo in Harare South, to expose the electoral fraud. This lesson was not lost on MDC leaders after the 2000 parliamentary elections.

However, opposition party difficulties were primarily the result of a political environment deeply alien to pluralism. ZANU-PF's political culture is built on imposed unanimity, ingrained intolerance to dissenting views, and some underlying violence.[78] This political culture crystallized during the liberation war, when dissenting voices among guerrillas or outside their ranks were systematically branded "traitors" and "sell-outs." During the liberation war, ZANLA guerrillas made an extensive use of the latter label to denigrate not only those suspected of having betrayed them to the Rhodesians but also supporters of other nationalist groups (Muzorewa's UANC or ZAPU). Alleged sellouts were severely beaten and often summarily executed to teach other villagers a lesson. Suspicion was a method of political control. Therefore, when government called its opponents "sellouts" in the post-independence era it had some sinister implications and went beyond the ordinary political slander.

The idea that those who do not fully support the regime set themselves automatically "outside the nation" remains a pillar of ZANU-PF political culture.[79] Like the FORUM and the MDC in later years, ZUM was lambasted in the government media and its members were dubbed agents of apartheid South Africa trying to return Zimbabwe to colonialism. For ZANU-PF any opposition party is by definition an enemy of the state and a lackey of the whites. In spite of the early years' "reconciliation" policy, white farmers were held in suspicion, especially at election time when they were portrayed as a fifth column. White human rights activists were branded "racist" Rhodesians seeking revenge, even though most of them had opposed Ian Smith's regime. This extremely intolerant atmosphere deterred many reasonable people from getting involved in politics. Sometimes retribution was not limited to words, and harassment could take the form of financial punishment, such as the problems Enoch Dumbutshena faced in 1995.[80] Genuine pluralism is something alien to this party because it never moved away from the war mentality of the 1970s. The one-party state was dropped as a constitutional project, but the mentality survived almost intact. ZANU-PF activists proclaimed during the election campaigns of 1985, 1990, and 1995 that various townships or neighborhoods were "one-party-state" or "no-go" areas. The infamous War Vets—members of ZNLWVA and ZANU-PF thugs—adopted exactly the same mantras to prevent the opposition from campaigning in the rural areas in 2000. Only this time the rhetoric was backed by widespread violence.

Mugabe and the party hierarchy always made it clear that they would never relinquish power to another political party and lose their privileges. In 1995 (at a time the country was described by many as undergoing a democratic transition!), the governor of Masvingo Province, Josiah Hungwe, emphatically declared: "Our party enjoys immense popularity. That is why we will put up resistance if the opposition wins the election. There is no way we are going to accept that result."[81] For anyone who paid attention, Mugabe consistently adopted the same stance. For example, in 1995 he demanded "a massive 99.9 percent vote to frighten away the fringe opposition."[82] Threats of "another war" form one of the most consistent elements of discourse of the ruling party leaders and Mugabe himself since April 2000, in order to intimidate the opposition parties and the white farmers.[83] When the old autocrat insisted that "the MDC can never, ever be the government of this country" at a meeting in Bindura on 7 April 2000, he was basically reemphasizing his long-established stance. Nowadays nobody doubts that ZANU-PF leaders are prepared to kill to prevent such an outcome, but this has not been a sudden change of heart.

Another leading factor often ignored by foreign observers was the CIO infiltration and its manipulation of potential divisions within the opposition. Many of the breakaway factions of the rising star of the moment (ZUM in 1990–91, FORUM in 1993–94) were in fact sponsored by the secret police. Margaret Dongo, a CIO operative herself until the late 1980s, confided that it was part of her assignment then to oversee trade unionists on the CIO payroll, and that she warned Morgan Tsvangirai in 1999 that the ZCTU was still seriously infiltrated by the CIO.[84] These fears were fully confirmed during the ZCTU congress in February 2001. According to Dongo, any new opposition party would be quickly infiltrated by several agents posing as opposition activists not only to spy on the party activities but with the aim of creating mayhem. The savagely violent anti-MDC campaign, led since February 2000 by the state apparatus (CIO, uniformed police, army, registrar general's office), sheds new light on this controversial subject. For example, it is alleged that among the people who in the mid-1990s repeatedly migrated from ZUM to FORUM and from the latter to UP, there were some CIO agents who played an active part in the opposition's internal quarrels.[85] The same maneuver was clearly at work in Margaret Dongo's ZUD in 1999. She eventually exposed the late Kempton Makamure (a frustrated former leftist activist with an antiwhite prejudice) whom she had trusted, unfortunately, with executive functions in the party. The CIO also dissuaded disillusioned ZANU-PF middle-rank cadres from crossing the floor to ZUD.[86] More recently the CIO has certainly played a role in the rift within the MDC (especially the origin of the money paid to unruly youths to attack members of what became the so-called "pro-senate" faction remains a mystery).[87]

ZANU (Ndonga)'s narrow tribal base did not make it immune from infiltration. Mugabe's security apparatus tried to destroy Ndabaningi Sithole's reputation through the years with all sorts of ludicrous accusations even though the historic figure was no longer a political threat. Mugabe never forgave him for resuming his political career when he came back from exile instead of joining ZANU-PF as Joshua Nkomo had done. After the Churu farm saga in the mid-1990s,[88] blown out of proportion to ruin Sithole's credit in the eyes of his own community, he was arrested in October 1995 for allegedly plotting to assassinate President Mugabe. A confession extracted from William Nhamakonda, a member of the so-called "Chimwenje" dissident group, formerly operating from areas held by the Mozambique National Resistance (RENAMO) in Mozambique, was used to implicate Ndabaningi Sithole.[89] Although the latter denied any link with the Chimwenje, he was convicted for treason in early 1997 and sentenced to two and a half years in prison. The verdict relied on forged evidence, part of which was obtained through the use of torture against his alleged accomplices. However, the judge suspended the sentence on account of Sithole's deteriorating health, and the sinister manipulation ended when Sithole died in December 2000. There is a striking similarity between Sithole's trial in 1996, the judicial charade whereby Tsvangirai was repeatedly accused of plotting against the regime, and the trials held against ZAPU leaders in the 1980s—in particular the joint trial of Dumiso Dabengwa and Lookout Masuku in 1983, or Sydney Malunga's trial in 1986.

ZANU-PF's top leadership has a particular taste for this method of ridding itself of opponents. The systematic harassment of all opposition, even before it becomes a significant threat to the regime, not only points to the existence underneath the surface until 2000 of a police state, but also underlines also the huge obstacles of any emerging force trying to compete with ZANU-PF. This was compounded by the ruling party's control over the media, which prevented the opposition parties from campaigning and reaching the masses. However, the biggest obstacle perhaps was the twisted constitutional and legal framework and the control it gave to Mugabe's cronies over the electoral process.

Controlling the State

Post-independence Zimbabwe was never a genuine pluralist democracy, and "democratization" was never on the ruling party's agenda, even in the 1990s after the one-party state proposal was reluctantly shelved. Since Mugabe became prime minister in 1980, he has consistently undermined the institutional framework contained in the Lancaster House agreement: a liberal constitution—not devoid of loopholes and weaknesses that civic organizations wanted to correct in 1999—that provided for a balance of powers, an independent judiciary, and multiparty and free elections. Not only did Mugabe change the constitution to suit his whims but he used Rhodesian legislation to serve his purpose: the Law and Order Maintenance Act (LOMA) and the State of Emergency—renewed every six months from February 1980 until July 1990—are cases in point.[90] The government made full use of the Emergency Powers Act (1965) to produce a wide range of regulations that amended existing legislation or imposed arbitrary measures. The end result was a thinly disguised authoritarian regime where power to decide, punish, or reward was ultimately concentrated in Mugabe's hands. In spite of the rhetoric, enhancing genuine popular participation was of no concern to him. On the contrary, the concentration of powers also allowed him to alter the electoral process in order to keep ZANU-PF in power forever.

Institutionalizing Personal Rule

The Lancaster House agreement of December 1979 provided for a Westminster type of parliamentary democracy with a ceremonial head of state, a prime minister with executive powers, a Cabinet responsible to the lower chamber (the House of Assembly), and a Senate as the second chamber. This format, common in former British colonies, did not fit with the one-party state project, and, more important, it hampered Mugabe's capacity to rule at will. Therefore, the party "chefs"[91] were eager to speed up the necessary changes. However, a two-thirds majority in Parliament was required for the most important ones. In 1987 ZANU enlisted the support of five white "independents" to pass Constitutional Amendment No. 6 abolishing the twenty parliamentary seats and the separate voting roll reserved for the whites.[92] The subjugation of ZAPU allowed more sweeping constitutional changes to take place in 1987. Constitutional Amendment No. 7 instituted an "executive presidency": Mugabe concentrated the powers of the former nonexecutive president and those of the prime minister in his hands.[93] In addition, many sections of the constitution were thoroughly rewritten by Eddison Zvobgo, Mugabe's legal expert and diehard supporter,[94] to enlarge the president's area of control, creating what an analyst dubbed "a presidential monarch."[95]

The president appointed and dismissed government ministers at will but hardly needed them to run the country. Although he could address the Parliament whenever he wished, he was shielded from the MPs' questions and was not responsible to the House of Assemby, which he could dissolve at will.[96] He enjoyed wide-ranging powers to institute new legislation without going through Parliament under the Presidential Powers (Temporary Measures) Act of 1986,[97] although he could not change the constitution without Parliament's approval. The president could veto any bill presented by MPs and the Parliament could overrule this veto only by a two-thirds majority of its total membership. Mugabe was virtually untouchable as he could dissolve the Parliament once the legal process to remove him from office had begun, thus effectively dissuading parliamentarians to ever think of such a prospect. Therefore, neither the separation of powers nor the principle of responsible government was guaranteed by the constitution.[98] Only the Supreme Court, through its power to interpret the constitution, offered limited safeguards. This move toward a presidency with near-absolute powers, and the subsequent weakening of Parliament and the judiciary has been a common trajectory in African postcolonial states.[99] However, because of delayed independence, it took place in Zimbabwe about twenty years after other authoritarian presidential regimes in Africa had been roundly criticized. ZANU-PF could have drawn lessons from their fellow Africans' mistakes, but constitutional reform was the first step toward the institutionalization of the one-party state.[100] The political surrender of ZAPU and the co-option of its leaders into the ruling party had actually removed the last significant force with a capacity to contain Robert Mugabe's near-absolute power.

Although President Mugabe reluctantly dropped the one-party-state project in September 1990, because it encountered vocal opposition both in the public opinion (stirred by ZUM) and within the ruling party, the "executive presidency" has remained the backbone of authoritarian rule in Zimbabwe. Constitutional Amendment No. 9 of 1989 abolished the Senate, originally intended to protect the political rights of minorities and counterbalance a more partisan lower chamber, removing another protection against power abuses. Through the addition of the thirty Senate seats it then expanded the House of Assembly to one hundred and fifty members, and the added seats were used for political patronage: Mugabe directly or indirectly—for the traditional chiefs[101]—appointed these MPs. This provided the ruling party with an unfair advantage since any other party winning a majority of the 120 elected seats could still find itself lacking an overall parliamentary majority, and moreover the majority to overrule his veto, remove him from office, or amend the constitution. On the contrary, Mugabe needed only 46 of the contested seats to retain an absolute majority in Parliament. Winning 75 seats of 120 was an impossible task to achieve for the nascent MDC in June 2000. Short of this a victorious opposition would have found it impossible to govern the country and legislate, and the ZANU-PF regime made sure it never came close to achieving such numbers.

The ZANU-PF regime reintroduced the Senate for political expediency as part of Constitutional Amendment No. 17, passed in late August 2005. Out of the 66 seats of the new Senate, only 50 were to be contested within a constituency system on the basis of 5 constituencies per province (which led to an overrepresentation of the rural areas in this chamber). Another 10 seats were reserved for chiefs selected by the provincial colleges of chiefs, and the last 6 were to be appointed directly by the president. This amendment was meant as a minimal gesture to accommodate those demanding constitutional reform, both inside and outside the country, while strengthening Mugabe's grip. A vote of no confidence was made more improbable with the requirement of a two-thirds majority in both houses.[102] The MDC would have to try harder to win majority in two houses rather than in only one. Moreover, the new Senate provided also semiretirement positions for aging ZANU-PF politicians at a time Mugabe once again wanted to rely on younger and more loyal figures, and some solace for the losers in the party primaries before the March 2005 general election.

The combination of extensive presidential powers and the ruling party's domination of Parliament has reduced the House of Assembly to a rubber-stamping role, with important bills being rushed through Parliament without much debate in the relevant parliamentary committees—or ignoring the latter's advice. In the few instances when backbenchers resisted the dictates of the executive they were soon whipped into line. They could only tackle the Cabinet minister during question time, the most lively part of the debates reported in the parliamentary gazette *Hansard*, and some of the backbenchers like Malunga excelled in this game. Some select committees produced useful reports rarely followed by any action. However, the growing dissatisfaction of the ZANU-PF caucus forced the Cabinet to agree to the establishment of a Parliamentary Reform Committee in early 1997. With the full support of the then speaker, Cyril Ndebele, the committee chaired by Mike Mataure, organized public hearings and produced some interesting proposals to increase the role of Parliament and improve the legislative process, including some constitutional reforms.[103] However, the report was tabled in Parliament only in 1999 and its recommendations were never fully implemented.

Important government decisions were made outside Cabinet meetings that endorsed the president's will—to a point that high ranking civil servants often ignored their own minister's instructions and rather obeyed orders emanating from the Office of the President,[104] which has been enlarged through the years operating like a parallel power structure with direct links to the permanent secretaries in the various ministries.[105] The latter are carefully selected ZANU-PF cadres and certainly not neutral functionaries. Mugabe has become extremely skillful at staging controversies over policy issues in the Cabinet or the party organs, which would appear in the media, thus enabling him to better impose his own will behind closed doors.[106] Those few of his lieutenants from the liberation war who can talk face to face with him and voice their concerns never confront him in public. Praise and reprimand are used alternatively to seduce or, on the contrary, destabilize Cabinet ministers and party officials. Often Mugabe has played younger generations against the old guard and vice versa, especially in Cabinet or Central Committee appointments. This balancing act has been necessary for Mugabe to control the factional struggles mentioned before, but it has also allowed him to keep the upper hand in Cabinet proceedings: any minister is worried enough to be constantly watching his back and lashing out at his colleagues, rather than colluding with others against Mugabe. Besides, the appointees perceive positions in a bloated government—around forty ministers in the 1990s—as a fast track to self-aggrandizement (see Chapter 7). Through this process and the sudden elevation of unknown cronies, and the equally abrupt disgrace of erstwhile close aides, Mugabe has become the untouchable cockerel (the ZANU-PF symbol) in the farmyard. The so-called succession debate further contributes to these dynamics.

Hegemony Through Manipulated Elections

Once he won the founding elections, Mugabe never had any intention of relinquishing power. Although he was obliged to shelve his plans to establish a formal political monopoly, all possible means were used to control the outcome of the general elections. Thus no elections in Zimbabwe have ever been "free and fair." Even the independence elections under international supervision were marred by violence and intimidation, mostly from ZANU-PF, a reality overlooked at the time by most diplomats and commentators. The outside world was quite happy to uphold the fiction of a multiparty democracy in the making until the trick was fully exposed by the political crisis that came in the first decade of the twenty-first century.

The conventional wisdom had it in the mid-1990s that the opposition parties' weaknesses accounted for the most part of their marginalization in Zimbabwean politics. On these grounds, most observers have discounted the claims from opposition parties and civic organizations that the electoral process was seriously flawed and the balance was heavily tipped in favor of ZANU-PF. Margaret Dongo's exposure of the rigging system put in place in Harare South by ruling party cadres and partisan civil servants and her subsequent triumphal election in a rerun ridiculed assumptions that ZANU-PF enjoyed undiluted electoral support.[107] However, many still saw the manipulation of the electoral process in Sunningdale as a series of isolated incidents. The reality is that the 1995 elections were rigged in the sense that the process was manipulated to ZANU-PF's advantage, from registration of voters to announcement of results. Had opposition party candidates done their homework, like Margaret Dongo, not to mention journalists from the independent press, the truth would have unraveled long before 2000.

Another common but inaccurate explanation was the so-called voter apathy in the post-1980 elections, both in terms of the numbers bothering to register as voters and in terms of the share of the latter actually voting. In the 1996 presidential election, Robert Mugabe was returned to power with the support of only 27 percent of registered voters. In fact, the large numbers that stayed away from the polls, especially in urban areas, did so to express their dissatisfaction with the regime and at the same time their frustration over the lack of a credible alternative. The opposition parties' attempts to dislodge ZANU-PF from power were seen as preposterous. By making sure these parties did not win constituencies—even though this would not have jeopardized ZANU-PF's hegemony—Mugabe's strategists cultivated popular beliefs that the electoral route was closed. The February 2000 referendum's results provided the breakthrough: the surprise victory of the "No" vote contributed to further mobilize the urban electorate in support of the MDC.

Indeed, the systematic rigging and the extent of intimidation that marred the 2000 and 2005 parliamentary and 2002 presidential elections came as a shock for many. It was then more obvious because the robust MDC challenge to the ruling party's grip provoked a panic reaction within the ruling elite. However, if there was a change of scale in the manipulation of elections after the lost constitutional referendum the means and methods were already in place before February 2000. The study of the 1995 general election already pointed to a sophisticated system of controlling all phases of the electoral process before and after election days. It is a system where the state security agencies are involved in the electoral process and work in cahoots with partisan civil servants such as Tobaiwa Mudede, the registrar general, and supervisory bodies lacking even a modicum of independence. Since 2000 the rigging strategy has been delineated in meetings of the Joint Operations Command (JOC), which comprises the army, police, prison authorities, home affairs officials, and the CIO, and is chaired by Mugabe. There have been numerous NGO reports (especially from the Zimbabwe Election

Support Network, a coalition of 35 organizations, and the Zimbabwe Human Rights NGO Forum, a coalition of 17 organizations), and some reports from international observer missions (EU in 2000, Commonwealth in 2002), which all pointed to the various techniques used by ZANU-PF to influence the election outcome. We will summarize their main findings that suggest a consistent, permanent, and now familiar pattern.

The registration of voters process, overseen by Registrar General Mudede, a functionary loyal to Mugabe and born in the same area, has been used repeatedly to increase the number of registered voters in the areas perceived as pro-ZANU-PF—such as the Mashonaland provinces—therefore allowing some gerrymandering to take place through the delimitation of constituencies (which is based on registration and not census figures). This manipulation has affected all elections since 1980, and once again in 2005 with three constituencies cut out of MDC strongholds.[108] Although Mudede has been ordered by the courts to clean the voter rolls and allow the public to check their accuracy, his office has deliberately kept the voter rolls in shambles,[109] in such a way that there was always a need for supplementary voter rolls, to which the opposition parties had no access and which were used to doctor ballot figures in selected constituencies. This supplementary voter roll was ruled illegal in 1995 and has been relentlessly criticized by human rights NGOs and election observers. As in the previous elections, there were between one and two million more people on the voter rolls in 2005 than the total number of potential voters in the country—given the rate of emigration and increased mortality linked to AIDS and malnutrition—with still many duplications and names of deceased people appearing on the rolls.[110]

For the presidential elections in 2002 a good number of white citizens were stripped of their Zimbabwean citizenship, hence of their right to vote on the basis of the Citizenship Act 2001. This policy was generalized prior to the 2005 general election: 150,000 lost their right to vote when descendants of migrant workers from the neighboring countries and Zimbabweans of European descent were declared noncitizens.[111] For the 2002 presidential election, proof-of-residency requirements, which had been tightened up, were used to disenfranchise thousands of urban dwellers—known to be massively pro-MDC—especially new voters. In rural areas, however, an oral confirmation by village headmen or farm owners was accepted as a proof of residence, allowing an easy registration of voters controlled by ZANU-PF. In addition, Mudede and his aides also made it as difficult as possible to opposition candidates to field their nomination papers at various elections.

In the run-up to all national elections, the state and the ruling party prevented the opposition parties from campaigning efficiently by enforcing a ban in the government media and using the new media legislation to weaken the independent press. Another means was the harassment of opposition supporters by the police and the ZANU-PF militias. This was particularly true in the June 2000 parliamentary elections and the 2002 presidential elections, when the rural areas in several provinces were sealed. To further curtail opposition parties' activities, new repressive laws were implemented, such as the Public Order and Security Act (POSA) of 2002, which replaced LOMA. It made it an offense to criticize the president and gave arbitrary powers to the police to ban opposition parties and civic organization meetings and demonstrations. POSA also prohibits public statements "inciting public disorder or public violence or endangering public safety."[112] The violence was turned down immediately before and during the 2005 parliamentary election, and the MDC was allowed to hold some campaign rallies as the government felt itself under the scrutiny of its Southern African Development Community (SADC) and African Union (AU) counterparts.

As stressed in the above-mentioned study of the 1995 elections, the ZANU-PF-controlled state has used various forms of patronage to control the vote in rural areas, such as free tillage, free seeds, and fertilizer packages. However, this blackmailing of the most destitute among the electorate reached a new low in the run-up to the 2002 and 2005 ballots. Known or suspected opposition supporters were denied food aid where it was most needed. The breakdown of the vote at the polling station level in 2005 allowed a fine tuning in the subsequent retribution against communities supporting the opposition, making the ruling party campaign threats more serious. The traditional chiefs and headmen, who are on the government's payroll, have been co-opted furthermore into the ZANU-PF machine since the passing of the 1999 Traditional Leaders Act. They received hefty pay rises before each general election and have been relied upon since 2000 to coerce their clansmen to vote in favor of ZANU-PF.[113]

On election days various techniques were used to tip the balance for ZANU-PF from one constituency to another, to increase the margins through tampering with the supplementary voter rolls. The number of polling stations for the presidential elections in 2002 was reduced in the big cities, to lower the effective turnout in opposition strongholds, and the MDC had to seek an urgent order from the High Court to have the polling stations reopened for a third day of voting (but even here, the registrar general did not fully comply with the order). Not every voter managed to cast a vote in the urban areas in 2002. The postal voting system also provides room for foul play: it is restricted to the members of the police, army, and public service who have "good reason" to be away from their constituency on the polling day, also government employees on a foreign posting, thus excluding more than three million Zimbabweans of the diaspora who are considered unlikely to vote for the ruling party. Opposition parties and civic organizations have no control over the postal voting process, and the government can tamper with these ballots and use them in areas where they can make a difference.[114] Similarly the provisions for assisted voting intended for illiterate or disabled persons are widely abused by presiding officers to influence the people's choice. Electoral officers are chosen according to their loyalty to the regime,[115] and include an increasing number of military, CIO, and War Vets.

Counting and announcement of the results offer also some good opportunities for rigging. Interference with the counting of ballot papers before counting was completed in selected constituencies in 2005 led to allegations of ballot box stuffing.[116] A statistical analysis conducted by the Zimbabwe Election Support Network (ZESN) on the basis of the data collected by its 6,000 observers deployed in the polling stations shows that the published election results did not make sense in nearly 30 constituencies.[117] The Zimbabwe Electoral Commission (ZEC) provided no convincing explanation for these inconsistencies, and it refused to release a detailed breakdown of the voting by polling station in the disputed constituencies. However, the Zimbabwe Human Rights NGO Forum concluded in its postelection report that these irregularities were "not significant enough to affect the result" and that "the MDC [did] not appear to have lost the election due to a rigged ballot."[118] The MDC defeat could be better explained by other government tactics such as the political use of food aid in the months prior to the election, effective propaganda linking the MDC to colonialist interests, and threats of retaliation.[119]

Despite Mugabe's endorsement of the Principles and Guidelines for Democratic Elections, adopted by SADC in August 2004, the amended Zimbabwean electoral law still did not comply with the minimum requirements for free and fair elections. In a typical window-dressing exercise the ZANU-PF introduced in December 2004 some limited reforms: a new ZEC, the reduction of polling days from two days to one, the creation of an Electoral Court, the use of translucent ballot boxes and the counting of votes at polling stations.[120] The new act was designed to legitimize the upcoming elections in the eyes of African leaders, and thus alleviate the pressure exerted on Mugabe by his SADC neighbors, without compromising his party's control of the electoral process. For example, Robert Mugabe appointed the chair after consultation with the Judicial Service Commission (JSC)—stacked with presidential appointees—while he also appointed the four other commissioners from a list of seven nominees submitted by a Parliamentary Committee dominated by ZANU-PF members.[121] This was a far cry from the independent commission demanded by SADC guidelines. Moreover, the ZEC did not carry out voter registration, which remained in the hands of the registrar general's office. There remained also many overlaps between the functions of the ZEC and the Electoral Supervisory Commission (ESC), existing under the country's Constitution—a source of confusion (they both appointed a chief elections officer in early 2005!) and an opportunity to evade further scrutiny. Had the government sought a compromise agreement with the MDC on the creation of an independent electoral commission, it could have succeeded in amending the constitution and removing the redundant ESC prior to the 2005 election. In any case, the electoral process became increasingly run by the military (even ZEC's chairman appointed in January 2005 was former army officer George Chiweshe),[122] with the police, and the CIO, under the National Logistics Committee and the JOC, rather than by the impotent rival electoral commissions.

The control of the electoral process by Mugabe's close aides has deprived the MDC of likely victories in all national elections since the June 2000 parliamentary elections, where it narrowly lost with 57 constituencies against 62 for the ruling party (in addition to the 30 MPs appointed directly or indirectly by the president), and one for the late Ndabaningi Sithole's ZANU Ndonga.[123] This remarkable achievement in a political climate of violence brought a real opposition back to Parliament for the first time since 1987, and deprived the ruling party of the capacity to further amend the constitution—a true embarrassment for Mugabe when the succession debate developed in 2003. Although ZANU-PF managed to retain all its parliamentary seats and gain a few more in subsequent by-elections between 2001 and 2004, the required two-thirds majority remained beyond its reach until the parliamentary elections of 2005. The MDC also gained control of local government in the country's six largest cities, through the mayoral and council elections between 2001 and 2003. However, in Harare, Chitungwiza, Chegutu, and Mutare, MDC-led councils were subsequently dismissed and replaced by government-appointed commissions or "caretaker" mayors, as part of ZANU-PF's attempts to regain control of the cities.[124] It is also likely that Morgan Tsvangirai was the real winner of the presidential election in March 2002, although Robert Mugabe's popularity had risen, after reaching a record low in October 2000. Rigging on a large scale, as reflected in the Commonwealth and Norwegian observer missions' reports—and countless reports produced by local NGOs—remained necessary to produce the official outcome (55.2 percent of the vote cast for Mugabe against 41.4 percent for Tsvangirai).[125] The MDC electoral petition filed in April 2002 contained ample evidence of such practices,[126] but it was ditched by a partisan High Court judge after months of procrastination.

According to the Zimbabwe Electoral Commission, ZANU-PF polled nearly 60 percent of the vote in March 2005, an increase of 11 percent over the 2000 results, and the MDC's vote fell 9 percent to 39 percent. MDC representation in the House of Assembly was therefore reduced to 41 seats. Whether these results were doctored or were the logical outcome of years of intimidation and propaganda, the MDC emerged severely weakened from its third electoral defeat in a row. The stunned opposition party then failed to formulate adequate responses to the Murambatsvina tragedy in May–July 2005; even the MDC-led municipalities could not protect the people from ZANU-PF's wrath. The general strike it co-organized with the ZCTU and the National Constitutional Assembly (NCA), on 9–10 June, was a dismal failure, highlighting the party's perennial organizational problems. In this respect, the controversy and factionalism that surfaced in October 2005, and which led to MDC's split into two rival parties in early 2006, was a symptom of the opposition's already weak position. With the MDC deeply divided, and through the use of its repressive legislation and the biased electoral system,[127] the government obtained the outcome it desired in the November 2005 Senate election. ZANU-PF won 43 seats and the "pro-Senate" faction of MDC 7 (of 26 candidates) in the context of a record low turnout since a significant share of the electorate heeded to boycott calls by the Tsvangirai-led MDC faction. At his faction's congress in March 2006 Tsvangirai announced a new strategy of "peaceful, democratic resistance" and the organization of mass protest to force Mugabe out power throughout the winter (June to September).[128] As so often in the past, nothing materialized on the ground because Tsvangirai's party did not have the grassroots political structures necessary to lead a sustained campaign of mass protest.

Enjoying a two-thirds majority in both houses of Parliament, the ruling party could then change the Constitution at will. However, Amendment No. 18 was passed on 19 September 2007 with the support of MDC, thanks to mediation by the SADC. The amendment synchronized the presidential and parliamentary elections (with the effect of forcing ZANU-PF parliamentary candidates to support Mugabe in the presidential contest), removed presidential appointees in the lower house, and increased the number of seats in both houses—a means to foster Mugabe's patronage, play on MDC's divisions, and dissolve potential opposition in a ZANU-PF dominated Parliament. Yet the real purpose of the Act was to provide for an election procedure of a successor to

Mugabe, through a two-thirds majority in the two houses, jointly sitting as an electoral college, should the president die, resign, or be impeached before the end of his term. The amendment also increased the powers of the Zimbabwe Electoral Commission—removing the redundant ESC and transferring formally to the ZEC the control over delimitation and registration—but fell short of the MDC's demands for a new constitution and a bipartisan electoral commission. ZANU-PF and MDC negotiating teams agreed on a draft constitution on 30 September 2007[129]—known afterward as the "Kariba draft"—but the relationship soured, and by the end of the year it was clear Mugabe would not countenance constitutional reform prior to the elections.

As a result of the Mbeki-sponsored talks, however, the Electoral Act was also amended to provide for electoral observers in polling stations; more transparent procedures for counting ballots at the polling station—immediately after the end of the vote and with the results being displayed at station's entrance—and the right to demand a recount; a guarantee of the opposition's right to campaign unhindered around the country; and a more flexible access to the state electronic media during the campaign period. These limited changes nevertheless had an impact on the outcome of the March 2008 elections (see Conclusion). However, the government remained firmly in control of the electoral process beginning with the appointment of ZEC members, all of them Mugabe loyalists who, as usual, worked closely with the registrar general and other partisan officials. Interference from the JOC in the electoral process also was as important as in 2005—as the run-off in the 2008 presidential election later demonstrated.

Through the years Mugabe has established his personal control over the liberation movement, and then the state and the political arena in Zimbabwe, leaving any opposition from within or from outside the ruling party without breathing space. For sure it was not outright dictatorship: Mugabe maintained the façade of parliamentary democracy (including the old-fashioned, English style opening ceremony of Parliament) and just enough political bickering within the ruling party, although no one dared to challenge him. However, the outer limits of freedom were reached very fast in the late 1990s, and it became obvious that a truly democratic constitution, free press, independent judiciary, and transparent and fair elections were not compatible with the perpetuation of Mugabe's rule. By closing the electoral route for the opposition, Mugabe has left the MDC without any viable, alternate strategy, and, incidentally, has dissuaded potential ZANU-PF dissenters eager to get rid of the aging despot from striking any deal with the opposition. By 2007 the divided MDC lacked viable political perspectives in spite of

Mugabe's fast-growing unpopularity. The cunning autocrat propelled the succession debate by suggesting repeatedly (as early as 1999 in ZANU-PF closed-door proceedings on the constitutional reform) that he would soon retire from active politics, but only to force his lieutenants to make their bids, and then play upon their rival ambitions. These factions' leaders know very well that Mugabe trusts nobody—in line with the political culture of recklessness and deceit he has promoted within his own party—and will expect to die in office. Therefore, they fight each other primarily to prevent their rivals' ascent to power, a fairly common sight in any decaying personal rule.

Chapter 2

Violence as the Cornerstone
of Mugabe's Strategy of Political Survival

Violence was crucial for ZANU-PF to secure victory in both the parliamentary elections in June 2000 and the presidential election in March 2002, and once again in the 2008 presidential run-off (although systematic rigging also played a determining role, especially in presidential elections). From a survey conducted of people coming out of the polling stations in June 2000, Professor R. W. Johnson estimated that up to 12 percent of the voters changed their vote from MDC to ZANU-PF as a consequence of the political violence inflicted on them during the electoral campaign,[1] a figure corroborated by an October 2000 survey using the same methodology. It could be argued that only a minority of the electorate was affected, but this violence then targeted primarily the swing vote in the twenty constituencies where ZANU-PF eventually won with a margin of 500 votes or less. Therefore, it is very likely that without inflicting such violence the ruling party would have lost its absolute majority in Parliament. Moreover, with 75 seats the MDC would have been in a position to amend the constitution or impeach Mugabe. There was no public opinion survey after the presidential election. However, since political violence intensified rather than abated between 2000 and 2002, it is reasonable to assume that state-sponsored violence kept Mugabe in power for the first decade of the twenty-first century.

Many observers were caught off guard by the violent character of the Zimbabwe crisis. It seems that the façade of urbane language before some audiences and institutionalized procedures deluded many foreigners, who failed to listen to opposition parties' pleas before 2000. "Political stability," hailed by Western resident diplomats up to 1997 and seen as a guarantee for the security of foreign investment, was also used as a convenient justification for authoritarian rule among academic commentators. The other face of the Mugabe regime was ignored, and the role of political violence and oppression was assiduously downplayed. However, violence has been part of the ruling party's political culture (even in the infancy of black nationalism in Rhodesia)[2] and government's policies from the outset. ZANU-PF leaders were not even secretive about it, and hundreds of actions and speeches can be cited from press reports over the last twenty-two years. Not a single electoral campaign since Independence has been free of violence, albeit with variable intensity and geographical extension.[3] That illusions about "democratization" and "reform" prevailed for so long over the grim reality can only be explained by the convergence of Western powers' constant search for an African showcase and the Third World's perceptions of Mugabe as a freedom fighter. Nevertheless, February 2000 was a turning point: the intensity of violence and, more important, the cynicism of the state's obvious involvement, its indifference for the law also meant that the regime had thrown off its mask in the fight for survival with no prospect of reversing such policy.

A Political Culture Rooted in Violence

Ruling party secretary for information Nathan Shamuyarira once cynically pointed out: "the area of violence is an area where ZANU-PF has a very strong, long and successful history."[4] Although Mugabe and his party enjoyed some strong support among the masses, especially in the early 1980s, and were able to mobilize the electorate in the rural areas until the mid-1990s, this popular backing was at best ambiguous since it was obtained partly through the use of political intimidation, sometimes through direct violence, but most of the time—until 2000—through innuendos and coded discourse, enough to remind the people what the ruling party was capable of doing. Along with the deep-seated intolerance against all dissenting voices (as seen in Chapter 1), violence is part and parcel of the "one-party-state" culture, which remains to date ZANU-PF's ideological mold.

Contrary to the dominant historical narrative and the apparent collective memory, the internationally monitored 1980 elections were far from being "free and fair." In fact, widespread intimidation played a major role in ZANU-PF's victory: between 4,000 (official British estimate) and 10,000 ZANLA fighters were not stationed in the assembly points when the December 1979 ceasefire took effect but were hidden in the villages to prevent other parties from campaigning,[5] telling people to vote for Mugabe's party or the war would resume. ZANU's Enos Nkala publicly confessed this in Matabeleland.[6] Authors of a biography of Mugabe, generally sympathetic to ZANU's leader, write the following on the basis of an election supervisors' interim report: "More than half of the people of Rhodesia were being intimidated by Mugabe's guerrillas and supporters, they said. Conditions for 'free and fair' elections did not exist in five of the eight electoral districts in the country. Contrary to the claims of Mugabe, the supervisors found little proof of intimidation by [pro-UANC] Rhodesian security force auxiliaries."[7]

Although in some areas of Manicaland and eastern Mashonaland Province, UANC youths also employed methods of intimidation, nothing could match ZANU-PF's "paramilitary campaign" carried on against the background of wartime coercion. In any case, the UANC auxiliaries were kept in closer check, by journalists and Commonwealth observers, than ZIPRA and ZANLA forces. In regions like Masvingo, the Midlands, or some Harare townships where ZANU-PF and ZAPU were in direct competition, or Manicaland, the UANC stronghold, intimidation was paramount: "voting in these areas took place in an atmosphere of fear and under evident compulsion."[8] Political murder and explicit threats of retaliation were rife. In more than a quarter of the country no parties other than ZANU-PF had been able to campaign for fear of reprisals. Joshua Nkomo warned, "People are being terrorized. . . . There is fear in people's eyes."[9]

Incensed by overwhelming evidence of ZANU-PF's violence and intimidation, Lord Soames—the British governor appointed to oversee the transition—confronted Mugabe but refused to ban his party from contesting or to nullify the poll altogether in the relevant districts, and for obvious reasons: when challenged, Mugabe had threatened to throw away the peace agreement and he was likely to resume war. The British government had no intention of taking that responsibility and risking an international outcry at the United Nations. It was not prepared to lose such a golden opportunity to rid itself once and for all of the Rhodesian problem, that thorn in the flesh of its African policy since the 1960s. These calculations took precedence over concerns for democratic elections. The fact that ZANU-PF, most probably, would have won the elections anyway, contrary to Ian Smith's claims in his memoirs, is beside the point. Even if intimidation accounted only for the difference between a simple majority and an absolute majority, it mattered politically. Mugabe's 57 seats made his claim to the premiership indisputable. He could form a government of his choice, even with apparent magnanimity, and Joshua Nkomo had to surrender.[10]

So the people voted for "peace" in 1980, for the party that could deliver the war end as they had done in April 1979—then in favor of Muzorewa.[11] Yet the founding elections set a terrible precedent: for Mugabe what matters is the balance of forces and the electoral process a mere technicality to emphasize power. Therefore, there is a continuity in behavior between the wartime violence against black peasants and the harsh tactics implemented since February 2000 against farmworkers and selected communities suspected of supporting the MDC. For many people who lived through the war in the rural areas, ZANLA surpassed all other sides in brutality.[12] Recent historiography on Zimbabwe's liberation war indicates that routine coercion was an important and in some areas crucial resource to obtain political support from the "masses":

> Parents, youth, and the rural elite had little choice but to identify with ZANU and provide logistical support for the guerrillas. . . . One dared refuse only at the risk of personal physical harm. . . . A war [village committee] chairman succinctly expressed the sentiments of others when he explained that "comrades would know if you refused the job and then you could get beaten. I never knew of anyone who did refuse. There was just that fear that if one did, one could get beaten." . . . Failure to conform with guerrilla demands might also result in death, usually with the same instrument with which the guerrillas beat people.[13]

Villagers would be beaten for being too slow to surrender their meager resources, for declining to attend political meetings, or for their lack of commitment to the war and ZANU-PF.[14] Punishment of "sellouts" more than once degenerated into collective retribution against whole villages.[15] This dreadful experience created the basis of the culture of fear that has pervaded Zimbabwe's politics since Independence. Therefore, the use of violent methods to ensure the ruling party's electoral victory in 2000 and 2002 does not come as a surprise. Victims describing war veterans' terror techniques spontaneously recalled their war experience and the mix of ideological propaganda and violence they endured in the notorious compulsory night meetings—called "pungwes."

Gukurahundi

In the post-independence era the worst example of politically motivated violence was the massacre of thousands of civilians in Matabeleland in an orgy of killing known as "Gukurahundi." As argued in Chapter 1, the main purpose of these deliberate killings, rapes, torture, and destruction of property (huts, crops, and cattle) was the elimination of ZAPU's popular following as a way to force the party's leadership into submission. What is striking though is the savagery of the onslaught by the North Korean-trained and Shona-recruited Fifth Brigade, the CIO, some other army units, and the ZANU-PF Youth League, which left thousands of people dead and many more maimed and marked for the rest of their lives, most families being affected one way or another.[16] "From about the beginning of 1983, the people of Matabeleland experienced once again military and political terror hardly distinguished from that inflicted on the people of Zimbabwe by the Rhodesian State."[17] There was a dimension of ethnic hatred that resembled the "ethnic cleansing" later practiced in the former Yugoslavia in the 1992–95 wars: Fifth Brigade members told the women and girls they raped that they would bear Shona babies to wipe out Ndebeles in Matabeleland. There is little doubt that ZANU-PF leaders encouraged this attitude.[18] To this date, some ZANU-PF leaders who took part in these crimes boast of having no regrets as "the Ndebeles got what they deserved."[19] According to Amnesty International (AI), "The abuses documented during this period by Amnesty International and other organizations, including torture, extrajudicial executions and 'disappearances,' are serious crimes under international law, and may amount to crimes against humanity, as defined in the Statute of the International Criminal Court, adopted in July 1998."[20] When one sees to what extreme Mugabe was prepared to go in 1982–86 to get rid of ZAPU, the terror campaign launched against MDC since 2000 fits in the pattern.

In rural Matabeleland, the memory of the Fifth Brigade and Gukurahundi has not faded yet and it forms the background of any political activity in that region and to a large extent in the southern Midlands to date. At election time, frequent references to the 1983–87 violence could be found in the government press and in the ZANU-PF leader's speeches. For example, government intelligence was leaked to the press in January 1994 revealing that "a security joint operation command (JOC) [had] been put on full alert [in Bulawayo] to deal with any disturbances that might occur following surfacing reports that a group of youths calling itself Super ZAPU [was] allegedly planning to terrorise non-Ndebele speakers."[21] It was a reference to the South Africa-backed guerrilla unit that infiltrated Matabeleland during the conflict of the early 1980s and that was accused of the worst of the atrocities perpetuated by the "dissidents."[22] The allegation that Super-ZAPU was revived fooled nobody but was meant to create a climate of fear in the region. During the 1995 campaign, several ZANU-PF cadres threatened a return of the civil war of the early 1980s if the people in Matabeleland voted for the opposition parties. There was also a veiled threat in the president's speeches when he urged the Ndebeles to preserve unity and support the ruling party if they wanted to keep the peace they had enjoyed since 1987. In other parts of the country, especially in Masvingo, Manicaland, and Mashonaland, which bore the brunt of guerrilla activity during the liberation war, similar threats to resume fighting if the ruling party lost the elections were routinely made during the election campaign in 1995, but observers easily dismissed them as mere political rhetoric.

The same threats were renewed, more aggressively this time, during the 2000 and 2002 electoral campaigns. Didymus Mutasa's public admission that party leaders "would be better off with only 6 million people, with [their] own people who support the liberation struggle"[23]—the current government—betrays the extent to which ZANU-PF hard-liners are prepared to go eventually to get rid of the opposition. The then ruling party secretary for administration alluded not only to farm workers, many of whom are of Malawian, Mozambican, or Zambian descent, but also to opposition supporters in the rural areas who have been deprived of food aid repeatedly by party militias from 2002 to 2005. Food as a weapon had already been used against alleged dissidents in Matabeleland during the Gukurahundi.[24]

Even after the Unity Accord and the end of the alleged Matabeleland dissidence, the 1990 general elections were marred by several incidents of violence. The worst was an attempt to murder Patrick Kombayi, then a ZUM candidate in Gweru, who was widely expected to win the constituency held by Vice President Muzenda.[25] Two of the culprits, the Midlands CIO chief who was in charge of the vice president's security and a ZANU-PF youth leader, were eventually convicted and sentenced to seven years in jail. Although the Supreme Court upheld their conviction, President Mugabe, using his presidential prerogative for mercy, pardoned both in 1993. Incidents of violence were less prominent in the 1995 elections, but were far more numerous than most observers assumed, in particular in the ZANU-PF primary elections. The impression conveyed by the Electoral Supervisory Commission and several reports from civic groups that had monitored the elections—with the notable exception of the informed judgment of the Zimbabwe Human Rights Association (ZIMRIGHTS)—that the 1995 elections were "free but not fair" because there was little violence does not reflect the reality. Violence was rife in areas of actual competition, hence in the ruling party primaries (disregarded by the ESC), which were the real elections in many constituencies. In these the MP was subsequently elected unopposed as a direct result of the opposition's partial boycott. There were a few constituencies where ZANU-PF encountered real challenges from opposition or independent candidates. Such was the case in Harare North, where Trudy Stevenson campaigned actively for the Forum Party—and was called a "dirty white pig" by ZANU-PF women—or in Harare South, where ZANU dissident Margaret Dongo was castigated as a "sellout" by her CIO-sponsored opponent. A real challenge to its power always generated a violent response from ZANU-PF. The above-mentioned study of the 1995 elections concluded that when facing a credible and organized national opposition—what the MDC happened to be—Mugabe and his lieutenants would not hesitate to resort to large-scale violent methods already tested in 1980, 1985, and 1990. Unfortunately this prediction was vindicated by subsequent developments.

Violence as a Tool for Electoral Campaigns and Political Retribution

Although originally located on the commercial farms, a wave of organized violence immediately followed the government's defeat in the 12–13 February 2000 constitutional referendum. This reveals its real motives. Whatever the misgivings Mugabe might have had about the Constitutional Review Commission (CRC) draft, and a reform exercise imposed on him, he did not take lightly to defeat. He knew very well that the people voted for change and against him and his government rather than against a constitutional proposal that only a few had read. The grass roots had been successfully mobilized by the National Constitutional Assembly (NCA) outreach program against a twisted process of constitutional reform and a draft entrenching the president's powers. However, the majority of the people were primarily concerned with bread-and-butter issues after the 1998 food riots and used their vote as a protest. Not only had ZANU-PF, for the first time since Independence, lost a poll at the national level, but demonstrators took to the street to show Mugabe "red cards" after a referendum result seen as the "yellow card," a now famous soccer-inspired metaphor to convey the message that the president's time had come to leave the playing field. This strong anti-Mugabe mood prevailing the country over—although stronger in the urban areas—was measured by the Helen Suzman Foundation opinion poll in late January and early February 2000.[26] Mugabe's compromising tone when he acknowledged the referendum results on television was not an admission of failure but rather a tactical retreat to prepare for the next step.

The first purpose of post-referendum violence was retribution: white farmers had to be punished for their support of the MDC/NCA. For the ruling party strategists, the latter's victory in the referendum was only made possible by white financial and logistical support (indeed farmers were shown in the media signing checks for the MDC after a meeting with Tsvangirai and ferrying their laborers in trucks to the polling stations). Farmers—and to some extent employers in the manufacturing sector—were accused of mobilizing their black workers in favor of the opposition, although the role of the trade unions was more decisive in this respect. All this provided a convenient excuse to duck the real issue:

the low popularity of the president and his party after years of corruption and bad governance. Besides, the "Yes" vote campaign led by Jonathan Moyo, Godfrey Chidyausiku, and Patrick Chinamasa of the CRC had already pointed to a "white plot," and targeting white farmers transformed the lunacy into a self-fulfilling prophecy. The "land clause" was inserted into the draft constitution to win War Vets' support but also to provoke the farmers into reacting en masse and to create the ensuing racial polarization. The white farmers felt Mugabe had reneged on his Independence reconciliation policy. They were suddenly in a weak political position, and campaigned against the adoption of the draft constitution to prevent the land grab from being legalized. So the farm invasions targeted first the farms of MDC sympathizers—in fact a minority of the white farming community—and the first farmers to be beaten or killed were also MDC local organizers, such as David Stevens, openly abducted from a police station and murdered on 15 April 2000, or known MDC supporters. In subsequent government and ZANU-PF discourse, the MDC was portrayed as the party that wanted to give the country back to the whites; moreover, the party leaders were "puppets" of the British government and therefore all MDC supporters were traitors to their country and to their race—in ZANU-PF's view, a justification of the harsh treatment they were to receive. However, as early as May 2000 the black casualties of this undeclared war greatly outnumbered the white victims.

The murders and beatings of white farmers had a second purpose in Mugabe's plan: they were meant to frighten them away from the land and make the land grab easier. There would be no more legal technicalities, no more judicial squabbles, they should simply give up their farms; this was the ultimate objective. That message came out loud and clear throughout the months after February 2000, and the façade of legal procedures maintained up to mid-2002 was merely a cover-up for a cynical instrumental use of terror. At the December 2000 ZANU-PF congress, Mugabe explained his strategy: "we must continue to strike fear into the heart of the white man, our real enemy,"[27] and he renewed his threats on many occasions during the following months. But the anti-white violence was even more important from a symbolic point of view: it illustrated and justified the government's racialist propaganda; all that it was about was the final battle against colonialism, the "Third Chimurenga,"[28] as Mugabe chose to call it. For a Pan-African audience that has little knowledge of what was (and is) really happening on the ground, the emotional appeal of this anti-colonialist discourse is undeniable, and it has been the basis of Mugabe's belief that whatever he did he would not lose the support of his African colleagues.

When the invasions began, most farm workers expressed solidarity with their bosses, in spite of their supposedly conflicting class interests and contrary to the assumption that all white farmers were necessarily unreconstructed racists—in most cases labor relations were of a benevolent paternalistic nature with farmers providing their workers with basic but precious services in housing, health care, food supply, and schooling for the children. In any case, workers reckoned that the farmers' source of income was also their means of a livelihood and their jobs depended on their capacity to operate—indeed, most of these workers have been laid off since mid-2000 and their families left destitute. Besides, many workers understood that it all amounted to a political gimmick—more than anybody else they knew how difficult it was to become a successful farmer—and that the land illegally appropriated would end up in the hands of Mugabe's cronies (as was the case from mid-2002 onward). In a few instances the workers sided with the invaders, becoming accomplices to acts of violence—sometimes exerting revenge for some unsettled labor dispute—taking advantage of farm looting or applying for plots on occupied land. All attempts to resist illegal farm invasions have resulted in savage punishment, since it did not follow the script written by ZANU-PF "chefs." When farm workers defended themselves or tried to retaliate—as was the case with Stevens's employees who tried to evict invaders from the farm after the militias had raped a worker's daughter—War Vets would come back later with reinforcements and there would be more severe casualties. Violence or straight evictions—usually accompanied by the looting and the burning of workers' houses—drove several thousands from their homes. But this was only the beginning.

Parliamentary Elections

It soon became obvious that the violence associated with the farm invasions also had a third and a more crucial purpose for the ruling party, namely, to win the 2000 parliamentary elections. Originally due in early April, they were conveniently postponed until June 2000 to allow the time for violence to produce the desired outcome. The big cities like Harare and Bulawayo, which massively rejected the constitutional draft—with 73.2 and 75.3 percent of the vote respectively—were written off by ZANU-PF strategists. However, CIO reports indicated that the MDC, though less than a year old, was also making significant progress in the rural areas, the traditional power base of ZANU-PF. The usual methods of election manipulation and inflammatory rhetoric, through which the ruling party had managed to dominate the political scene since independence, were not going to work this time: outright but controlled violence was crucial to cow the rural masses back into submission. The margins might be too narrow and with a still relatively independent judiciary, postelectoral litigation could be—and indeed was—used by the MDC. Successful legal challenges might then reverse an election victory obtained through rigging. In other words, the façade of legalism more or less maintained until February 2000 had to be dropped for a more offensive campaigning.

Mugabe made his intentions clear in March 2000 when he declared at an official ceremony: "Those who try to cause disunity among our people must watch out because death will befall them."[29] The Zimbabwe Human Rights NGO Forum final report on the parliamentary elections is based on 1,000 statements from victims. Providing only a glimpse of the massive scale of political violence it stated:

> ZANU-PF supporters and many state organs were engaged in a systematic, premeditated campaign to terrorize local communities into voting for the party or not voting at all. . . . One independent report has estimated that there were well over 200,000 cases of political violence in the first half of 2000. . . . The evidence clearly supports the view that there was a systematic campaign of organised violence and torture perpetrated against all opposition political parties and their supporters. The physical acts of violence conform to the definition of torture contained in the UN Convention Against Torture.[30]

International observers from the Commonwealth and the European Union concurred with the NGOs on the role of violence that prevented the opposition from campaigning openly and the electorate from voting freely.[31]

Intimidation followed a pattern: elements of the ZANU-PF militia called War Vets, armed mainly with knives, spears, axes, machetes, batons, and a few firearms, would round up the farmworkers—wives, the elderly, and children included—frog-march them to the militia's nearby camp (usually an invaded farm), and beat them at random, force them to sing pro-ZANU-PF chants, keep them at all-night "political education" meetings reminiscent of wartime *pungwes*, while some MDC activists would be singled out to be tortured, beaten, and sometimes killed. Workers would be released only once they had pledged to vote for ZANU-PF and were threatened by War Vets with severe punishment if they did otherwise. The violent campaign moved from one farming district to another, probably because the party strategists lacked the resources (manpower and finances) to operate simultaneously in all areas. For many farmworkers with little education and no access to independent information, the threat was credible enough, given the fact that the police refused to act when violence was reported to them or often sided with the War Vets, who clearly enjoyed full government support. How could you believe your vote to be secret, as NCA, MDC, and election monitors had told voters, in circumstances where the whole state apparatus colluded with the perpetrators of violence? This terror campaign extended to some mining camps in the Bindura area and forest plantations in the Eastern Highlands.

The same violence fell upon MDC activists in Harare's high-density suburbs like Mbare, Mufakose, and Budiriro, this last being the locality of War Vets leader Chenjerai "Hitler" Hunzvi's private surgery, which was used as a torture chamber and murder arena by ZANU-PF activists, with the complicity of elements of the police and the army.[32] All around the country, MDC local officials were beaten and maimed and saw their houses and other properties destroyed as the campaign expanded from the commercial farming areas to the communal lands (the former tribal reserves where blacks peasants were confined prior to 1980) and small towns. Testimony gathered by human rights groups shows that victims were sometimes chosen haphazardly but more often were carefully identified on preestablished lists, suggesting that the War Vets benefited from intelligence sources—although one of the purposes of the torture sessions was to extract more inside information from alleged MDC members. In the rural areas, ZANU-PF militias were tipped off by headmen and traditional chiefs. Several opposition party members were abducted and subsequently killed, such as MDC candidate David Coltart's electoral agent in Bulawayo and an MDC activist in Mberengwa. The June 2000 MDC candidate standing against Emmerson Mnangagwa in Kwekwe went into hiding after surviving an assassination attempt and seeing his house burned down by ZANU-PF thugs,[33] only to reappear when he won the election—to his own astonishment. MDC candidate for Bindura, Elliot Pfebve, narrowly escaped several attempts on his life but his look-alike brother was murdered. There were 40 deaths countrywide in the run-up period, 36 of them MDC supporters.[34]

Some constituencies were put under siege, with War Vets and other party militias manning roadblocks to prevent MDC activists from campaigning and creating "no-go areas," not only for MDC but also for independent press reporters, church and NGO activists, and election observers—in particular in the three Mashonaland provinces. In the rural areas and small towns, various categories of people perceived as potential opposition supporters (like schoolteachers, council employees, doctors, and nurses) were systematically assaulted or driven away.[35] They took refuge in towns as dispossessed farm workers had done and were not able to vote in the elections. Although MDC, seen as the main political threat, was also the main target, other opposition parties were treated in the same fashion, such as UP in the Mudzi area. In May and early June 2000, most MDC candidates could not hold campaign meetings in the rural areas or townships without been physically attacked by the War Vets or brutally dispersed by the riot police. Several ZANU-PF candidates took an active part in the violence—some of them using firearms against their opponents—and were later rewarded by Mugabe for their zeal.

State Sponsorship and Impunity for the Criminals

That Mugabe condoned such deliberate and often carefully planned violence was made clear from the very beginning. In public speeches he downplayed the importance of the murders and other incidents of violence, claimed on several occasions that the farmers or the MDC activists had "provoked" the War Vets, stopped the police from acting against perpetrators of violence when they were linked to ZANU-PF, and threatened on various occasions, including formal party meetings or state functions, to crush the white farmers and all political opponents. Plans for the violent invasions had been drawn in advance and bore no resemblance to the spontaneous occupations that had taken place from time to time since independence and were always ended by a timely police intervention. The coordination of the farm invasions, in particular the choice of the first targets, bore the mark of the CIO.[36] The strategic planning at the highest level was entrusted to the JOC, which acted under direct instructions from Mugabe and involved minister of justice Emmerson Mnangagwa; the national security minister (Sydney Sekeramayi and from July 2000 Nicholas Goche); the head of the CIO; chief of staff of the Zimbabwe Defence Forces (ZDF) General Zvinavashe; notorious former head of the Fifth Brigade General Perence Shiri; War Vets leader Hitler Hunzvi, and Border Gezi. This committee became the real power behind ZANU-PF's Politburo and the Cabinet. Only a few high-ranking chefs close enough to Mugabe—not even all Politburo senior members—were privy to its decisions.

The executive branch of the state fully supported the violence against the opposition, and the CIO was behind several cases of abduction and torture. The murder of Martin Olds in April 2000, with its bizarre modus operandi, was the work of either the CIO or the military intelligence. A paramilitary unit came from outside the Nyamandlovu area—perhaps from Harare—and its obvious purpose was to kill the farmer (they started to shoot shortly after arrival). The uniformed police stopped neighboring farmers who responded to Olds's urgent call on the road to his farm and intervened only after the death squad had left the scene. The operation was staged on Independence Day, when Mugabe was delivering his speech on television, and was meant to terrorize the white farmers.

According to Amnesty International, "impunity has become the central problem in Zimbabwe, where state security forces—police officers, army officers or agents of the CIO—commit widespread human right violations without being brought to justice."[37] Although statements from victims gathered by the Human Rights NGO Forum and witnesses who testified in the election challenges at the High Court named some perpetrators of violence, very few were subsequently prosecuted. The General Amnesty for Politically Motivated Crimes, which was enacted on 6 October 2000, absolved most of them. As a matter of fact, violence with impunity is part of ZANU-PF's political culture: a general amnesty was granted after both the liberation war[38] and the Matabeleland massacres,[39] allegedly in both cases in a spirit of reconciliation but effectively preventing any accountability on the part of combatants and officials involved. In any case, the Emergency Powers (Security Forces Indemnity) Regulations, enacted in July 1982, which were similar to the indemnity law passed by the Smith government in 1975, had in advance indemnified subsequent unlawful acts perpetuated by government officials and security forces. The report of the commission of inquiry set up in November 1983 to investigate human rights abuses by the Fifth Brigade during the Gukurahundi—the Chihambakwe Commission—was never released by Mugabe, and when human rights groups went to court in 1999 to compel the government to publish it, minister of justice Emmerson Mnangagwa—one of the officials implicated in the killings and abuses—claimed the document was missing and could not be located. The "dissidents" who surrendered to the police benefited from the amnesty, but civilian victims and their families received no apologies, and the issue of appropriate compensation is still pending as of this writing.

Another sign of this culture of impunity entrenched in the ruling party is the extensive use of presidential pardon;[40] as earlier stated, the two who made an attempt on Kombayi's life in 1990 were pardoned. Edgar Tekere, ZANU-PF secretary general and a Cabinet minister, who took part in the murder of a white farmer in 1980, benefited from an indemnity law passed by the Rhodesian regime to protect its soldiers who had committed atrocities from prosecution. Similar methods were used to protect some of Mugabe's henchmen in the last two years.

Although murder, robbery, rape, indecent assault, and possession of arms were formally excluded from the October 2000 amnesty, very few ZANU-PF criminals have been prosecuted and none convicted. Mberengwa War Vet leader Wilson "Biggie" Chitoro, who coordinated the terror campaign against the opposition in the district,[41] was arrested after the parliamentary elections and remained in prison for more than a year, charged with torturing to death an MDC activist at Texas Ranch

Farm militia camp. However, he was released on bail in November 2001 and has not yet stood trial. He allegedly resumed his activities in December the same year and set up another militia base at Chingoma Secondary School in preparation for the presidential election.[42] When the Buhera North election challenge was heard in the High Court, judge James Devittie requested that attorney general Andrew Chigovera arrest and prosecute the known suspects (one a local War Vet and the other a senior CIO operative in Chimanimani) for the murder of two MDC officials campaigning for Tsvangirai who were burned alive in their car on 15 April 2000. The police were tasked in July 2001 to investigate the case but to this date the docket is blocked by the police chiefs in Harare, and the killers remain at large, perpetrating violence (one of them was briefly detained by the police and then released). The impunity granted by the police to criminals from ZANU-PF militias extends to uniformed police officers who committed human rights violations voluntarily. Indeed, impunity creates a sense of solidarity and common belonging between the two, in the process further damaging the police as an institution of the state.

Moreover, the presidential amnesty covered only the period between 1 January and 31 July 2000. However, political violence, including murders, committed since then was not attended to by the authorities either. In instances when perpetrators of violence were arrested and stood trial, they happened to be MDC members. This was a deliberate attempt to portray the opposition as violent—a recurrent claim of the government press—while ZANU-PF militias, responsible for close to 90 percent of the incidents, and all of the most serious, enjoyed impunity. The latter were clearly encouraged by party leaders to terrorize again in preparation for the 2002 presidential poll. In addition, victims seeking redress or witnesses giving evidence in the High Court when MDC's electoral petitions were heard were assaulted again and some had to go into hiding.[43] Those arrested who had benefited from the amnesty then took their revenge against the people who reported them to the police.

From the 2000 to the 2005 Elections and Beyond

Violence abated for a couple of weeks before the 24–25 June 2000 elections, and the months of July and August were relatively calm. However, retribution violence against farmworkers never stopped completely. In Harare high-density suburbs that had returned MDC members of Parliament with huge majorities (80 percent or more), riot police and army units were deployed in early October 2000 to quell some public unrest over the rising food prices and started a door-to-door campaign that lasted until the end of November to beat people at random. Perpetrators did not hide the political motives of this retributive violence. In February 2001, an MDC MP in Chitungwiza and the party security chief, Job Sikhala, and his pregnant wife were assaulted in their house at night by soldiers. Another MDC MP Willias Madzimure was attacked by ZANU-PF militias twice (in May and July) and his house was ransacked while he was sitting in Parliament.[44] Once again between late February and 20 March 2001, army units were deployed in several townships and raided beer halls, streets, and private properties to beat people and force them to chant slogans in support of Mugabe and ZANU-PF.[45] The same scenario repeated itself in July, in response to a two-day general strike organized by the ZCTU.[46]

Throughout 2001, random beatings, abduction, and torture of MDC supporters went on sporadically. Gokwe saw some of the worst violence between the parliamentary elections and the presidential ballot, with a record number of schools closed as War Vets attacked scores of teachers and forced them to flee to Harare.[47] The latter were told that as civil servants they should not hold political views different from those of the government. The minister of Foreign Affairs warned: "You are going to loose your jobs if you support opposition political parties in the presidential election. . . . You can even be killed for supporting the opposition and no one would guarantee your safety."[48] This was a constant view shared by ZANU-PF leaders, as illustrated by the public controversy over civil servants' political neutrality in 1995.[49] Back in 1990–91, Cabinet ministers declared that civil servants should be card-carrying members of the ruling party.[50] In all instances of violence (including rape) inflicted on teachers since February 2000, often in front of their pupils, the regional and national authorities of the Ministry of Education failed to stand up for the rights of the victims and provide them security. Not only were the teachers perceived as a natural ally of MDC since their union leaders had taken an active part in ZCTU and the foundation of the party, but they were seen by ZANU-PF as spreading wrong ideas contradicting the ruling party's propaganda—thus explaining MDC's growing success among the rural youth.

The June 2000 parliamentary elections established a pattern of extremely violent behavior that was to be repeated in by-elections thereafter, all of them "won" by ZANU-PF, including the presidential election in March 2002. Burning MDC members' houses and other properties and harassing their families became permanent features of ZANU-PF's modus operandi in 2001 and 2002. On several occasions, campaigning MDC convoys faced a coordinated assault of ZANU-PF youth, War Vets, and police, some of whom used firearms. This was the case during the Bindura parliamentary by-election campaign, on 22 July 2001, but also during the presidential campaign in Nkayi in an incident involving soldiers using AK47 rifles. MDC campaigners were routinely assaulted or abducted to be tortured and killed. Such was the fate of Ephraim Tapa, president of the Zimbabwe Civil Service Employees Association, a ZCTU member union, who, with his pregnant wife, was abducted on 16 February 2002 by ZANU-PF militias. He was held in the militia camps around Mutoko for almost a month, during which time he was severely beaten and tortured. The couple were rescued by the police, which for once implemented an urgent order from the High Court, when their captors were about to kill them.

Violence intensified again in late 2001 when a new militia, the National Youth Service, was deployed in preparation for the presidential election. The categories of people already targeted in 2000 were once again assaulted on a larger scale between December 2001 and March 2002. According to the NGO Forum, 31 people were killed between 1 January and 1 March 2002, including one former MDC candidate in the 2000 parliamentary elections.[51] However, on the eve of the ballot, violence focused on MDC polling agents, many of whom were abducted and severely tortured. Some others were caught after the presidential election in retribution for the MDC vote in a specific area. Month after month, women became increasingly the victims of sexual violence, including gang raping and tortures affecting the genitals, inflicted by ZANU-PF militias, policemen, and soldiers in retaliation for their political support of the MDC. Rapes involved girls as young as twelve and were sometimes performed in public to increase the humiliation and "teach a lesson" to the whole community.[52] The pattern emerging from NGO interviews of rape victims suggests a deliberate and systematic policy of terror covertly promoted by the top echelons of the state, which went on long after the 2002 presidential election.

What has taken place in Zimbabwe since 2000 has nothing to do with ordinary interparty violence as might be observed in hotly contested ballots the world over. The ANC official who compared Zimbabwe's situation to the political violence in South Africa during the transition period, prior to the 1994 democratic election, was wrong. Indeed, the violence that engulfed Zimbabwe after February 2000 was deliberate (Hunzvi boasted that he led a revolution that required violence to succeed), state-sponsored, carefully planned, and perpetrated by party militias acting in concert with state security agencies.[53] It was a war of attrition against the opposition, and anyone in civil society expressing dissenting views was thus perceived as an enemy of the ruling party. It was a "revolutionary war" with tactics very similar to those used to erode ZAPU's popular base in Matabeleland in the early 1980s.

Violence became more sporadic after the presidential elections, surging again when there was a by-election or during the rural and urban council or mayoral elections in 2003–4.[54] For instance, MDC MP Job Sikhala and his lawyer Gabriel Shumba were detained during three days in January 2003 and tortured at the CIO underground torture chambers at Goromonzi—to force them to confess a plot to kill Mugabe.[55] During the 2004 parliamentary by-election in Zengeza, on the second day of polling, ZANU-PF Cabinet minister Elliot Manyika was accused of having killed MDC activist Francis Chinozvina in public with a gun. The minister was never prosecuted and the opposition candidate filed an electoral petition in vain.[56] The campaign for the March 2005 general election was less violent than the 2002 and 2000 ballots (as noted in Chapter 1), but there were still provinces like Mashonaland Central where the MDC candidates could hardly set foot in early 2005, let alone campaign normally. Moreover the ZANU-PF candidates—including several prominent Cabinet ministers—who had sponsored violence in 2000 in twenty constituencies, and had not been held accountable by the courts, were standing again in 2005.[57] The impunity they enjoyed sent a dreadful message to the electorate and was an effective deterrent to opposition sympathizers.

Persecution against the MDC went on after 2002. Its leaders and MPs, including Morgan Tsvangirai and party treasurer Fletcher Dulini Ncube, were detained on spurious grounds. The incident most publicized outside Zimbabwe was the persecution of Roy Bennett, the popular (white) Chimanimani MP. In 2000 his farm was invaded and his workers assaulted. In April 2004 he was evicted from the property in spite of five court orders prohibiting the farm's compulsory acquisition, and his cattle and farming equipment were confiscated. Following a brawl with Patrick Chinamasa in Parliament in May 2004 after the minister of justice had insulted him, Bennett was unfairly sentenced to fifteen months in jail, with a three-month suspension—an unusually harsh punishment for such a light offense—and was taken into custody on 28 October.[58] Detained in squalid conditions (now a common fate in Zimbabwe prisons) and denied food and proper clothing, Bennett was freed on 28 June 2005.

In March 2006 an alleged plot—again to assassinate Mugabe—was fabricated by the CIO to implicate Giles Mutsekwa, MDC MP for Mutare North, whose contacts in the army were feared in a volatile political climate.[59] But the prosecution abandoned the case for lack of incriminating evidence after some of the accused claimed to have been tortured to extract their confession. In the meantime, Roy Bennett, who had been cited by the government press as one of the alleged plotters, fled to South Africa in fear for his life. There his application for political refugee status was first rejected by Pretoria on the grounds that the courts in Zimbabwe upheld the law (!) but eventually accepted after he went to court.

After the parliamentary elections in 2005, the usual political retribution was unleashed on communities that had voted for MDC, its polling agents, and some of its candidates—some were arrested and tortured.[60] In addition, this time there was a concerted assault on the MDC's primary constituency, the urban poor. On 25 May 2005 the police, supported by the army, embarked on Operation Murambatsvina (Restore Order)[61] allegedly to clean up the cities, implement urban planning and curb the black market and other crimes.[62] The massive destruction without due notice of makeshift houses and other "illegal structures" erected in the city suburbs countrywide left about 700,000 people homeless and destitute in the middle of the Southern Hemisphere's winter. Thousands of informal traders were detained by the police, and an estimate of 2.4 million were affected in one way or another—including losing their only source of income. In addition, an estimated 500,000 children were forced out of school or had their education seriously disrupted. The operation, widely condemned (outside Africa) for the violence with which it was carried out, ended officially on 27 July 2005, although sporadic destruction and many arrests continued. Beyond its stated aim of "cleaning" the cities, Murambatsvina had a middle-term strategic dimension also: by destroying the homes and businesses of millions of people in the MDC strongholds, the government wanted to force them back into the ZANU-PF controlled rural areas where they would become dependent on government food aid. Sometimes the displaced persons were rounded up and bundled in police and army trucks to be dumped hundreds of kilometers away from their home.[63] Subsequently some of the victims were sent to rural "re-education camps" run by the security services and militias. It is possible that depopulating opposition enclaves was meant to weaken the opposition votes in the following parliamentary and presidential elections and in the meantime jeopardize the ability of the urban poor to stage organized protests against the government.

In an attempt to legitimize Murambatsvina as an operation aimed at improving urban settlements and to counter the international outcry, in late June 2005 the government launched Operation Garikayi/Hlalani Kuhle (Live Well), and claimed that it would build 300,000 houses before the end of 2005, and a total of 1.2 million by the end of the program in 2008.[64] Despite a UN offer to assist, the achievements of this policy, riddled with mismanagement and corruption from the outset, were limited, and after a year most of the victims remained homeless, as a few thousand houses had been built countrywide.[65] In May 2006, a follow-up Operation "Round-Up" forcibly transferred about 10,000 homeless and street kids from Harare to country farms where they were dropped without food, water, sanitation, or proper equipment. They were held on the farms, destitute and frightened.

Throughout 2006 there were renewed threats from Mugabe or his security minister to violently suppress any attempt from the opposition groups to protest in masses in the streets. MDC and civic organizations were again under assault in early 2007: on 11 March, the riot police brutally disrupted a prayer meeting held by civic organizations, killed one activist and injured many, and arrested more than fifty leaders, including Tsvangirai. They were severely beaten while in custody, while others were abducted by the CIO and tortured.[66] Violence has remained the cornerstone of the government's attitude toward any form of perceived dissent or criticism.

The ZANU-PF Militias

In line with its tradition of violence, ZANU-PF always had a tendency to use certain party organizations to exert coercion and intimidation on its opponents, in addition to or in conjunction with state security agencies. Hence the Women's League and the Youth League were mobilized as the party shock troops during electoral campaigns. The ZANU-PF youth and women's leagues have been used in the past to intimidate opponents in the high-density suburbs and the rural areas in what was euphemistically called "door-to-door" campaigning, a tradition going back to 1963, when ZAPU and ZANU were fighting for political control of the African townships and their rivalry left hundreds of people maimed with property destroyed as the Rhodesian police stood by. The same tactic was employed again in 1980 and 1985, against ZAPU, and in 1990 and 1995, against ZUM and other opposition parties. ZANU-PF youth and women's leagues disrupted opposition party rallies and serious violence erupted; they also harassed people at night.[67]

The violent behavior of ZANU-PF youth and women was at that time already openly condoned by Mugabe who even asked his supporters to intensify the door-to-door campaign. When FORUM leaders said that their supporters were entitled to defend themselves since the police remained inactive, Mugabe responded during a central committee meeting of his party with a thinly veiled personal threat: "In that dangerous game our side would certainly have more and better arrows and spears than Dumbutshena [Forum president], now nicknamed Dumbutshaka, and his handful of warriors can ever hope to wield. Will the former chief justice really be able personally to avoid and duck those arrows he is inviting?"[68] Alleging that the leader of the FORUM, dubbed a party of European settlers by government's propaganda, was manipulated by whites, the president added: "They will come off, in a contrived violent conflict situation, not second best, but not best at all. Let them be warned."[69] This was in 1994. Already the same Mugabe who would claim in 2001 that he and his party had "degrees in violence." The ZANU-PF Youth League had also taken part in the Gukurahundi along with the Fifth Brigade and the CIO, and a lesson had been learned then: mass repression can be more easily denied when performed by "uncontrolled" militias rather than the regular army. However, before February 2000 there was nothing on the scale of the War Vets and the militias called "green bombers," who have since waged the sustained, nationwide campaign of violence detailed above. It seems necessary therefore, to look at the creation and dynamics of the ZANU-PF militias,[70] the shock troops of the Third Chimurenga.

War Vets

When Hitler Hunzvi and his supporters of the Zimbabwe National Liberation War Veterans Association (ZNLWVA) rioted in the streets of Harare, in July–August 1997, after the plundering of the War Victims Compensation Fund[71] by the regime's "big men" was revealed, press commentators mistook them for the most determined opponents of the government and were astonished to see ZNLWVA members spearheading the farm invasions. Although the fiction that they were acting independently from the government soon dissipated, their exact relationship with the ruling party is still contested and has evolved since 2000.[72] War Vets invading the farms were transported in army, police, or District Development Fund trucks (the DDF having been for a long time a ZANU-PF instrument of patronage in the rural areas) and were given army tents and food rations. Money from the president's office was channeled to the War Vets by party officials (Z$20 million was allocated for the 2000 elections campaign and another Z$15 million was budgeted in 2001). ZNLWVA operated from two-story headquarters in a government building in Harare, and its shock troops were hosted during much of 2000 and 2001 by the ZANU-PF headquarters, where some offices were used to torture people. Indeed, ever since 2000 War Vet leaders repeated that they would use all means to keep Mugabe in power.

ZNLWVA was formed in the early 1990s under the ruling party's patronage, as part of a constellation of similar groupings to promote the economic emancipation of former war combatants[73] and their social and welfare needs. Although many of them were employed in the police and the army and others had sought education abroad and found jobs in the state apparatus or the private sector, some remained destitute ten years after independence and grew very bitter when witnessing the social impact of ESAP and the blatant corruption of the ruling elite. Although ZNLWVA once claimed a 40,000 strong membership, it is difficult to assess its popularity among ex-combatants. Some ZANU-PF backbenchers like Margaret Dongo and Ruth Chinamano promoted the association's agenda in Parliament as a convenient political resource against the party "big men." Dongo's vehement accusations against minister of social affairs Nathan Shamuyarira, of neglecting the war veterans' welfare was one of the reasons for her fall from favor in 1995. Indeed, since Independence, Mugabe has made use of former guerrillas in the army, the police, and the CIO to drive out ZAPU/ZIPRA in the 1980s[74] and prevent this constituency from developing as an independent power base within or outside of the ruling party.

There was a new turn of events, however, when the ambitious "doctor" Hunzvi was elected chairman of ZNLWVA in 1995. Despite his claims, Hunzvi had no war record since he had spent most of the war years abroad—in Romania where he contracted his unconditional admiration for the communist dictator Ceausescu, and in Poland where he did medical studies. He was briefly employed in a government hospital when he returned from Poland in 1990. Hunzvi, a racist by his own admission, proud of his chosen Chimurenga name "Hitler," claimed at the same time to be a dedicated communist. However, his Polish former wife publicly denounced his male chauvinism and domestic violence. Hunzvi had become popular with the ZNLWVA rank and file by granting them medical certificates of disability to support their bogus claims of war injuries submitted to the War Victims Compensation Fund. Hunzvi also obliged the ruling party "big men" and some of their relatives, who never saw action or were too young during the liberation war, with even more dubious certificates that enabled them to claim unreal percentages of disability. For good measure Hunzvi included himself among the disabled veterans and was granted a total of Z\$517,536 for a 117 percent disability.[75] Thus, Hunzvi actively participated in the plundering of the fund at the expense of the real victims as the government commission of inquiry, headed by Judge Godfrey Chidyausiku, later established. However, when payments were suspended in mid-1997, the ZNLWVA leadership cleverly deflected the anger of those who had not yet benefited by encouraging them to take to the streets and to squeeze concessions out of Mugabe, holding him hostage while he attended a meeting at the ZANU-PF headquarters in August 1997. A package of a Z\$50,000 gratuity and a Z\$2,000 monthly pension was awarded to each registered veteran.

Mugabe's first reaction was to punish Hunzvi, who was the only person cited in the Commission's report to be subsequently prosecuted by the state and held in jail for a time in 1999. Soon after this, war veterans were co-opted into the grand strategy of farm invasions. Instead of receiving more gratuities that the public treasury could not afford—as the lump sums granted in 1997 had already been eaten up by inflation—Hunzvi's militant faction of ZNLWVA would spearhead the campaign of violence and be rewarded with land. This was to become the most critically damaging of their actions. A brilliant ploy of enrolling this discontented fringe of the regime into the president's political survival campaign was to follow in order to channel their frustration toward the whites and the MDC. It prevented a sizable constituency within ZANU-PF from becoming a powerful internal opposition, while at the same time the president could use this ruthless mercenary force to fight his enemies. More important, as the farm invasions commenced, Mugabe could pretend to dissociate himself from these activists and claim that he could not order the police to remove them from the farms without risking a bloodbath. More brazenly, he observed that they were merely "demonstrating" for their right to land. By constantly denying the obvious links between his government and the militias he obscured his ultimate responsibility for the beatings and murders. By so doing, Mugabe could dupe, at first, his SADC and other African colleagues into believing that the state was not behind the human rights violations. Moreover, when the MDC challenged parliamentary election results in 38 constituencies on the basis of the violence perpetrated by ZANU-PF militias, the concerned ruling party candidates conveniently denied any link with these activists.

Once they moved onto the farms, the core of ex-combatants were joined by ZANU-PF youths, along with unemployed urban people who were attracted by the daily allowance and, in a few instances, by some communal farmers enticed by the prospect of being awarded a piece of land. They soon formed a ragtag militia known as "War Vets," which perpetrated most of the atrocities of 2000 and 2001. Some MDC supporters were forced into joining the militia and taking part in violent campaigning to avoid being beaten up themselves.[76] Initially the War Vets and party youths were paid for their performance, fed (although they often demanded food from the white farmers whose farms they occupied), and given free alcoholic beverages—in some places they took *mbanje* (marijuana)—and they often went out beating people while drunk or high on drugs. They were confident that Mugabe had granted them impunity as long as they obeyed the directives of the central command. Their leader, Hunzvi, who toured the invaded farms to keep the militias on the upbeat, fast became a central figure of the regime, whose word would take precedence over the vice presidents or Cabinet ministers, even though he had never held office in the party or the government, other than by becoming an MP. Hunzvi's lack of a war record and his original affiliation to ZIPRA rather than ZANLA made him more malleable by Mugabe, who always feared high-profile former guerrillas with an independent power base. Contending factions in ZANU-PF courted Hunzvi, and Solomon Mujuru offered him the Chikomba constituency that the retired general had held in a previous Parliament. No one dared oppose Hunzvi's nomination in the ZANU-PF primaries. The MDC was not allowed to campaign in that area and Hunzvi was elected by a large majority. He had hoped for a junior Cabinet position in the July 2000 reshuffle but was still more useful to Mugabe outside government, propping up ZANU-PF campaigns—for example, against the independent judges. When Hunzvi died suddenly on 4 June 2001, officially of cerebral malaria but most probably of AIDS, he was buried in Heroes' Acre—the national monument for liberation war heroes—and Mugabe read his eulogy, with all the ruling elite behind him, posing as grief-stricken comrades. Though dispensable as an individual, Hunzvi was a useful pawn in the autocrat's power game. No other ZNLWVA leader since has displayed his skillful and charismatic demagoguery.

"Green Bombers"

The death in a car accident in May 2001 of Border Gezi, minister of youth development, gender, and employment creation, whose role in the 2000 election campaign had been decisive, was another important setback for Mugabe. But Gezi was replaced in the redundant Cabinet position—a means to channel public resources to the ruling party—by Elliot Manyika, also a young Turk from Mashonaland Central, where he had succeeded Gezi as governor, and whose violent campaign in the Bindura by-election had been hailed as a model by ZANU-PF hardliners. Manyika went on with Gezi's plan to establish the "green bombers" militia under the guise of a six-month National Youth Service. The first battalion of approximately 1,000 volunteers completed training in the Border Gezi Training Center (a militia camp established at Mount Darwin, near Bindura) by the end of November 2001 and was deployed in the rural and suburban areas in December and January 2002. They were placed under the local War Vets' command to bolster ZANU-PF's campaign effort. The rationale for the creation of such paramilitary units lay in the fact that ZANU-PF youths and ZNLWVA elements originally mobilized in the farm invasions and the 2000 parliamentary elections were too few to cover the whole country and were poorly organized. Although in September 2000 the War Vets became a "reserve force" of the national army, in a move to instill some discipline into their ranks, on the ground they remained uncontrolled and dangerous.

The new force was summarily trained by CIO and military officers in military discipline, drilling, counterinsurgency, and terror tactics, and duly brainwashed to regard the MDC, whites, and Western countries as enemies of Zimbabwe.[77] Initially ZANU-PF supporters joined the "green bombers" en masse, but some other youths, with no particular political affiliation, were lured into the force by promises of cash and future jobs in the police and the army. As time went on some were forcibly drafted into the militia especially as a means to destroy support for the MDC among the rural youth. These units were equipped with olive green uniforms—hence the popular nickname alluding to the containers of an insect-killer spray—fed and paid with the taxpayers' money, which was particularly attractive for ZANU-PF leaders at a time when the ruling party's coffers were empty. Although this ostensible National Youth Service was inaugurated to provide community services countrywide (to give credibility to the official stance some did sweep the streets and public squares with much publicity provided by the government press in December 2001), the militia inflicted the worst violence before and after the March 2002 presidential election as noted by the Commonwealth Observer Group.[78] Being de facto a branch of the state, they could operate in broad daylight with every pretense of legality.

With these two militia forces used in tandem, the regime militarized the rural areas, establishing illegal roadblocks to stop "undesirable" people, confiscating ID cards (which were needed to be able to vote) from real or alleged opposition supporters, rounding up and beating villagers and raping or killing at will. Their camps, which were scattered around the countryside, became feared centers of torture, the practice of which intensified as the presidential election drew to a close. In Matabeleland their behavior reminded people of Gukurahundi. The "green bombers" tried to emulate the abuses of the ZANU-PF youth brigades of the 1980s. They were "fighting the enemy" again with a similar excuse of protecting national sovereignty. There were no limits because impunity was guaranteed. Abducted young women and girls, supporters or relatives of MDC supporters, were gang raped and reduced to the status of sex slaves by the militias, often contracting AIDS in the process in a country where 20 percent of the adult population is HIV positive. As in the liberation war, when rape and abduction of teenage girls for sexual services were sometimes perpetrated by the guerrillas, these are another feature of the culture of violence. The Zimbabwe Women Lawyers' Association estimated in mid-2002 that some 1,000 of these women had been held in militia camps.[79]

As a result of this policy, many districts became "no go areas" for the opposition in late 2001 and early 2002, and people were effectively intimidated into voting for Mugabe at the presidential election. Although the ruling party had managed to retain the majority in Parliament in June 2000 and win subsequent parliamentary by-elections, it had lost the towns to the MDC in the mayoral elections in Masvingo in mid-May 2001 and in Bulawayo—the second largest city in Zimbabwe—in early September. With Zvobgo's influence, Masvingo Province was no longer secure and ZANU-PF's full control was only assured in rural Mashonaland where the MDC had been eradicated in May–June 2000. Therefore, in a national ballot such as the presidential election, a total control of rural areas was necessary to counterbalance the numbers of mobilized MDC voters in urban areas. It was the militias' task to create a permanent climate of fear among rural communities, and they thoroughly succeeded.

Collapse of the Rule of Law

Besides its immediate impact on the political opposition and civil society, the long-term disruptive effect of state-sponsored violence should not be ignored. Two years of systematic violence singling out specific groups of people had already transformed the postcolonial state. The Police Support Unit (notably in the repression of various demonstrations in the mid-1990s and of the food riots in January 1998) and the CIO and the Police Law and Order Section have been used in partisan ways since 1980. Previously the uniformed police, the Zimbabwe Republic Police (ZRP), were seen generally as a professional and politically neutral force but this is no longer the case. The commissioner of police, Augustine Chihuri, himself a former combatant in the liberation war, claimed in January 2001 that he was a ZANU-PF member and later in the same year that he would not obey the orders of an MDC president. Police station commanding officers were under instructions not to assist assaulted MDC members and not to act against ZANU-PF supporters acting violently.[80] In the few instances when police officers tried to protect MDC people from ZANU-PF's thugs, they themselves were assaulted. One constable was murdered by War Vets when conducting an inquiry on an invaded farm, and his superiors made no attempt to arrest the culprits. Members of the force feared the ZANU-PF militias that enjoyed such political protection. But the collusion between the security forces and the War Vets also stemmed from ZNLWVA's 1997 campaign for payment of war services to all former guerrillas, including those employed in the state apparatus.

Therefore, in most instances, police officers stood by when MDC

members were assaulted, only to charge the victims themselves for allegedly "inciting violence" or to refuse to take reports from the victims
(which enabled the police spokesman to declare afterward that he knew
nothing of the incident since it had not been reported to the police!).
Sometimes they would say that the docket was lost so that police investigations would not lead to prosecution. Arbitrary detention without
charge increasingly became a pattern of police behavior toward the
MDC in 2001 and 2002. Some police officers took an active part in the
harassment of opposition supporters or human rights activists in several
cases documented by human rights groups,[81] and this behavior tended
to spread as time went on, while increasing numbers of War Vets were
drafted into the force and speedily promoted. By mid-2002 the riot
police and some officers from rural police stations were involved in torture cases against the opposition members. Police officers also colluded
with militias looting the properties of MDC supporters or the white-
owned farms by providing transport for the looted goods and sharing
the spoils.

Between 2000 and 2002 a minimum of 2,000 police officers were
transferred. Suspected MDC sympathizers—or just politically neutral
officers—were purged, posted in bureaucratic assignments (the infamous "Commissioner's pool" in Harare headquarters for senior police
officers), or kicked off the force. Others resigned out of frustration or
in fear of harassment, while War Vets in the police were promoted to
the head of rural police stations in order to cooperate with ZANU-PF
militias.[82] Chihuri's excuse for purging senior officers—that they were
remnants of Rhodesian Selous Scouts and British South Africa
Police[83]—betrays the war mentality still dominating ZANU-PF leadership. All these "political policemen" report to Mugabe directly rather
than to their commanding officers. When the station head is a professional officer, his orders might be overruled by a deputy or junior officer
who is a War Vet, especially when incidents on white-owned farms or
politically motivated violence are involved. As if a legitimate excuse, the
phrase "it is political" became the customary, official response when
police were criticized for inaction as the crisis mounted. More War Vets
and ZANU-PF youth were recruited by the police, hastily trained, and
dispatched in the rural areas prior to the presidential election at a time
when scores of professional policemen had left the force. Through these
changes in both personnel and behavior the ZRP was transformed into
another de facto party militia and all pretense of impartiality has been
dropped. On several occasions, assistant police commissioner Wayne
Bvudzijena professed no knowledge of cases of assault and torture documented by NGOs and lately cynically dismissed numerous reports of
politically motivated rapes as "cheap propaganda," when in fact many

victims who reported to the police were sent back and told that they or their parents should not have voted for the wrong party. The police as a major institution of the state has been compromised and corrupted for political expediency, thus destroying the underlying basis of the rule of law. The police nowadays tend to ignore court orders when they are opposed to the government's interests, and they see themselves increasingly as being above the courts.

The same process has affected other branches of the state. Army generals see themselves as above the law since the abduction and torture of two independent journalists by military intelligence in January 1999. Officers suspected of supporting the opposition have been removed from commanding positions, sometimes paid their salary but with no duties to perform, or transferred to lower-status postings. Others have been forced into early retirement, while less qualified former guerrillas were promoted ahead of them.[84] The promotion of noncommissioned and junior officers on the basis of political loyalty rather than professional ability has eroded the army as an institution of the state. In the process the amalgamated national army created in 1980 is being transformed into a partisan private army to serve Mugabe's interests.

Other segments of the public service have been targeted by retribution violence and have ceased to function normally, including the educational system with about 48 rural schools closed down by mid-2002 in various parts of the country—since assaulted or raped teachers had fled to safety—especially in MDC electoral strongholds. The health care delivery system and several rural councils were also affected. However, the lack of funds and shortage of qualified people also played a role in the collapse of these services. The idea was to destroy MDC's local organization to leave no dissenting voice in the rural areas so that government officials (including chiefs and headmen on the government payroll) would cow the people into voting for Mugabe, but the purge went on until well after the presidential ballot. The district administrators of Matobo and Umzingwane—who are the representatives of the state in the local arena—were pushed out of their offices by War Vets in July 2002 after Minister Chombo accused civil servants of delaying the land redistribution exercise. As in a Maoist-style "Cultural Revolution," nobody is untouchable except Mugabe's inner circle. Thus continuing violence is eroding the effectiveness of state institutions. Zimbabwe was, up until the mid-1990s, a relatively well administered state in comparison with many African countries (petty corruption was contained, law and regulations were enforced and records more or less kept), but in the future, incompetence and arbitrary rule might prevail. Violence is also damaging the fabric of society, undermining values such as justice, truth, and accountability. The longer this situation endures the more strenuous it will be to restore law and order afterward. Under these circumstances the government is likely to find that it has opened a Pandora's box that will be hard to close again.

Civil War or Militarized Autocracy?

A neglected aspect of the crisis so far is the potential loss of control by Mugabe and his lieutenants of these party militias created to fight the opposition and chase the whites away from the land. Although the government had no difficulty in reining in War Vets from invading businesses in Harare when it suited its interests, this does not mean that the state could evict them from the farms or disband them without provoking violent reactions. State-sponsored violence might then evolve into outright anarchy in the wake of the state collapse if not into a full-fledged civil war.

After the death of Hunzvi, the ZNLWVA was rocked by quarrels between individuals who vied for the top job (Andrew Ndlovu, Andy Mhlanga, Patrick Nyaruwata, or even Harare-based Joseph Chinotimba) and by corruption scandals. It transpired that the mismanagement of Zexcom, the ZNLWVA investment fund in which most members had invested the gratuities received in 1997, would cost most members their savings. ZANU-PF strategists preferred to delay the ZNLWVA congress, which was due to elect a new chairman, and they confirmed Hunzvi's deputy as the acting chairman. In late July 2002, the inquiry into the misappropriation of ZNLWVA's funds led to the imprisonment for embezzlement of Andrew Ndlovu,[85] the acting chairman. Hunzvi had also been charged with defrauding Zexcom of Z$3 million. Factional strife among the War Vets was a logical development of the competition for spoils but may also have been fanned by the CIO as a control technique. Although there were places like Nkayi and Lupane in Matabeleland North where the local chapters of ZNLWVA were less prone to violence during the parliamentary election campaign,[86] this situation changed radically later and these two districts saw the worst incidents of violence during the presidential ballot. Some of the War Vets' victims mention Ndebele speakers alongside Shona speakers among their torturers, thus indicating that wartime political cleavages were less relevant among ex-combatants. This does not necessarily preclude an ethnic rift from developing in the future.

As ZNLWVA squabbles proceeded, a movement that had begun during the farm invasions developed very rapidly: every district chairman or local prominent War Vet became a law on to himself and tended to act independently from the organization's leaders in Harare. If the Third

Chimurenga was a new kind of war, some of the War Vets certainly behaved like local "warlords"—a media catchword to suggest autonomy and paramount authority in a certain territory. A notable example was former army captain "Comrade Chiweshe," who terrorized the Marond-era farming area during election campaigns, acting as if he was the true local government authority, helped by young militiamen to implement his decisions. Others enjoying various degrees of autonomy were "Comrade Jesus" in Kariba and "Biggie" Chitoro in Mberengwa. Taking their line from mysterious national directives coming from Harare, War Vets masquerading as "land committees" made arbitrary decisions regarding farms: closing down offices and schools, sacking civil servants and teachers, and, without any proof, telling people that laws and statutory instruments had been rescinded. The district administrator was usually powerless to stop them.

Farm invaders ceased to be paid daily allowances, as had been the case at the beginning of the invasions, because the government ran out of funds. The War Vets invented various strategies to secure new sources of income: extorting payment from frightened farmworkers for ZANU-PF cards that never materialized, selling "permits" to communal farmers and other hangers-on applying for plots of land, selling crops (an estimated 50 percent of the maize crop in 2001 was stolen or destroyed by squatters) and equipment impounded on the farms, and later, "managing" food aid. In so doing, their interests were competing with those of the ZANU-PF "big men" who intensified their land-grabbing after the presidential poll. On several occasions after March 2002 squatters were evicted by the riot police when they were told that the farm they had occupied was "earmarked" for a party official or a general. It became impossible to ignore the prospect of violent confrontations between government and embittered militias.

After two years of activity, ZANU-PF militias became accustomed to enjoying impunity when beating, looting, and robbing alleged MDC supporters, especially as the police pronounced them "untouchable." The "green bombers" frequently complained quite openly that they had not been paid—being provided only with food and beer (and some say drugs)—and claiming that their crucial role in Mugabe's election victory had not been adequately rewarded. Many had joined the National Youth Service because they were unemployed school graduates or had lost their jobs. The promised positions in the army, police, or civil service were not forthcoming (although some were hastily drafted into the police to enforce the August 2002 farmers' evictions). They have been increasingly driven to use their special status for survival and behave like criminal gangs, especially in urban townships. For example, a militia group attempted in July 2002 to extort "security fees" from vendors at the Mbare Musika vegetable market in Harare.[87] Violence is becoming a way of life for these young people[88] in a process similar to the building up of militias in other war-torn African countries.

War veterans do not form a social class or even a cohesive group inter-acting as such with government and party leaders. Indeed, many genuine former combatants of the liberation war do not feel represented by the ZNLWVA criminal leaders[89] and disapprove of the organization's endorsement of ZANU-PF's political agenda and the War Vets' thuggish behavior. Some regrouped in May 2000 to form the Zimbabwe Liberators' Platform (ZLP) with a view to challenging ZANU-PF's monopolization of the liberation legacy. Their spokesman, Wilfred Mhanda (alias Dzinashe Machingura in the war), was a former ZANLA commander victimized by Mugabe.[90] Mhanda claims that the bad publicity attracted by ZNLWVA's violent actions, which put the war veterans in disrepute, prompted him with his colleagues to form the ZLP. At the outset, he said, most members of the organization, who "range from company directors, to magistrates, to high-ups in the army and the police . . . even within the intelligence services," are now sympathetic to the MDC although not aligned with it. They hoped for its victory in the past elections and claimed to support a democratic constitution and the restoration of the rule of law. Some war veterans even joined the MDC, such as Sarodzi Chavakanaka (alias Zulu in the war), a former intelligence officer for ZANLA who retired from Mugabe's presidential guard in 1997 and became an MDC organizer in Mashonaland Central in April 2000. So effective was he that Joyce Mujuru allegedly offered a reward for his assassination.[91]

Conflict Scenarios and the Army's Role

The Mugabe clique's war of attrition against the MDC increasingly tested the party's commitment to a legalist and peaceful course of action. The number of violent incidents initiated by MDC people rose significantly during the parliamentary by-elections in 2001 and the presidential and Kadoma mayoral elections in 2002—though still far below violence coming from the other side—and there were more ZANU-PF/ ZNLWVA members among the casualties. Cases of arson on ZANU-PF activists' properties were also on the increase. MDC supporters were desperate after years of suffering and three stolen elections, and some MDC youths and a good number of party cadres wanted to fight back. As matter of fact, many MDC activists were defectors from ZANU-PF who carried with them the ruling party's culture of intolerance and violence. This violent behavior was also manipulated by certain party leaders to settle scores in internal squabbles, and, as we will see, it played a role in the split of the MDC in 2006. However, the ruling party might also split along regional/tribal lines. Contending factions led by regional "big men" are likely to fight over shrinking economic resources and attempts to preempt Mugabe's succession. Therefore, a civil war would not necessarily pit the MDC against ZANU-PF but rather various factions of disintegrating political parties.

The future attitude of the army will be crucial in this respect. Certain units like the presidential guard division have already participated in retributive violence in Harare high-density suburbs in late 2000. Elements from the air force were used to quell a strike in August 2001 and to occupy the local MDC MP farm in Chimanimani. Some soldiers were also seen beating up people in Masvingo in the run-up to the mayoral election. Others were seen manning roadblocks alongside the CIO and the police. However, it is difficult to establish the facts accurately because CIO operatives sometimes dress as uniformed police or military as a cover: it is in the regime's interest to project the impression of a police and an army united behind ZANU-PF if only to preclude dissidence in these corps. The head of ZNA and now chief of staff general Constantine Chiwenga toured the barracks prior to the presidential elections to urge the military to vote for Mugabe. The commanders of the armed forces claimed before the 2002 and 2008 presidential elections that they would not salute Tsvangirai if he won. There has been a policy of politicizing the army ever since Independence, especially during the Matabeleland "disturbances" when ZANLA elements in the integrated national army illegally discharged ZIPRA ex-combatants, including superiors in rank, and were promoted according to their political loyalty.[92] War Vets leaders had threatened to "declare a military government" if the MDC won the parliamentary and then the presidential elections and vowed to fight to defend ZANU-PF.[93] Promotion in the military and the police force, and even the prison corps, favored former ZANLA guerrillas politically loyal to the president. The upper levels in the military establishment share with ZANU-PF politicians and high-ranking civil servants the same political culture and they have the same vested interest in perpetuating Mugabe's regime.

There have been, however, some signs of sympathy for the opposition: some army rank and file waved in support to NCA/MDC demonstrations in 2000, and some army units intervened to stop ZANU-PF violence in the run-up to the parliamentary elections in Mashonaland Central. There was also sporadic unrest in the barracks after the intervention in the DRC, rumors of mutinies in late 1998, and protests over the high level of casualties. Only a minority of high-ranking or well-connected officers got rich from business deals in the DRC and the prevailing mood among the military was probably not at variance with public opinion: most soldiers suffer as much as the rest of the people from the inflation and the food shortages. In July 2001, according to the South African press, some unnamed junior brigadiers had offered to depose Mugabe if they received South Africa's political and logistical support. Mbeki is said to have rejected this proposal as premature, too risky, and projecting a bad international image. Whether the story is genuine or not, the dissatisfaction of the military from junior brigadiers down to privates has increased along with the worsening economic and social situation. The ZLP offered to broker contacts between the MDC and the army chiefs like Perence Shiri or retired general Solomon Mujuru to have them switch sides, to no avail. Conversely, staging a coup is made more difficult by the army's organizational structure:[94] distribution of food rations, fuel, and ammunition is closely monitored on a short-term basis to control the units' operational autonomy. Planning even limited troop movements would quickly attract suspicion from headquarters.

Besides, the military intelligence is fully at work to uproot any feeling of dissent or unrest in the defense forces, as was apparent in the unlawful detention and torture of the two *Zimbabwe Standard* journalists in 1999. In addition the government tries to keep the armed forces happy to be able to rely on them to nip in the bud any popular uprising. Provisions for defense in the state budget have always been high since independence to keep the generals happy. Army and police personnel's wages were raised significantly before parliamentary and presidential elections, again in April 2006 and July 2007 (by 900 percent!).[95] However, these pay rises failed to catch up with inflation, and there have been reports of army and CIO personnel resorting to crime to make up for their shrinking income while others deserted to South Africa.[96] Some officers have also been rewarded with land as more and more farms were confiscated after 2002. In August 2006 the government spent millions of foreign currencies to buy cars for middle level police and army officers to buy their loyalty to the regime.[97] By mid-2006 the army had recruited new soldiers to expand the existing force of 30,000 to 35,000.[98] However, Mugabe does not need many troops to shoot disarmed civilians; he can rely on his presidential guard and the 20,000 ZANU-PF youth militias, which have been used in the past to quell opposition protest marches.

What is happening already is the increasing militarization of the regime.[99] Mugabe has relied increasingly on military officers to deliver the 2002 presidential election and 2005 parliamentary elections, which were run as military operations: service army officers supervised the administration of the ballot, including the counting and centralization of results, and retired officers packed the Electoral Supervisory Commission (ESC). Head of the ESC and later attorney general Sobuza Gula-Ndebele was a former military intelligence officer, while former High Court judge George Chiweshe, who became chairman of the Zimbabwe Electoral Commission (ZEC) in 2005, was an army officer before being appointed to the bench in 2001. Military officers were appointed to run strategic parastatals such as National Oil Company of Zimbabwe (NOCZIM), Grain Marketing Board (GMB) and the Zimbabwe Broadcasting Corporation (ZBC) under the excuse of fighting corruption or red tape, some others were assigned to ministries or diplomatic missions abroad. Military officers even held positions in the Zimbabwe Revenue Authority and the Central Bank. It betrayed Mugabe's need either to control access to rare commodities—such as gasoline—or to use policy tools—such as selling grain—for political benefit, but also to gather information to rein in rival party factions.

The armed forces were also involved in the infamous Operation Murambatsvina (or "Drive Out Trash") from May to July 2005 and committed numerous human rights violations. Interministerial Committees (IMCs), headed by high-ranking military officers, have been set up in all major towns and provinces to oversee the Hlalani Kuhle reconstruction exercise; they have taken over some of the city council functions. In November 2005, the government launched Operation Maguta/Sisuthi ("Operation Eat Well"), using the military to stem food shortages by helping resettled farmers in tilling the land, planting, and harvesting on underused land. But again the army personnel acted without restraint and often brutalized villagers,[100] and the command-style campaign failed to increase the agricultural output significantly, rather, the contrary. Soldiers forced the farmers to plant maize for the GMB and destroyed small vegetable gardens to render the farming communities dependent on their political support for the ruling party. The farmers were obliged to work all day almost at gunpoint and without food, and the whole operation disrupted farming activities rather than enhanced production—a typical ZANU-PF program.

The Joint Operations Command recreated by Mugabe at the beginning of the Third Chimurenga has played an increasing role. "The JOC has replaced the cabinet as the primary policy-making organ, briefed on and approving major measures before ministers implement them."[101] It organized the terror tactics against the opposition, defined the attitude toward the South African mediation, and was to play a central role in organizing Mugabe's illegitimate reelection in 2008. Whatever the rumors of military commanders dictating their terms, this inner circle is dependent on Mugabe for protection and is content to enjoy his patronage through which it has amassed unbridled wealth.[102]

According to a 2005 survey, "There are no official figures of those killed in political violence, but human rights groups estimate that over the past seven years over a thousand have died. The actual figure could be much higher as parts of the rural areas are now inaccessible to NGOs and indeed to anyone who is not overtly pro-ZANU-PF."[103] Many more were injured or maimed, some of them handicapped and psychologically traumatized for the rest of their lives. Mugabe is personally responsible for this nightmare, all the political crimes perpetrated in Zimbabwe since March 2000, and he should be held accountable in a court of law. Beyond the horror, what was striking in the developments since February 2000 was the cynicism of Mugabe and the ZANU-PF ring leaders using violence as a political means. Indeed they never parted with their wartime political culture.[104] That war was their deep-seated vision of politics was embodied in a statement from Mugabe in a radio broadcast in 1976: "After all, any vote we shall have, shall have been the product of the gun. . . . The people's votes and the people's guns are always inseparable twins."[105] Ruling party leaders have kept their supporters mobilized during two and a half decades by using bellicose language and creating situations of violent confrontation with ZAPU, ZUM, FORUM, MDC, whites, the West, or "paper tigers" such as the IMF or British colonialism. Mugabe and his lieutenants have never moved into a true culture of peace and democracy.[106] Their vision is supported by the War Vets: since ZANU-PF won the right to rule through the blood spilled and not through elections, why should they hand over power to another party that has not defeated them in war? Mugabe, who claimed that his August 2002 government was a "war cabinet," and his two deputies who threatened the MDC with bloodshed would certainly welcome a violent confrontation that they are confident of winning. In Mugabe's mind the Lancaster House agreement in 1979 left unfinished business: he always longed for a "crushing" victory on the battlefield.

Chapter 3

Militant Civil Society and the Emergence of a Credible Opposition

Although some opposition parties existed prior to 1999, none succeeded in breaching the ZANU-PF monopoly. Indeed, the Movement for Democratic Change is "the first substantive opposition party to emerge [in Zimbabwe] in the last 20 years."[1] However, the positive legacy of the failed opposition of the 1990s should not be underestimated. Not only had these parties contributed to the democratic struggle at a time when many civic and union leaders claimed to remain "nonpartisan" and avoided harassment from the state, but the MDC also drew some precious lessons from their pioneer work. By its near success and the sheer scale of its challenge to Mugabe's rule, however, the MDC is unique in Zimbabwe's history.

Civil Society Moves from Passive Resistance to Politicization

The limits and failures of opposition political parties in the 1990s, partly attributable to their lack of impact at the grassroots level, left civil society as the only effective source of opposition to ZANU-PF's neo-authoritarian rule.[2] If indeed Mugabe's regime was not at that time just another African autocracy, it was largely attributable to a lively civil society and its almost twenty-year resistance to incorporation or control by the state. This militant civil society later became the cradle of the MDC, the emergence of which incidentally tends to defeat the notion of civil society's ingrained political impotence. The trade unions and their sustained struggles to achieve and maintain their autonomy, as early as 1988, played a pivotal role in this transformation. The contributions of the private media and independent-minded judges are also key factors in understanding how civic organizations managed to counter ZANU-PF hegemony.

Whether or not theoretical debates on the concept of civil society validate its use in an African context,[3] there is, in countries like Zimbabwe, a reality that needs to be assessed. A wide range of nonstate actors (sometimes called "civic organizations"), differing in significance, stated objectives, and structure, are active in the public sphere in competition and/or in collaboration with the state. Some are seen as formulating primordial identities (class, religion, or ethnic affiliation) or as protecting sectional interests (professional lobbies), but others, such as various advocacy groups on the environment, human rights, women's conditions, or HIV/AIDS, are providing services yet also promoting a public debate on policy issues. They try to force government to take into account all stakeholders or, more specifically, the marginalized sections of society.[4] Some play a unique social or economic role; others raise the people's political awareness. This broad category of organizations operating outside the realm of the state includes urban resident rate-payer associations, trade unions, churches, and the independent media—although the latter also functions as a business.

Contrary to common stereotypes on African NGOs (bad governance, organizational dependence on donors) most Zimbabwean voluntary, not-for-profit organizations do not exist only by virtue of external funding or as mere subsidiaries of international NGOs, though local organizations had to make up for the state's diminishing financial capacities in the 1990s and became privileged recipients of foreign donors' funds.[5] Lately there has been a trend—as elsewhere in Africa—among former civil servants whose salaries had declined in real terms or among university graduates seeking employment whereby the creation of a new NGO became a source of income generation or a substitute for formal employment. However, many civic organizations have a long history. Some existed long before independence: the Association of Women's Clubs—originally a Rhodesian organization for the advancement of black women—is an example. Certainly, if foreign donors withdraw from an NGO project that is indeed "donor-driven," the organization's financial viability is often at stake. When a donor imposes a specific project framework as a condition for funding, it does not necessarily imply an attempt to control the organization's overall policy—though there have been instances of donors withdrawing support because of an NGO's controversial image. Some of these local NGOs are affected by corruption, as is the rest of society, especially when they become the vehicle of some big men's accumulation strategies. However, most advocacy NGOs are led by dedicated activists who spend their time—and often their own money—promoting their cause in spite of potential risks to themselves, and many of whom have experienced crude violence at the hands of ZANU-PF militias and state security agencies since February 2000. For example, the Zimbabwe Human Rights Association (ZIM-RIGHTS), founded in 1992, boasted 4,000 members in the mid-1990s and was involved, under a dynamic leadership, in monitoring elections, documenting cases of torture and abduction linked to the past Matabeleland disturbances, defending the workers' rights in various industrial actions, and conducting various civic education programs.

There was initially an ideological connivance between the state and the numerous development NGOs that sprang up in the early 1980s insofar as the latter believed in the progressive ideals ostentatiously publicized by the ruling party. However, by the end of the decade, the revelations of government corruption and the policy move toward structural adjustment prompted many civic organizations to become far more critical of the government. Many drifted away or were demonized by party "chefs" when they began to address sensitive issues. For instance, the Africa Community Publishing and Development Trust, which produced civic education material for the poor in vernacular languages, was initially accommodated in a government building, and it worked closely with various government departments until the mid-1990s. However, it was seen with growing suspicion, especially when it published civic awareness material on constitutional reform for the outreach program led by civic organizations. The Legal Resources Foundation (LRF), a private trust founded in the late 1980s with respected public figures sitting on its board, provided legal services to the socially marginalized or specific groups of victims and conducted legal training for state employees. Although it supported constitutional reform and the independence of the judiciary and published articles critical of the government in its austere *Legal Forum*, it maintained until the late 1990s a nonconfrontational approach. Indeed, the minister of justice made a point of addressing its annual fund-raising dinner. However, this working relation was irremediably jeopardized in 1997 when LRF copublished with the Catholic Commission for Justice and Peace (CCJP) the damning *Breaking the Silence* report on the Matabeleland massacres.

The CCJP, created in 1972, was a strong proponent of majority rule during the Rhodesian Front's UDI regime and initially welcomed the black nationalist government. When atrocities were committed in Matabeleland, they were condemned in general terms through a pastoral letter released in 1983. However, the CCJP, which had been put under a closer check by the Catholic bishops in 1981, did not publish its detailed reports on the disturbances (allegedly to protect its personnel in the missionary stations in Matabeleland from reprisals by the state) in sharp contrast with its previous practice under the RF regime. The bishops opted to lobby government for a change of policy although the violence went unhindered on the ground until well after the 1985 elections. Since ZANU-PF was anxious to keep the Matabeleland crisis out of public debate and had imposed a blackout of information on the military operations there, a more militant attitude certainly would have led to a confrontation the Catholic Church was eager to avoid.[6] Another rationale was to remain sufficiently neutral in order to broker political discussions between ZANU-PF and ZAPU—although many observers attribute the achievement of the 1987 breakthrough, leading to the Unity Accord, to former non-executive state president Canaan Banana.

Overall, the state had little to fear from national civic organizations until the last year of the first decade of Independence, not only because some ideological naïveté and cooperative mood still prevailed in this milieu, but also because the concentration of resources in the hands of the ruling party—including its political legitimacy grounded in the liberation war and the 1980 election victory—dissuaded potential dissenters. This began to change with the students' movement in 1988–89 and the debate on the institutionalization of the one-party state. At its annual meeting on 10–11 March 1990, CCJP issued a strongly worded statement—later published as an advertisement in the press—against Mugabe's plan and in defense of "the supremacy of Parliament over the ruling party and the separation of powers." This was "an unusual display of open church opposition to ZANU-PF on political matters"[7] just before the general elections and in the midst of the independent press's relentless campaign on the same issue. Immediately afterward, CCJP was involved in the monitoring of the parliamentary elections—again in 1995—and denounced the violence during the campaign period. Both in 1989 and 1992 the CCJP criticized the heavy-handed police repression against the students' movement. CCJP also criticized the Land Acquisition Act (1992) and Mugabe's confrontational approach to land reform. Not surprisingly, the government reacted by castigating "individuals masquerading as human rights activists, ivory tower intellectuals and some foreign mass media correspondents dedicated to sowing seeds of national despondency, racial and ethnic hatred and conflict," targets he also accused of "destabilization maneuvers."[8] The evolution of the trade unions seemed to fit perfectly with this conspiracy theory.

The Zimbabwe Congress of Trade Unions' First Encounter with Civic Organizations

The Zimbabwe Congress of Trade Unions (ZCTU) was created in 1981 as a wing of ZANU-PF[9] in order to unite the trade union movement—

divided at independence into six different groupings, some of them linked to political parties—but also to ease the implementation of government's policy and curb the movement of spontaneous industrial action witnessed at independence. Throughout the decade, ZANU-PF labor policy became increasingly authoritarian, enforcing a more stringent legislation such as the Labour Relations Act of 1985, which aimed to ban strikes de facto and increase the discretionary powers of the Ministry of Labour and Social Affairs (including the power to rescind a union acting outside its mandate), in order to strengthen government's control over the labor movement and prevent the ZCTU from crossing into the "political agora."[10] Trade union membership remained marginal and the ZCTU leadership's enjoying state patronage had little support within an organization where internal democracy left much to be desired.[11] In the second half of the decade, however, the workers saw their initial gains of the first five years—such as wage increases and some access to social services—eroded by recessions. Thereafter they could be mobilized more effectively.

In 1988 the ZCTU elected the young Morgan Tsvangirai, a self-educated former mine worker, as its secretary general. The expanded and restructured organization became openly critical of the government's labor policies but also broadened the scope of its actions. From September 1988 the demonstrations and criticism of university issues and of state corruption by the radical Students' Representative Council (SRC) of the University of Zimbabwe (UZ) were vindicated both before and after the Willowvale scandal was exposed. Violent police repression of students fighting what was seen as a legitimate cause and the arrest of their leaders brought them widespread support, including from the ZCTU, which openly criticized the government closure of the University on 4 October 1989.

Morgan Tsvangirai had his first taste of punishment at the hands of the security agencies when he was illegally detained later in October 1989 despite several High Court orders for his release. He had already displayed his leadership qualities and personal bravery. It was clear that any attempt to question the regime's actions on security matters—as Mugabe perceived them—would meet a merciless response from the state. Then, in spite of backbenchers' protests in Parliament and demonstrations organized by the Association of University Teachers, the government introduced the University of Zimbabwe Amendment Act 1990. This removed what was left of university autonomy through the appointment of the vice-chancellor by the head of state. Now 65 percent of the University Council members would be appointed by the relevant minister.[12] The authoritarian nature of the ZANU-PF regime was increasingly apparent to many in the academic community.

During the May Day celebrations in 1990, the ZCTU also made public its opposition to Mugabe's one-party state project, which was indeed totally in contradiction with the unions' newly acquired independence.[13] Numerous students and university lecturers who had lived through the UZ crisis joined Tekere's ZUM during the 1990 election campaign but the ZCTU leadership stayed out of party politics, sparing itself the huge disappointment created by ZUM's defeat. The same year, the launch of the neoliberal Economic Structural Adjustment Program (ESAP) shifted the union's agenda back to labor-related socioeconomic issues such as wages and retrenchments. But a new anxiety for the ruling party came into view: worried by Kenneth Kaunda's 1991 electoral defeat at the hands of the trade union-led Movement for Multiparty Democracy (MMD) in Zambia, ZANU-PF chefs then decided to strike at the nascent workers' power. In April 1992 the government introduced an amended labor relations bill that aimed to weaken ZCTU federal structures, increase government interference in labor issues, and authorize the formation of splinter unions and rival federations. In the midst of a drought and food crisis that year, the ZCTU organized a successful protest on May Day, once again with the support of a newly elected SRC, but the police, invoking the Law and Order Maintenance Act (LOMA), stopped workers' demonstrations staged on 13 June—on the heels of the students' riots—and the new labor law was enacted in January 1993. Mugabe subsequently refused to attend the May Day celebrations and accused the ZCTU of "turning itself into a political party."[14] If indeed the ZCTU leadership had entertained such ambitions in mid-1992, the government's successful handling of the food crisis with massive foreign aid and its fomenting of divisions among the trade unions—on both financial and political issues—effectively prevented any move in that direction.

By late 1992, the students' movement was in disarray in part because activists were discredited by the May 1992 riots, their rude public language, and their use of intimidation to enforce class boycotts.[15] More fundamentally, however, the majority of the student body did not support the SRC's leftist, confrontational agenda. Therefore, the SRC leadership could not capitalize on its moral victory when in April 1993 the Supreme Court ruled against its suspension by the UZ Council. However, these five years of relatively successful collaboration between the students' and lecturers' movements and the trade unions over political issues such as state governance, human rights and basic freedoms, the multiparty system, and the rule of law in some measure prepared the ground for the enlarged civic alliance of the late 1990s.[16]

Government Attempts at Controlling the NGO Sector

In its attempts to impose its hegemony on society as a whole, the ZANU-PF regime stepped up its all-out interference with NGO operations, even seizing or regaining control of some of these organizations through intimidation and legal or illegal means. Although this policy was inaugurated in the 1980s with the merger of the black farmers' unions,[17] there were renewed interventions in the 1990s, when the government wanted to silence the growing criticism over its ESAP policies. One after the other, the ZCTU, the students' movement, CCJP, ZIMRIGHTS, and later the Gays and Lesbians of Zimbabwe (GALZ), and the Association of Women's Clubs were targeted. The National Association for Non-Governmental Organisations (NANGO), the state-sponsored umbrella NGO organization, became more tightly controlled by government when the foreign affairs minister's wife Eunice Mudenge became its chairperson in the late 1990s. Although the NGO sector remained structurally weak and most development and advocacy NGOs tried to maintain viable relations with the state by the end of the 1990s,[18] as a whole, civil society mounted stiff resistance to attempts by the government to control them.

When Mugabe viciously attacked the homosexual community in August 1995, at the official opening of the Zimbabwe International Book Fair—the theme of which was "Human Rights and Justice"—many progressive activists in Zimbabwe were flabbergasted. The government forced the fair's organizers to ban the Gays and Lesbians of Zimbabwe (GALZ) exhibit, a harmless display of educational material on HIV/AIDS, at a time the government would hardly acknowledge the importance of the pandemic in Zimbabwe. Again at the 1996 book fair, GALZ's rented stall was forcibly closed down when an angry ZANU-PF-sponsored mob stormed the Harare Gardens, even after a restraint issued by the Ministry of Home Affairs was declared illegal by the High Court.[19] The uproar, in Zimbabwe and abroad, that followed Mugabe's statements in 1995 were useful diversions, after the president's adulterous affair with Grace Marufu had been revealed (see Chapter 4) and at the time the judgment on the Harare South court case came out revealing the fraud in the parliamentary elections. For weeks the public controversy focused on GALZ and the homosexual community with racist undertones: homosexuality was "un-African," according to Mugabe, and imported by the white man, a stereotype in total contradiction with the ethnic mix in GALZ's membership. Mugabe repeated his homophobic remarks ad nauseam to restore his battered popularity by flattering a prejudiced public opinion. He received the sycophantic support of several small Protestant denominations and traditionalist African churches.

This issue was also a golden opportunity for him to embarrass the human rights groups and the independent press, which hesitated to go against the society's widespread bigotry. Issues were blurred since a case of freedom of expression was deliberately misrepresented as a moral choice between virtue and perversity. CCJP and ZIMRIGHTS bravely condemned Mugabe's language and defended gay and lesbian citizens' rights against a regime that wanted to persecute them. The president's cynical attitude was revealed when the crimes of the Reverend Canaan Banana became public knowledge. While in office as the ceremonial president of Zimbabwe from 1980 to 1987, Banana had abused his position by sexually harassing at least one of his military bodyguards—a crime on which Prime Minister Mugabe chose to keep quiet not only to avoid scandal but also to have a means of controlling Banana. Belatedly prosecuted,[20] Banana was later convicted for sodomy (when it should have been for rape).[21] Mugabe's attacks on GALZ diminished (until British gay activist Peter Thatchell attempted his citizen's arrest of Mugabe in October 1999), but the government press chose again to vilify homosexuality in Banana's criminal case, rather than to criticize the obvious abuse of power and question Mugabe's complicit silence.

To stifle civil society's growing criticisms against government policies and the corruption at the top echelon of the party and the state, the cabinet moved in early 1995 to replace the pre-Independence Welfare Organisations Act, which governed the relations between the various NGOs and associations and the state, by a tougher piece of legislation. The Private Voluntary Organisations Act gave the minister of Labour and Social Welfare extensive powers to approve or reject registration of these organizations at his/her discretion. Section 21(1) of the Act entitled the minister to interfere with the internal proceedings of any registered NGO, including the right to "suspend all or any of the members of the executive committee of a registered private voluntary organization from exercising all or any of their functions in running the affairs of the organization." It amounted to giving the minister license to take control of a targeted organization using flimsy excuses such as fighting "illegal activities," redressing "maladministration of the organization," and protecting the "public interest." To decide whether this was "desirable," he did not need to consult anybody, nor was he obliged to justify in more precise terms the reasons of his actions. In terms of section 22 of the Act, he could then appoint trustees of his personal choice to replace the suspended members and administer the affected organization according to his instructions. These arbitrary powers violated the freedom of association and assembly and the freedom of expression enshrined in the constitution.[22] It sounded like beating the war drum against the militant wing of civil society.

The first test of the new legislation came in November 1995 when minister Nathan Shamuyarira suspended all but two members of the executive committee of the Association of Women's Clubs (AWC), appointed some trustees and ordered that the allegations of misuse of funds made against the AWC executive be investigated. ZANU-PF cronies (women) were put at the head of the organization with the result that foul play was suspected. The AWC is one of the oldest and most powerful women's NGOs in the country, claiming up to 40,000 members, and as expected, the allegations against it turned out to be baseless. The minister wanted not only to control the organization but also to get his hands on the U.S.$9.5 million grant pledged by foreign and local donors to support AWC's development projects in rural areas.[23] However, the deposed chairwoman, Sekai Holland, and eleven other suspended members took the case to the Supreme Court in May 1996. The judgment delivered in February 1997 declared section 21 of the Act in contravention of the Bill of Rights, ordered that the AWC executive members illegally suspended be reinstated and the costs be paid by the Ministry of Labour and Social Welfare.[24] This landmark judgment brought about a welcome relief in the confrontation between civil society and the state. However, the fact that civil society relied on costly litigation—thus on a still independent judiciary—to defend its autonomy against a government waiting in permanent ambush, producing new legislation and sponsoring its own brand of civic organizations, showed that the need to strengthen Zimbabwe's legal and constitutional framework remained paramount. This explained why many civic organizations were eager to participate in the constitutional reform movement that began to crystallize in 1997.

Despite the appearance of a series of fake NGOs (such as the Heritage Foundation), sponsored by ZANU-PF "big men," noisily displaying their support for the regime, the most representative civic organizations found themselves increasingly in conflict with Mugabe and his lieutenants. By then ZIMRIGHTS was active and vocal: it defended striking nurses, was agitating for compensation for Matabeleland victims, and had produced the most critical report on the 1995 elections. Logically it became the target of CIO destabilization. The strategy succeeded in 1998 when outgoing chairman Dr. Reginald Matchaba-Hove was replaced by Nick Ndebele. Ndebele was perceived by many as a CIO plant after he blundered over the nurses' strike in 1995.[25] Previously he had fallen out with CCJP, where he was accused of embezzling funds. The controversial election and the new chairman's statements in support of the government (for instance of Mugabe's decision to intervene in the DRC or of his land reform) led to a bitter internal squabble in 1999 as Nick Ndebele joined the government constitutional commission while David Chimini, the executive director and a former Teachers' Union official, represented ZIMRIGHTS in the NCA task force. Eventually, Chimini was sacked, but Ndebele failed to have the organization boycott the NCA. These developments and the lack of financial transparency in the management of ZIMRIGHTS led most Western donors to withdraw support in 1999 and 2000, and ZIMRIGHTS was in disarray for several years.

In 1999 leading civil society activists Mike Auret and David Coltart were viciously attacked in the government press, in a pattern similar to the pre-election period in 1995. Auret, who had been in conflict from late 1996 with the Bishops' Conference over the publication of the *Breaking the Silence* report, the content of which was leaked in February 1997 to the South African press and made available on the Internet, came under strong pressure from a group of bishops led by Archbishop Patrick Chakaipa, Mugabe's friend, for his involvement in the NCA and in the tortured journalists' case. When Auret, a long-time director of the Catholic Commission for Justice and Peace, was publicly vilified in a presidential address in February 1999, the bishops remained silent but later announced a "redirection" of CCJP, which prompted Auret to resign from his office of director.[26] In addition to ZIMRIGHTS, a second human rights watchdog was effectively silenced. However, these developments strengthened civil society activists' perception that their basic rights were threatened by a government violating its own laws. In this respect, their involvement in the NCA and later the MDC (see below) was largely Mugabe's own making.

From Constitutional Reform to Opposition Politics

The case for the Movement for Democratic Change (MDC) as a labor-based party is argued by Brian Raftopoulos and Peter Alexander in separate works.[27] They both underline the pivotal role of the ZCTU and its then leadership in forming the backbone of the new party. However, the contribution of the civic organization-led constitutional reform movement was also crucial, in terms of both timing and inspiration, to coalesce traditional issue-oriented workers' demands into a national agenda of political transformation. A wealth of individual competences in law, organization, publicity, and fund-raising could be tapped from civic organizations, some of which had never worked with the unions before 1998.

The constitution inherited from the Lancaster House agreement had been by 1999 significantly altered by fifteen amendments—especially Amendment No. 7 (1987), which introduced the executive presidency— and suited Mugabe's interests almost perfectly. He and his cronies repeatedly stated that there was no need to change it in the face of NCA demands. Constitutional reform had featured prominently in the political agenda of the opposition parties as early as 1993–94, and several of them gave the fundamental flaws of the Electoral Act and the Constitution as the main motive behind their boycott of the 1995 and 1996 elections. Donor-funded workshops organized by various civic organizations such as ZIMRIGHTS from 1994 up to 1997 came invariably to the conclusion that a new constitution was a prerequisite for democratic political change and built up public awareness on this issue while providing the preparatory ground for a coalition of civil society and trade unions. As the economy and the social situation worsened, following the government's controversial policy decisions in 1997–98, opposition parties and civil society argued that governance and constitutional issues were closely related: Mugabe's deaf ear to criticism was rooted in ZANU-PF's hegemonic position, guaranteed by entrenched clauses. This was one of the causes of ZCTU's full backing of the movement and willingness to work with opposition parties and other civil society organizations.

The National Constitutional Assembly task force—NCA as it came to be known in the press[28]—was initiated in May 1997 by several civic and church organizations but was relaunched in a more effective way in January 1998, with a full-time secretariat, thanks to some Western donors' support. Originally, the task force intended not to work as an autonomous constitutional commission and produce an alternative draft (as it turned out), but only to lobby for a democratic and all-inclusive constitutional reform process. Although trade unions were only one stakeholder among the 96 organizations involved at the peak of NCA success, the ZCTU organizational capacity and national network were crucial when the NCA started to consult the people on the need to promote a participatory framework for constitution making. After the successful stay-away of December 1997, when Tsvangirai gained a wide audience outside of his traditional ZCTU constituency, it seemed logical that he should take the chair of the NCA, which he retained until August 1999 when he resigned to assume MDC's leadership. The ZCTU was adamant that tiny, noisy opposition parties should not hijack the NCA and use it as a partisan platform. It is also likely that Tsvangirai had in mind the next step: the subsequent formation of the MDC.

Its pivotal role notwithstanding, the constitutional reform movement cannot be reduced to a ZCTU strategy to broaden its alliances. The large support NCA enjoyed in various sectors of society as a whole was crucial in stirring up public debate about Zimbabwe's lack of democracy and the faults in the constitution outside the tiny circles of the educated urban class. It had a dramatic impact on the maturation of public opinion and contributed to delegitimize Mugabe's regime in the eyes of the common man. Scores of public meetings and the successful outreach program from July to September 1999 liberated public discourse as many citizens seized the opportunity to voice criticisms and anger toward a government that had betrayed all their aspirations. The consultative workshops mixed socioeconomic issues with the denunciation of the chefs' arrogance and proper constitutional issues but somehow, in the confusion, certain themes came out loud and clear: limitation of the powers of the president and of the number of possible terms in office with the unanimous cry "Mugabe must go now," introduction of checks and balances with more powers for Parliament, strengthening of the Bill of Rights, entrenching the independence of the judiciary and the media. In other words, a truly democratic constitution. The NCA got a clear enough picture to produce a constitutional draft, but the outreach program had wider implications: it crystallized the anti-Mugabe and antigovernment feeling across the country. Indeed the ZANU-PF barons spotted the danger and consistently denigrated the NCA as "an opposition party in disguise." This was not yet true although many task-force members thought it would be the logical next step.

The NCA had begun to exert serious pressure on Mugabe's regime in a dramatic context: the food riots in January 1998, the ZCTU-sponsored stay-away protests, and the military intervention in the Democratic Republic of the Congo in August 1998. Criticism mounted from within the ruling party from disgruntled backbenchers and provincial leaders who thought that the government's policies were catastrophic and were shocked by the marginalization of the Parliament and the party caucus when major decisions with financial implications were made. Some of these dissenting voices bravely raised the issue of Mugabe's retirement and saw constitutional reform as a way to achieve this aim. In February 1998 Dzikamayi Mavhaire, ZANU-PF chairman for Masvingo Province and Eddison Zvobgo's close lieutenant, moved a motion in Parliament in favor of constitutional reform, specifically the limitation of the president's terms of office. "The president must go," Mavhaire said bluntly and was predictably suspended from the party structures for two years.[29] However, it seemed Mugabe could not easily quell the wave of unrest in his party. Several ZANU-PF backbenchers protested in the party caucus and through the press against the president's decision to intervene militarily in DRC without the Parliament's endorsement. Therefore, during the ZANU-PF annual conference in December 1998,[30] Mugabe tactically relented and assented to a review of the existing fundamental law—not the election of a constitutional assembly to write an entirely new constitution as demanded by the NCA. That constitutional reform was forced upon Mugabe explains in part why he was not genuine in this exercise and did not want it to succeed.

Zvobgo, a former Cabinet minister and also secretary for legal affairs in the party Politburo, was tasked to discuss with the NCA the formation of a broad-based commission to draft the proposed changes. It seemed an awkward choice at first look, since Zvobgo, a lawyer by training and Mugabe's legal adviser during the Lancaster House negotiations, masterminded the "executive presidency" and other important amendments to the constitution meant to pave the way for the one-party state. However, Zvobgo then a minister without portfolio, was already sidelined and reduced to the status of a regional leader controlling the party apparatus in Masvingo Province. In 1996, in the hope of boosting ZANU-PF's popularity after the low turnout in the presidential election that year but also to hedge his bets in the succession race, he proposed a limited constitutional reform. He suggested the restoration of the abolished Senate—as a halfway retirement for the ruling party "deadwood"—and the office of prime minister for himself, obviously to counterbalance the president's excessive powers, attracting only raised eyebrows from Mugabe and his cronies and criticism from the opposition, which found the proposal too tame. Many saw Zvobgo's car accident later the same year as a clear warning signal from the top (an interpretation based on his intriguing statements while in health care in the UK, promising to tell everything once back in Zimbabwe, which he did not do, of course). Zvobgo's image as a reformer made him the best placed Politburo member to approach the NCA and entice its members to join the presidential commission.

In fact, Zvobgo had already held a meeting with NCA leaders in November 1998,[31] and discussions went on for most of the first half of 1999, even after the government commissioners were sworn in. The two sides came close to an agreement once, but Zvobgo himself was kept on a short rein by ZANU-PF "hawks." The late involvement of some of Mugabe's close aides (Chen Chimutengwende and Ignatius Chombo in particular) in the negotiations and the tense political climate arising from the arrest and torture of the *Zimbabwe Standard* journalists in January that year did not help to bridge the gap between ZANU-PF and the NCA, particularly on the question of the government's Constitution Commission's membership. The NCA demanded a civil society-dominated Commission, and more important, insisted on Parliament passing ad hoc legislation empowering the Commission to produce a draft that would then be adopted through a national referendum, with limited government interference. ZANU-PF ministers were inflexible on using the Commissions of Inquiry Act as the legal framework. Under the Act Mugabe enjoyed a discretionary power to appoint people of his choice (indeed many commissioners identified by the government press as "businessmen" or "civil society leaders" were primarily Mugabe's cronies), to give the Constitutional Review Commission a restrictive mandate (a mere "review" of the existing constitution) and to accept its report, reject it or amend it. The president could revoke the proclamation establishing the commission at any time and was not compelled under the Act to make public the Commission's findings.[32] As a matter of fact, a good number of commissions of inquiry had been established in the past, and their reports had been withheld indefinitely by Mugabe. This near-absolute power of the president under the Act was the stumbling block for the NCA—when the negotiations collapsed irrevocably— since the civic coalition was genuinely committed to a transparent exercise that would empower ordinary Zimbabweans, as was pledged solemnly at the People's Constitutional Convention (PCC) convened at the Chitungwiza sports complex, in June 1999, and attended by more than 4,000 people of all walks of life.

Most NCA task-force members were from the beginning suspicious of Mugabe's motives. Besides, Zvobgo's real mandate was obviously to co-opt NCA members into a government-controlled process, not to empower the people, through civic organizations, to produce a people's constitution—the stated NCA philosophy. Mugabe was seeking to relegitimize himself by capitalizing on Zimbabweans' aspirations for change, while outmaneuvering a potentially powerful opposition and obtaining a constitutional draft accommodating his interests. When the Constitutional Review Commission (CRC) was announced on 28 April 1999 and sworn in the following month, NCA fears were vindicated: the plethoric 400-member commission was packed with ZANU-PF MPs, provincial governors, Central Committee members, "traditional" chiefs, and hand-picked supporters with little consideration for political, social, or gender balance. A few people with a reputation of independence and integrity, such as former UZ vice-chancellor Walter Kamba, were expected to give credibility to the exercise and attract some donor funding since the inflated provisional budget of the Commission rose to Z\$600 million, only Z\$50 million of which was provided by the state budget. Civil society was clearly marginalized in spite of the addition of a handful of white farmers, businessmen, lawyers, and consultants happy to be sworn in at State House and who pathetically stated afterward that they believed then they could make a difference.[33]

Only a few individual members of the NCA joined the government commission, some of them lured by the promise of hefty sitting allowances. The Zimbabwe Council of Churches (ZCC), which had played a pivotal role in facilitating the formation of the NCA but not without much ambiguity and second thoughts, defected to the CRC, arguing that it could not stay out of the legal process of constitutional reform.[34] However, the real reason might have been the need to preserve the unity of member churches since some of the evangelical denominations were close to ZANU-PF leaders. The CCJP remained in the NCA, but some Catholic bishops (to start with, Archbishop Chakaipa) participated in the CRC. Similarly, most Christian denominations were divided between CRC and NCA. Women's organizations, however, resisted the government's attempts to divide them. The Zimbabwe Union of Journalists (ZUJ), whose membership spanned both the government and the independent press, saw it as its duty to counter the government's projects to control the press through a Mass Media Trust, whether or not the framework was totally satisfactory.[35] Some organizations like ZUJ had a foot in both the government CRC and the NCA camps, although that position became increasingly difficult to maintain as time went on and the public confrontation built up.

Many observers then believed that the NCA had made a strategically wrong decision in boycotting the government-sponsored constitutional reform process and in rejecting in advance the subsequent CRC draft. Critics claimed it was unrealistic to lobby for constitutional reform in Zimbabwe and refuse to discuss it with the incumbent party, which had all legal powers either to block or to ease the process. Better work from within, it was argued, to influence the CRC proceedings and the wording of the new constitution. According to this line of analysis, it was wrong to assume that the draft was already written, as some NCA activists claimed, and that the whole exercise amounted to mere window dressing. The NCA, it was alleged, should have made tactical use of the divisions within a ruling party that was no longer monolithic. As a matter of fact, some "reformist" ZANU-PF MPs like Dzikamayi Mavhaire, Mike Mataure, and Rita Makarau,[36] who had grown bolder during the Fourth Legislature, having worked in the Parliamentary Reform Committee led by Speaker Cyril Ndebele, were the most vocal commissioners in plenary sessions and pushed for a more radical agenda within the CRC.[37] They insisted that Mugabe should commit himself to implementing the CRC's final report without alterations and to organizing a referendum to formally adopt the new constitution.

Even at the time one could guess that Mugabe would have appointed more party stalwarts to the commission if NCA members had joined en masse, as there was no ceiling in its membership. NCA members' mere presence would not have stopped the manipulation of the Commission's proceedings, the careful selection of the chairpersons of its thematic subcommittees (when independents insisted on a formal vote they were defeated by ZANU-PF majorities).[38] As soon as actual work began in June 1999 the decision making in the commission appeared very centralized in the hands of the small group of people within the coordination committee: the CRC chairman Judge Godfrey Chidyausiku, the spokesman Jonathan Moyo,[39] attorney general Patrick Chinamasa, and CRC finance secretary Ibbo Mandaza.[40] The whole organizational chart of the CRC was designed to allow significant technical debate in subcommittees, but arbitration and editing were done within the coordination committee, which was kept under control by Charles Utete from the President's Office. Besides, supervision of the CRC was taken over by Mnangagwa because it fell under his portfolio, and he interfered significantly with the writing of the draft. Independent members of the CRC and critical backbenchers were smartly outmaneuvered.[41] Objections raised at CRC's plenary sessions were ignored or the decision was set apart for further consideration never to be heard of again. Contrary to the original rules of operation, commissioners did not have any opportunity to discuss and vote section by section on the draft. On the final plenary session on 29 November 1999, the draft concocted by the executive committee was adopted by acclamation according the CRC chairman with cheers from a ZANU-PF packed meeting, where the voice of the independents was silenced when Chidyausiku cut short the proceedings to rush to State House for a prearranged meeting with the president.[42] Twenty-eight members of the Commission sent a strongly worded petition to Mugabe on 17 November to protest over the contents of the draft that did not reflect the views expressed by the people. Later published in the *Zimbabwe Independent*, the document pathetically underlined the fact that they had been used to give some credibility to a flawed process.

Who could have prevented Mugabe from amending the draft anyway? This he proceeded to do in January 2000, by including the "land clause,"[43] since he was entitled to do so by the act under which the CRC had been established. Even if a strong NCA element had succeeded in polarizing the CRC, it is likely that, on important issues such as presidential powers and terms of office, the "reformist" ZANU-PF MPs would have toed the party line as they had done before whenever their leaders cracked the whip. Indeed, none of these so-called reformers uttered a word of protest against Mnangagwa's last-minute intervention to discard clauses of the transitional arrangements that would have barred Mugabe from standing for another term of office in 2002 (one of the most widely expressed demands emerging from the popular hearings). Yet this effectively dashed their hopes of the president's swift exit to allow a new generation to take over the party. Nor did they protest when the draft was amended without consulting Commission members. The CRC final draft was very similar indeed to the outline discussed and endorsed by ZANU-PF Central Committee earlier on and the whole exercise appeared largely deceptive. Although the constitutional proposal contained useful clauses, such as the suppression of the thirty appointed MPs, an Independent Electoral Commission or a Senate hearing for high-ranking civil servants before their appointment, it disregarded civil society's demands in terms of independence of the judiciary and the limitation of presidential powers. The president retained the bulk of his executive powers. Consequently, the prime minister's office, the Senate, and other checks and balances inserted into the constitution would have been of little significance: in a case of conflict between an opposition-dominated Parliament and the president, the latter would have prevailed.[44]

During the second half of 1999, the NCA had been heavily criticized even in the independent press and had lost some donors' trust—also money, which was shifted toward the CRC coffers—while the propaganda machinery of the ruling party forcefully attempted to discredit the coalition. However, the very intensity of the anti-NCA campaign in the state media was a testimony to the coalition's efficiency in questioning the CRC's legitimacy.[45] The CRC further tarnished its own image with corruption and financial profligacy when it was alleged in the press that Ibbo Mandaza[46] and Jonathan Moyo had granted themselves unjustified hefty allowances in U.S. dollars from the Commission's budget—typical ZANU-PF behavior. On the contrary, the NCA operated on a shoestring and was accountable to donors. Throughout the period, the NCA went on with its work of educating the people on constitutional issues and the shortcomings of the government-sponsored commission and setting up an alternative constitution-making process as it was mandated to do by the June 1999 People's Constitutional Convention. The network of provincial and district committees it built countrywide was later used to successfully campaign for the "No" vote in the referendum.

The amendment of article 57 allowing the confiscation of farmland without compensation, unless the former colonial power paid for it, was the final indication that Mugabe was gearing himself for a serious confrontation. With such a clause he would have a legal excuse to expropriate white farmers and win the following elections on a populist/racist line. With the draft rejected by the electorate, as it happened, he would claim the whites and their "stooges" plotted to protect the farmers' property rights, leaving him with violent farm seizure as the only option. No wonder the campaign for the "Yes" vote—led by the executive committee of the disbanded CRC—was so openly racist, presenting the constitutional referendum as a choice between "real independence" and the return to colonial rule. Not only was Mugabe to win both ways, but also he had turned the constitutional reform process to his advantage. However, the controversy over the "land clause" and the lack of transitional arrangements to bar Mugabe from standing in 2002 rescued the NCA from a difficult position: its rhetoric on the need of a transparent process had become less audible—if not less relevant—and the delay in producing an alternative draft proved counterproductive. In a matter of weeks the "No" campaign developed beyond initial NCA expectations and led to the resounding defeat of the government project in the February 2000 referendum: the draft was rejected by 54.7 to 45.3 percent of valid votes, although with a low turnout. In tactical terms, the NCA campaign and the subsequent government defeat in the referendum gave considerable momentum to the nascent MDC during the first six months after its inception.

The ZCTU's Role in the Creation of the MDC

If the involvement of the trade unions in the creation of an opposition party appears in retrospect to have been quite natural, it was largely the unforeseen result of a shift in the strategy of the unions. As Raftopoulos correctly analyzes, it was a transformation of the workers' movement philosophy that consumed the best part of the 1990s. In the early years of that decade, the ZCTU focused on criticism of ESAP and its dramatic social consequences for the working class, both the decline of its revenues in real terms and massive cutbacks in the workplace. The ZCTU saw its mandate primarily as protecting the workers from the worst impact of ESAP while trying to influence policy making in view of the preparation of the second phase. The original program was primarily a product of the Ministry of Finance's technocracy without any attempt at consultation. The trade union movement wanted to be part of the formulation of the second phase of ESAP, which was to begin in 1995, an objective that obliged the ZCTU to maintain a working relationship with both the government and the business organizations.

By then, ZCTU's outright hostility to ESAP and its neoliberal economics had changed into a more constructive attitude: the need to adopt a development strategy to alleviate poverty and provide new jobs for laid-off workers.[47] More emphasis was also put on government's inadequate fiscal and budgetary policies, seen as the root cause of the decline of services in health care and primary education as well as the decline of investment in the productive sector. By the mid-1990s, ZCTU's leadership was still eager to enter into a collaborative relationship with the government and to develop collective bargaining. Mugabe attended May Day celebrations in 1995, for the first time since 1991, and trade unions remained politically neutral during the 1995 and 1996 electoral campaigns, although, during the same period, the ZCTU actively supported strikes in the public sector and expanded union affiliation in the civil service.[48] Although acknowledging already in private the need to form a strong labor-backed opposition party, Tsvangirai stressed that the situation at that time was not yet ripe for such a bold move.

However, the political climate worsened rapidly with the acceleration of Zimbabwe's economic and social decline, following Mugabe's series of calamitous policy decisions. The unbudgeted allocation of financial packages to the war veterans in August 1997 and the publication of a list of farms to be forcibly acquired plunged the economy into disarray and precipitated a sharp fall in the value of the dollar in November the same year. When the government introduced new taxes to finance the war veterans' pensions, the ZCTU organized the most successful strike in Zimbabwe's history on 9 December. This attracted mass support throughout the country including from white farmers and businessmen. The withdrawal of a government tax proposal was attributed to ZCTU's forceful response, although ZANU-PF's party congress also jettisoned it. The government attempted to undermine this emerging alliance between traditionally antagonistic social classes using threats and launching a tripartite National Economic Consultative Forum. But the ZCTU quickly boycotted this "talk shop." On 11 December 1997 Tsvangirai was the victim of an assassination attempt in his Harare office that was commonly attributed to the CIO.[49]

In January 1998 a number of sharp price increases for basic commodities prompted spontaneous "food riots" in the Harare high-density suburbs, which left at least twelve people dead and several hundred injured.[50] It indicated how desperate the urban poor had become but also reminded union leaders that the ZANU-PF regime would not balk at shooting innocent people to protect its power position. Although the March 1998 stay-away action was a resounding success with a whole country virtually paralyzed, it was obvious that no change of government policy would be obtained by this method. On the contrary Mugabe's decision, in August 1998, to intervene militarily in the DRC demonstrated that he was prepared to strain public finances even more and further jeopardize Zimbabwe's economy for the sake of the personal interests of the ruling elite. The government was prepared also to ban all strikes—but there would be two others in November 1998—and to enforce a de facto state of emergency, and the ZCTU leaders, to whom everybody by then turned for political guidance, had no contingency plans for such confrontation. Further improvisation would have cost many more lives—a fundamental concern for the future MDC as well. It was time to offer a political perspective for the people before public anger led to uncontrollable violence.[51] The success of the stay-away actions, in particular in towns, proved that ZCTU could mobilize far beyond its working-class constituency. This it had done by articulating the concerns of a majority of Zimbabweans over economic and political policy issues, as well as by linking "good governance" with constitutional reform and civil rights (including the right to go on strike and the right to demonstrate peacefully).

With the ZCTU being fully involved in the NCA, the constitutional debate further raised Morgan Tsvangirai's profile as the potential opposition leader. The unions resolved to launch a parallel process to produce a global political alternative to ZANU-PF. In February 1999, the ZCTU convened a National Working People's Convention, in order to identify the problems affecting Zimbabwe and the solutions that could be envisaged. The well-attended meeting brought together unionists and a large array of civil society groupings, including churches, NGOs, human rights groups, but also representatives of the lawyers and other professionals, business leaders who had supported the general strikes. Even white farmers, who were being increasingly vilified by Mugabe, had established a working relationship with the agricultural workers union (General Agriculture and Plantation Workers Union of Zimbabwe, GAPWUZ). This deliberate eclecticism was reflected in the name of the convention. Although the debates and final resolutions adopted focused primarily on the dramatic socioeconomic situation, the convention recommended the creation of "a vigorous and democratic political movement for change" to lead the country out of the crisis.[52] After consulting with the grass roots the Convention met again in May 1999 and mandated that the ZCTU leadership facilitate the formation of a political party. This decision was formally endorsed by a ZCTU special congress in August the same year—despite a significant pro-ZANU-PF element within the trade unions[53]—as Tsvangirai and Gibson Sibanda, the organization's largely ceremonial president, wanted to carry as many as possible of the union cadres into the new party to establish its structures nationwide. The MDC was formally launched on 11 September 1999 at Rufaro Stadium in Harare, to the cheers of an enthusiastic crowd.

The entire ZCTU leadership moved into the MDC executive. Tsvangirai, the former ZCTU secretary general, became the president of the party, and Sibanda his vice president. First, Tsvangirai as a younger yet more experienced leader in politics was needed to be the MDC's candidate at the presidential election. Second, Zimbabwe's post-Independence political tradition required that the position of president go to a

Shona speaker and the vice presidency to a person from Matabeleland. The MDC national chairman was logically Tsvangirai's former deputy in the ZCTU, Isaac Matongo, and a majority of the seats in the provisional National Executive Council (NEC) went to unionists whom Tsvangirai and Sibanda fully trusted. However, during the first congress in Chitungwiza on 29–30 January 2000 the top six posts in the MDC—later known as the Management Committee—were filled by a democratic ballot and the delegates sometimes voted for NCA people with a human rights or civic NGO background. The core of the NCA task force was included in the MDC apparatus, shadow cabinet, and subsequent parliamentary caucus. Indeed, most of the MPs elected in June 2000 belonged to the middle class (a good number being teachers and lawyers) rather than the working class.[54] There was occasional tension at the party primaries held in each constituency between unionists and would-be candidates with another background. Hence, to the apparent fury of middle-ranking union bureaucrats and various leftists left out of the party leadership, the MDC is definitely not a true workers' party. It is not even a labor party such as the British Labour Party in the 1960s, because trade unions do not organically control the party structure and dual party/union membership is encouraged but not compulsory. This is perfectly logical since some of the unions' membership opposed the creation of an opposition party, but also because Tsvangirai wanted to attract people from all walks of life as a workers' movement alone could not deliver a majority at the polls. The strength of the rural electorate and the lack of union penetration in communal areas warranted such a strategy.

The ZAPU Legacy

The MDC achieved a tremendous success in the June 2000 parliamentary elections in Matabeleland. It won every seat in Bulawayo and Matabeleland North and all but two in Matabeleland South (one in Beitbridge, a ZANU-PF stronghold where the minority Venda tribe historically resented Ndebele hegemony, the other in Gwanda), in most cases with huge margins, including in rural areas. This achievement can only be understood through Matabeleland's particular history and the legacy of ZAPU, the mass support of which went across the rural/urban divide. However, Jocelyn Alexander and JoAnn McGregor point out that the ZCTU structures in Matabeleland North, as elsewhere in Zimbabwe, constituted the backbone of the party organization, especially in the Hwange area with its strong mining community.[55] There was also in Bulawayo a long history of coordination between the nationalist movement and the trade unions as Joshua Nkomo had begun his career as a railway union activist. In Matabeleland and southern Midlands, the MDC is widely perceived as the natural heir of Joshua Nkomo's organization. On the other hand, some former ZAPU guerrillas (including 1980s dissidents who benefited from the amnesty) sided with pro-ZANU-PF War Vets against the new MDC opposition. However, the MDC leaders skillfully exploited strong anti-ZANU-PF feelings during the electoral campaign, making specific references to Nkomo as the "father of the nation" and claiming to be the true heirs of ZAPU (MDC's open palm symbol reminded elderly people of early ZAPU meetings using the same sign).[56]

Ever since the 1995 parliamentary elections, Matabeleland had been seen as a region where support for ZANU-PF was dropping fast,[57] but Joshua Nkomo was still a respected figure and the lack of a nationwide alternative to the ruling party prevented that disaffection from materializing. The "father of the nation" died on 1 July 1999; beyond the feeling of sorrow and after the mourning period, the Ndebeles and Kalangas from Matabeleland, who had remained loyal to his person, felt free to shift allegiances. They always resented the Unity Accord imposed on them by Mugabe but did not dare voice their disapproval as long as Nkomo was alive. The vivid memory of the Gukurahundi massacres, which reentered the public debate after the publication of the CCJP/LRF report in 1997, and for which apologies and financial compensation were long overdue but still rejected by Mugabe (he lamely regretted the "madness" at Nkomo's official funeral), underlined the region's deep distrust of ZANU-PF. There was also a widespread perception in Matabeleland that the region's economic crisis was worse than in the rest of Zimbabwe and that the area was kept undeveloped almost deliberately by the ruling party. The pressing issue of water supply and the delayed Matabeleland-Zambezi Water Project, which was to link the river to Bulawayo, illustrated such alleged neglect by the central government.

Some civic groups sprang up in the late 1990s to defend the Ndebele cultural heritage but acted also as advocacy groups, mobilizing mostly urban youth and especially encouraging them to register on the voters' roll and fight political apathy.[58] Imbovane Yamahlabezulu,[59] launched in 1998, organized some public debates around the Gukurahundi massacres in various well-attended meetings in Bulawayo, and some of its members later joined the MDC. Its leader, Lovemore Moyo, who went to Zambia in 1977 to be trained as a "political commissar" for ZAPU,[60] became a member of the Bulawayo-based Open Forum (but not of the FORUM), was elected MDC MP for the Matobo constituency in June 2000 and eventually Speaker of Parliament in 2008. ZAPU 2000, a group of young people questioning their fathers' compliant attitude toward ZANU-PF and their lame acceptance of the Unity Accord, later changed itself into a political party called ZAPU, deliberately using Nkomo's ZAPU symbols such as the bull in order to revive the nationalist legacy and chase away the fear from the people's minds. The new ZAPU fielded some candidates in Bulawayo and in some districts of Matabeleland North but failed to attract a significant share of the vote despite the involvement in the party of the charismatic director of Bulawayo's Amakosi Theatre, Cont Mhlanga. Also from Matabeleland, the Zimbabwe Liberty Party (ZLP) competed to reclaim old ZAPU inheritance. The new ZAPU and ZLP demanded a federal organization of the state to protect regional interests from "Shona chauvinism" and bring government closer to the people. However, the people from Matabeleland favored the MDC in all elections since 2000, because it was credible enough to win and bring about immediate change at the national level. Therefore the very existence of the MDC contributed to the containment of separatist ambitions in Matabeleland far more than ZANU-PF repressive policies could ever have done.

Those ZAPU leaders who had joined ZANU-PF in 1987, like John Nkomo and Dumiso Dabengwa, remained loyal to Mugabe after Joshua Nkomo passed away; they were decisively defeated by MDC candidates in the June 2000 election in Bulawayo. Vice President Joseph Msika, who was strikingly unpopular in Bulawayo, where he antagonized the voters during the 1995 elections, did not dare to stand in any constituency. Former Matabeleland North governor Welshman Mabhena, one of the few who could have rescued ZANU-PF's battered image, had fallen out with Mugabe. If the top leaders were too corrupt to quit the ruling party, many former middle-level ZAPU cadres, however, who had been out of active politics for some time, joined the MDC. Such was the case of NCA member Paul Themba Nyathi, a former director of elections in Matabeleland South for ZAPU in 1980, Bulawayo's new mayor Japhet Ncube, and the first party treasurer Fletcher Dulini Ncube. Yet, very few cadres crossed the floor directly from the ruling party to the MDC. In any case the MDC hierarchy was determined to exclude aspiring candidates with a known ZANU-PF past. Apart from helping win the elections in three provinces, this ZAPU component was also useful on the diplomatic scene. ZAPU's historical links with the ANC during the anti-apartheid struggle—at one time Mugabe's ZANU-PF had closer links with the South African Pan Africanist Congress (PAC)—were put to use in early 2001 to open channels of communication between the MDC leadership and Thabo Mbeki's government. With support in both Shona-populated areas and Matabeleland, the MDC was able to bridge regional differences and prevent an ethnic polarization of Zimbabwe politics, whereas none of the previous opposition parties, including ZAPU, had been able to establish a permanent presence in all provinces.

MDC Weaknesses and Eventual Crisis

Unlike most of the previous opposition parties, which had a strong urban middle-class bias, MDC tended to cut across the entire spectrum of Zimbabwe society, and this diversity, in itself a source of strength, also generated difficulties. The MDC was a "patchwork" party, associating people from various backgrounds (social, racial, professional) and with different political creeds, from conservative farmers and neoliberal businesspeople on one end of the political spectrum to Trotskyite activists on the other. There was also a strong Christian element. Former CCJP director Mike Auret and one ordained minister joined the parliamentary caucus in 2000, and several party leaders were devout—sometimes born-again—Christians. Several Catholic and Anglican clergy were accused by the government of supporting the opposition, and the election of the Anglican bishop, when Bishop Peter Hatendi retired, became a political contest. The NCA held weekly multidenominational prayer meetings at the Anglican cathedral in Harare throughout 2000 to protest ZANU-PF-sponsored violence, and the renewed effort to unite the opposition in late July 2006 was sponsored by the Christian Alliance—a grouping of civic organizations and churches. However, this heterogeneous background led to differences over policy formulation and, more important, left a legacy of different political cultures and strategic vision. These problems were contained as long as other pressing issues absorbed the leadership's energies, but they resurfaced in 2004.

There has been a confused debate over MDC's policy orientation. Some critics pointed out the neoliberal flavor of the emergency measures presented at a press conference in March 2000 by Morgan Tsvangirai's newly appointed economic adviser and MDC economic spokesman Eddie Cross. A white businessman, once a vice president of the Confederation of Zimbabwe Industries (CZI) and a former member of earlier opposition parties, Cross was held responsible by some observers for the MDC's alleged shift to the right. His stance was allegedly at variance with the party provisional manifesto released in August 1999, which advocated "social democratic, equitable, human centered development policies" and with the resolutions approved by the National Working People's Convention in February 1999.[61] However, being a mere adviser with useful contacts in the donor community, Cross was never in a position to dictate the economic policy of a future MDC government. Besides and contrary to the contentions of anti-white MDC members,[62] Cross is not the typical conservative white settler promoting his class interests. He was an opponent to Ian Smith's UDI and policies, an organizing secretary of the Centre Party with other "white liberals" who supported the "one man, one vote" principle and thus were harassed by Ian Smith's government. Many of the older whites that joined the MDC belong to that stock and not to the "racist Rhodies" group as alleged by ZANU-PF propaganda.

As a whole, the core white support for the party comes from the middle class, especially people with an NGO or human rights background such as three of the four white MPs elected in June 2000. The fourth, Chimanimani farmer Roy Bennett, was known for his progressive social ideas, fluency in Shona, and good interaction with his black farm workers and communal land peasants who chose him as the party candidate. This is precisely why he was persecuted by the regime until he fled the country in 2005: he was living proof that blacks and whites could work together in the rural areas to improve the lot of the majority. Contrary to the government's propaganda, most whites from big business sat on the fence, and some openly supported Mugabe, such as the former pro-Smith sanctions-buster John Bredenkamp, the corrupt Billy Rautenbach, or Nicholas van Hoogstraten, a British real-estate millionaire convicted and jailed for "manslaughter" in the UK (although subsequently released by clever legal argument). The rogue capitalist element is rather on the ZANU-PF side.

Moreover, MDC's early policy documents such as the 1999 manifesto, produced six months before Cross was appointed, showed the same commitment—arguably less clearly stated—to financial discipline.[63] The policy statement released in April 2000 did not bear major differences, although it spelled out more coherently the detailed economic measures for the first hundred days in power,[64] with the hope of securing donor financial support. When challenged on the policy orientation of the MDC,[65] Tsvangirai endorsed the need to implement strong orthodox stabilization policies to restore the financial credibility of the government and attract private investment in order to create employment. It is this compromise between the people's demands (needs) and the economic constraints that Tsvangirai calls "social-democracy."[66] The party line is largely the product of the changing economic thinking within the trade union movement in the 1990s, rather than the sign of a takeover by right-wing businessmen. The "Beyond ESAP" document was a landmark step in this process, when the ZCTU supported the notion of a "social contract" to alleviate the burden of structural adjustment on the poor. The policy also rests on the assessment of the failure of ZANU-PF "socialism" and its interventionist policies in the 1980s. In this respect, the MDC took into account the achievements of successful black entrepreneurs like Strive Masiyiwa, some of whom support the party finances behind the scenes.

Inasmuch as policy proposals incorporated the business community's concerns, it was in accordance with the Working People's Convention and its "all stakeholders" approach that led to the foundation of the party. MDC is meant to bridge ethnic, regional, and class divides—the "unholy alliance" (between business and union leaders) vilified by ZANU-PF's propaganda as early as 1997. Beyond the principles of democratic participation expressed in the Manifesto, ZCTU leaders acknowledged realistically that they could not rid the country of ZANU-PF's twenty-year domination alone: a narrowly defined workers' party would have left out the urban middle-class and the rural areas. When business leaders, fed up with Mugabe's erratic economic policy and arbitrary governance, supported the general strikes in 1997 and 1998, it was not out of sheer class interest, but with a sense of urgency to spell out a common strategy against the government. Personal contacts between business and union leaders built through the years made it easier. Although the two partners in the alliance believed that employers' and workers' interests remained substantially different and partly antagonistic, there was room for consultation and negotiation in the interests of the country and its economy.

Another alleged shortcoming is the absence of a clear land reform policy, supposedly because the MDC leadership could not reconcile the interests of its financial backers (the white farmers) and those of its rural support base (the masses supposedly crying for land). However this approach is biased and plays upon the cynical manipulation of the land issue, which is discussed in Chapter 6. The alleged dilemma is largely fictitious. The MDC denounced the violent and illegal farm invasions to defend fundamental principles such as upholding the rule of law and the constitutional rights of both commercial farmers and farmworkers. From the outset too the MDC was concerned about the damaging impact of farm invasions on the economy. Mugabe's propaganda machinery could not substantiate its claims that the party leadership is a "puppet of the whites" as only a minority of white farmers supported the MDC financially. The same argument was invoked against the FORUM in 1995, since some people in ZANU-PF cannot accept that there could be a party in which blacks and whites work together as equals for a common purpose. In fact, the MDC stated several times that it supported a legal, well-planned process of land redistribution, with enough technical and financial support to the new farmers. However, all MDC leaders might not be in agreement on specific aspects of the land tenure policy, whether, for example, the communal land system should be scrapped in favor of freehold tenure with some security for landowners as suggested by independent economist John Robertson— and endorsed by MDC's Eddie Cross—or whether they should opt for long-term leases while retaining communal property. Such a policy debate is perfectly legitimate in any democratic party and does not imply that this party cannot make clear decisions once in power.

Moreover, crafting a convincing political manifesto with detailed policies is not the crucial factor for electoral victory, especially when fighting against an authoritarian regime. ZANU-PF did not "win" successive elections from 1980 on the basis of its manifestos that abounded with unfulfilled and contradictory promises. It dominated the polity because it controlled the rural vote through a diffuse mix of coercion, unchallenged propaganda, and clientelism. Election studies show that most people don't read manifestos in detail, they react to short slogans, advertising logos, and images, which encapsulate the policy orientation and the priorities of the party. The MDC slogan "Chinja Maitiro!" (Change your way of doing things) successfully challenged the ZANU-PF's aggressive "Pasi ne . . ." (Down with . . .). The December 2002 general election in Kenya was a further example when "bring change" and "no corruption" rallying cries laid the basis of President Kibaki's victory. Similarly, most Zimbabweans have long been tired of arbitrary rule, violence, corruption, and economic chaos, and the MDC slogan perfectly encapsulated this feeling.

MDC's Fledging Allies: The ZCTU and the NCA After 2000

When Tsvangirai left the NCA task force, his deputy, feminist activist Thoko Matshe, with whom he had a good working relation, took over and led the coalition on the same track while maintaining its independence.[67] Task force members who had accepted positions in the MDC resigned from the NCA. The NCA task force produced a draft constitution in early 2000 and circulated it nationwide to get feedback from the people. However, in the growing climate of violence after the referendum and with the country's attention focused on elections for the following two years, mobilizing for constitutional reform was no longer seen as the priority. It also became far more dangerous. A peaceful, well-attended march organized by the NCA on 1 April 2000 was violently suppressed by ZANU-PF militias who viciously targeted white demonstrators with the active support of the riot police, effectively closing the road for civil-society-led constitutional reform. With its own constitutional draft rejected, ZANU-PF was not prepared to accept a new one on NCA's terms. From then on and until the presidential election, the NCA, like most other civil society organizations, focused on voter education and election monitoring under the umbrella coalition Zimbabwe Election Support Network (ZESN).[68]

Not all NCA members joined the MDC in 1999–2000, and it would be wrong to describe the civic body as a mere satellite of the party. The nature of structural relations between the two was left unsettled and was put to the test during the NCA general assembly in July 2001. A new task force chairperson and deputy were to be elected to replace departing Thoko Matshe. Morgan Tsvangirai's maneuver to get his candidates elected, but, more important, to bar Matshe's former deputy, Lovemore Madhuku, from taking over, was resented by many delegates as undue interference. The MDC leadership's hostility toward Madhuku arose from the latter's alleged criminal record—as a junior lawyer he was accused of embezzling funds in a law firm and was barred from practicing law—but also from his difficult relationship with several members of the MDC leadership and the outgoing NCA task force.[69] Many in the MDC believed that the ambitious Madhuku wanted to use the NCA as a platform to create a rival opposition party. That he had campaigned in the provinces to mobilize votes and that his supporters in the general assembly attempted to use what was dubbed "ZANU-PF tactics" to prevent their opponents—such as Tendai Biti or Trudy Stevenson—from entering the premises did nothing to alleviate the MDC leadership's fears. As the result of this politicking, an NGO-supported candidate with strong MDC connections, Dr. John Makumbe, was defeated by Madhuku. Although the election was endorsed by MDC leaders to avoid further public controversy, in August 2001 pro-MDC civic leaders launched a new, enlarged umbrella coalition, the Crisis in Zimbabwe Group (CZG), purportedly to bring together all civil society,[70] in the spirit of the all-stakeholders conferences organized by the NCA in 1998–99. CZG was to lobby foreign governments and international organizations so that they would exert mounting pressure on Mugabe prior to the presidential election. In addition, the group would keep in check Madhuku's NCA.

The latter's renewed attempts to take to the streets in April 2002, after Tsvangirai's defeat in the presidential election, can be seen in the light of this nascent competition. After the presidential elections, the NCA revived its campaign for a democratic constitution and organized several street protests in Harare that were always fiercely repressed. Madhuku was detained and beaten several times, but these brave challenges to the police state achieved very little. Once again his alleged appetite for power was denounced by some NCA members when Madhuku fiddled with the organization's constitution to seek a third term as the task force chairman at the end of May 2006,[71] as he vowed to lead the NCA until the democratic constitution was in place. Although the civic coalition continued to appeal to the radicalized urban youth, it alienated sizable constituencies with its leadership squabbles.

In the meantime, the NGO sector deemed to be pro-MDC became

the target of state repression. In November 2004 a new Act was passed in Parliament, giving the government extensive powers to monitor NGOs, ban foreign financial support for local organizations involved in human rights and governance, and criminalize many advocacy groups that had been very critical of the government.[72] Because the act had been labeled "unconstitutional" by a parliamentary committee and attracted much adverse publicity abroad, Mugabe stalled signing it into law. However the Private Voluntary Organisations Act gives already wide-ranging powers to the government to harass NGOs and suspend their leadership. Since March 2005 it tasked CIO operatives to audit the accounts of some NGOs to intimidate their leadership.

The formation of the MDC also created a leadership drain and power vacuum in the Zimbabwe Congress of Trade Unions. Moreover, it raised the question of the relationship between the two parent organizations. Though its leadership was drawn largely from ZCTU, the MDC was not formally controlled by the unions. Some workers began to criticize policy statements and to remind the party leaders "where they came from." As a matter of fact, ZCTU always included members with various political affiliations, including a significant number of ZANU-PF stalwarts who were not prepared to implement the MDC's political agenda. Reciprocally, the trade unions were jealous of their autonomy, but the MDC still needed the backbone of the unions to reinforce its own organization nationwide, and its leaders could not afford an adverse takeover of the union movement by ZANU-PF. Government propaganda tried to widen the emerging rift by stressing that the MDC had betrayed the workers by aligning itself with "white capitalist interests." Eventually, the ZCTU congress was held in February 2001 to elect a new leadership and remobilize the union movement. The CIO was accused of having bribed some delegates and helped indebted unions to pay arrears in order to allow them to vote in the congress. However, a ZANU-PF takeover was avoided. Isidore Zindoga was then said to be ZANU-PF's supported candidate for the secretary general post, against Nicholas Mudzengerere, a member of MDC's national executive.[73] Eventually the overtly pro-MDC candidates were not elected, but all those promoted to key positions had some sympathy for the MDC and its chairman. New secretary general Wellington Chibhebhe was close to Tsvangirai, with whom he had worked in the NCA task force. President Lovemore Matombo was also pro-MDC, while head of the MDC women's league, Lucia Matibengu, was elected first vice president of the ZCTU.[74] ZANU-PF candidates were defeated, but with relatively small margins, a testimony to ZANU-PF's intense lobbying.

Following its failure to take over ZCTU, ZANU-PF appointed in April 2001 a labor committee, led by members of the new executive of the ruling party in Harare province, War Vet leader Joseph Chinotimba (political commissar) and Chris Pasipamire (vice-chairman). In an attempt to win back the workers' political support, this labor committee began in May to interfere with labor disputes in private companies, hospitals, charity organizations, and foreign development agencies, exploiting the dysfunctional system of settlement of workers' grievances under the auspices of the Ministry of Labour and Social Affairs. ZANU-PF militias raided the companies and assaulted the managers, some of whom were taken to ZANU-PF headquarters to be beaten or even tortured. Millions of dollars of "retrenchment packages" were extorted through these methods, and the militias retained a share of the bounty as a reward for their services in what had become, by the end of May 2001, a systematic financial racket for the benefit of Hunzvi and Chinotimba. But this attempt by Harare-based War Vets to hijack the trade unions' agenda backfired: not only did it not win a single voter to the ruling party since the affected businesses closed down and retrenched more workers, but there was a wave of international protests as some foreign nationals and organizations were affected by this thuggish behavior.[75] The government for once decided to rein in the War Vets and blamed "rogue elements" among them. The labor committee was dissolved and a few arrests were made, but prosecution was subsequently dropped by the state—a recurrent policy—and the main instigators were never questioned.

The subsequent strategy was to speedily develop the rival Zimbabwe Federation of Trade Unions (ZFTU) by encouraging ZANU-PF supporters to form break-away unions. In late 2001 and 2002 the ZFTU led by Joseph Chinotimba became more aggressive, claiming thirteen member unions. The incorporation of ZFTU in the ring of ZANU-PF satellite organizations betrays the chefs' persistent dream of a subservient civil society that would toe the line, another remnant of the "one-party state" culture. During the same period, the ZCTU was weakened by a huge loss of membership, given the near collapse of Zimbabwe's manufacturing sector, hence of formal employment, and also by the dramatic impact of political violence on member unions like GAPWUZ in agriculture or the Teachers' Union, whose officials were killed, went into hiding, or fled abroad. A new stringent labor legislation was put in place in 2001, forbidding strikes and threatening unions of deregistration if they did not comply, leaving no doubt that the government regarded the ZCTU as an enemy of the state on the same footing as the MDC.

Since its congress, the ZCTU has remained actively involved in NCA, ZESN, and the Crisis in Zimbabwe Group. It lobbied South Africa's Congress of South African Trade Unions (COSATU) for support and backed Tsvangirai's bid at the presidential election. State and ZANU-PF-sponsored violence—in particular the September 2001 punitive beatings in the high-density suburbs following a ZCTU-sponsored general strikes the previous July—as well as the dramatic downward spiraling of the economy, with rapidly rising inflation and the widening shortfalls in basic commodities, kept the union movement in a close strategic alliance with the MDC. The ZCTU naturally condemned the official results of the presidential elections, adopting MDC's stance in their analysis of the fraudulent ballot, and it tried to organize in April 2002 a three-day strike in protest, but without much success. The preparations derailed by the actions of the police, which interfered with a meeting of the ZCTU national executive, alleging it was a political meeting. Under the new Public Order and Security Act, police had to be notified in advance of all political meetings, and the government interpreted this as the power to ban all public gatherings. Lacking underground structures and with a shrinking membership base due to the economic melting, the ZCTU has remained ill-prepared to resist systematic harassment and organize effective mass action—as illustrated once more by the arrest and beating of its leaders in September 2006 when they attempted to stage a protest.

From Political Tensions to Effective Split

From the outset the MDC was burdened with organizational problems that have never been properly overcome and that were compounded by the state violence that has destroyed party structures in the provinces.[76] In addition, the hastily formed structures at the province and constituency level were bound to include many opportunists with hidden agendas, such as Sekesai Makwavarara. A Harare deputy mayor elected on an MDC ticket in 2002, as a councillor in the township of Mabvuku, she switched allegiances to ZANU-PF in April 2003, when executive mayor Elias Mudzuri was suspended on spurious grounds by the minister of local government.[77] A docile acting mayor, she was rewarded with a commercial farm in September 2004. In December 2004 Makwavarara was appointed chairperson of the Harare Commission by the minister, when the elected city council was disbanded by the government for alleged mismanagement. The ZANU-PF plant endorsed Operation Murambatsvina without hesitation in May 2005, and her mandate was further prolonged in June 2006 in spite of her disastrous management of city affairs.

In Harare province, the expectation of an easy victory at the 2000 parliamentary elections, given the referendum results, generated fierce political competition in the high-density suburbs with accusations of rigging and intimidation traded between rival aspirants to office. Some of the MPs subsequently elected displayed erratic behavior, such as Munyaradzi Gwisai, self-proclaimed leader of the leftist International Socialist Organisation (ISO). Gwisai made several provocative statements supporting Mugabe's land policy and accusing the party leadership of being dominated by "bourgeois and petty-bourgeois elements" and whites.[78] In February 2001, the government press published a document presented as Gwisai's speech in an MDC closed seminar, where he accused his party of abandoning the working class to please the business class, commercial farmers, and Western countries. Morgan Tsvangirai then hinted that the discontented MP could leave the MDC if he "felt at variance with the policies of the party."[79] Eventually, and following fresh public criticisms of his party's leadership, Gwisai was expelled on 22 November 2002. He automatically lost his parliamentary seat and was trounced by the MDC official candidate in the March 2003 by-election, obviously enjoying no support in the working class he purported to represent.

The clash of personal ambitions that delayed the election of a permanent provincial executive in Harare until January 2002 also tainted the MDC's selection of its candidates for the executive mayor and Harare Council elections, to be held at the same time as the 2002 presidential election. After years of bickering with the ZANU-PF Harare Commission, David Samudzimu, former chairman of the Combined Harare Residents Association (CHRA), which had been criticizing the mismanagement of city affairs since the mid-1990s, seemed to be best qualified to stand for the MDC in the mayoral contest. However, in the meeting convened in January 2001 by the interim MDC Harare province executive Samudzimu lost to Elias Mudzuri, the relatively unknown former deputy city engineer and union official, in a climate of cheap politicking and racial slurs: some of Mudzuri's supporters accused the CHRA of being a "white middle class" organization from low-density suburbs and Samudzimu of being a "puppet of the whites." According to eyewitnesses, vote buying, intimidation, and other typical ZANU-PF methods of canvassing support were used.[80] The party national executive was divided over the issue as the national chairman supported Mudzuri against the MDC director of elections' advice, and Tsvangirai eventually endorsed Mudzuri's nomination. As a result of the incident, the director of elections, Paul Nyathi, was moved to the post of party spokesman in the September 2002 reshuffle, after the sudden death of Lovemore Jongwe. For the first time, a rift crystallized at the top echelons of the party, more or less along the lines of the future contending factions.

Exhilarated by their referendum victory, MDC leaders imagined they could win the June 2000 elections, block repressive legislation, and confront the executive.[81] Through 2001 they naively hoped to detach anti-Mugabe MPs—especially Eddison Zvobgo—from the ZANU-PF caucus to vote the old president out of office.[82] Once again and although the constitution and Electoral Act remained the same, with the addition of repressive legislation, the MDC hoped to mobilize enough voters to win the 2002 presidential election. The party's strategy relied too heavily on the world's will to force Mugabe to accept truly democratic elections and step down from power. After the MDC's defeat in the crooked ballot, the South African government's endorsement of the results while the Western powers seemed powerless, and with low expectations of a better outcome in the 2005 general election, there were growing tensions within the top leadership over the party's strategy. Although in August 2004 the party's Management Committee endorsed the compromise constitutional draft negotiated with ZANU-PF under the auspices of South Africa's Thabo Mbeki, the leadership was in fact divided. Welshman Ncube, who had led the negotiations on the MDC side, was the driving force behind this attempt to settle the national crisis through pacific and legal means. But national chairman Isaac Matongo, who was said to hate the secretary general—and the Ndebele at large—accused him of accepting a power-sharing arrangement, with the MDC as the junior partner, in the hope of being appointed to the position of prime minister.[83]

The 2005 elections were another bone of contention. Members of what would become Ncube's faction always argued for contesting elections and never ceding an inch of political ground to the ruling party without a fight. It was a matter of credibility and consistency with the party line: change through pacific and legal means only. The opposite faction that included most former union leaders no longer believed in the electoral route for change, given the Mugabe regime's ability to manipulate elections, especially when the opposition could not even challenge results in the courts. Although this group advocated mass action, neither the MDC and the ZCTU nor the NCA were ever able to set up successful strategies to this end. Beyond the "democratic space" argument, Ncube and his allies did not believe that MDC structures could carry on mass action in a nonviolent and effective way.[84] Besides, if the MDC and its civil society allies used violence, they would be crushed by the regime's security apparatus: Mugabe would have loved to have an excuse for mass murder—such as was the case with the "insurgency" in Matabeleland in the 1980s. Since 2002 Tsvangirai vacillated between the two strategic options, and on 24 August 2004, the MDC announced that it would not take part in subsequent elections unless the just-adopted SADC guidelines for democratic elections were fully implemented in Zimbabwe—only to reverse this stance in early February 2005, giving in to international pressure and fears from part of the leadership that a boycott would demoralize grassroots members and entrench Mugabe's rule. After another defeat in the March 2005 elections, once again the election boycott advocates became more vocal when the Senate election issue came up.

In the meantime factionalism within the MDC had taken the more vicious form of violence orchestrated by Tsvangirai's "kitchen cabinet," a group of personal advisers sometimes referred to by opponents as the Masvingo "tribal clique," who have built a parallel party structure allegedly to improve the implementation of the president's directives, but in a broader perspective to improve efficiency in a party seriously disrupted by ZANU-PF violence.[85] They came in direct conflict with the members of the official MDC secretariat when they started a smear campaign to unseat Ncube and his allies.[86] "Kitchen cabinet" members crossed the red line on 28 September 2004, when they had some party youths beat Peter Guhu, MDC director for security, nearly to death, and again in mid-May 2005, seriously assaulting MDC staff members loyal to Ncube at Harare party headquarters, in the Bulawayo Provincial Office and in Gwanda. Although these delinquent youths were expelled from the party in May 2005 and one member of the "kitchen cabinet" was suspended in June, senior members of the MDC who allegedly manipulated these youths escaped sanctions.[87] That this internal violence was not dealt with in the appropriate manner left many National Council members with serious misgivings: if the culprits enjoyed impunity they would resort to violence again. As Brian Raftopoulos noted, "Most of the energies of these [parallel] structures have thus been turned on those perceived as enemies within the party, rather than to developing a strategy to confront the Mugabe regime . . . for Ncube and his supporters the use of the parallel structures within the party [was] largely a means of isolating and pushing them out of leadership positions at the next congress."[88] Tsvangirai's stubborn refusal to address these serious concerns, brought up again in July 2005 by four members of the Management Committee, and his refusal to disband his "kitchen cabinet" laid the ground for the subsequent bitter controversy.

It was in this climate of intimidation and distrust that the Senate elections debate took place in the National Council (NC) on 12 October 2005. While Ncube and Sibanda argued that the MDC might gain enough seats to deprive Mugabe of a two-thirds majority and the capacity to change the constitution at will, Tsvangirai and his allies claimed that ZANU-PF would rig these elections as they had done with the 2005 House of Assembly election and that the MDC should no longer legitimize such fraudulent exercises. After the Management Committee failed to reach a consensus, the NC voted 33–31 (with two spoiled ballots)[89] to contest the elections, and the decision was endorsed by four of the top six leaders. But not Tsvangirai, who walked out of the meeting and rushed to the press, claiming that the National Council vote was deadlocked at 50–50, and that he had then used his "casting vote" to decide against participation. The Management Committee published a statement to correct the facts after a failed attempt to have the president backtrack, a move which further confused the situation in the public's mind. That Tsvangirai knew perfectly what was at stake is obvious in his final words when he left the NEC meeting: "If the party breaks so be it. I will answer to congress."[90] This explains why he subsequently resisted all mediation attempts (including by Thabo Mbeki) in the following months.

Tsvangirai refused to budge, and the two factions drifted away, trading insults and accusations in the media. Tsvangirai or some members of his faction suggested that Ncube and his colleagues were on CIO payroll to plot against the party president and that they wanted to sign a new unity accord with ZANU-PF.[91] There have also been disturbing occurrences of racist abuse against white members of the Sibanda/ Ncube faction. The latter for its part was adamant that Tsvangirai had violated several clauses of the party's constitution and the National Disciplinary Committee, chaired by Sibanda, subsequently suspended the MDC president, who convened an NC meeting on 1 December 2005 to nullify these proceedings and expel the rebels from the party. For the so-called "pro-Senate" faction, the issues of violence and violation of the party rules, which were downplayed by the Tsvangirai group, were the fundamental causes of the split rather than the difference over the Senate election. Therefore it was a matter of political ethic and internal democracy, of observing the founding values of the MDC: nonviolence, leadership accountability, and strict adherence to the rule of law. The Tsvangirai faction found it legitimate to bend the rules to accommodate political expediency, since their view of the Senate election was allegedly in the party's real interest and they had correctly read of the minds of their fellow citizens. Tsvangirai claimed that he was directly answerable to the people at large and, as the party president, above the dictates of the NEC. His opponents retorted that he had become "another Mugabe," a law unto himself.

Although some other factors such as the Shona/Ndebele antagonism played a role, the lack of a common, democratic culture—rather than a common ideology, as often stated—is the main cause of the MDC split. Under duress and as their commitment to the cause was increasingly put to test, the leaders could not agree on fundamental principles and rules to guide their political behavior. The two factions held separate congresses in early 2006, thus hardening the split to the shock of Zimbabwe's civil society. It was obvious first at its March congress and then in a series of public rallies that Tsvangirai's faction (MDC-T) attracted a wider audience outside Matabeleland. The president was followed by the majority of NC members and of the party membership and by about half the party caucus in the House of Assembly. This is not surprising in view of Tsvangirai's trade union connections and the large number of former ZCTU cadres in the party structures. He also retained the backing of major civic groups, including the NCA and the ZCTU. Female unionist Thokozane Khupe (MP in Bulawayo) was promoted to deputy-president for the women's rights, and the ambitious Lovemore Moyo (MP in Matabeleland South) was elevated to the position of national vice-chairman. These concessions to ethnic/regional balance could not hide the fact that the most senior leaders from Matabeleland were aligned with the Ncube faction, and unfortunately the two parties were likely to reproduce the ZANU/ZAPU ethnic divide of the late 1970s.

At its Bulawayo congress in February, the "pro-Senate" faction elected Professor Arthur Mutambara as president, acknowledging the fact that the faction needed a charismatic Shona leader to stand in a presidential election. A former SRC leader in the late 1980s, who had obtained a doctorate in robotics in the United States, Mutambara was not tainted by the opposition's internal squabbles and was expected to rejuvenate the MDC. At the same time, by mixing pragmatic economics with an anti-imperialist discourse Mutambara could blast the ZANU-PF-constructed view of the MDC as a "white puppet." In April 2006, however, Mutambara's party (MDC-M) was weakened by a series of defections to the rival MDC-T, namely its director of elections and his deputy, Blessing Chebundo and Sipepa Nkomo, and the party national chairman, Gift Chimanikire—the latter having resented Mutambara's ascent to the top position that he coveted. With too few Shonas remaining among its leaders the MDC-M was not able to retain its seats outside Matabeland in subsequent electoral contests. The MDC-T trounced its rival in the Budiriro by-election in May 2006, but with a diminished margin (64 percent of the votes cast, against 82 percent in 2000 and 78 percent in March 2005) and a low turnout pointing at the party's failure to fully mobilize its electorate (its candidate gathered less than half of the votes the MDC had received in 2000). Both factions lost some urban council seats to ZANU-PF in the course of 2006, a warning signal of shrinking popularity in former opposition strongholds.

Violence remained endemic in the MDC-T and partly condoned by the leadership as evidenced by the campaign for the Budiriro by-election where the winning candidate, Emmanuel Chisvuure, was one of the two party officials suspended for two years in June 2005.[92] MDC-T's chairman for Harare province made public statements reminiscent of

ZANU-PF intolerance toward any opposition. In early July 2006, veteran MP for Harare North Trudy Stevenson and three other provincial executive members of the MDC-M were severely assaulted and injured by Tsvangirai's party thugs in Mabvuku. Although MDC-T's secretary general Tendai Biti denied any link between the party and the attack, Stevenson recognized some of her assailants as people previously involved in intraparty violence. This assault was allegedly sponsored by Timothy Mubawu, a local MDC-T MP with a personal history of violence, known for operating outside the local party structure, and with close connections to a CIO officer.[93]

There are no real ideological differences between the two MDC wings, and the Ncube faction by no means embodies the "right" as opposed to Tsvangirai's alleged progressive wing. Maybe the MDC-M is more concerned with the justice due to the victims of the dictatorship and would strongly support the establishment of a truth commission to investigate all human rights violations. In this matter, the other MDC is keen to offer Mugabe immunity from prosecution as part of an exit package. But above anything else the violence and ensuing accusations and counter-accusations, as well as differences over the political strategy, impeded cooperation between the two parties up to the 2008 elections. Discussions held in late 2006 and again after March 2007 in view of forming an alliance against ZANU-PF did not overcome the widening breach between the sister organizations. A coalition agreement was announced in April 2007 but soon collapsed on differences over its implementation, and the Mutambara faction withdrew its signature in July the same year, announcing it would present its own candidates in the March 2008 elections. At that time the MDC-T was again thinking of a boycott if the Mbeki-sponsored talks (see Chapter 8) failed to produce a satisfactory constitutional and legal framework.

The repeated setbacks suffered by the opposition from June 2000 to May 2008 should not obscure the impressive achievements of the MDC during its ten years of existence in spite of the state's relentless violence and crude propaganda. Although the MDC was not the first opposition party in Zimbabwe history to struggle for democracy and better governance, it was the first to seriously challenge Mugabe's personal rule and the ZANU-PF mafia's grip on Zimbabwe. Its significant presence in Parliament—although eroded in 2005—lent credibility to its claims of representing a large section of the people. By its campaign activities inside the country and its contacts outside, the MDC has lodged at the heart of the national agenda, and ZANU-PF with all the resources of the state apparatus and a reckless use of violence failed to dislodge it. The MDC has successfully questioned ZANU-PF's claim of an inherent right to rule.

Through building close ties with a vast array of civic movements, including the NCA and the ZCTU, the MDC leadership laid the foundations for a true political alternative. Its incipient capacity to bring together people from different social and political backgrounds, with an agenda of change by peaceful, legal means would have been a recipe for success in any normal political environment with a reasonably level electoral framework. However, from stolen electoral victory to crushed demonstrations and strikes, the bitter struggle has had the divisive impact that Mugabe's strategists expected, especially on a party that was not set up to fight a war. MDC leaders were not prepared to counter the deluge of violence and treachery they have faced since February 2000. Like an acid, terror has dissolved the party's fabric and left behind the altered components, including personal ambitions, racial and ethnic prejudice, and greed.

Chapter 4

The Media Battlefield:
From Skirmishes to Full-Fledged War

A feeling of freedom flourished when, at Independence, the ZANU-PF government announced its determination to remove the Rhodesian Front regime's strict state controls on the media. "Not only will the media be genuinely free in an independent Zimbabwe; they will also be responsible as well as responsive to the will of the majority," promised Nathan Shamuyarira, minister of information and tourism and former journalist.[1] However, this spirit of goodwill was short-lived and the media soon became another contested terrain between the government and civil society. Notwithstanding individuals such as respected nationalist and journalist Willie Musarurwa, Mugabe's regime was and has remained profoundly hostile to a pluralistic system of information. This intolerance took various forms in the 1980s and 1990s, although at the time there was the widespread illusion entertained by civic activists and journalists that private-owned media was strong enough to safeguard the freedom of information and keep the government in check.

In the context of the economic and social decline of the late 1990s, the tense relationship between the small but dynamic private press and the government escalated into open confrontation, first in January 1999 and again after the February 2000 constitutional referendum, as part of the whole political crisis. From then on the government waged war on the independent media, using an impressive range of weapons such as verbal abuse and threats, random violence by militias, sabotage, and the recourse to a new, oppressive legal framework. But before we turn to the ongoing clampdown on press freedom, we need to survey briefly the media scene since independence.

Government Media Policy After Independence and into the 1990s

The first decade of majority rule saw the large state-owned print and electronic media becoming increasingly politically controlled, leaving a very limited space for a few private newspapers and magazines. The second decade saw a significant expansion of the private print press, both in terms of the number of titles published and circulation figures. This was certainly a source of irritation for the ruling party bosses but did not change the overall balance between the large government-owned media and a few independent voices, if only because the president successfully resisted the pressure to liberalize television and radio ownership.

In 1981, the Zimbabwe government received a U.S.$5 million grant from Nigeria to buy out Zimbabwe Newspapers (1980) Ltd., known as Zimpapers and formerly the Rhodesian Printing & Publishing Company Ltd., a subsidiary of South African Argus Printing and Publishing Company. At the time, the purchase of the Rhodesian Printing & Publishing Company seemed justified from the nationalist point of view as part of the decolonization policy. However, it must be said that the *Herald* and the *Chronicle*, which were owned by Zimpapers, were frequently censored under Ian Smith's regime, and many (white) journalists fought to preserve editorial independence. These papers were not just propaganda mouthpieces of Smith's government, unlike Rhodesian television and radio. The Mass Media Trust (MMT) was created in January 1981 to handle the Nigerian grant and ostensibly to act as a buffer between the government and Zimpapers.[2] The same year Minister Shamuyarira boasted to the Zimbabwe Union of Journalists, "We created the MMT so that the media would be in neutral hands and not business tycoons or the government—that would quash the free voice of journalists."[3] A rather ironic statement in view of what is happening today, a betrayal of promises that does not seem to bother Shamuyarira—no longer a cabinet minister but a long-time ZANU-PF secretary for information. Admittedly some safeguards were introduced in the Trust's constitution to protect journalists against state and ruling party interference. For example, members of Parliament, civil servants, and uniformed services people could not be appointed as trustees. Originally the MMT had a controlling share of 43.42 percent in Zimpapers, and it was only after 1986, when the country was apparently on the path to the one-party state, that the MMT secretly acquired an absolute majority—about 51 percent of the equity.

Since 1981 Zimpapers has controlled the major part of the print press: two dailies, the *Herald* in Harare and the *Chronicle* in Bulawayo, with their respective sister Sunday papers, the *Sunday Mail* and *Sunday News*. For most of two decades the *Herald* and the *Chronicle* were the only daily newspapers circulated in the country. The absence of an independent daily to counter the *Herald*'s fables—the *Daily Gazette* notwithstanding— was a major constraint on public debate on government policies and a major handicap for the opposition parties. Zimpapers also published regional papers such as the *Manica Post* in Mutare and the *Gweru Times* in the Midlands. Government papers were widely distributed in the rural areas in particular through the local government apparatus. In the early 1990s the government set up, with the support of the United Nations Educational, Scientific and Cultural Organization (UNESCO), the Community Newspapers Group, which included six papers reporting in vernacular languages. The government also controlled production of news stories through the national wire service, Zimbabwe Inter-Africa News Agency (ZIANA), established in 1981 as a nonprofit public service. For good measure, the ruling party's impressive Jongwe printing press later published a party magazine, the *People's Voice*, originally edited by Charles Ndlovu (alias Webster Shamu), a protégé of Shamuyarira. The crude Marxist-Leninist terminology used by government papers and Ministry of Information apparatchiks, purporting to reflect "development journalism" and reverence to the "masses," conveniently disguised the oppressive nature of the political order. As in the Soviet Union under Stalin, the reality was likely to be significantly different if not the complete opposite of what was printed or broadcast, but only Zimbabweans with alternate sources of information and some education could decipher the truth. Most visitors and newly arrived expatriates would also be easily deceived by the façade of professional reporting and apparent reliability of the state media.

By the mid-1980s it was already obvious that the MMT was not the impartial autonomous body the government had claimed. The MMT trustees were appointed by the government on Shamuyarira's recommendation. He handpicked people—some qualified, others not—with no personal power base who would depend on him, and he deliberately excluded trade unionists, prominent human rights activists, ZAPU people, and vocal war veterans. A ZANU-PF cadre, Dr. Davison Sadza, was appointed chairman of the Trust and of the Zimpapers group that functioned de facto as a parastatal. Therefore, it is not so surprising that in 1990 the supposedly nonpartisan MMT, like other parastatals, made a substantial financial donation to the ruling party's parliamentary elections campaign. Zimpapers was put under tight control of the Ministry of Information and the ruling party, with the active complicity of the MMT chairman. In addition, MMT's growing financial and administrative dependence on the state made it easier for the minister to interfere with its management: without constant financial and administrative support from the government, the MMT would have collapsed entirely by the mid-1980s. Similarly, ZIANA operating under the nominal control of the Mass Media Trust was in fact strongly influenced by the government because the agency was dependent on state budget subsidies for its daily operations.

In the early 1980s, the ruling party entrenched loyalists in key posts within Zimpapers and ZIANA to act as a kind of "political police"—or as one former Zimpapers chief executive and then ZANU-PF supporter referred to them (including himself in the group), "ZANU's hatchet men."[4] The minority shareholders of Zimpapers had no voice in the selection of the group's managing director and that of the various newspapers' editors. According to Richard Saunders, the government was able to "simultaneously penetrate, encircle and marginalize the effective supervisory role of the MMT within the media, while continuing to assert the legally enshrined independence of both the Trust and the media under its control."[5] Political activist Judith Todd, then a member of the Zimpapers board (her mother, wife of Sir Garfield Todd, being on the MMT board), later recalled how the rules were twisted to accommodate both ZANU-PF and some corrupt managers.[6] Indeed, Nathan Shamuyarira, first as minister of information, and later as the ZANU-PF secretary for information, interfered directly in the appointments and dismissals of newspaper editors from February 1981. As Saunders noted, "Between 1985 and 1989, for example, three editors at the MMT-dominated Zimpapers were summarily fired on ZANU-PF orders for political offences, without objections from the MMT. Many other journalists in less senior positions were regularly subjected to reprimand, warnings and other forms of intimidation."[7] Basically the MMT never performed the role it was supposed to play according to ZANU-PF's deceptive rhetoric.

When the editor of the *Sunday Mail*, Willie Musarurwa, a former friend and appointee of Shamuyarira, was unceremoniously relieved of his post, the minister was quoted as saying that the president wanted to appoint a "true and trusted cadre."[8] A Princeton-trained journalist and PF-ZAPU secretary for information, Willie Musarurwa was jailed for nearly a decade under the RF government. His refusal to renege on his loyalty to Joshua Nkomo during the Gukurahundi and the assault against his party made him a liability for Mugabe's regime. Besides, Musarurwa would not go along with the one-party-state project. In 1989,

Geoffrey Nyarota, editor of the *Chronicle*, was moved to a meaningless administrative position in Zimpapers' Harare headquarters after he exposed the Willowvale corruption scandal (see Chapter 7). Nyarota had not only seriously embarrassed the regime but mentioned Shamuyarira's name in connection with the scandal. Shamuyarira also sued the *Chronicle* for defamation and won his case since his name was not cited in the Sandura Commission of Inquiry report on the Willowvale scandal, despite insistent public rumors.[9]

Government-owned newspapers, especially the *Sunday Mail* under Willie Musarurwa's editorship, enjoyed a certain degree of editorial autonomy backed by some professional reporting until the mid-1980s.[10] However, this was valid as long as they did not challenge ZANU-PF's power. This relative freedom was progressively eroded through the years and in the late 1980s—much earlier as far as the Matabeleland disturbances are concerned—it was obvious that the government press toed the party line. This became ominous during the confrontations between the students and trade unions on the one hand and the state on the other in 1989–92, and of course during every election campaign. Elias Rusike, being a Zezuru and a friend of Shamuyarira, was appointed managing director of Zimpapers in 1984, and then chief executive officer. However, he resigned in 1989 over this growing political interference in the day-to-day running of the company and conflicts with partisan editors such as Charles Chikerema. When the latter was appointed editor of the *Sunday Mail* in 1987, thanks to his family ties with Mugabe, the newspaper became a propaganda mouthpiece. In the 1990s, both the *Sunday Mail* and the *Herald* demonstrated unconditional support for the president, although some of his cabinet ministers were sometimes criticized. Even self-censorship did not shield Zimpapers' editors from the government's wrath: in January 1998 the editor of the *Herald*, Thommy Sithole, was removed (and "promoted" as the group director of business projects and public relations) for sharp editorial comments following the food riots.[11] Although Sithole was a ruling party stalwart, the *Herald* had developed from 1997 a more critical style of reporting in the context of the ZCTU-sponsored strikes and with the competition from the private press.

The state monopoly on radio and television in Zimbabwe was another legacy of the Rhodesian era that the ruling elite was happy to retain. Since Independence the Zimbabwe Broadcasting Corporation (ZBC) has been fully owned by the state and operated the four—legal—radio stations and the two existing television channels. Governors on the ZBC board, its director-general, and other directors were political appointees. The ZBC programs were under surveillance of the Ministry of Information ever since 1980. According to direct oral testimonies, the minister gave instructions to ZBC directors on what could or could not be broadcast. The news bulletins were oriented to convey the same message on the various channels. The electronic media were powerful instruments for political propaganda. If only 25 percent of households owned a television set in the 1990s, most were able to listen to the radio, and programs in vernacular languages on Radio 2 were popular in the rural areas.

The political bias was particularly obvious at election time, a situation that has been repeatedly criticized by human rights groups.[12] Opposition parties were given a ridiculously short space on radio and television—certainly not sufficient to compensate for years of biased reporting—while ZANU-PF enjoyed unlimited access. During the 1995 election campaign the ruling party's coverage in the news bulletins was thirty times bigger than that of all the other opposition parties. ZBC's reporting of political meetings was systematically hostile to the opposition and sycophantic for the president, vice presidents, and Cabinet ministers. This pattern was not seriously altered during the 2000 referendum campaign: although the NCA obtained more significant space on national television, ZBC refused to take its paid commercials—in the past the government print press too had refused to publish political advertisements from opposition parties—while it willingly broadcasted the government Commission's propaganda. The NCA had to go to court to force the ZBC to air its advertisements. The Media Monitoring Project of Zimbabwe (MMPZ) gave a thoroughly researched assessment of this bias: ZTV allotted 16.12 hours to pro-CRC programs as compared to 1.33 hours to the NCA, and only 1.2 hours of general information about the constitutional issues.[13]

There were occasional loopholes in this policy when more lively and free-speech programs were allowed on the airwaves, such as the four "Meet the President" TV shows in 1994, but this experiment was terminated before the 1995 elections. These programs were invariably interrupted after a while by some phone calls from ZANU-PF "big men." The BBC African transmissions and those of SABC and satellite television were, for a time, the only sources whose broadcasts exposed Zimbabweans to some alternative news and views. Political interference also brought about mismanagement of the corporation and corruption as in other Zimbabwean parastatals. By 1997, ZBC was virtually bankrupt; its huge debt enhanced by arrears due by the state (estimated then at Z$100 million). Its debt servicing and administrative overhead absorbed 63 percent of its earned income.[14] Therefore the corporation was even more dependent on the state for its very existence, a situation unlikely to foster editorial independence.

Although the black nationalists had criticized racism in the Rhodesian media, with good reasons, the government media followed the ruling party chefs' increasing tendency to discriminate against white political opponents, civic leaders, and farmers. White bashing was present in columns written by external contributors but also in the *Sunday Mail* editorials under Charles Chikerema and in advertisements published by indigenization lobbyists such as Philip Chiyangwa and Roger Boka, material that only the government press accepted. Clothed in approximate Marxist discourse—whites being equated to the ritual bourgeoisie —these racist ravings revealed the hatred that some ZANU-PF ideologues and journalists nurtured against segments of the population and which would burst into the open in 2000. Although most commentators in the 1990s downplayed these "excesses," which they attributed to lunatics and fanatics, it must be noted that neither Mugabe nor his Cabinet ministers disavowed these abusive comments. It was originally perceived as part of a xenophobic and paranoid attitude toward Western countries and their media, to be understood in the context of cold war global politics and the struggle against the apartheid regime. However, in the late 1990s and by contrast with a democratizing South Africa, this racism appeared deeply embedded in ZANU-PF political culture.

Strenuous Development of the Private Press

From independence up to 2000, a small but vibrant independent press was tolerated by the ruling party because it did not enjoy mass circulation and could not compete with the government's propaganda machine. Being weekly papers or monthly magazines published in English for the urban middle class, and devoting only part of their editorial space to political issues, they did not affect ZANU-PF's monopoly of information in the rural areas. Conversely, the existence of a few titles under close watch by Western donors gave some credibility to the regime's claims of upholding freedom of information. The truth is that a vast majority of Zimbabweans had never read, or even heard of, these papers at least until the *Daily News* appeared on the newsstands. Therefore, while the political importance of the independent press in the first two decades cannot be ignored, its significance for assessment of democracy in Zimbabwe should not be overstated—as done by many foreigners. Otherwise, the sudden change of course in 2000 would be inexplicable. This change will be addressed in the next section.

When Elias Rusike left Zimpapers he bought Modus Publications, with the help of two other black businessmen. Modus, owned since 1979 by a group of "white liberals," published the country's major independent weekly the *Financial Gazette*, whose editor from 1982 was Clive Wilson.

He had significantly upgraded this business-oriented newspaper (increasing its circulation from 4,000 to 20,000). However, Geoffrey Nyarota, the new editor appointed in 1989, gave it a new dimension as the most articulate critic of government policies, in particular in economic and social matters. It benefited from young professional reporters and excellent columnists, although the so-called progressive forces did not acknowledge its contribution because it defended market-oriented policies—especially ESAP. Modus Publications also published from 5 October 1992 to 25 December 1994 the *Daily Gazette*, an intended competitor to the *Herald*. With a tabloid format and a taste of sensationalism, the new paper targeted a popular readership. However, the newspaper lacked the resources to undertake investigative journalism as its editor intended to do. With a weak financial basis from the outset it never succeeded in overcoming its original problems and when it folded Modus was debt-ridden.[15] Whatever its shortcomings, the *Daily Gazette* offered a breathing space to civil society and the opposition parties, something the ruling party could not tolerate in the run-up to the 1995 elections. State and private companies were warned against advertising in the newspaper and rumor had it that a British investor had been dissuaded from coming to the rescue.

Modus Publications was shaken in 1995 by attempts by the government to intimidate *Financial Gazette* journalists.[16] The publisher, the editor, and one of his deputies were arrested and indicted for criminal defamation for alleging a secret marriage of President Mugabe to his secretary Grace Marufu, with whom he had been having an affair—and two children. An informant they refused to name had fed the journalists a false story, and they were ultimately convicted in 1996 when they refused to name their source. At the same time some financial pressure was exerted on Modus through the government-owned Zimbank to which the group was indebted. The Modus Group's chief executive officer and majority shareholder Elias Rusike closed down his loss-making *Sunday Gazette* and decided to revamp the profit-making *Financial Gazette*. This questionable project and the legacy of the criminal defamation case soured Rusike's relations with the paper's editor, Trevor Ncube, who was suspended. In early 1996 Ncube resigned with Iden Wetherell, whose column "Muckraker" had been scrapped from the new formula because he was both white and very critical of the president and the Cabinet.

These developments damaged the independent media's image in the public eye—which was part of the CIO's plan. They also led to speculations about the ultimate loyalties of the Modus chief executive. Elias Rusike was a ZANU-PF cardholder in the 1980s and he once ran—unsuccessfully—in the ZANU-PF parliamentary primaries in Goromonzi. It is alleged by former combatants that during the liberation struggle he was part of group of Zezuru cadres (the "21 Zezurus") working as a brotherhood to advance the interests of their clan in a liberated Zimbabwe. Some people found it hard to believe also that Rusike had secured a Zimbank loan to buy the *Financial Gazette* in 1989 without political patronage, hence with strings attached to it. Others remembered how the then *Financial Gazette* editor, Nyarota, was dismissed without explanation in 1991. For several months after the departure of Ncube and Wetherell there was an unmistakable tuning down of *Financial Gazette* editorials to appease the ruling elite. For example, this paper remained almost silent on the CCJP/LRF report on the Matabeleland atrocities released in 1997, probably because Mugabe's personal responsibility was at stake. By late 2002, Rusike sold his shares to the newspaper editor and other investors, including Gideon Gono, a relative of Mugabe who had appointed him governor of the Reserve Bank.

Other attempts in the early 1990s to publish popular independent newspapers such as the *Sunday Times* or the *People*, failed after a few months or even weeks in circulation. Some monthly magazines, though not focusing primarily on politics, made useful contributions on political issues. Published by the Catholic publishing house Mambo Press, *Moto* criticized corruption and human rights violations. *Parade* and *Horizon* covered mainly sports and musical entertainment. However, *Parade* in the 1980s, and later on *Horizon* created in 1991 by *Parade*'s former editor Andrew Moyse, reported on some serious political issues. For example, *Horizon* covered the run-up to the 1995 election and Dongo's saga more fully than other publications. However, their finances were uncertain and *Horizon* folded in early 2000 (its situation being worsened by the cost of lawyers after a series of defamation cases brought against the magazine by ZANU-PF "big men"). *Parade* survived thanks to the support of its owners Thomson Publications. There have been many other privately run general news magazines in Zimbabwe, but they have offered no or very little coverage of political issues. *Social Change* was a quarterly publication aiming to promote socialism in Zimbabwe but had a very limited readership. *The Worker* monthly issued by the ZCTU addressed mainly labor issues although its editorials were increasingly critical of the government.

The launching on 10 May 1996 of a new weekly newspaper, the *Zimbabwe Independent*, brought about some useful competition to the *Financial Gazette*. Founded by the white investors who had sold Modus to Elias Rusike, the *Zimbabwe Independent* hired Trevor Ncube as its chief editor and Iden Wetherell as his deputy. This unexpected competition stimulated the *Financial Gazette* and by the end of the 1990s the pink-colored newspaper, geared by its able editor Francis Mdlongwa, was once again critical of the ruling party and the president. A new Sunday paper, the *Zimbabwe Standard*, hit the newsstands on 13 April 1997. Owned by the same group as the *Independent*, but with a separate editor and its own team of reporters, it provided a welcome alternative to the *Sunday Mail.*

The *Zimbabwe Standard* was the focus of a major attack on the freedom of the press on the eve of the new millennium. In January 1999, two *Standard* journalists, editor Mark Chavunduka and reporter Ray Choto, were arrested following the publication of a story alleging that an attempted military coup had been severely repressed in the army. The two journalists were illegally detained in a military camp for ten days by the military police (which has no authority over civilians) and severely tortured by the military intelligence to force them to reveal their sources in the army. When they later recounted their ordeal, their revelations shocked the public at home and abroad: for most human rights watch-dogs the ZANU-PF regime had shown its true colors. In the sensitive context of Zimbabwe Defence Forces intervention in the DRC, the security agencies displayed an obvious contempt for press freedom, indi-vidual rights supposedly guaranteed by the constitution, and the law itself. The newspaper's major shareholder and CEO, Clive Wilson, was also detained over a weekend when he went to the police station to inquire about the fate of his journalists. Although Chavunduka and Choto were eventually released on bail and later cleared by the courts, this unprecedented act of intimidation of the media was a sinister fore-warning of what was to come. In a television broadcast on 6 February 1999, Mugabe lambasted the independent press and linked it to "Rho-desians and neo-colonialists," a tirade that was to become the dominant line of government discourse after 2000.

Although the deteriorating economic conditions made life increas-ingly difficult for independent papers depending largely on advertising revenue, the prolonged crisis, both political and economic, into which Zimbabwe entered in the late 1990s created also a public demand for more independent reporting and analysis. Launched on 31 March 1999 by the Associated Newspapers of Zimbabwe (ANZ), a consortium of Zim-babwean businessmen backed by foreign press groups from the UK, New Zealand, and South Africa, the *Daily News* emerged on the eve of impor-tant political developments. This attracted fierce criticisms from the government and the information minister at the time, Chen Chimuteng-wende, threatened in 1999 to ban foreign investments in Zimbabwean media and donor interference in the sector.[17] The *Daily News* ran into financial difficulties as early as September 1999. It was then rescued by a soft loan from the Southern Africa Media Development Fund (SAM-DEF)—a program linked to the Media Institute of Southern Africa

(MISA). However, the *Daily News* benefited from its experienced editor Geoffrey Nyarota.

By late 1999 the paper was already a success: it took advantage of the vibrant public debate stirred by the confrontation between the CRC and the NCA. When the government press was busy tarnishing the NCA's image, the civic leaders were able to put the record straight in the independent daily. NCA's public meetings received good coverage and the newspaper vividly reported the exchanges in the respective CRC and NCA awareness programs. It made a huge difference, in the urban areas at least, especially during the constitutional referendum campaign. In the run-up to the 2000 general elections the *Daily News* regularly covered the MDC's election campaign at a level never seen before by any opposition party. It also documented ZANU-PF militia violence. By late June 2000 the independent daily had overtaken the *Herald* in circulation numbers (129,500 versus 87,647 copies) and attracted significant advertising. The people were so upset by the *Herald*'s pro-ZANU-PF bias that they began to cancel their annual subscriptions, and advertising orders plummeted.[18] This infuriated the ruling party, which attempted to influence SAMDEF into calling the ANZ loan in November 2000.[19] This time ANZ was saved by a consortium of indigenous entrepreneurs led by Strive Masiyiwa's Independent Media Group, which recapitalized the newspaper group, thus bringing the level of foreign shareholding down to 30 percent. However, the daily newspaper was a primary target of the war of attrition against the independent press in 2001–2.

The success of the independent press incited some scheming ZANU-PF supporters to join the fray. Ibbo Mandaza, CRC treasurer and long-time friend of Nathan Shamuyarira, already owned a magazine, the *Southern Africa Political and Economic Monthly*, the editorial line of which was rather ambiguous. Claiming to be independent from the government, his Southern Africa Printing and Publishing House (SAPPHO) launched the *Zimbabwe Mirror* in December 1997—later called the *Sunday Mirror*—and the *Daily Mirror* in December 2003 after a false start earlier on. In 1998 Mandaza posed as an independent and his newspaper, the *Mirror*, engaged in some bold reporting—however not always credible professional journalism—which landed the editor in jail for a few days in February 1999. Subsequently these newspapers were used by Mandaza to attack the MDC and sometimes to settle scores with other members of the ruling elite (for example, on the land issue) until the CIO covertly took control of Mandaza's heavily indebted Zimbabwe Mirror Group of Newspapers (ZMGN) in 2008.[20] Other publications[21] generally perceived to be beneficiaries of government patronage included the *Weekend Tribune* and the *Business Tribune* published by the Media Africa Group (later Africa Tribune Newspapers), although its chairman,

Tapiwa Matangaidze, hotly denied this allegation. There was certainly a double-edged strategy used by the ruling party since the 1980s to undermine the free press. However, drawing lessons from the past twenty years, no newspaper is likely to survive without attracting readers, regardless of the amount of "secret funds" wasted on them.

Moyo's Turn to Autocratic Control and Assault on Freedom

A former political science associate professor who began his public career as a severe critic of the ZANU-PF regime but rallied behind Mugabe in 1999 (see Chapter 3), Jonathan Moyo was appointed to the Cabinet after the June 2000 elections, as a minister of state in the president's office, at the head of the Department of Information and Publicity, which replaced the former Ministry of Information. He was rewarded for his pro-Mugabe activism within the CRC and subsequently his active part in the referendum and parliamentary election campaigns. His mission was to muzzle the independent press, curtail the activities of foreign journalists in Zimbabwe, and make sure that the state media would toe the party line. Thereafter he worked to outflank the ruling party hardliners, becoming an unconditional supporter of Mugabe's plan to stay in power at all costs. This included advocating the violent suppression of the opposition. Clever, unscrupulous, and a mischief maker, Moyo implemented his master's wishes to the letter[22] until he fell out of favor in late 2004.

Although ZTV and the radio channels never practised political balance and unbiased reporting, especially at election time, this pattern was strikingly accentuated during and after the June 2000 parliamentary elections. Jonathan Moyo put the state propaganda machine to full use and the government media assumed under his close monitoring a distinct Orwellian character. Moyo's outrageous lies were repeated ad nauseam to become the official truth and any dissenting view was derided as unpatriotic or treasonous. Black-on-white racism increasingly purveyed in the state media from the early nineties was cynically stepped up in 2000 to a black-on-black oppression, with black supporters of the opposition being called "Uncle Toms" and stooges of "Western enemies": Britain, British prime minister Tony Blair, the United States, Europe in general and whites, especially commercial farmers. An era of unremitting attacks on any dissenting voice came gradually to dominate the columns of Zimpapers and ZBC services.

From then on radio and TV news bulletins were routinely edited in Jonathan Moyo's office—not without frequent blunders though—and ZBC journalists as well as editors of government newspapers lost the last vestiges of their independence. The Mass Media Trust was dissolved in December 2000 as it was no longer necessary to hide the government's tightening grip. Those who dared protest against blatant political interference were unceremoniously fired and replaced by junior staff, owing their promotion solely to their allegiance to Mugabe and to Moyo himself. Deprived of any power base in the ruling party—he was appointed to Parliament by Mugabe, having no electoral constituency—the minister used the state media as his personal political capital in the factional struggle. By mid-2004, however, even before the Tsholotsho plot, his extremely partisan treatment of the news had infuriated several ZANU-PF big men who demanded that Mugabe rein in his chief propagandist. But it is his involvement in the succession struggle that led to Moyo's downfall. Needless to say, partisan reporting went on unabated afterward, especially during election campaigns: in 2005 ZTV devoted 82 percent of its election coverage to ZANU-PF and only 18 percent to the MDC, although it was a slight improvement from 2002, when Mugabe received 97 percent of the coverage as opposed to 3 percent for Tsvangirai.[23]

Moyo's intolerant, autocratic behavior was not limited to news bulletins. There were advertising jingles used to demonize political opponents but also all the people the minister disliked. Patu Manala's "phone-in" radio program, which allowed some political discussions, was abruptly closed after the minister of information was severely criticized on air by members of the public. Mnangagwa's associate Mutumwa Mawere saw his National Democratic Association (NDA)'s contract to air serious debate on national issues summarily and illegally canceled by ZBC on Moyo's instructions. The prospects of privately owned Joy TV bringing improvements and proper competition to ZTV faded after the major shareholder and licensee James Makamba, a businessman well connected in the ruling party's hierarchy, was forced to close down this channel in mid-May 2002. Moyo enforced a provision of the Broadcasting Services Act (BSA) passed in 2001 that made it illegal for the ZBC to continue leasing a channel to any other station. That Joy TV broadcasts included the BBC news programs in particular scandalized the minister of information. This second channel had also provided all-party panel discussions and personal interviews.

After the cancellation of the Joy TV lease, the ZBC remained the only television broadcaster in Zimbabwe, since no other station has been licensed to date. Although ZBC has become the Zimbabwe Broadcasting Holdings (ZBH),[24] a commercial public company with nine subsidiaries, this did not alleviate political control over the television and radio programs. In 2003, the Parliament's Portfolio Committee on Transport and Communications conducted an enquiry into the ZBH operations and slammed government's interference in broadcasting, its abuse of airtime and the lack of balance of the news coverage.[25] Its recommendations, in particular the limitation of the minister's powers to appoint members of the ZBH board and the company's senior management, were never implemented. However, Moyo's policy has had a severe adverse impact on the quality of both print and electronic government media and caused advertisers to desert in droves. Shares in Zimpapers fell from 25 Zimbabwe dollars to 25 cents in 2001, as the group was shielded from bankruptcy only by state subsidies. In the urban areas the *Herald* was then eagerly sought after not for its sheer contents but as a kind of political talisman to be displayed as protection when passing through a police or militia roadblock.

As early as 1999, during the CRC sessions, the ZANU-PF government indicated its intention to discipline the media through the creation of the media council and the promotion of "smart" or "patriotic" journalism, the official excuse being the need to bring an element of "ethics" into Zimbabwean journalism. At the time, the Zimbabwe Union of Journalists (ZUJ) adopted a somewhat ambivalent attitude that, to a certain extent, reflected its politically mixed membership.[26] In January 2002 the Parliament passed the Access to Information and Protection of Privacy Act (AIPPA), crafted by Jonathan Moyo and signed into law on 15 March. It did not go through smoothly, and Eddison Zvobgo, the ZANU-PF chairman of the Parliamentary Legal Committee, described the bill in its original form as "the most calculated and determined assault on our (constitutional) liberties, in the 20 years I served as Cabinet Minister."[27] Eventually, Zvobgo toed the party line and let the bill go only slightly amended. Government justified the new legislation by the "war situation" (a reference to the Third Chimurenga) and the alleged use of the press by foreign powers willing to overthrow the government (see Chapter 8). ZANU-PF has far outpaced the previous regime of Ian Smith in the oppression of journalists. AIPPA and other repressive laws have been used to ban de facto independent newspapers such as the *Daily News*.

Contrary to its very name, the AIPPA severely curtails publicaccess to information by shielding many government activities from media investigations. The protection of privacy is a convenient excuse for the imposition of tight controls on the press activity. In late 2002, the Independent Journalists Association of Zimbabwe (IJAZ),[28] supported by the Media Institute of Southern Africa (MISA), challenged sections 79, 80, 83, and 85 of AIPPA in the Supreme Court as being in breach of the Bill of Rights, in particular the freedom of expression. Altogether these sections compel all journalists in Zimbabwe, whether citizens, permanent residents, or visitors[29] to seek accreditation by the government-appointed

Media and Information Commission (MIC), where independent media professionals are not represented. The MIC enjoys discreet power to deny them accreditation, suspend existing accreditation, or revoke it at any time with a wide range of grounds to do so (limited however to those listed in section 71). The Media and Information Commission was chaired until 2008 by Dr. Tafataona Mahoso,[30] former head of the government's mass media training school, former chairman of the ZBC board, a regular television panelist, and a sycophantic columnist in a government weekly newspaper. His partisan and often erratic conduct of MIC proceedings was highlighted by several court cases in 2005 and 2006, when its prejudice against independent journalists and the publishers of the *Daily News* was exposed.

In addition journalists must pay high registration fees. All newspapers and magazines must also register with the MIC. It is a criminal offense under section 72 to publish without accreditation and registration: journalists and media house directors are liable to up to two years in prison and severe financial penalties. In addition section 80(1) of AIPPA provides for punitive measures for what is called "abuse of journalistic privilege." AIPPA is clearly designed to tame the independent journalists and prevent them from reporting political violence and other news putting the government into disrepute. However, this section was nullified in the 2004 Supreme Court judgment—without much impact on the security forces' harassment of journalists.

The Act also forbids ownership and funding of Zimbabwean media by foreign companies or public agencies, in an attempt to give some credibility to ZANU-PF's propaganda, which has repeatedly claimed that independent newspapers were subsidized by some Western secret services. The AIPPA was amended in June 2003 by Parliament, allegedly to ease the restrictions on media activity as a response to demands from AU and SADC leaders. However the main provisions of the Act remained unaltered until 2008, and some legal experts argue that the amended sections promulgated in October 2003 strengthen the powers of the MIC and broaden the definition a "media house" and "journalist," thus further tightening government control over the media. In February 2004 the Supreme Court rejected IJAZ's application both on the obligation to register and on the constitutionality of the MIC. In January 2005 a new amendment of AIPPA introduced penalties for unlicensed journalists. Subsequently the police raided the offices of local journalists working for international news organizations, who had to flee abroad for their safety.

The Act encompasses advertising agencies, publishers and news agencies, the production as well as the dissemination of news. The term "mass media" is so broadly defined in section 2 of the Act, and so vague that it could be used to control personal communications by e-mail and Web postings, any information disseminated through the Internet—undoubtedly an effective channel used by the MDC and civil society since 2000. Indeed, by mid-2004 the government was moving toward controlling these private communications by exerting growing pressure on Zimbabwean service providers. Some users were arrested and indicted for writing e-mail messages allegedly insulting the president. The Department of Information was said to be spending billions in acquiring sophisticated software to monitor the Internet.[31] It has become the "Big Brother is watching you" syndrome, revealing Moyo's megalomania and the regime's dictatorial inclinations.

The independent newspapers had until a 31 October 2002 deadline to register their companies and their journalists with the MIC. Although many vowed to resist this unconstitutional obligation, most did comply to be able to operate. Some independent journalists, especially reporters working for the *Daily News*, resisted at first but then applied to see their applications turned down by the MIC. Hence they cannot work for the media in Zimbabwe. This mechanism is also an effective means of controlling journalists working in the state media, as they can lose accreditation if their articles do not please the Minister.

In the late 1990s the government promised to amend the old Broadcasting Act, last amended in 1974, to open the airwaves to competition but the reform was postponed several times. In late September 2000, however, a private radio station, Capital Radio, successfully challenged Section 27 of the Broadcasting Act in the Supreme Court still chaired by Chief Justice Gubbay. The court ruled that the state monopoly over the establishment and operation of signal transmitting stations contravened the freedom of expression and information guaranteed by the constitution and authorized Capital Radio to operate a broadcasting service within the country. The government's response was swift and stern: the Presidential Powers (Temporary Measures) Broadcasting Regulations promulgated on 4 October 2000 temporarily deferred the Supreme Court judgment, established the Broadcasting Authority of Zimbabwe (BAZ) as a government-appointed regulatory body, and gave the Minister of State for Information and Publicity the ultimate authority to issue broadcasting licenses. All independent radio stations were thereby declared illegal.

The Broadcasting Services Act (BSA) was enacted on 4 April 2001, to replace the temporary regulations on which it was based, and gives the Minister sweeping powers over the broadcasting sector, for example, the granting of licenses (after consultation with the Broadcasting Authority), the power to interfere with the content of the programs and ban a broadcaster in the name of national security.[32] Instead of liberalizing the broadcasting sector, as required by the 2000 Supreme Court ruling, and as civil society and opposition parties demanded, the BSA consolidated state control. The BSA prohibits political organizations (including civic groups involved in the public debate) from controlling broadcasting stations, limits the number of operators and restricts broadcasting licenses to resident citizens. The Act banned all unlicensed private radios, including those operating from outside the country, and transmitting to Zimbabwe "by satellite or any other means,"[33] a clear violation of international law.

A Systematic Onslaught on the Independent Media

In crisis time (such as the Gukurahundi, the 1990 elections, the 1998 food riots and strikes), the government's propaganda was fast to blame international media for painting an unflattering picture of Mugabe and the ZANU-PF regime. Although adverse reporting in the Western press, especially British newspapers, especially after 2000, was conveniently dismissed as "biased" and "neocolonialist," it irked Mugabe and it embarrassed the government for its potential impact on the regional leaders. As soon as he took up his portfolio, Jonathan Moyo moved to get rid of the most talented foreign correspondents. Within a few months Joseph Winter from the BBC (later all BBC reporters were banned from entering Zimbabwe), Mercedes Sayagues, and David Blair from the *Daily Telegraph* saw their work permits summarily canceled and were subsequently deported. In October and November 2002, two journalists of the Agence France Presse (AFP) were denied extensions on their work permits and ordered to leave Zimbabwe. However, when ZANU-PF strategists realized that the AU and SADC heads of state had swallowed Mugabe's story—that is, that the conflict was about land and that he had pitted an African nation against the formal colonial power and its local allies—public opinion outside Zimbabwe was regarded as less important.

Prior to and after the 2002 presidential election, the ruling party's first objective was to cow the Zimbabwean people into submission and to convince them that "there is no life outside ZANU-PF." Hence the brutal offensive directed toward the local press and "unpatriotic" journalists. The *Daily News,* being perceived by ZANU-PF strategists as a potent force favoring the opposition, became a priority target. In late January 2001, powerful bombs destroyed the *Daily News* printing presses a few hours after Minister Moyo had vowed on TV to "silence" the newspaper. Although the police never concluded proper investigations, there were clues pointing to the state security agencies. In February

2002, the newspaper's Bulawayo offices were gasoline-bombed. Until late December 2002 *Daily News* editor Geoff Nyarota had to cope with state-orchestrated harassment: a bomb that damaged his own office and personal death threats. Marauding "war veterans" or "green bombers" frequently destroyed copies of the *Daily News*—and occasionally the *Independent* and the *Standard*. Its vendors and sometimes readers were physically attacked, and the distribution of the paper in ZANU-PF rural strongholds became virtually impossible.[34] These restrictions in the circulation of independent newspapers were meant to prevent rural voters from accessing information from other than the government media. Violence was used also against journalists to prevent them from doing their job, especially in the period between June 2000 and March 2002: "In 2001, Amnesty International documented harassment, beatings or death threats against more than 40 journalists from privately-owned newspapers who tried to report on political or human rights issues, or who filed reports critical of the government."[35] In 2002 alone, approximately 44 media workers were arrested and five were physically attacked.[36] This kind of harassment diminished after 2004 without disappearing altogether and intensified again during and after the presidential rerun in 2008.

Capital Radio, the first to bravely defy the state monopoly on electronic media, was able to broadcast only for eight days before it was muzzled by the police and its transmitter confiscated—in violation of a High Court injunction. In May 2002 Capital Radio again challenged the constitutionality of the BSA in the Supreme Court when Jonathan Moyo refused to grant it a license. In September 2003 Chief Justice Chidyausiku struck section 6 of the Act, which makes the minister the licensing authority, because it undermined the Broadcasting Authority's independence and violated the freedom of information. However, other sections of the act were upheld and no private radio was ever granted a license by a Broadcasting Authority whose members are government appointees. In August 2002, the Harare office of another independent broadcasting organization, Voice of the People (VOP), was gasoline-bombed. On 29 August 2003 a midnight bomb explosion destroyed VOP's office once again. VOP then operated from a secret location in Harare and was transmitted over shortwave on a Netherlands radio platform. Gerry Jackson's SW Radio Africa was forcibly shut down in January 2002 and exiled to transmit nightly from London over shortwave. A third station, Studio 7, was transmitted, according to the government, through a Voice of America transmitter based in the Botswana mining town of Selibe-Phikwe—allegations denied by Gaborone. These radio stations, popular with those Zimbabweans aware of their existence, have been jammed intermittently since March 2005.

AIPPA was immediately put to use to harass journalists and editors of the independent papers.[37] Geoff Nyarota, one of his reporters, Lloyd Mudiwa, and Andrew Meldrum, correspondent of the *Guardian* and the *Observer* were all indicted under section 80(1)(b) of AIPPA for reporting or publishing false news. Meldrum filed a dispatch on the Internet quoting a story in the *Daily News* alleging ZANU-PF activists beheaded a woman in front of her children in a remote village in Mashonaland West. On discovering the story was false, the independent daily published an apology, as did the *Guardian*. A magistrates' court acquitted Meldrum in July 2002 but the home affairs minister ordered his deportation within twenty-four hours, an order suspended by the High Court. Although the courts upheld Meldrum's rights as a permanent resident in Zimbabwe for twenty-two years, he was arbitrarily arrested and deported on 16 May 2003, a few hours after his resident's permit was illegally revoked by immigration officials. Moyo's grudge against the American-born journalist was such that the security organs were prepared to ignore all court rulings to have him out of Zimbabwe.

Geoff Nyarota was also arrested in April 2002 for publishing allegations that Registrar General Mudede announced conflicting results in the presidential elections and suggesting that this proved foul play from the registrar general's office. Later Bornwell Chakaodza, the newly appointed editor of the *Standard*, also suffered the same fate,[38] and over a dozen journalists and editors have been arrested and charged under the same section of AIPPA since March 2002. In the meantime, the *Daily News* lawyers had challenged the constitutionality of section 80 in the magistrates' court and the case was deferred to the Supreme Court. The state did not oppose the application, conceding the unconstitutionality of the section. The Supreme Court made an order by consent on 7 May 2003, thus extinguishing legal action against *Daily News* journalists. Accordingly the relevant section of the Act was rewritten in the June 2003 amendment (henceforth it specified that intent was a prerequisite for the publication of falsehood—now more clearly defined—to be an offense). These were setbacks for the government but most sections of AIPPA remained in force, and the vicious and arrogant Media Commission was in place until late 2008.

The Associated Newspapers of Zimbabwe (ANZ), the company publishing the *Daily News*, also challenged several sections of the Act, including section 65, which forbids foreigners to own or hold shares in Zimbabwean mass media. The partisan Supreme Court ruled on 11 September 2003 that the news group was not entitled to challenge the constitutionality of the Act as its paper was illegally published, having not complied first with registration by the end of 2002. This ruling ran against all logic, since the purpose of the application was precisely to challenge the provisions on registration, but it gave a pretext to the police to raid the *Daily News* offices on 12 September 2003 and close down the newspaper—an action reminiscent of Ian Smith policies in the 1960s. The police began to remove equipment illegally from the newspaper's offices on 16 September and never returned them in spite of an urgent order granted by High Court judge Justice Omarjee on 18 September, an order that also allowed the paper to resume publication by virtue of section 8(2) of AIPPA.

Subsequently the ANZ applied to the MIC but was denied registration. ANZ journalists were first charged for practicing without accreditation and later denied application because they worked for a nonregistered media house. However, a senior judge at the Administrative Court, Michael Majuru, ruled on 24 October 2003 that the MIC was not properly constituted and had shown bias in denying a registration certificate to the *Daily News*. The Commission was ordered to issue a license to the ANZ by 30 November, failing which the paper would be deemed to have been registered. But the Commission's appeal to the Supreme Court suspended the effect of the judgment. The newspaper nevertheless resumed publication for a day in late October 2003, on the basis of the Administrative Court's judgment and section 8(2) of the Act which provides that once applications for registration have been submitted the media house can carry on with its activities pending the determination of the application. However, the police intervened to arrest the newspaper's directors who were subsequently prosecuted for publishing illegally. Interestingly, Judge Selo Nare, who took over the case from Majuru, also ruled in favor of the *Daily News* on 19 December 2003. Once again the police raided the newspaper's offices to prevent the staff from working in violation of the court ruling. Although the Supreme Court on 25 March 2005 nullified the 2003 MIC decision (if only to convey a favorable impression to SADC and AU observer missions), the partisan judges upheld the controversial provisions of AIPPA, and the ANZ had to reapply for registration. Mahoso waited until well after the rigged elections and predictably rejected the application in July 2005. After the High Court nullified the MIC decision on the basis of Mahoso's perceived bias in February 2006, the legal wrangle shifted toward the Ministry of Information. However, the minister claimed the AIPPA did not empower him to appoint an independent committee as a substitute for the discredited MIC. In May 2007, ANZ once gain failed to obtain a High Court order to be duly licensed and remained banned.[39]

The independent daily had been the main alternative view to ZANU-PF's propaganda, and its absence impeded the civic organizations' struggle and the MDC's 2005 electoral campaign. Since the closure of the

Daily News, the government-controlled media have had a free hand in omitting or distorting important news—there is abundant evidence of this in MMPZ reports. The *Weekend Tribune* also fell victim to government censorship, although it was owned and edited by Kindness Paradza, a former journalist who was elected ZANU-PF MP for Makonde in 2000. It could hardly be seen as pro-MDC in spite of its increasingly critical coverage of the government and Paradza's public criticisms of the AIPPA. The newspaper was closed on 10 June 2004 when the MIC canceled its license on the usual spurious grounds. Paradza was also expelled from the ruling party by the Mashonaland West provincial chairman. Although the publisher appealed against the MIC decision in the High Court, Justice Tendai Uchena rejected his application, arguing that the law gave discretionary powers to the MIC to punish violations of the Act.[40] A fresh application was again rejected in July 2005, although Paradza had complied with all AIPPA provisions.

In addition to the AIPPA, the government routinely uses the Public Order and Security Act (POSA), a tougher substitution for LOMA enacted in January 2002.[41] The Act criminalizes "false statements prejudicial to the state." By publishing a "false" statement likely to "incite public disorder, affect the defense and economic interest of the country, or undermine public confidence in the police, armed forces or prison officers," a journalist may be sentenced to up to five years in prison. Section 16 makes it an offense to make a public statement with the intention of or knowing there is a risk of "undermining the authority of or insulting" the president. Since 2002, journalists have been routinely arrested and beaten by the police and charged under some provisions of POSA. Although most cases never reach the stage of trial, this harassment is meant to intimidate them to the point of self-censorship.

In spite of its lawyers' stamina and the determination of its editors and journalists to resist government's encroachments, the threatened independent press has become weakened after four years of constant onslaught. The *Financial Gazette* turned down the tone of its editorials and reporting after Gideon Gono, governor of the Reserve Bank and a relative of Mugabe, became its majority shareholder and liberal Francis Mdlongwa was kicked out. Only the two newspapers owned by Trevor Ncube's media group remain totally independent and unrelenting in their criticisms of Mugabe's regime. As the editor of the *Zimbabwe Independent*, Iden Wetherell, who was detained for 48 hours with two of his colleagues in January 2004 over a story published in the paper, admitted: "we know they are out to get us."[42] Their capacity to expose the government's misdeeds was increasingly curtailed also by fast-deteriorating economic and social conditions. Running a paper as a business—meeting printing costs and selling enough advertising to cash-strapped commercial enterprises and raising circulation among impoverished citizens—is an almost impossible task. By 2007 the few remaining weekly papers on sale in the streets of Zimbabwe were far above the means of most Zimbabweans, including the urban middle class. The Internet offered a useful alternative, but Internet access is almost nonexistent outside the main towns and service provision proved increasingly unreliable as the economy melted down and power cuts became recurrent.

Having trampled on the country's laws and constitution to silence the *Daily News*, nothing could stop the ZANU-PF government from closing down all independent media if needed. In 2003, the International Committee to Protect Journalists listed Zimbabwe among the ten worst offenders of press freedom in the world.[43] The implementation of this policy of information control is an essential component of the ruling party's authoritarianism. An opinion survey conducted in mid-2004 revealed that Robert Mugabe's popularity was higher than in 1999: trust in the president went up from 20 percent in 1999 to 46 percent, and the proportion of those satisfied by his job performance rose from 21 percent to 58 percent.[44] The same survey revealed that the people's trust in Morgan Tsvangirai (18 percent) and in the main opposition party (14 percent) remained low if only because they were still unknown to the majority in the rural areas—or known only through twisted portrayals by the state media. Although Zimbabweans blame the government for their declining living standards, their opposition to one-party rule fell from 74 percent of respondents in 1999 to 58 percent by 2004, and those "committed to democracy" (an indicator built by the researchers) to 28 percent compared with 50 percent. Zimbabweans increasingly associated multiparty competition with violent conflict and seemed to acquiesce implicitly to ZANU-PF's dominance. Among the factors tested to explain this attitude the authors' statistical analysis shows that "political propaganda is by far the most important determinant of presidential approval." ZANU-PF's desperate efforts to control and influence the flow of information has paid off, especially when combined with politically motivated violence.

In retrospect, Zimbabwe's relative freedom of the print media in the 1990s was a mirage, a façade largely for foreign consumption or to accommodate local business and farming communities when "reconciliation" was still the official motto. The mask was thrown away in 2000 and furthermore in the following years. Although the pluralism of information never really fitted in the ruling party's political culture, it is the threat of a credible opposition with a popular leadership that prompted the avalanche of repressive measures and the heinous attacks against the independent media. This tactic succeeded to the extent that ZANU-PF has prevented the MDC from getting out its message to the electorate, and this has further polarized the society. These tactics guaranteed ZANU-PF a victory in the 2005 parliamentary elections, but in the long run even government propaganda failed. By 2007–8 the dramatic economic and social decline—affecting also the operations of the state media outlets—became so blatant that every Zimbabwean could experience it directly, whatever the fairy tales broadcast on ZBC.

Chapter 5

The Judiciary: From Resistance to Subjugation

Since Independence the judiciary has often been under attack, including the harassment of individual Supreme Court and High Court judges, some of which was documented by human rights NGOs such as the CCJP and LRF.[1] In fact, Mugabe's regime never really accepted the principle of the separation of powers and often singled out white judges for abuse. Being a seasoned tactician, Mugabe's abiding by the law has always been qualified and calculated. However, the assault against independent judges—many of them blacks—commencing in late 2000 is unprecedented in its violence and duration. The courts have been purged and subsequently staffed with demonstrably pliant judges. As part of this campaign the authority of the courts was systematically undermined by government speeches and actions. These were not regrettable "excesses" but a sustained and deliberate assault against the judiciary.

It cannot be explained by a sudden and somewhat mysterious change of mind on Mugabe's part, nor can it be understood as the unfortunate by-product of the political and social conflict building up in 2000. Here again the land controversy operated as a mere smokescreen for a deliberate sabotage of the judicial system. In other words, the courts were coerced into subservience—though not totally—because it was the logical conclusion of a long-standing albeit controlled hostility and a prerequisite for the preservation of Mugabe's political power by all means. Therefore this process belongs to a two-decade confrontation between the judiciary and the executive. At the same time it is an essential part of the survival plan worked out by Mugabe and the small clique surrounding him. An independent judiciary would never have sanctioned the violence and manipulation surrounding the elections that were the only means for ZANU-PF to avoid resounding defeats in 2000 and 2002.

Through the years, the High Court and the Supreme Court (court of last appeal and constitutional court)[2] have managed to resist several government attempts to interpret the law to its exclusive benefit. Given Mugabe's autocratic stance, his inclination to use violence against his opponents, and the intolerant political culture of the ruling party, it is surprising that the judiciary retained its autonomy for so long. To explain this somewhat miraculous survival of an independent Judiciary until 2000, in the context of a neo-authoritarian regime, one must take into account several factors. Constitutional and legal safeguards played a role but cannot fully explain the judiciary's ability to resist the executive's encroachments. For example, the provision enabling the president to appoint to the Supreme Court as many judges as he pleases—without a number ceiling—was in the constitution from 1981 but was never used until 2001. Therefore, one must understand what made Zimbabwe's judges resilient and willing to uphold the rule of law against political interference and what process led to the final showdown.

Constitutional Protection

The Supreme Court has played a decisive role in safeguarding individual and collective liberties through an overall liberal interpretation of the Declaration of Rights included in the Summary of the Independence Constitution attached to the 1979 Lancaster House Agreement. The Declaration of Rights was said to be "fully justiciable," and the Supreme Court had the authority to rule in favor of anybody alleging that his or her rights under the Declaration were infringed.[3] Consequently the Declaration had a superior value in comparison to other sections of the constitution and all the laws. Derogations were only admissible "within specified limits, during periods of emergency." The Declaration was de facto untouchable for ten years: a bill amending the Declaration— unless it was meant to expand the rights already stated—required the unanimous vote of the House of Assembly and the votes of not less than two-thirds of the members of the Senate, when an ordinary constitutional bill would pass in the House with 70 percent of the members' support.

Although this provision has often been vilified because as a consequence white farmers' property rights were safeguarded, it has been instrumental in enabling the courts to protect Zimbabwe citizens from ZANU-PF arbitrary power. Not surprisingly the ruling party attempted to erode this judicial protection with Constitutional Amendment No. 9

(Act 31 of 1989) that entered in force in 1990. If the land issue had been the unique concern of the government, it needed only to repeal the original paragraph E-29 of the Lancaster House constitution while keeping the restrictive provisions for the amendment of the Declaration of Rights. On the contrary, by making an amendment of the Declaration easier the ruling party intended to undermine the constitutional power of the Supreme Court. The same intent presided over the attempted deconstitutionalization of the Declaration of Rights through Amendment No. 14 (Act 14 of 1996), which modified section 11 of the constitution. This section corresponded to the first part of the Declaration and formed the basis of Supreme Court protection of individual liberties. A synthesized version—hence far less precise—formed the introduction to a restructured chapter III, and it was presented as a mere set of principles with no obligatory consequences.

The original Lancaster House constitution ritually proclaimed the independence of the judiciary in section 79-B. There were, however, more practical and apparently effective guarantees. The chief justice, the keystone of the judicial system, was appointed by a then purely ceremonial president formally on advice of the prime minister, but on the basis of the recommendations from the Judicial Service Commission (JSC), a professional body headed by the chief justice, the independence of which was sanctioned also by the constitution. In practice, this meant that the new chief justice was chosen from among candidates recommended by his predecessor for their competence in judicial matters. Whenever the prime minister departed from the JSC recommendations Parliament was to be informed prior to the appointment. The potential public controversy was deemed to be a strong enough deterrent. The appointment of other Supreme Court and High Court[4] judges by the president, on the recommendation of the JSC and without interference from the prime minister, was a purely formal prerogative.

There is near consensus that in the early years Mugabe endorsed the JSC recommendations and did not seek to impose partisan judges, although nothing in the constitution barred him from doing so. Enoch Dumbutshena once recalled a case when he was a JSC member under Chief Justice Fieldsend. The candidacy of a relative of first lady Sally Mugabe working in Botswana was deemed unsuitable by the JSC without provoking any reaction from Mugabe.[5]

Others believe that Mugabe patiently built a clientele in the judicial profession as everywhere else. For example, Justice Adam, who nullified the elections of Bulawayo and Harare executive mayors in 1996 on the FORUM party's request but declined to examine the constitutionality of the Presidential (Emergency) Powers Act, the main point raised in the application, was said to be connected to ZANU-PF through his family.[6]

Most people at that time were not aware of the social and political connections of potential appointees. Few blacks had sufficient experience in the legal profession at independence. Many of those who had trained in law were involved in nationalist politics at one point or another; it did not make them necessarily "political" judges aligned to ZANU-PF—Dumbutshena, for example. The career of current chief justice Godfrey Chidyausiku is fairly typical in this respect. Deputy minister of local government in 1980, then of justice in 1981, Chidyausiku was appointed attorney general in 1982. On ZTV in 1983 he pleaded for "an independent judiciary rather than one that panders to the wishes of the government . . . a judiciary that is prepared to make a decision that will be unpopular with the government."[7] He was appointed to the High Court in 1987, a decision not perceived then as politically motivated. Although he was part of the ZANU-PF patronage network, he met the criteria of professional experience. Seven years as an advocate were required in the 1980 constitution; Amendment No. 2 (Act 25 of 1981) relaxed this rule, taking argument from a reform of the legal professions, and included any "comparable" experience in the legal profession to qualify for such a position. The position of attorney general, who did not sit in Cabinet at that time, was then differently perceived. However, Chidyausiku's later promotion to judge president of the High Court raised some eyebrows as it did not follow the order of seniority.

The delicate constitutional equilibrium was significantly altered with Amendment No. 7 (Act 23 of 1987), which changed, among other things, the conditions of nomination of the High Court and Supreme Court judges (section 12), without provoking much reaction at the time. The word "recommendation" was deleted and replaced by a mere "prior consultation" of the JSC. Moreover, whenever the JSC and the president disagreed, the Parliament would have to be informed "as soon as possible" and no longer prior to the nomination, making the fulfillment of this provision almost pointless. It was unlikely that a de facto one-party state Parliament would reverse judicial appointments made by the president thus contradicting the advice of the JSC, which would already have taken effect. The JSC was from then on limited to a formal verification of the professional abilities of the candidates. Besides, the JSC had already been enlarged to include the attorney general and three instead of two qualified persons (Amendment No. 4), while the required number of years of working experience in the judicial profession had been reduced from seven to five and now included all kinds of professional experience in the legal professions (Amendment No. 1).

From this sketchy analysis of the successive constitutional amendments it can be safely concluded that even before 1987 the executive had a hand in the JSC proceedings and after 1987 could do without JSC approval. Another example is the suppression of the Senate through Amendment No. 9 (Act 31 of 1989), inasmuch as the Senate could delay the adoption of a constitutional bill for up to 180 days. Similarly, separate political representation for the white minority—removed by Amendment No. 6 (Act 15 of 1987) after the stipulated seven years— although betraying the "one man one vote" principle, helped contain the ruling party's propensity to amend the constitution for political expediency. Until 1987 white MPs and senators could, together with ZAPU legislators, block any constitutional bill deferred to Parliament.

Judges in the High Court and the Supreme Court were appointed for life or until retirement or voluntary resignation. Amendment No. 4 (Act 4 of 1984) enabled the president to appoint some judges for limited periods of time—therefore making them presumably more subject to political influence—and established a retirement age limit of sixty-five. However, most judges could be removed only through a lengthy and restrictive procedure where the final decision was reached by an ad hoc court, the verdict of which the president had no option but to endorse (section 87). It has been used twice since independence.[8] In the first case the judge was found guilty of misconduct and dismissed. In the second instance Justice Fergus Blackie from the High Court in Bulawayo was accused by the government press of having presided over a "kangaroo court" in February 1995 and having colluded with human rights lawyer David Coltart in doing so. Coltart, who represented a white farmer illegally detained at a rural police station over a conflict with some black farmers from a nearby communal area, obtained an urgent order from the High Court judge to release his client on bail. Justice Blackie was suspended for "misconduct" by request of the attorney general, but was later cleared by the ad hoc court set up to investigate the matter and was reinstated. Although the constitutional guarantee operated with no further interference, the whole story was regarded as a deliberate attempt to intimidate a judge seen as too outspoken. Besides, the government press was looking for an opportunity to discredit opposition lawyer David Coltart. A former RF MP under Ian Smith's regime, Justice Blackie conveniently fitted with the fanciful Rhodies' plot allegation that government propaganda attempted to spread time and again, especially when some potential opposition had sprung up—first from the FORUM and now the MDC.

The Judicial Culture

The shortage of experienced black lawyers at independence meant that the first judges to be appointed to the High Court and Supreme Court were either white or Asian advocates who had worked under the previous regime. Some of the whites were former RF supporters, but others had defended black political prisoners under Ian Smith's regime. Justice Nick McNally, a Supreme Court judge in the late 1990s, was a "white liberal," formerly deputy president of the small, multiracial Centre Party, and one of many lawyers who argued in 1968 that UDI was unconstitutional and therefore Ian Smith's regime was illegal. However, once appointed to the bench, they all upheld the Declaration of Rights and the Constitution of Zimbabwe, if necessary against the will of the ruling party. Beyond their different backgrounds and political opinions, they played a crucial role in giving the Zimbabwe judiciary a common professional ethos, on which a corporate solidarity could be based. Younger black judges recruited through the years naturally acquired this judicial culture.

It is important to stress that apart from occasional racial slander on the part of ZANU-PF leaders, the High Court and the Supreme Court were not polarized along racial lines up to 2000. Some judges were more conservative than others—black and white—when it came to women's rights or the death penalty. Some were politically closer to the ruling elite, but until 2000 all behaved professionally in their judicial capacity. This does not mean that their actions were always above reproach. For example, Justice Wilson Sandura did a poor job at the head of the Delimitation Commission in April–June 2000, where he covered up gerrymandering by ZANU-PF civil servants. Justice Paddington Garwe played according to ZANU-PF's script in the criminal defamation case against *Financial Gazette* editor Trevor Ncube in 1995. But the very existence of a judicial community in a context where the law was largely enforced had a regulatory effect on individual behavior.

Reading the current conflict between the government and the judiciary as one between black nationalists and British-born white judges, as Mugabe and War Vet leaders would have us believe, is misleading. Dumbutshena, who died in December 2000, was striking evidence of the opposite. Being the first Zimbabwean black chief justice, from 1984 to 1990,[9] he contributed decisively to the formation of this judicial culture promoting the absolute sovereignty of the law by which all powers must abide. His jurisprudence at the head of the Supreme Court was enlightened and distinctly progressive in matters such as personal liberties, women's rights, and social affairs; hence he was immensely respected in the legal profession. Born in 1920, he joined the nationalist struggle in 1947 but was never a member of ZANU. Originally a ZAPU cadre, he was a legal adviser to Muzorewa's UANC at the time of the Lancaster House conference. Trained in law in the UK in the 1960s and having practiced in Zambia during the 1970s, he was one of the few black advocates at the time of Independence. He was appointed to the Judicial Service Commission and then to the Supreme Court; his career owed nothing to political patronage. Although a Zezuru from Zvimba, Dumbutshena was not part of Mugabe's clientele. When the constitution and universally accepted principles of justice were involved, Dumbutshena was inflexible and did not hesitate to tackle the government in court.

This culture was effective also because a vibrant and organized legal profession exerted some degree of control over the judges. The minister of justice or the attorney general would avoid antagonizing professional bodies such as Zimbabwe's Bar Council or the Zimbabwe Law Society, which would not hesitate to criticize the executive's encroachment in the domain of the judiciary, including some legal and constitutional changes. After 2000 the Law Society chastised on several occasions the decline of the rule of law, police inaction, and the lack of proper implementation of court decisions—though with far less impact than before. NGOs formed in the 1990s such as Zimbabwe Lawyers for Human Rights (ZLHR)[10] or the Legal Resources Foundation (LRF), the board of which was packed with lawyers and which helped to publish the law record as well as a small law journal, *Legal Forum*, also played an important bonding role in the legal profession and a useful watchdog role vis-à-vis the government. To protest against the illegal detention and torture of the *Standard* journalists and the president's callous response, the legal fraternity led by Kevin Lauer of ZLHR organized a march in downtown Harare that was violently repressed by the police. As long as the minority of human rights activists were respected professionals they enjoyed the de facto solidarity of their colleagues.[11] This is not to say that there were no political divisions within the legal fraternity: some lawyers were definitely pro-ZANU-PF. But the common professional ethos implied that even the latter would abide by a technically faultless judgment. There was also a deep understanding and mutual respect between experienced lawyers, especially constitutional law experts—such as Adrian de Bourbon or Chris Andersen—and the judges of superior courts. This is why some prominent lawyers from the ZLHR and the Law Society were harassed by the police after 2000—some of them beaten while in police custody—or prosecuted on trumped up charges.

The Conflict Building in the 1990s

Amendment No. 7 (Act 23 of 1987), which concentrated executive powers in the hands of Mugabe and saw the adoption of a unicameral Parliament of 150 seats—all but 3 controlled by ZANU-PF after the 1990 elections—opened an era of more direct confrontation between a more assertive president and a judiciary on the defensive. Not that there were no occasions of conflict prior to 1987, but Mugabe had other priorities. If on the one hand the judiciary refused to be dragged into his vicious vendetta against ZAPU and discharged most of its leaders when brought to trial in the 1980s, on the other hand the courts were not a serious impediment, especially as the state of emergency was kept in force until 1990. Security agencies were seen as above the law and Gukurahundi victims had little hope of getting redress through the courts. The concentration of powers in the hands of Mugabe and his avowed plan to establish a one-party state, the absence of opposition in parliament and the exposure of the corruption at the top of the state opened a period of tension in 1988. The students took to the streets with the support of the unions, and the new secretary general of ZCTU was illegally detained as mentioned before. As civic organizations turned to the courts to shield themselves from the wrath of government repression, ZANU-PF leaders became increasingly frustrated with what they perceived as the partiality of the courts.

Sensitive issues such as general elections when the ruling party's interests were at stake provided opportunities for the judicial system to demonstrate its integrity and independence. In this respect the High Court ruling that set aside the results of the April 1995 legislative election in Harare South was a milestone. The subsequent rerun was won by the applicant, Margaret Dongo.[12] ZANU-PF leaders were stunned by her temerity in challenging the results with documented arguments. The government was infuriated by Justice George Smith's criticisms of the electoral process, which vindicated claims by opposition parties that elections were rigged in favor of ZANU-PF. This landmark judgment opened the way for a series of court cases in parliamentary and local council elections. However, it must be said that Justice Smith remained cautious in his approach to the case. He did not accuse Registrar General Tobaiwa Mudede of rigging the elections—in spite of the evidence available, including the excess number of ballot papers in the ballot boxes—but claimed that the process was mismanaged and ruled that Mudede did not have to bear the costs of the trial. Consequently the state and Mudede did not oppose the ruling. Justice Smith knew very well that Mudede was close to Mugabe and that the court should not go too far.

Some other court rulings underlined the willingness of judges to resist pressure—mostly indirect—from political power, such as in Strive Masiyiwa's four-year battle to secure a cell phone license against the vested interests of ZANU-PF big men. Another landmark case was the Supreme Court's nullification of the illegal suspension of the whole executive of the Association of Women's Clubs by the Ministry of Social Affairs in

February 1997. The 1995 Private Voluntary Organisations Act, the provisions of which were used by the minister to base his decision, was in breach of the constitutional freedom of association. One of the bones of contention was the increasingly arbitrary use of the Presidential Powers (Temporary Measures) Act (1986), normally limited to emergency situations. Mugabe used it several times in the Fourth Parliament to speed up the process against hostile public opinion and reluctant ZANU-PF backbenchers. Such was the case in 1995 for the amended Urban Councils Act, creating the executive mayors. When ruling over these distortions of the normal legislative procedure the Supreme Court declared such legislation unconstitutional, which was interpreted in State House as a slap in the face of the president.

One of the forms of the confrontation was the Mugabe government's inclination to amend the constitution to overrule a Supreme Court ruling that ran against the government's will, thus undercutting the judiciary's efforts to enforce the constitutional protection of citizens' freedom. Of the sixteen amendments to the constitution adopted from 1980 to 2000, five—passed by Parliament after 1987—contained one or several provisions overturning Supreme Court rulings. Amendment No. 11 (Act 30 of 1990), for example, includes one paragraph contradicting a Supreme Court ruling over corporal punishment inflicted on children and another one anticipating a Supreme Court decision on hanging as a method to execute the death penalty. In another instance, given the amount of public controversy stirred by the Land Acquisition Act (1992) over the compensation of white farmers whose property was compulsorily acquired, and after the chief justice firmly stated the farmers' right to a fair compensation and confirmed the authority of the courts to hear these disputes, the government introduced successively Amendment Nos. 12 (Act 4 of 1993), 13 (Act 9 of 1993), and 14 (Act 14 of 1996) to further restrict the ability of the courts to hear complaints over both the compulsory acquisition and the amount of compensation offered by the state. These early skirmishes with the judiciary over the status of land acquisition take a new significance in view of what happened in 2000–2001.

Although occasionally the issue at stake in these legal battles was not directly political, it was either a matter of resisting the inherent tendency of the executive to use its powers arbitrarily (as illustrated by Amendment No. 7, Art. 31K, stating that exclusive powers of the president were not subject to judicial interference) or a matter of protecting fundamental freedoms enshrined in the Declaration of Rights. The Supreme Court did not bow to intimidation. When Amendment No. 14 (Act 14 of 1996) withdrew the right to permanent residence and the right to be granted citizenship for spouses or concubines of a Zimbabwe citizen, reversing a well-established jurisprudence of the Supreme Court, the latter restated in 1997 (*Kohlhaas v. Chief Immigration Officer and Others*, S-183–97) the right for a foreign spouse of a citizen to live permanently in Zimbabwe by virtue of the right to a normal family life.

The 1999 Crisis

Prior to 1999, attacks on the judiciary were largely limited to ad hominem smear campaigns in the government press or the odd slander by a minister—not necessarily with Mugabe's endorsement. However, it seems clear in retrospect that independent judges and the ruling party were on a collision course throughout the 1990s as government increasingly threatened to ignore hostile court rulings. January 1999 was possibly the turning point—rather than 2000—because this was the first time Mugabe directly attacked the judiciary as an institution and hinted at the need for a purge. This proves that the later assault was premeditated and not only the side effect of the land reform controversy. Three urgent orders for the release of two *Standard* journalists illegally detained delivered by the High Court were ignored by government security agencies. Only when Justice George Smith threatened to arrest minister of defence Moven Mahachi for contempt of the court were the journalists brought before a court, indicted for the "propagation of wrongful information" under the LOMA, and released on bail. The judge's boldness was commendable, a tribute to the judicial culture mentioned above.

However, government refusal to abide by the law and the deliberate inaction of the police force when human lives were at stake were worrisome issues and a bad omen for the future. In addition, Defence Minister Mahachi's and his permanent secretary's defiant statements alleging that the army was above the law pointed at a new and now recurrent pattern of behavior. They echoed ZANU leaders' discourse during Gukurahundi, and the same claim would be made again in 2000–2002 to cover up the War Vets' violent actions. The public was understandably worried, and the judicial authorities saw the danger. The three Supreme Court judges then present in the country (only one being white) sent a solemn letter to the president in late January 1999 to stress how these developments ran against the notion of the rule of law, threatened a good administration of justice, and ultimately would lead to anarchy. Judges demanded that the president dissociate himself from these actions and institute an impartial inquiry.

Mugabe's answer took the form of a television broadcast on 6 February 1999. He claimed that the journalists had provoked the army and should not be surprised by the treatment they received at the hands of the military. Judges were advised to stay out of politics and refrain from "instructing" the president since this "outrageous" behavior compromised their judicial function. The speech ended with a vitriolic attack against whites of British descent, who were accused of committing sabotage, rebelling against the legitimate government, and plotting against national unity. Mugabe named two white owners of private newspapers, David Coltart, who had been instrumental in compiling and publishing *Breaking the Silence, Building True Peace*, the report on the massacres in Matabeleland, and Mike Auret, then director of CCJP, which had cosponsored the report. In a single speech the president targeted the judiciary, the free press, and human rights activists, all of whom would be harassed in the following years. Thus the autocratic nature of ZANU-PF's regime was fully revealed before the farm invasions began, unlike what the AU and many African governments repeatedly claimed after 2000.

These tirades on "whites living in a Rhodesian past" and attacks against the judiciary were reiterated on 21 February, during Mugabe's ritual "birthday" TV interview. He bluntly demanded that the Supreme Court judges resign. The twenty-five judges—eight of whom were whites—of the High Court and the Supreme Court, who sat together for an unusual meeting chaired by the chief justice, reaffirmed the independence of the judiciary and rejected presidential suggestions that they should leave office. Even pro-ZANU-PF judges could do nothing but support this show of strength, which forced Mugabe to back down. Because the lawyers defending the two journalists invoked the unconstitutionality of the LOMA, the case was referred to the Supreme Court, which ruled that the relevant sections of the Act were outside the Constitution as they contradicted the freedom of expression and dismissed the charges. The journalists' lawsuit against the army and police did not get very far since the police refused to cooperate and conduct a proper investigation in spite of Chief Justice Anthony Gubbay's injunction to do so.

This conflict between the executive and the judiciary in the first quarter of 1999 not only announced the dramatic developments of the following three years, but it signaled that Mugabe's attitude toward the judiciary was radically changing. ZANU-PF's political hegemony was challenged by the strength of civil society movements like the NCA, the vigorous private press, and soon the opposition MDC. Mugabe's political survival required that in the future the judiciary should not be a recourse for his numerous opponents. Although the courts then won a respite, the stage was set for a final showdown in 2000–2001. As long as a token respect for the independence of the judiciary and the rule of law brought more benefits (including a positive image in the West) than costs, Mugabe had complied with most court rulings and therefore accepted some temporary setbacks. However, there was no love lost between them. Mugabe never recognized any authority above his own, and the "rule of law" has always been a political philosophy alien to him. On 29 July 1982 he stated in Parliament: "The Government cannot allow the technicalities of the law to fetter its hands." Again, throughout the year 2000, Mugabe made it clear that he was no longer prepared to abide by court decisions or uphold the rule of law. He warned at the ZANU-PF congress in December 2000: "The courts can do whatever they want, but no judicial decision will stand in our way. . . . My own position is that we should not even be defending our position in the courts."[13] Indeed, the time had come to discipline the judges and get rid of "untrustworthy" elements.

The Great Purge in the Supreme Court

If the contest over land reform offered a convenient excuse to target the Supreme Court it was all too logical to strike first at the head of the judicial system in order to destroy it. Unable to get several High Court judgments enforced, the Commercial Farmers Union (CFU) had brought the matter before the Supreme Court. On 10 November 2000 the Supreme Court upheld previous High Court rulings declaring the farm invasions illegal and ordering the police to evict the squatters. Ministers and provincial governors involved in the fast-track program were to stop implementing it until all the legal requirements and procedures had been fulfilled in compliance with the provisions of the Land Acquisition Act. As in the High Court, government consented to the judgment but took no action.

On 24 November about two hundred War Vets invaded the premises of the Supreme Court, noisily declaring that Mugabe, not the courts, made the law, and police intervention was delayed for two hours. No investigation or prosecution of the perpetrators of this major offense was initiated and no action was taken by the minister of justice or attorney general to protect the judiciary (as noted by the International Bar Association).[14] On 21 December the Supreme Court ruled that although land reform was necessary, the government must abide by the laws enacted for this very purpose in accordance with the provisions of the Constitution. Any new compulsory acquisition was illegal and unwarranted but the government was granted a six-month delay to restore the rule of law on the farms and present by 1 July 2001 a workable plan of land reform as required by section 16A of the Constitution. The judgment also pointed at the culprits: "Common law crimes have been, and are being, committed with impunity. Laws made by Parliament have been flouted by the Government. . . . A network of organizations, operating with complete disregard for the law, has been allowed to take over from Government. . . . [Invaders] have been supported, encouraged, transported and financed by party officials, public servants, the CIO and the Army. The rule of law has been overthrown in the commercial farming areas."[15]

In practical terms the Supreme Court rulings ruined Mugabe's strategy to grab land hurriedly and without restraint. In the meantime, another Supreme Court decision infuriated the president and his supporters: by a statutory order signed on 8 December 2000, by virtue of the presidential powers under section 158(1) of the Electoral Act, Mugabe attempted to put an end to all judicial proceedings related to the 39 challenges launched by the MDC against the parliamentary elections results. Against much evidence to the contrary, the president claimed that the elections were "held under peaceful conditions" and the outcome represented "a genuine and free expression of the people's will." He dismissed the MDC challenges as frivolous and undermining peace and stability. On 30 January 2001 the Supreme Court ruled unanimously that the executive order was unconstitutional and upheld the rights of the applicants "to challenge the result of an election which was claimed to have been tainted by corrupt and illegal practices, and to seek practical and meaningful redress" in the courts.[16] Mugabe's motive was to save several ZANU-PF MPs from an ignominious nullification of their election and prevent the erosion of the ruling party's small majority in Parliament. Indeed the MDC later won seven cases in the High Court. If Mugabe could control the Supreme Court, he could paralyze the judicial process as ZANU-PF appealed systematically against the High Court rulings. Indeed, the new chief justice, appointed in March 2001, shelved the appeals indefinitely and the MPs whose election was nullified remained in Parliament until 2005.[17] Judging from the chronology of events one gets the impression of a confrontation gaining momentum. The attack on the judiciary was clearly planned in advance (probably in February 1999). As early as April 2000 "Hitler" Hunzvi had claimed that the "courts were part of the old colonial order" and that the whole judicial system "should be revamped [because the judges] are undermining the powers of the executive."[18] Six months later these views were expressed publicly by Mugabe and his aides.

In late November 2000 Hunzvi threatened the white judges with death unless they resigned, and he was even more blunt on 3 March 2001: "If [the judges] want us to use violence, we are going to use that." Also in November Jonathan Moyo called upon the chief justice to resign. Some

ZANU-PF MPs urged the president to set up a Commission of Inquiry to investigate the judges. The "traditional" chiefs stirred by ZANU-PF also joined the fray in January 2001. Mugabe accused the judges of protecting "white racist commercial farmers." Although the whites were publicly slandered for propaganda purposes, all independent-minded judges were in fact targeted by this public campaign of harassment.[19] In January, in an unprecedented move to further his chances of promotion to the Supreme Court, Judge President Chidyausiku accused the chief justice of bias in favor of the white commercial farmers, citing Gubbay's public remarks on the Land Acquisition Act (1992), which sought to remove the power of the courts to decide fair compensation for the farmers. This vicious political attack was a clear breach of Justice Chidyausiku's constitutional duty. He also resented the formal reprimand he received from the chief justice for his refusal to abide by a Supreme Court judgment on the farm invasions. He was reminded that a High Court judge had no power to suspend a decision by the highest court of the land. Although it transpired that Justice Chidyausiku misunderstood the implications of the original Supreme Court ruling, his primary motive was to please his political masters.[20]

Initially Anthony Gubbay, who called in vain on Mugabe to rein in the War Vets, had resolved to stay put,[21] but the beleaguered sixty-eight-year-old man eventually gave way to the combination of direct pressure from the government and renewed death threats from the War Vet leaders, including Joseph Chinotimba, who walked into his office and directly threatened to kill him. He was even accused by a ZANU-PF MP close to Mugabe of working for British intelligence to overthrow the government. The convergence of these attacks revealed a deliberate and determined attempt to unseat the judges. After the interior and justice ministers had both hinted in February that they would do nothing to protect him, the chief justice had no other option but to go into early retirement. Formally, he was put on leave on 1 March—allowing Mugabe to appoint the sycophantic Chidyausiku as acting chief justice—and retired officially on 1 July 2001. The constitutional protection theoretically guaranteed to members of the judiciary is effective only when the police abide by the law. Hunzvi and Chinotimba should have been immediately arrested for their criminal offense. That it did not happen meant that their actions were condoned at the highest level of government.

Striking at the head was logical not only because of the pivotal role of the chief justice but also because it sent a clear message to the others: if the police would not protect the embodiment of the judiciary, what about ordinary judges? Indeed, most members of the 2000 Supreme Court left within a year following Gubbay's forced retirement. Justice

Simbarashe Muchechetere, who was seriously ill, died in December 2001. Justice Nick McNally refused to resign in February despite threats by the minister of justice, but he reached the age limit in December and eventually retired in January 2002. Justice Ahmed Ebrahim, originally a supporter of Mugabe, who had made him attorney general in 1980 and appointed him to the Supreme Court in 1990, also bravely resisted the pressure but resigned in March 2002. A member of the Asian minority, Justice Ebrahim certainly felt weaker and more exposed to retaliation than other judges. Only Wilson Sandura remained of the old Supreme Court, and there was little he could achieve alone.

Mugabe was then in a position to shape the new Supreme Court at will. The ruling of 2 July 2001 upheld that of December 2000, which had declared the compulsory acquisitions illegal, since government had not presented the required credible resettlement plan by the fixed deadline, and Chief Justice Chidyausiku was the dissenting voice with the four other judges united against him. It was imperative for Mugabe to reverse the majority decision that had been made in the Supreme Court. In late July 2001 he appointed three new judges: Misheck Cheda, Vernanda Ziyambi, and Luke Malaba, expanding the court from five to eight judges. Malaba, a former war veteran, had a reputation as a dedicated ZANU-PF supporter, as did Ziyambi—the first woman appointed to the Supreme Court. Cheda had been permanent secretary in the Ministry of Justice (by late the 1980s all permanent secretaries were ZANU-PF stalwarts). Although Justice Ziyambi's record in the High Court was more balanced than one would believe[22] and Justices Cheda and Malaba produced fair judgments in the Bulawayo High Court,[23] they were political appointees: they were selected on the basis of their opinion on land reform and without taking seniority in the High Court into account. Indeed both Cheda and Malaba were on the list Margaret Dongo had released in 1999 of Mugabe's protégés who had received a commercial farm.

In December 2001, the Supreme Court, composed of Chief Justice Chidyausiku, Misheck Cheda, Vernanda Ziyambi, Luke Malaba, and Ahmed Ebrahim reversed the previous judgment by four votes against one, the dissenting voice now being Ebrahim. The "fast-track program" of land distribution was no longer in contradiction with the constitution and farm occupations were retroactively legalized. That three of the senior judges (Sandura, Muchechetere—though ill—and McNally) were left out for political convenience was a clear indication of Chidyausiku's intentions. On important constitutional issues the chief justice had discretion to call a full bench as Gubbay would certainly have done. The last opportunity for the former judges to overcome Chidyausiku in a constitutional case was in November 2001, when the Supreme Court cleared Tsvangirai of accusations to plot to overthrow Mugabe through the use of violence, following a controversial statement made in a public meeting in September 2000.

After December 2001, the new Supreme Court became a pliant tool in Mugabe's hands, especially when the full bench sat for constitutional issues. However, in February 2002 the court nullified the General Amendment Act, which amended forty different laws. These included several changes to the electoral law, which effectively forbade local civic organizations to provide voter education and monitoring of the presidential election for the ESC, authorized the registrar general to make changes on the voters' roll, and deprived Zimbabweans living abroad of their right to vote—among other treacherous provisions. Justices Cheda and Ziyambi concurred with Justice Ebrahim—giving his last judgment—against Justice Malaba, to rule that the Act was improperly passed in Parliament. However, the Act was nullified only ten days before the election and it was too late for that decision to have an impact on voter education, monitoring, and even postal voting. Besides, these provisions were immediately reenacted by the minister of justice and President Mugabe, using their extensive powers under the Electoral Act (sections 157 and 158 respectively).

When at first look a decision seemed favorable to the opposition, civil society, or the independent press, a string was usually attached to it. For example, when the Supreme Court ruled in May 2003 that section 80 of AIPPA contravened section 20 of the Bill of Rights, the judgment was not opposed by the attorney general. He had admitted in November that section 80 of the Act should be rephrased in an amendment that was still in preparation. Other constitutional challenges of AIPPA were shelved by the supine chief justice. From then on successful appeals against High Court judgments would depend entirely on who heard the case and what was at stake. When the government appealed against a High Court ruling in favor of Judith Todd, granting her the right to a Zimbabwe passport,[24] the chief justice reversed that judgment in February 2003. Like her father, the liberal prime minister of Southern Rhodesia who had strongly opposed Ian Smith and protected some black activists, Judith Todd was a symbolic and popular figure. A supporter of the nationalist government in the early years, she became a fierce critic of corruption and authoritarianism in the late 1990s. Besides, the potential deprivation of citizenship affected not only 40,000 whites but also the black farm workers of Zambian, Malawian, and Mozambican descent, with wider implications for electoral politics. These examples show how the appointment of partisan judges on the bench undermines the Supreme Court's crucial role in the enforcement of the Declaration of Rights.

A Still Restive High Court

The purge in the High Court was less severe if only because there were more people to deal with. The overall objective remained to cut down the number of independent-minded judges who might rule against the interests of ZANU-PF or a particular faction within the party. That alone would intimidate the remaining judges. Judgments that would have passed almost unnoticed five years earlier were now deemed anti-government, such was the polarization of politics. Justice James Devittie was pushed out with death threats in May 2001 with effect by 30 November, but he was immediately removed from presiding over election challenges after he nullified in April 2001 the June 2000 election of ZANU-PF candidates in three constituencies, Hurungwe East, Mutoko South, and Buhera North.[25] He vowed to "uphold the truth . . . and uphold the oath of his office" and stated that "violence and intimidation have no place in a democratic society." The fact that in Buhera North Devittie's ruling favored Tsvangirai probably infuriated Mugabe and his cronies. Justice Michael Gillespie resigned in early September 2001. The ruling party objected to his comments during the 2000 electoral campaign to the effect that the use of violence was a cause for election nullification (ironically this is precisely what the Electoral Act says). Gillespie also delivered several judgments favorable to dispossessed white farmers. In his final judgment the learned judge stated the reasons why he could no longer act as an independent judge in contemporary Zimbabwe: "Manipulation of court rolls; selective prosecution; and the packing of the Bench of the superior courts are techniques which provide a government determined to do so with the opportunity to subvert the law while at the same time appearing to respects its institutions."[26] A black judge, Justice Esmael Chatikobo also left the bench in May 2001. The previous October he had ruled in favor of the first private radio station in Zimbabwe, Capital Radio, attracting a fierce reaction from Jonathan Moyo's office. Justice Chatikobo also delayed in February 2001 the deportation of two foreign journalists residing in Zimbabwe whom Moyo sought to punish for their adverse reporting.

Justice Fergus Blackie was also compelled to resign, in July 2002, and Justice George Smith remained the only white judge in the High Court until he reached the age limit. Although he submitted his resignation, Justice Blackie was further harassed through spurious accusations of obstructing the course of justice: just before leaving his judicial office he acquitted a white woman whom the government press later misrepresented as his mistress—in fact they had never met before the court hearing. There was apparently a blunder in the paperwork giving Blackie's colleague Justice Makarau cause to complain. More important, the judgment annoyed a black lawyer close to ZANU-PF who had accused the woman of stealing her employer's money. A case was fabricated out of a petty wrangle by the judge president and the chief justice, and Blackie was detained in squalid conditions by the police for three days in September 2002. The arrest was illegal since the correct procedure of an internal inquiry conducted by the judiciary, as spelled out by the constitution, was not followed. The uproar in the judicial and legal professions was such that the state withdrew the case in July 2003. Beyond the purge, it was all a matter of revenge. As mentioned earlier, Justice Blackie had been under attack before. He had ruled over several corruption cases involving some ZANU-PF big men—such as Christopher Ushewokunze—in the 1990s and had made many enemies in the ruling party, including Chinamasa, the former attorney general and then minister of justice. When the latter ignored repeated summons to appear before the High Court (in relation to the case of three American missionaries unduly detained in July 1999), Blackie ordered his arrest though to no avail, and, on 17 July 2002, fined him and sentenced him to three months in jail for being in contempt of court. Although it was ignored by the police, a humiliated and fuming Chinamasa appealed to the "new" Supreme Court, which overturned Blackie's ruling on 22 August.

As he had done in the Supreme Court, Mugabe hastened to appoint new judges to the High Court: four in December 2000 and three others in 2001. Some are undeniably pro-ZANU-PF judges, such as Ben Hlatshwayo or Anne-Marie Gowora, who spent most of her career in the attorney general's office and received a farm in October 2005.[27] A law lecturer at the University of Zimbabwe with ZCTU connections, and one of the few individuals to defect from the NCA to the government-sponsored CRC, Ben Hlatshwayo worked very closely with Jonathan Moyo in the Secretariat of the CRC and during the referendum campaign. Once appointed to the High Court, he delivered several controversial judgments in cases involving the Combined Harare Residents Association and the MDC. The MDC rightly protested in June 2001 when Justice Hlatshwayo was assigned some electoral lawsuits previously attributed to Justice Devittie. He refused in particular to nullify the June 2000 election in Mberengwa East, although some MDC activists had been tortured to death by local War Vets during the campaign, and he dismissed the MDC petitions in Goromonzi and Murhewa North, where violence had also been pervasive.[28] By stating that the War Vets' violent assaults on MDC candidates and activists were linked to the land reform and not the elections, he legitimized de facto private violence against the country's laws. No wonder the opposition leaders complained when Justice Hlatshwayo was assigned to hear MDC's petition on the 2002 presidential election. The MDC pointed out that both Hlatshwayo and Justice

Garwe were partisan judges as they both benefited from the landgrab.[29] Hlatshwayo's private behavior betrays little respect for the law and a lack of integrity.[30] Justice Hlatshwayo also granted the government on 1 June 2003 an urgent order—said to be fraught with many legal defects—to stop the week-long series of general strikes and demonstrations planned by the MDC from 2 to 6 June on the grounds that the opposition party intended to "oust a legitimately elected president."

A former permanent secretary in the Justice Department, Paddington Garwe also showed his ZANU-PF affiliation in a 1995 criminal defamation case. He was cited by the press as having illegally benefited in 1995–96 from a public housing scheme meant to help low-ranking civil servants. He acquitted Hunzvi, who had been accused of defrauding the War Victims Compensation Fund, using an extremely dubious argument. In March 2000 he ruled the farm occupations illegal and specifically directed the police commissioner to evict the War Vets. Yet in the election challenge cases he presided over he ruled in favor of ZANU-PF, alleging a lack of evidence of violence and rigging. Appointed judge president in February 2001, he influenced the distribution of sensitive cases to trustable colleagues and set the dates for hearings. The former rotating system had been abolished by his predecessor Godfrey Chidyausiku, who began to allocate cases arbitrarily, thus indirectly affecting the judgments' substance. In the wake of several rulings in favor of MDC parliamentary candidates in the first half of 2001, the new judge president delayed the hearing of the other electoral petitions or assigned the cases to "political judges."[31] This contradicted the Electoral Act that requires that election petitions be expedited speedily—if only to limit the time period during which an illegitimate MP may take part in the legislative process. This deliberate obstruction and the appeals indefinitely postponed in the Supreme Court quashed the MDC hope of changing the outcome of these elections through litigation: not even one of the MDC electoral challenges was ever resolved by the judiciary. Justice Garwe's docility was rewarded by his elevation to the Supreme Court in July 2006.

By mid-2002 the MDC finances were heavily dented by Tsvangirai's defense in the "treason" trial and by the preparation of the petition instituted on 12 April 2002 to obtain nullification of Mugabe's reelection. The MDC also challenged in the courts government decisions at various stages of the preparation of the presidential contest, including the constitutionality of sections of the Electoral Act and late-hour amendments to it by the president.[32] Even when the MDC applications were successful, the court orders were ignored by the executive or the contentious legislation was reenacted by the president through statutory instrument. The registrar general and the Electoral Supervisory Commission conspired, in violation of High Court orders, to frustrate the MDC from establishing the facts through an analysis of the voters' roll and the used ballot papers. Similarly the hearing of Tsvangirai's election petition was deliberately delayed for more than a year.

However, the MDC's tenacity paid off when Justice Hlatshwayo granted on 4 July 2003 an order sought by the MDC to reiterate Justice Garwe's ruling in January 2003 to compel the registrar of the High Court to allocate a date for this hearing. Therefore, the first stage of the presidential election challenge case, which dealt solely with legal and constitutional issues, was argued in early November 2003. Yet Justice Hlatshwayo, who was assigned to the case and whose track record was known by then to everybody, delayed judgment for seven months and then summarily dismissed the petition without providing his reasons. Neither Mugabe's counsel at the hearing nor Justice Hlatshwayo in his judgment bothered to rebut the petitioner's arguments.[33] The second phase scheduled to hear the evidence of violence, intimidation, corrupt and illegal practices, and various forms of rigging never materialized. In 2005 a frustrated MDC, citing the High Court's inability to finalize the matter, deferred its petition to the Supreme Court where it was left pending.[34] Obviously the judges' obstructive maneuvers were meant to spare Mugabe the embarrassment of a nullification of the presidential election—an indictment of the lack of independence and integrity of these now political judges.

The MDC was not any luckier with its electoral petitions following the March 2005 elections. The new election court packed with political judges delivered a series of partisan rulings: even when acknowledging the evidence of ZANU-PF's violence and the politicization of food aid the judges ruled that they had no impact on the results.[35] The court's lack of independence was established in March when jailed MDC parliamentarian Roy Bennett first obtained an order allowing him to stand in his Chimanimani home area and postponing the ballot in that constituency until 30 April, but then saw the election court reversing its ruling and suspending its order after the Chairman of the Zimbabwe Electoral Commission (political judge Justice George Chiweshe) filed an urgent application to this end. In the meantime Mugabe, who disliked Roy Bennett personally, had threatened to appeal the initial judgment—presumably in the Supreme Court—although the law states that the election court's decisions cannot be appealed. As the result of this gross interference and intimidation of the voters, the MDC lost the seat to ZANU-PF.

Several of the new High Court judges suspected of political bias delivered some honest, brave judgments in electoral disputes and in media cases.[36] Rita Makarau, one of the twelve MPs directly nominated by

Mugabe during the Fourth Parliament, took an active yet ambivalent part in the work of the CRC in 1999. Justice Makarau handed down several judgments favorable to the MDC in preparation for the 2002 presidential election. She also nullified the parliamentary elections in the two Gokwe constituencies in January 2003 because of the violence used by ZANU-PF against MDC members. However, she upheld the results in Mount Darwin South and Mwenezi on the basis of a narrow reading of the Electoral Act and in spite of the violence perpetuated by ZANU-PF. Justice Makarau eventually toed the line when appointed to the controversial electoral court in May 2005, and she was appointed judge president in July 2006 to succeed Justice Garwe. Although at the official opening of the legal year 2007, in a surprising gesture of independence, Justice Makarau criticized the appalling state of the judicial system—including cases of corruption—she reacted sternly at the beginning of 2009 to local lawyers' and the International Bar Association's criticisms of several High Court rulings related to wrongfully detained civic activists.[37] Even political judges are willing to maintain a pretense of legality.

The harassment of High Court judges did not cease with the purge of the white members in 2001, but targeted afterward some judges who had dared to deliver judgments that annoyed the president or some ruling party big men. Such was the case of Justice Benjamin Paradza when he ordered the immediate release from custody of Harare's MDC mayor, who had been arrested by the police in January 2003 under the spurious accusation that a public meeting with the Harare residents' association at the town hall had violated the POSA. Mayor Mudzuri was locked at the time in a bitter wrangle with local government minister Ignatius Chombo. Paradza's ruling, coming after his August 2002 judgments favorable to white farmers, also irritated top government circles, which expected a more cooperative attitude from a war veteran. He had also instructed the authorities to stop withholding Judith Todd's passport. Paradza soon found himself implicated in a case—a concocted case, according to him and many human rights lawyers—of corruption of justice and was illegally arrested in February 2003 (the same modus operandi as with Blackie). On bail since then, he was convicted in January 2006 and fled abroad. Another High Court judge, Lawrence Kamocha, was threatened by CIO officials when he released James Makamba from jail in August 2004.[38] The "political businessman" close to the Mujuru family had been arrested in January 2004 for violating exchange control regulations, but unverified rumors suggested that he had had an affair with Grace Mugabe.[39] In Zimbabwe today the judiciary is expected to espouse Mugabe's personal vendettas.

Another landmark judgment was delivered on 5 August 2004, when

Justice Sandra Mungwira ruled in favor of the six MDC members accused of murdering Bulawayo War Vet leader Cain Nkala. Nkala had been arrested in connection with the disappearance of Patrick Nabanyama, MDC MP David Coltart's polling agent, in 2000. In November 2001 Nkala was abducted from his home in broad daylight and soon after was found dead in a shallow grave. According to some family members, he had resolved a few days before his death to reveal in the courtroom that top members of Mugabe's party were also involved in Nabanyama's murder. His elimination was probably an insider job, but it was used by ZANU-PF to discredit the opposition; in particular, Mugabe, who presided over Nkala's funeral, used the occasion to lambaste the "MDC terrorists." The accused were illegally detained, some of them for more than two years, in defiance of High Court and Supreme Court orders for their release. Among them diabetic sixty-two-year-old Fletcher Dulini Ncube, popular MP for Lobengula-Magwegwe and MDC treasurer, was kept in police cells without medication and lost an eye as a result.[40] The state was so desperate to have the opposition activists convicted that one of the accused, Khetahini Sibanda, was tortured to extract a confession implicating the others. However, in March 2004 Mungwira castigated the police officers for the falsified evidence produced in the court, labeled it "works of fiction" and "fraught with conflict and inconsistencies," and ruled that confessions obtained through torture were not admissible as evidence in a court of law.[41] Consequently the prosecution's case appeared totally empty, as MDC lawyers argued from the outset, and the accused were freed.

These admirable gestures of independence on the part of a few newly appointed High Court judges should be viewed in relation to the above-mentioned judicial ethos that operates as a constraining factor: they do not want to lose all credibility in the legal profession by appearing too subservient to the ruling party. Among the newly appointed, those who spent part of their career in private practice before they joined the bench have a tendency to write more robust judgments and adhere to a more coherent vision of the law. They also have a better knowledge of the jurisprudence on which to base their decisions.

Another factor could be that even people with a ZANU-PF background were genuinely horrified by Mugabe's increasingly violent and arbitrary rule. Even the overtly partisan judges had to remain cautious. Justice Hlatshwayo reluctantly granted an urgent order sought by the MDC to have the polling stations reopened for a third day of voting during the March 2002 presidential elections, and only after he was flown over the city in a helicopter to assess the numbers still lining up (a fact obvious to anybody else). Similarly Justice Susan Mavangira, elevated to the High Court bench in 2002 straight from the attorney general's office (a fairly bad omen), hesitated a fortnight before granting bail to Morgan Tsvangirai when he was once more arrested and indicted for treason in early June 2003. Nevertheless Tsvangirai was freed—though with extremely tough bail conditions—and Justice Mavangira saw no legal basis for prolonged detention of the MDC leader, contrary to the prosecution's line of argument. The judicial culture that had taken root in Zimbabwe in the 1980s is strong enough for political judges to find it tricky to drift away from jurisprudence and legal reasoning. The support from the human rights NGO sector, locally and abroad, and the legalistic approach adopted by the MDC and sister organizations such as Crisis in Zimbabwe and the NCA, where professional lawyers are numerous, has been crucial also to encourage judges—sometimes—to make a stand.

The best lawyers work for the opposition and ridicule the accusers when cases are not documented and supported by credible evidence.[42] A striking illustration is provided by Morgan Tsvangirai's treason trial, which dragged on from early February 2003 to October 2004. The team of lawyers led by South African advocate George Bizos (Nelson Mandela's lawyer in the landmark Rivonia trial)[43] established that charges against the MDC president, MDC secretary general Welshman Ncube and MDC MP Renson Gasela were trumped-up, as the state's case relied on flimsy evidence: inaudible sound tapes, a doctored videotape of a meeting where the plot was supposedly hatched, and some witnesses totally lacking credibility, especially Canadian businessman Ari Ben-Menashe.[44] Allegedly a former Israeli spy until 1987, subsequently involved in many shady deals around the world, and a man a U.S. congressional committee described in the 1980s as a "talented liar," Ben-Menashe was paid by Mugabe's CIO more than U.S.$500,000 to frame the MDC leadership. The incrimination was meant originally to prevent Tsvangirai from standing in the 2002 election and to ruin his political career, but the maneuver backfired when the court proceedings received extensive international media coverage and the Mugabe regime's political motives were fully exposed.

Having established that the charges were fictitious, the defense team requested the High Court to discharge the accused. Judge Garwe himself described Ben-Menashe, the main prosecution witness, as "rude, unreliable and contemptuous." The embarrassed judge president ruled on 8 August 2003 that Welshman Ncube and Renson Gasela should be acquitted. But he then rejected the application to discharge Tsvangirai in order to accommodate the ruling party's demands. At the time Mugabe was adamant that the MDC should withdraw its presidential election petition. Yet Justice Garwe, who had ruled several times in favor of the accused throughout the proceedings, was obviously at pains to find grounds for Tsvangirai's conviction. The judgment was set for 29 July 2004, but was postponed when the two assessors, Justice Misheck Nyandoro and Justice Joseph Dangarembizi, allegedly refused to concur with Garwe's verdict of guilt.[45] If matters of law—in particular the appropriate punishment to be imposed—are at the discretion of the presiding judge, questions of fact must be resolved by a majority of the panel of three. Tsvangirai's acquittal on 15 October 2004 was the logical outcome of this two-and-a-half-year saga since "the State has failed to prove any conspiracy to assassinate Mugabe or to bring about a coup d'état," as advocate George Bizos noted in his closing address.

However, the conclusion of this highly publicized trial cannot be cited as evidence that Zimbabwe retains an independent judiciary. Truly independent judges would have thrown out the fraudulent charges from the beginning. Besides, Mugabe's real aim was to harass Tsvangirai, sap his morale, and exhaust MDC funds and political energy, which would have been better used to solve the party's internal problems that surfaced in late 2004. In this respect the plot largely succeeded. In addition, the opposite verdict with the mandatory life imprisonment sentence would have elevated Tsvangirai to a Mandela-like status, that of a martyr to ZANU-PF tyranny, thus further attracting adverse international attention at a time Mugabe was pretending to adhere to SADC elections rules and to stabilize the political situation. This judgment, therefore, underlines how deeply politicized the judicial process has become in Zimbabwe.

The Last Barrier to Dictatorship

The rule of law has been seriously undermined since 2000, although the situation was far from perfect before, and the actions of the government and the ruling elite have been increasingly tainted by illegality and impunity. The lower circuits of courts have not been spared from gross interference. Several magistrates and prosecutors have fallen victim to harassment and sometimes violence orchestrated by ZANU-PF militias and elements from the security forces.[46] In spite of the ZANU-PF regime's effort to "re-mould the legal system into the pliant instrument of State power,"[47] the judicial arena has remained up to now a site of struggle for democracy and the rule of law. However legal victories for the opposition and human rights defenders have become less and less relevant given the propensity of Mugabe and his aides, his supporters, and partisan civil servants to ignore court orders not in the government's favor. The police's reluctance to abide by court decisions, originally limited to the land issue, but later on in any case politically sensitive—anything related to the MDC, the NCA, or the independent media—created opportunities for ruling party militias to take the law into their own hands. There is little the remaining professional judges can do about the arbitrary behavior of politicized security forces. Besides, the independent judges' rulings can be overturned sooner or later by a "political judge." If it was not his desire to maintain a façade of respectability and legality, at least in the eyes of his SADC and African Union colleagues, Mugabe would certainly have done without the courts altogether, thus ending more than twenty years of uneasy cohabitation with an institution he does not trust or like. Still, defending the independence of the judiciary in Zimbabwe remains a matter of crucial importance: not only does it enable the opposition and the civic organizations to survive without having to go underground, but it provides a modicum of the rule of law as the last barrier to a full-fledged dictatorship. Thus the MDC and various civic groups persevered in taking government to court on various issues in spite of limited chances of success.

Chapter 6
The Land "Reform" Charade and the Tragedy of Famine

"Land reform" is an inappropriate name for a political strategy that has little to do with rural development or the black peasants' alleged hunger for land. Reclaiming the land has been a mobilization slogan ever since the liberation war,[1] and it is now a political weapon against the regime's perceived enemies. The technical/developmental approach of resettlement adopted in most of the literature on the land controversy,[2] useful as it may be when dealing with a planned and rational resettlement program, does not address the core issue: the politicization of the land question from the outset and its harnessing, in the current crisis, to serve the political survival of Mugabe's regime.

Just as in other British settler colonial states in Africa such as Kenya and South Africa, with a history of land appropriation by whites and dispossession and forced relocation for blacks, the ownership of arable land has always been a contentious issue in rural Zimbabwe.[3] In addition, the Shona cult of the ancestors' spirits (Mhondoros), with symbolic territories dividing up the country, underlined the people's spiritual relationship to the land that was as important to them as its utilitarian value. Although land was underutilized and less densely populated in precolonial Zimbabwe,[4] an argument used by white settlers to legitimize their landgrab, there are countless stories of traditional shrines and sacred sites that were forcibly incorporated into white-held farms and are still claimed today by local black peasants or displaced communities. In 1980 white-owned commercial farms occupied 39 percent of the land (the well-watered richer soils between 1,000 and 1,500 meters above sea level), against 42 percent allocated to the communal areas (former tribal reserves mostly in the dryer lowlands),[5] 15 percent was state-owned and state-managed, and 4 percent was set aside for small-scale (black) commercial farming.[6] Both ZANU and ZAPU committed themselves to radical land redistribution, seen in the early 1980s as a genuine policy priority, a requirement of economic justice and a rural development issue.[7]

However, ZANU-PF's official history portraying a militant peasantry as the backbone of ZANU and the land as the cause for which the libe-ration war was fought is largely self-serving propaganda.[8] It provides a convenient legitimization of the ruling party's twenty-year political hegemony and nowadays of the ruthless confiscation of white-owned farms. From the outset, the issue of land redistribution to black farmers was politicized in such a way that policy implementation has been under-mined by political expediency and ideological posturing. Therefore the so-called fast-track land reform in the the first decade of the twenty-first century[9] was only the latest—admittedly the most tragic—development of twenty years of policy blunders, bureaucratic procrastination, and political propaganda. That the much-vaunted "revolution" to empower poor rural blacks at the expense of "British colonialists" led to the largest landgrab ever performed by the ruling elite and to mass starva-tion of black peasants is more evidence of Mugabe's brutal cynicism.

The Resettlement Policy from Accommodation to Conflict

At the Lancaster House negotiations Ian Smith—himself a farmer—made it a condition for any agreement that white farmers' property rights be entrenched in the constitution of the new Zimbabwe for a minimum of ten years. Beyond the economics the farming community impersonalized the myths at the core of Rhodesian identity and the typi-cal white lifestyle.[10] It is now fashionable to criticize the Lancaster House agreement, but the compromise on land seemed at the time a reason-able trade-off for majority rule and a peaceful transition.[11] Mugabe lamented in June 2000: "Perhaps we made a mistake by not finishing the war in the trenches. We were modest and rushed [sic] to Lancaster [House]."[12] However, the Smith regime had contained the guerrillas on the battlefield and both sides were pressed to negotiate by their own allies. Besides the Declaration of Rights attached to the Independence Constitution contained provisions for "compulsory" acquisition of "underutilized land" for resettlement on condition of "adequate com-pensation and, where the acquisition is contested, that a court order is obtained" (Section 5.1).[13]

White farmers were effectively shielded from outright confiscation by the nationalist government, which could also purchase land on a willing seller/willing buyer basis, thus at market prices, and indeed there have always been more farms on offer than the government could acquire.[14] The Commercial Farmers Union estimated that up to 83 percent of commercial farms in Zimbabwe have changed ownership since independence. Most white farmers in the late 1990s had bought their land with the government's approval, having obtained "Certificates of no Present Interest"—meaning that the land was not needed for resettlement— issued by the Ministry of Agriculture. By 1990, only 3.5 million hectares had been bought—25 percent of the commercial farming area at Independence—only 2 million had been used to resettle 71,000 families,[15] with uneven economic success.[16] The resettlement program had come almost to a halt because the government did not provide the expertise, training, farming equipment, and infrastructures needed. With the shift in Mugabe's economic policy,[17] resettlement was no longer a priority the rhetoric set aside.

At the end of the ten-year period a constitutional amendment (1990) provided for compulsory acquisition of the white-owned farms and the amended Land Acquisition Act (1992) limited the farmers' right to compensation and to appeal to the courts—allegedly to accelerate the acquisition process of half of the 11.5 million hectares of commercial farms left. The CFU led a civic campaign against these sections of the Act and the Supreme Court warned that they would be in breach of the constitution. Eventually, Mugabe backtracked. The courts subsequently ruled that compensation offered by the government was inadequate in most cases.

Pledges to speed up the land redistribution process featured prominently in ZANU-PF's election campaigns ever since independence— only to be played down in the interval. Prior to the 1990 elections the ruling party announced a "revolutionary land reform program."[18] Although it took the form of a constitutional amendment and the promulgation of the above-mentioned Land Acquisition Act, there was not much change on the ground, except when the government compulsorily acquired farms belonging to its political opponents.[19] The 1995 parliamentary election campaign was dominated by the "indigenization" of the economy theme, but the land rhetoric came back in full force during the presidential election campaign in 1996, with stingingly racist undertones at odds with official "reconciliation policy" and threats to seize white-owned farms without compensation on the grounds that the colonial settlers had not paid any to indigenous inhabitants.

The aggressive rhetoric that has become so pervasive in the ZANU-PF discourse from 2000 was used in public in 1996 as if to test the waters. At the time, it was dismissed as an electoral gimmick by most observers.

A vocal member of the indigenization lobby close to the ZANU-PF hierarchy, Roger Boka, then building a controversial tobacco auction floor to capture the lucrative trade monopolized by white-owned businesses, was also a founding member and a financial backer of the Indigenous Commercial Farmers Union (ICFU). Boka's and ICFU's newspaper advertisements openly supported a straightforward eviction of the whites from their farms without compensation.[20] Often ridiculed by the independent press, Boka enjoyed behind-the-scenes political backing as his well-attended funeral revealed in early 1999.

The Land Acquisition Act (1992) contained also criteria for selection of qualified blacks, targeting agricultural college trainees, to enter commercial farming on the acquired properties. However, this efficiency-oriented approach in line with both the liberal turn of ESAP and the "indigenization" policy was to provide a smokescreen for the first wave of large-scale landgrabs. Press reports revealed in 1994 that the government had doled out land purchased for resettlement of landless peasants to members of the ruling elite as a means of Mugabe's patronage. Following these allegations, the British government, having paid £44 million for land reform since independence[21] suspended funding in 1995,[22] and was accused after 1999 of having provoked the Zimbabwe government! Although Mugabe claimed, ahead of the 1995 general elections, that the 1993 controversial leases were nullified, nothing changed on the ground, and the independent MP Margaret Dongo produced a fresh list of farm recipients in 1999. By the end of the decade corrupt appropriation of land had become part of the ZANU-PF big men's strategy to access wealth.

The issue of land redistribution was reignited when militant war veterans demanded farmland in addition to other benefits in mid-1997.[23] Although the War Vets leadership were seen as a threat to the government, Mugabe used their demands to put pressure on Western donors and hedged his bets in early November 1997: white farmers would not be compensated—except for "infrastructural developments"—unless Great Britain, the former colonial power, provided the necessary funds. He received a stern rebuttal from Clare Short, British minister for development cooperation in the incipient Blair Cabinet, in a letter that many perceived as tactless and that prompted the alleged moderates within ZANU-PF to align with the "radicals."[24] The government issued on 28 November 1997 a list of 1,471 farms to be expropriated to appease the War Vets—a move immediately countered by the farmers in the courts and strongly castigated by the donors.

At the September 1998 all-stakeholders conference on land reform, Western donors committed themselves to funding land redistribution, provided that it was based on the "willing seller, willing buyer" principle, conducted in accordance with the law and the constitution, and benefited primarily the landless peasants and the rural poor. Pledges of up to U.S.$200 million were made in view of resettling 150,000 families with the essential infrastructure to be provided over several years (an ambitious enough target given the government's lack of implementation capacity). Transparency was demanded in the acquisition and distribution of land in a clear reference to previous land grabbing by the regime's protégés. This program certainly seemed reasonable and Mugabe could have claimed a major success had he been really interested in land reform. A first inception plan for a two-year period was launched in March 1999 with the acquisition of some 118 farms already identified with CFU help, and the UNDP was tasked to coordinate donors' efforts with government departments. However, it soon surfaced that once again some of the farms purchased under the new scheme had gone to political cronies, allegedly for lack of suitable candidates for resettlement, while the government complained that the money pledged by donors was not disbursed.

From Referendum to Farm Invasions

The repeated attempts by Mugabe's pawns in the CRC to introduce the "land clause" in the constitutional draft and the eventual "correction" to that effect in January 2000 meant that from the regime's viewpoint the September 1988 deal was already dead: had the draft constitution been approved in the February referendum, Western donors would not have been more forthcoming. Therefore, Mugabe's claim, sheepishly endorsed by SADC heads of state at the Victoria Falls Easter 2000 summit, that the violent farm invasions were the desperate response of the "masses" to an international community reneging on its 1998 promises is deceptive. Mugabe deliberately dumped the negotiated resettlement program for political expediency. By March 2000, the UNDP coordinating unit had ceased to function properly because officials of the Ministry of Land excluded foreign experts from their planning meetings and suddenly refused to communicate relevant information.[25]

During the referendum campaign, led on the government's side by the CRC secretariat and in particular by Jonathan Moyo, the land issue was key in the government's propaganda blitz. Sloppy slogans such as "land is the economy and the economy is the land" proliferated, as if other sections of the draft constitution did not really matter. This deliberately polemical discourse claiming nationalist authenticity portrayed any compromise on farm acquisition as a betrayal of Zimbabwe's independence and a return to colonial rule. The media campaign had an openly racist component as the whites were singled out and held responsible for the land reform deadlock and equated to alleged British colonial interests. Not only were their economic interests threatened by the clause inserted in the draft constitution, but their citizenship was denied. Most of them were born in Zimbabwe and Britain owed them nothing.[26] These fears were later confirmed by the Citizenship Act (2001), which stripped most whites of their Zimbabwean citizenship, unless they could prove that they had renounced their rights to any other nationality.

Many whites who had believed the "reconciliation policy" rhetoric in the 1980s were taken aback when Jonathan Moyo blamed them for the "No" vote in the referendum.[27] In fact white farmers had acquired a false sense of security when Dennis Norman, the pre-independence chairman of the Commercial Farmers Union (CFU), was minister of agriculture from 1980 to 1985. Leaders of the farming industry (CFU and the powerful Zimbabwe Tobacco Association, ZTA) had easy access to Cabinet ministers, and even the president, and were able to influence agrarian policies.[28] Party big men mingled with whites in various business ventures. While staying away from active politics, especially opposition parties, white farmers often contributed to ZANU-PF election campaigns either in money or in kind—providing transport and food for meetings held on their farms or nearby. Some farmers and businessmen boasted friendly relations with some cabinet ministers or governors as if it constituted a life insurance policy.

The hatred speech against the whites, which became routine after 2000, was not utterly new and was in line with the search for scapegoats such as "imperialism" and the West to hide the regime's failures over the years. Whenever the ruling party's grip on power was remotely threatened, the hostility would quickly resurface with threats and abusive language. For example, at the peak of the students' movement in October 1989, Mugabe accused white University of Zimbabwe lecturers of "belonging to Ian Smith," of feeding the young blacks with propaganda, and of plotting to "destroy the government."[29] Ironically most of these white academics were initially staunch supporters of majority rule and ZANU-PF. When Edgar Tekere launched the Zimbabwe Unity Movement (ZUM) in the run-up to the 1990 general election, Mugabe branded him a "front for Apartheid forces." The then information minister Nathan Shamuyarira threatened the whites for allegedly funding ZUM's candidates. Mugabe stated bluntly: "If the whites in Zimbabwe want to rear their ugly terrorist and racist head by collaborating with ZUM, we will chop that head off."[30] Since 1980 white activists opposing the government have received more than their share of abuse, as was the case with FORUM party candidates in 1995. The political tensions over the amended Land Acquisition Act (1992) had also led ZANU-PF leaders to slip into racist, abusive language.

Although the president pretended to accept the referendum results on television, the "No" vote in the referendum underlined his fast dwindling popularity and called for a strategy to spare the ruling party a crushing defeat in the following parliamentary elections. Indeed the farm invasions began almost immediately,[31] and Mugabe hastened to bless the movement in his televised birthday interview on 20 February. From the outset, it was obvious that the land drama was neither a spontaneous social movement[32] nor a radical move to solve the land issue once and for all, but rather an example of political manipulation hiding the planned violent assault against the political opposition. This became increasingly obvious with Mugabe's rebuttals of foreign donors' numerous overtures, from the British in May 2000 and September 2001—including assurances that £37 million were immediately available for a peaceful and legal land reform—as well as from the high level UNDP mission sent by UN secretary general Kofi Annan, which recommended a return to the September 1998 agreement. The Zimbabwe government had many opportunities to backtrack on the land issue if Mugabe so wanted.

The 2000 farm invasions were strikingly different from the localized incidents of squatting by landless peasants that took place shortly after independence and again in the 1990s, when rural areas felt the brunt of the 1992 drought and later, the impact of ESAP. In the past, the police had forcibly evicted spontaneous squatters coming from adjacent communal areas, sometimes without the need for the farmer to go to court, with a government reiterating its adherence to property rights and the rule of law.[33] In 2000 the farm invasions went on all over the country, following a concerted plan superseding local initiatives.[34] They were coordinated by War Vets, police, and CIO officers[35] using state resources, and they received extensive and favorable coverage in the state media. Rather than being disavowed and lambasted by the ruling party leaders, land invaders were overtly sponsored by Cabinet ministers,[36] and the operations were planned by a secret committee comprising Mugabe's closest aides. The president and his ministers condoned the violence against white farmers (they claimed against all available evidence that the victims had provoked the War Vets), and cold-blooded murders became an all too frequent component of the modus operandi in sharp contrast to previous squatting experiences.

While the previous squatter phenomenon was directly linked to local conflicts over land, from the outset the 2000 farm invasions assumed another dimension. Although the rhetoric emphasized the belated conclusion of the "liberation struggle" and the need to deliver the land to those who fought for it, there were more sinister motives. Attacking the farms became part of a ZANU-PF strategy aimed at crushing the opposition. Some white farmers and businessmen backed the broad multi-stakeholder and trans-class-based coalition that the MDC had crystallized, and this was precisely what Mugabe wanted to break. Indeed local War Vet ringleaders who spearheaded the occupations were also the main perpetrators of violence against MDC candidates and supporters in the run-up to the June parliamentary elections. Labeling such campaigns the "Third Chimurenga" was an attempt to link it to the past anticolonial struggle and justify the War Vets' role—the subtext being that some violence against civilians was deemed justifiable during a war (see Chapter 2).

In many places communal farmers were conspicuously absent from the invaded farms, especially during the first few months, although they were the alleged beneficiaries of the land reform. Among those eventually seen on the farms, in particular after April 2000, many had been coerced to join the movement by War Vets and ZANU-PF officials. Many of the genuine farmers trickled back to the communal areas in 2001 and 2002 when it became obvious they had been dumped on the farms without tools and other necessities, not even a functioning well to get some drinkable water, and with no hint of the legal status of their newly owned plots. Indeed, many resettled black peasants were evicted in late 2002 or 2003 to make room for ZANU-PF big men, who were taking advantage of the final phase of the landgrab. Black farmworkers in most instances did not join the invaders and they remained loyal to their employers, sometimes even attempting to evict the War Vets. Although exploitation and racism did exist on white-owned commercial farms, most owners provided decent living conditions for their employees—by African standards and compared with what they would have obtained in many communal areas. The most active pro-MDC white farmers—such as Roy Bennett—had established better working relations and militancy created a new bond across the race divide.[37] In addition, many black farm owners had a worse record, and the newspapers occasionally reported squalid conditions and labor disputes on commercial farms owned by ZANU-PF big men.[38] Black farmworkers were immediately the target of abuse and intimidation, what War Vets labeled "political re-education," in order to foster a stronger racial polarization that suited government propaganda.

Farm occupations were declared illegal by the High Court on 17 March 2000, and the police were ordered to move onto the farms to evict the invaders within seventy-two hours.[39] Police Commissioner Chihuri first alleged that he did not have the manpower to evict the War Vets—although less than a few thousand were permanently staying on the farms. He subsequently argued that the occupation was a political matter needing a political solution in spite of a renewed court order. Although the home affairs minister Dumiso Dabengwa claimed in early March that the white farmers enjoyed the protection of the law, he was contradicted the same day by Mugabe, who stated that he would not stop the "peaceful demonstrations" by the War Vets on the farms. When the latter began to commit murders on the farms the High Court urged the president on 13 April to abide by court judgments and order the police to act.[40] Mugabe rebuked the judges and declared that the land was not a matter to be solved by the courts, a reminder of earlier statements of the same kind.[41] All these and subsequent orders by the High Court and the Supreme Court were ostensibly ignored by the government and the police. Although the constitutional draft rejected in February was dropped, Mugabe made sure that the controversial land clause was inserted in the Lancaster House constitution through Amendment No. 16 (Act 5 of 2000)—passed before the general election—with its claim of the British government's obligation to compensate the farmers. The Land Acquisition Act was subsequently amended in late May 2000, using provisions from the Presidential Powers Act, in an attempt to give a legal basis to the "fast-track" resettlement program that had begun in the form of a chaotic occupation of the farms. Finally, Amendment No. 17, passed on 30 August 2005, made constitutional the acquisition of all farmland without compensation and without legal recourse for the commercial farmers for "whatever purpose." The ZANU-PF government effectively relieved itself of the difficulties of implementing its own legislation.

Despite government's propaganda about the "land hunger" in the country, findings from various surveys draw a starkly different picture. Zimbabweans do not make land redistribution a priority: only 30 percent of respondents in a nationwide survey in January 2000 supported the compulsory acquisition of white farmers' land to facilitate land reform and a large majority of the people were against it, including respondents who said they would vote for ZANU-PF in the following elections.[42] A study of rural poverty in Zimbabwe conducted in 1995 and endorsed by the government suggested that access to land was a priority for only 2 percent of communal area peasants and 3 percent in resettlement areas. On the contrary, access to cheap loans, tillage, and low-cost irrigation was seen by these farmers as paramount to increase the agricultural output. Land distribution was rated among the least important items, far behind access to formal employment—a widespread aspiration among the rural youth—as a means to fight rural poverty.[43] Zimbabwe's communal farmers know very well, after twenty years of resettlement experiments, that the land is nothing without the means to

farm it. This is why it was easier for Mugabe's henchmen to enlist destitute urban people with no farming experience in the land invasion
instead of genuine communal farmers. Throughout the first months,
hired farm invaders received a daily allowance, and some got tents, blan-
kets, and food from the ZNLWVA, army, or local authorities.

The farming community showed much restraint and did not recipro-
cate violence despite repeated provocations and murders.[44] Unfortunately that moderation was taken as a show of weakness by the regime.
Not only was justice never rendered to the families of the murdered
farmers but even those who preached a conciliatory attitude eventually
lost everything. Since the beginning of the farm invasions in 2000, the
CFU leadership was unable to work out a cogent strategy, alternating
between negotiating with the government in the hope of limiting the
extent of the damage and taking legal action to defend the rights of
the farmers.[45] Initially, only a minority of farmers felt the brunt of the
invasions, others went on with their business and even planted 10 percent more wheat in 2001 compared to 2000. Outside the few MDC active
members and a handful of ZANU-PF-connected individuals, most farmers vowed to remain apolitical, but they largely misunderstood what was
really happening. They failed to learn from past experience and always
expected a return to normalcy. Typical of this wishful thinking was Colin
Cloete's attempt to adopt a low profile in order to "go around the presidential election" and buy some time.[46] The CFU chairman, elected in
August 2001, was convinced that "land reform" was a political gimmick
meant to win Mugabe a new term of office. The biggest farmers, many
of whom had invested in other countries in the region, and particularly
leaders of the Zimbabwe Tobacco Association (ZTA) publicly rejected a
"confrontational" and "political" attitude on the part of white farmers,
with the obvious calculated intention of saving their own farms. Therefore, in May 2001 the CFU endorsed the Joint Resettlement Initiative
(JRI) sponsored by ZANU-PF's friends—themselves farm owners—Nick
Swanepoel and John Bredenkamp. The technical proposal was realistic
but the initiative was politically damaging. The contrite admission that
"the organized farming community had contributed to the impasse with
Government" was unwarranted. Besides, the pledge that "CFU would
not pursue further litigation against Government" put the farmers in a
weak bargaining position.[47] The JRI petered out after a couple of highly
publicized meetings with Vice President Joseph Msika, when it became
clear that Mugabe was not at all interested in a compromise. According
to the CFU, a total of five million hectares—one million to be handed
over immediately—were offered to the government for resettlement,
but the proposal was scoffed at. JRI promoters failed to take into
account the desperate nature of Mugabe's strategy and his pressing

need for more land as a resource for his grandstanding acts of patronage.

When the land grab accelerated after the presidential election in 2002, it became clear to many that the CFU leadership's compromising approach had completely failed. Justice for Agriculture (JAG) was formed in June of that year as a breakaway from the CFU to fight the evictions in court. At the CFU's 59th annual congress in early August 2002, Cloete disowned JAG and sheepishly claimed that CFU leaders still wished for dialogue with the government.[48] The CFU dissociated itself from the court cases supported by JAG. This split within the farming community sprang from differences not only over correct strategy but also over some fundamental values. As early as 2000 the MDC had begged the white farmers to stand for their rights and show that they were prepared to uphold the law and constitutional principles of the country they belonged to. By doing so in a polarized society JAG had aligned itself de facto with the opposition and civil society fighting for democracy, while the CFU leaders remained, to the end, blinded by the hope of safeguarding their property and continuing farming. They resorted to their traditional tactic of sponsoring ZANU-PF election campaigns in order to buy protection.[49] But this lame-duck attitude did not always protect them from occupation and seizure. In 2004 JAG was still calling on the demoralized white farmers to stay on in Zimbabwe to help rebuild the country when the political conditions would become more favorable, but the farmers' resistance had become irrelevant. Those who, after the presidential election, attempted to compromise by negotiating a subdivision of farmland and the downsizing of their operations were no more successful in the long run.[50]

As early as June 2000, during the parliamentary elections campaign, and the following December, at a ZANU-PF congress, Mugabe had vowed to take all the land owned by the "white devils," but he waited until after the 2002 presidential election to implement this project in full. The return of the army from the DRC and the need to reward loyal military cadres provided another incentive to move forward. Following an amendment to the Land Acquisition Act rushed through Parliament in May that year, a first wave of 2,900 white farmers received eviction orders. Farmers were forbidden to tend their lands and take care of their livestock after 24 June. By midnight on 8 August 2002 they were to surrender their farms, including the homestead, to the government without any financial compensation. According to JAG, 1,740 white farmers decided to stay put and fight the orders in court, but the government threatened to arrest them (a few were indeed arrested and fined) and send them to jail. Some farmers won their cases in the Administrative the High Court. For example, Justice Charles Hungwe ruled on 7

August 2002 that a mortgaged farm might not be seized if the mortgage company had not been served with the same notice as the farmer, since creditors who had been given title deeds as security had the first claim to the farm. JAG also brought test cases questioning the constitutionality of the May amendment to the Act but they were never heard in the Supreme Court. The government hastened to amend the Act once again in September 2002.

Besides, in most cases the farm invaders and the police alike contemptuously ignored the court orders. In any case Mugabe had warned that the government would only comply with court decisions when they were deemed acceptable to the state. Some white farmers were ordered at gunpoint to vacate their properties, whether or not the farm was actually listed and the farmer had actually received his eviction notice. As the year went on the process became more anarchical and arbitrary. Instead of being conducted in accordance with the existing legislation by the Agricultural Land Settlement Board, the allocations were made by Land Task Force committees chaired by provincial governors and nationally by the minister of local government, Ignatius Chombo. Political interference was rife and the process was deeply corrupt, since members of the Land Task Force committees began with granting themselves some farms (see below). Moreover, the beneficiaries received "allocation" letters signed by the minister of agriculture that were of no legal effect. Title deeds were not properly transferred (except for about a hundred farms) because the government to speed up the acquisition had circumvented the lengthy legal procedure. Thus scores of people were "officially" resettled on land to which they had no rights. However, in 2006 the government legalized these acquisitions through ninety-nine-year leases that would provide security of tenure while the government retained the ultimate right to reallocate the land.

The land reform debate had been dominated, during the 1990s, by the issue of fair compensation for the white farmers. However, the violence directed toward the white farmers and their black workers and the unlawfulness of the "fast-track" program whereby the government violated its own legislation, even before the ink was dry, have offset this alleged focal point. ZANU-PF propagandists repeatedly claimed that it was a war—the Third Chimurenga—hence the need to keep their supporters upbeat by pointing at the enemy and keeping the conflict seemingly intractable (from the outset the British government made clear it would not accede to Mugabe's blackmail, not only because of the large sums involved but as a matter of principle). The freezing of donor support gave the Zimbabwe government a ready excuse to seize the farms without payment. The farmers' passive resistance and the confrontational atmosphere seemed to justify the case for breaking the law "for a good cause." Yet behind this politicized land expropriation and beyond its instrumental use for election purposes, there was the largest asset-grabbing exercise ever conducted in the country's history.

The Indecent Landgrab by the ZANU-PF Elite

After the presidential election and the May 2002 acceleration of farm confiscations there was a rush to the rural areas as anybody with some leverage in the state or the party apparatus claimed a farm, and top ZANU politicians were busy accumulating several of the best ones. Those ministers, Politburo members and generals who had already received leases at very low rentals in the previous phases of the land-grabbing saga also came for a second helping. By mid-2002, the list of land predators read like a ZANU-PF who's who: the two vice presidents, most ministers, deputy ministers, permanent secretaries, MPs, governors, provincial and district administrators, generals, CIO chiefs, police officers, ambassadors (Zimbabwe's envoy to Washington Simbi Mubako), connected businessmen such as Enoch Kamushinda, ZNLWVA leadership, and quite often members of their families. Also on the list was a prominent bootlicker and ZBC presenter, so partisan he could not set foot in Harare townships without being assaulted by the public. Farms were also allocated to pro-Mugabe ex-Anglican bishop Norbert Kunonga and the top civil servants suspected of organizing the electoral fraud, Dr. Mariyawanda Nzuwah, chairman of the Election Directorate and the Public Service Commission, and Tobaiwa Mudede, registrar general.

The greed was greatest among the top echelon of the ruling party. Grace Mugabe received a farm with a twenty-seven-room mansion worth an estimated U.S.$100 million.[51] Of course, Grace and Robert Mugabe's siblings and their respective offspring got the lion's share, including the first lady's brother Reward Simbarashe Marufu, who had made a killing in the plundering of the War Victims Compensation Fund in the 1990s. Marufu grabbed Leopardvlei Farm from Bob Duncan and violently expelled the 200 farm workers on 23 July 2002. Menacing people with a gun like a common criminal, the president's brother-in-law had the workers' huts and belongings burned down by his security guards and some ZANU-PF youths. The ruling elite indulged in a desperate looting frenzy, which had little to do with any rational policy to restructure the ownership of agricultural land. With the collapse of the economy, there were less state resources left for Mugabe to reward his patrimonial clients. Land was a convenient accessible asset left for patronage, and the president announced in August 2002 that officers who fought in the DRC would also receive a piece of land.[52] Although Mugabe claimed that the land reform had been completed by December 2002, and the government encouraged remaining white farmers to plant (with a guarantee of no political interference) to alleviate food shortages, the seizure of almost all remaining white-owned farms, some as small as 60 hectares, went on up to now, although at a slower pace.[53]

Squatters on invaded farms began to realize that they had been used to spearhead the farm invasions for the ruling elite's benefit. Prominent politicians loyal to Mugabe now control scores of farms illegally acquired, while many poor blacks are stranded on arid stretches of land without adequate water or sanitation. As Wilfred Mhanda of the Liberators' Platform hinted, "all the prime land [was] for the politicians and their cronies."[54] Besides, by late 2002 and through 2003 ZANU-PF big men who coveted particular farms got the War Vets and peasants who had been squatting on them since 2000 or 2001 forcibly evicted, sometimes with the help of the riot police or the army. This development dramatically highlighted the lack of tenure security on the land redistributed under the "fast-track" program. In the worst of these incidents five thousand settlers were told to vacate eleven farms in Zvimba District to pave the way for members of Mugabe's family, including his sister Sabina, on land reclaimed in 2000 by Chief Nyavira and his clan with government approval.[55] This shows how the ruling class cynically understood ZANU-PF's own slogan "empowering the people."

Moreover, few of the alleged new owners began farming in spite of the government's threat to repossess the farms if left idle. Not only are most of them without any agricultural skill or sense of farming vocation, but they often lack the capital required to engage in large-scale farming. Besides, the possession of a farm is an element of prestige for the elite dubbed "weekend farmers," and many were interested in land only as collateral to secure loans from the banks. They found it difficult to obtain new lines of credit as the farms had been mortgaged to the banks by their previous owners, and title deeds had not been properly transferred. Judging from past experience altogether there is little hope of seeing a dynamic, "indigenous" commercial agriculture emerging from this process: ZANU-PF big men who have received farms in the last twenty years were, for the most part, thoroughly incompetent managers and used their rural properties as weekend retreats rather than as holdings for agricultural production. Incidentally, the implementation of the Land Acquisition Act's criterion for underutilized and derelict properties led to the designation for compulsory acquisition of 20 black-owned farms in 1992 and 250 more in 1997. Of course, the indigenization lobby succeeded in getting them delisted. In the same vein, black commercial farmers from ICFU—then chaired by a member of Mugabe's family—lobbied the government in May 1998 to stop the introduction of a tax on underutilized land (when the white-dominated CFU was power-less).[56] To avoid dereliction and abandonment, some of the self-proclaimed new commercial farmers have resolved to rent out their farms to agribusinesses. For example, FSI Agricom Holdings has entered contractual agreements with about 400 War Vets, ZANU-PF officials, and political businessmen to operate their farms obtained through the "fast-track" land reform in exchange for a rental payment.[57] Far from herald-ing the emergence of a new agrarian class this is a typical rent-seeking behavior.

The public scandal caused by the indecent landgrab by government and senior ZANU-PF officials prompted Mugabe to order an audit. Pre-liminary findings put together by Flora Buka, minister of state for the land reform program, were leaked to the international press before hav-ing been discussed in cabinet.[58] Her report confirmed that people already resettled have been illegally displaced as well-connected indige-nous businessmen acquired the farms. Matumwa Mawere's company FSI Agricom was cited as an example. Ministers were accused of using their influence over district land committees to have certain properties listed and then allotted to them in total violation of the stipulated policy. ZANU-PF officials such as Chris Pasipamire and Mike Moyo or military officers such as Air Marshal Perence Shiri assaulted legally resettled black farmers to have them vacate the farms, which the former wanted to acquire. In the Insiza District, Sithembiso Nyoni, then minister for small and medium enterprises development, was accused in the report of having hired thugs to intimidate settlers and land committee mem-bers. Even so-called moderates such as the minister of mines Edward Chindori-Chininga took part allegedly in this free-for-all. The report mentioned that these decisions were endorsed in Mashonaland Central by Governor Elliot Manyika and presaged a feud between regional bar-ons in Mashonaland West when they could not agree among themselves in sharing the spoils. Finally the report contained a list of thirty promi-nent people who held more than one farm (including Ignatius Chombo, Sabina Mugabe, Perence Shiri, Jonathan Moyo, and assistant commissioner of police W. Bvudzijena), and pointed out that it was only the tip of the iceberg, as many people interviewed were too scared to volunteer names, fearing retaliation from these big men.

Of course, when the report was leaked, those implicated denied its authenticity and claimed it was a political maneuver (some press reports suggested that the list of offenders was carefully edited as part of ZANU-PF factional infighting). However, in July 2003 a preliminary report of the Presidential Land Review Committee, officially appointed by Mugabe and chaired by Charles Utete, confirmed that the "one man, one farm" policy had been widely abused. Subsequently Mugabe ostensibly ordered those who had acquired more than one farm to relinquish the other properties for resettlement.[59] A list compiled by the Joint Operations Committee on Land in Matabeleland North revealed the extent of the landgrab and the corrupt practices at all levels of the ruling party's hierarchy: five farms in the three southwest provinces for Kembo Mohadi, the minister of home affairs, three farms for Jonathan Moyo, two for John Nkomo, the ruling party's national chairman and minister of special affairs, and two also for Vice President Joseph Msika, and so on.[60] Although some local ZANU-PF officials might have been forced eventually to surrender some ill-acquired properties, provincial land officials interviewed by the newspaper were adamant that cabinet minister and Politburo and Central Committee member cases were to be referred directly to the president's office, thus effectively shielding Mugabe's closest allies from public scrutiny. The presidential directive merely intended to redeem the regime's shattered public image. There was no real intent to restore an orderly and legal process at a time when Mugabe's family was at the forefront of land grabbing. Besides, as opposition critics pointed out, multiple farm grabbers would have registered their properties under various family members' and friends' names, a common practice within the state bourgeoisie. The "one farm only" policy has never been seriously implemented, although it has been used to target specific individuals who had fallen into disgrace or become casualties in the factional struggle within ZANU-PF.

The Destruction of a Viable Agriculture and Economy

In addition to its violence and lawlessness, the confiscation of white-owned farms and the haphazard process of land redistribution that took place between 2000 and 2003 destroyed the commercial farming community and had a very predictable negative impact on the country's economy. Mugabe could not claim ignorance of this most predictable outcome since it was one of the major warnings advanced by Samora Machel and others in advising him not to grab the white-owned land upon independence. Therefore, the president bears personal responsibility for the ruin of Zimbabwe's economy and the food crisis that followed and is now a permanent feature. The consequences of his cynical survival politics will be felt for many years to come.

The combination of state-sponsored plunder, arbitrary violence, and the Citizenship Act (2001) had the desired effect, from ZANU-PF's viewpoint, of forcing many white farmer families to emigrate, mostly to South Africa, Australia, and New Zealand. However, some farmers resettled in neighboring Mozambique and Zambia and even Nigeria, under long-term lease contracts. Indeed these countries were eager to benefit from their farming expertise, which had sometimes accumulated through several generations. It is precisely this expertise and the knowledge of the climate and soil conditions in Zimbabwe, on the basis of which a planned, orderly land reform should have capitalized, that is now lost to the country. Contrary to Mugabe's early claims that only those with more than one farm faced eviction, JAG estimated in 2003 that 1,480 farmers who had only one farm lost it through compulsory acquisition. Another 1,200 white farmers, constituting 30 percent of the total, whose land had not been listed, were forced out of their farms. By mid-2003, according to the CFU, fewer than 400 white farmers remained on their property unaffected by the land acquisition, while another 800 had retained part of their farm and were still farming. By early 2004 the number of white farmers was down to 600 and there were renewed land seizures after the March 2005 parliamentary elections and well into 2006, bringing the number down to 300 with regional differences.[61] Those who lost their farms lost everything as they fled to the cities and then went abroad. Only a handful of them (126 exactly, according to the CFU) actually received some compensation—though the amounts were totally inappropriate—for improvements and farming equipment as provided for by the law.[62] Those farmers chased from their homesteads from August to November 2002, sometimes at gunpoint, were allowed to take only their personal belongings. Most of them were prevented from selling their crops already harvested or their cattle thus losing millions owed to the banks. Billions of Zimbabwe dollars' worth of movable assets have been illegally impounded or stolen since February 2000, and what was not looted was often vandalized, such as tobacco barns or irrigation equipment.

Commercial agriculture was Zimbabwe's biggest private employer (one-quarter of formal employment), providing accommodation for about 350,000 farmworkers and their families[63]—a total of 1.2 million people—as well as schooling for 500,000 children and basic health care. They fled for their lives when ZANU-PF militias looted and then burned down their houses. The vast majority of these workers had already been forced from their homes before the end of 2002,[64] and some went to crowded squatter camps near the cities in the hope of assistance. However, most of the displaced farm workers' families remained in the rural areas looking for food or some source of income. Some refugees fled to Malawi and Mozambique, or crossed illegally into South Africa to work for farmers there. Others were allowed to resettle in communal areas—especially in the Zambezi Valley—where they started farming activities. Even those allowed to stay in their quarters lost their jobs, as only 10 percent of the new large-scale farmers have absorbed some of the original workforce, and only 60,000 to 80,000 workers were still employed on the original commercial farms by mid-2003—and far fewer by the end of the decade.

In most cases farm workers were excluded as the beneficiaries of land redistribution either because they were perceived as supporting the white farmer or the MDC, or because they were seen as aliens (about one fifth were of Zambian, Malawian, or Mozambican descent). Away with white bosses went some social services such as health clinics and schools provided by the farmer or his spouse in places where the state was unable to do so. A statutory instrument introduced by President Mugabe before the presidential election in 2002 obliged evicted farmers to pay their farmworkers terminal benefits (though some farmers had no cash available to do so), and it was an effective tool in eroding the mutual trust and understanding between the two groups.[65] But this was only a short respite, and jobless farmworkers were exposed to starvation in 2002 and 2003 and were often excluded from food aid by the ruling party militias. The most glaring achievement of Mugabe's land policy has been to plunge this one million people into absolute poverty and hunger.

Productive land reform requires adequate funding and extensive initial support in terms of seeds, fertilizers, draft power, irrigation, and infrastructure (schools, hospitals, roads, and so on). None of this was made available to resettled farmers during the years following the land grabbing. For example, a district council administrator complained that there were only eight tractors running in the whole Makonde District in August 2002, not enough to service all "new farmers" in time for the planting season. The shortage was compounded by the lack of spares and fuel.[66] Imported tractors intended for resettled small-scale tobacco growers were snatched instead by high-ranking ZANU-PF officials and civil servants, including the president and Cabinet ministers, to service their farms or to resell at a profit (one official allegedly allotted thirty-five tractors to himself).[67] In mid-2002 it was estimated that only 20 percent of the then pegged farms—half of the total seized—were taken up by people attempting farming and most of the designated farms remained unused and for the most part derelict. Therefore, the agriculture minister Joseph Made's claim that 300,000 black farmers were resettled by the end of 2002 was absolutely fanciful: certainly less than half of this number ever began to work on their plots. The Presidential Land Review Committee's report submitted to Mugabe on 11 September 2003 established that only 130,000 peasant families had been allocated land (under the A1 scheme) on 4 million of the 11 million hectares confiscated, and 15,000 under A2 (large-scale farms).[68] In most areas land was not ready for the November 2002 planting season and by no stretch of the imagination could a bumper harvest have been expected in 2003 as Made had so foolishly boasted.

The government-proffered fiction that Zimbabwe could at least be self-sufficient without a vibrant large commercial farming sector does not stand up to the evidence, as large-scale (white) commercial farms have always been crucial in meeting the country's food security. Yet, communal areas' output increased significantly after independence—in what was hailed as an "agricultural revolution"—as the result of high agricultural prices from the state purchasing agency, the Grain Marketing Board (GMB), and subsidies provided by the state.[69] Peasant farmers' share of the maize delivered to the GMB rose from 11 percent in 1980 to a record 41 percent in 1984. However, that proportion dropped again in the 1990s. The 1992 drought was blamed but also the decline of state-provided extension services and inputs. This model was not sustainable without a high level of public expenditure no longer available under ESAP—even more so since 1997 with the economic downslide. The GMB purchase prices did not catch up with the soaring inflation of recent years, subsidies like free seeds and fertilizers or free tillage have been removed, and extension services have collapsed. Even in the peak years, only about 11 percent of the total one million communal farms produced a marketable surplus in the 1990s, with the top 8,000 producing 45 percent of the marketed crop. On average, about 50 percent of the other communal farms were just self-sufficient (far less in drought years) while the remaining 39 percent did not produce enough maize for their own consumption and either had to buy the shortfall on the market or permanently depended on drought relief handed out by the government.[70] About 20 percent of peasant farmers relied on food aid, even when harvests were excellent, and ZANU-PF has always used this as a political tool. Although low productivity among communal area farmers is usually attributed to poor soils and inadequate rainfall, there is no guarantee that these farmers would be more productive once resettled on better lands. In addition, even the better-off communal farmers are highly dependent on the rainfall while many white commercial farmers relied on expensive irrigation systems. Constructing and operating these facilities requires time, training, and capital.

In 1999, agriculture accounted for 20 percent of Zimbabwe's gross domestic product (GDP). A year later, the figure had dropped to 11 percent, and it has continued to decline: indications from farmers suggest a 50 percent fall in 2002. Tobacco production fell by an estimated 60 percent between 2000 and 2003 (tobacco export earnings well above U.S.$600 million in 1999 and 2000 had fallen to under U.S.$100 million a year in 2005). CFU's figures show that the commercial cattle industry dropped from 1.2 million head in 1999 to below 200,000 in 2003. Farmers evicted in late 2002 were forced to abandon their cattle, most of which were later slaughtered by invaders or marauding gangs while foot-and-mouth and other diseases spread throughout the country. The United Nations Food and Agriculture Organization (FAO) and World Food Programme (WFP) estimated in June 2003 that the total output of remaining large-scale commercial farms during the 2002–3 farming season was only 10 percent of what was produced in the 1990s.[71] It is estimated that there was a loss of 30 percent of the GDP between 2000 and 2005, during which the ruin of commercial agriculture and its subsequent impact on all other sectors is seen to have been the main cause: the business cycle in Zimbabwe has always been closely connected to the agricultural output. The fall of agricultural exports, which once accounted for nearly 40 percent of the total foreign currency earnings, explains in part the acute shortage of foreign exchange gripping the country since mid-2002. This, of course, was combined with the decline of the industry strangled by the government's fiscal and monetary policies and the adverse impact on tourism of Zimbabwe's international image—including some incidents of violence toward foreign visitors. The agricultural crisis also precipitated the closure of at least 3,000 companies directly or indirectly dependent on this sector. This downward spiral of the economy could have been largely avoided had the land reform been implemented according to the 1998 international agreement.

An Enduring Food Crisis

The accelerated expulsion of white farmers not only directly affected agricultural production dramatically but also worsened the impact of a severe drought during the 2001–2 farming season. The production of maize (corn)—the country's staple food—plunged by nearly 70 percent in 2002, according to the United Nations. The production of winter wheat harvested that October was down by as much as 40 percent compared to 2001, as many farmers were prevented from harvesting before leaving their confiscated farms. In 2003 the CFU estimated that the wheat production was down by 90 percent compared to 2000. The WFP estimated that almost half of Zimbabwe's 12.5 million people needed food aid until the end of the 2002–3 rainy season. Despite the government's bold assurances that newly resettled farmers would produce enough food in 2003, UN Humanitarian Assistance early estimates of agricultural production found that the country faced another 1.3 million metric ton deficit for the 2003/2004 marketing year.[72] The government had to swallow its pride in July and make an urgent appeal to the international community to assist with the importation of 700,000 metric tons of maize. By July 2003 the UN agencies warned that Zimbabwe faced a major humanitarian crisis in late 2003 early 2004, and that about 5.5 million people would need food aid until June 2004.[73] Although the situation was better by late 2004, 3.3 million people were still in need of food aid in early 2005, and Mugabe himself acknowledged the shortage of maize.[74] In August 2006 the Vulnerability Assessment Committee comprising representatives of the government, the UN Agencies and the NGOs conservatively estimated that 1.4 million people in rural areas needed food aid until the following year, as they could not purchase the maize even when available on the market.[75] In addition there were thousands of hungry poor in the cities, whose situation became dramatic in 2007–8 with the hyperinflation and the loss of value of the national currency. With good rains in late 2005, President Mugabe had boasted that Zimbabwe would no longer need international support, but the food crisis has become a permanent feature of this fast collapsing economy.

Although the climate was widely blamed for failed maize crops in 2002 (particularly in Matabeleland, the Midlands, and Masvingo provinces) and the whole Southern Africa region was affected, the land seizures and especially the atmosphere of violence and arbitrary rule surrounding them had a significant impact. The remaining white farmers were allowed to plant only a tiny proportion of their arable land—sometimes none—by aggressive squatters and ZANU-PF militias. Before the land crisis, commercial farmers produced 40 percent of Zimbabwe's maize and almost all the wheat and soybeans, as well as most of the beef, pork, poultry, and dairy products. Moreover, drought was endemic in the south and southwest of Zimbabwe, and the Grain Marketing Board (GMB) was entrusted with the task of maintaining strategic reserves of grains, but it was seriously mismanaged and failed in doing so. In 1992 a drought of the same proportion had been properly addressed—nobody died of hunger—through a combination of the GMB strategic reserves, an expansion of grain production by commercial farmers, and the timely import of supplementary grains. In the first decade of the twenty-first century the first two options were unavailable and the lack of foreign currencies for massive food imports made the situation impossible, hence the call to the international community. In this respect, the food shortage was indeed the product of Mugabe's policies, although the UN agencies claimed that only a quarter of the two-million-ton shortfall in Zimbabwe's food supply in 2002 was the direct result of the destruction of white commercial farming.

The time of trial came in 2003, with better rains—though still below normal in the southwest—but with most farms left idle by the so-called new farmers. Bread shortages worsened as the latter could not match the level of production of the former commercial farmers. The degree of disorganization in the agricultural sector was such in the winter of 2003 that only 6 percent of the usual surface was planted in wheat—50 percent for barley—according to a CFU survey. By mid-2003 it was estimated that only 23 percent of previously existing irrigation schemes, essential for winter crops, were still functioning, as a result of theft and vandalism.[76] Although the small-scale black farmers' organization ZFU claimed that many of its members planted wheat, production was limited and mainly for household consumption. Hundreds of thousands of tons of wheat had to be imported to provide for sufficient bread at a time foreign currency was increasingly scarce.[77] The UN has pointed at the government's policy of controlling food prices, which encouraged the black market in the context of rocketing inflation. Inept currency exchange rates strangled any attempt at profitable farming. However, the supply of wheat became inadequate primarily because the land under cultivation shrank significantly.

The most affected by food shortages were communal area dwellers from drought-prone regions, displaced former farm workers, and the jobless urban poor. Ironically, the beneficiaries of the "fast-track" program have not been spared the consequences of the mayhem they helped to create in Zimbabwe's productive agriculture. By mid-2002 many of the resettled peasants dumped on A1 farms suffered from hunger like most of the rural dwellers in the south and southwest, and they loudly complained that they had never received the free grain from the GMB, which the government had pledged to supply until the following harvest.[78] Although some of the resettled peasants managed to survive by resorting to traditional subsistence farming, others poached wild animals, heavily depleting this valuable resource. This was particularly true on private conservancies, which were not suitable for commercial agriculture but were meant for safari hunting and other tourist-oriented activities. Elsewhere, the slaughtering of the white farmers' cattle or the systematic felling of trees to produce wood for sale were other unfortunate means of survival, a trend on the increase in early 2004 after a third season of poor rains. By the middle of the first decade of the twenty-first century it was obvious that farm invaders' poverty and ignorance created lasting environmental damage. As one resettled farmer admitted, "Sometimes we fear the farms we got will end up barren like the reserves [communal lands] from where we came."[79]

The humanitarian crisis of food shortage was addressed by the UN agencies and did not result in millions of casualties because of Western countries' timely response to WFP calls. To speed up the distribution process a U.S.$85 million hard cash basket fund was provisionally set up in July 2002 by UNDP to provide private sector firms with foreign currency to import about 400,000 tons of food. However, Mugabe's government stopped the fund from operating, insisting on retaining the Grain Marketing Board monopoly of food importation, using the excuse that private sector companies would speculate and increase prices beyond the reach of ordinary Zimbabweans. In fact, through the GMB, Mugabe's supporters were able to control the allocation of the staple food (mealie meal)[80] in the country. Besides, the food crisis was perceived by cynical ZANU-PF big men as a potential profit-making opportunity. Shuvai Mahofa, the deputy minister of youth development, gender, and employment creation, was accused of buying GMB-subsidized maize to sell for a huge profit on the black market.[81] A few select companies owned by political cronies were licensed to import food into the country.[82] The insistence of the government on retaining its monopoly of maize and wheat imports and marketing has been an aggravating factor in the recurrent food crisis.

The United States had donated 17,500 metric tons of corn that was blocked in Durban for several weeks in July 2002 because Harare claimed it was genetically altered. It was finally delivered through the WFP to the government to be milled before distribution.[83] Obviously Mugabe's aides did not take kindly to donors' demands that the grain should be delivered to starving Zimbabweans through NGOs when the government insisted on controlling distribution. The real stake behind this diplomatic row was the ruling party's ability to use hunger as a political weapon.[84] ZANU-PF officials doling out food favored the party faithful, while families of MDC members or alleged supporters were denied access to cheap grain. Either the militias prevented them from buying the grain from the GMB (in Masvingo, Mhondoro in Mashonaland West, Gokwe, and Matabeleland South),[85] or they blocked feeding programs implemented by Western donor agencies for high-risk groups (in Binga and Insiza).[86] In mid-October 2002, the WFP suspended food aid in Insiza District, citing political interference with food distribution ahead of the parliamentary by-election: ZANU-PF had seized three tons of maize from the international agency to distribute to government supporters.[87] Headmen were asked also to exclude MDC supporters when drawing WFP feeding lists. Children from families perceived as pro-MDC were excluded from the feeding scheme put in place in rural schools, although local and foreign NGOs attempted to defeat this maneuver. In several districts MDC supporters were also excluded from government-sponsored "money/food for work" schemes or were cheated at the time of payment.

This political manipulation of food was widespread, as it has been documented for eighteen districts and urban centers in five provinces. It was directly linked to parliamentary by-elections or rural district council elections in September 2002.[88] The blackmail was quite blatant: vote for ZANU-PF or be starved to death, and in several districts food was used for vote buying. This ostracism also applied to black farm workers still employed by a white farmer.[89] Similar methods were used in the past by the government to fight an enduring opposition: for example, food was withheld from Matabeleland in 1984, during a severe drought, as part of the terror tactics against the PF-ZAPU support base. The politicization of food aid was used again before the 2002 presidential election, the 2005 parliamentary election, and ahead of the 2008 harmonized election, with ZANU-PF youths supervising the distribution of maize in the rural areas and some ZANU-PF candidates threatening that the communities would not get food if they voted for the MDC.[90]

Although the invasion of white-owned farms played a key role in Mugabe's political survival strategy and was the curtain raiser for the broader confrontation with local and international opponents, the land issue was not at the core of the crisis, as many foreigners were led to believe. The deadlock in Zimbabwe's land reform program, which was largely the product of years of government mismanagement and neglect,[91] could have been amicably and rationally resolved on the basis of the 1998 stakeholder conference agreement. As a matter of fact, the Third Chimurenga was not about land reform but was primarily a propaganda act. It conveniently obfuscated the violence against the opposition in a cloud of "revolutionary" posturing, and purported to convince the rural masses that ZANU-PF was, at last, fulfilling the promises of the liberation war. From the punitive farm invasions to fix the white "enemies," to the politicization of food aid to "teach MDC supporters a lesson," it was Mugabe's political survival that was at stake, not the needs of "land hungry" peasants.

A secondary objective was the appropriation of some of the best farms by the ruling elite and its clientele, as a means to solidify state bourgeoisie support for Mugabe and make up for the overall economic meltdown. It is significant that in spite of the rehashed revolutionary rhetoric in government circles, the largest land estates owned by transnational corporations or foreign businessmen with political or economic leverage—such as Nicholas van Hoogstraten and the Oppenheimer family—were barely affected.[92] Some of them were in business partnerships with ZANU-PF politicians; others had the means to strike a mutually beneficial deal with the government.

As the evictions continued unabated until after the 2008 elections, seventy-nine white farmers turned toward the SADC human rights tribunal based in Windhoek. It ruled on 28 November 2008 that Zimbabwe land seizures were discriminatory—on the basis of race—and unfair for lack of compensation, and therefore against international law including several SADC treaties.[93] Naturally, the Zimbabwe government did not recognize the tribunal's jurisdiction and went on with its landgrab. When challenged, the High Court and Supreme Court stated the country's constitution took precedence over the SADC tribunal ruling—a clear rebuff of Harare's propaganda on land reform since 2000. Zimbabwe's neighbors were no longer deceived.

As a whole, Mugabe's survival tactics played havoc in the agricultural sector and generated a structural food crisis and unprecedented suffering, sending thousands into exile. Food aid has become a permanent element of Zimbabwe's political economy as the FAO announced in June 2008 that this agricultural year was the worst since 1992. In spite of the president's populist claims, Zimbabwe's poor have been the most affected by a retrogressive policy perpetrated in the name of the masses.[94]

Chapter 7

The State Bourgeoisie and the Plunder of the Economy

It is difficult to reconcile Stephen Chan's recollection of the simple life-style in 1980 of Teurai Ropa (Joyce Mujuru) and her husband Rex Nhongo (General Solomon Mujuru)[1] and their current position as prominent businesspeople.[2] In their own way they exemplify the success of the ZANU-PF elite. In the early literature on Zimbabwe great emphasis is put on the nationalist/socialist project carried by both guerrilla movements ("pro-Russian" ZAPU and "pro-Chinese" ZANU), and a great deal of intellectual debate focused in the 1980s on whether or not ZANU-PF had engaged Zimbabwe on the path of a socialist revolution. Most observers then took at face value the black nationalist elite's ostentatious revolutionary commitment and egalitarian ethos.[3] That ruling party leaders genuinely sought socioeconomic development and the welfare of the masses, as illustrated by the high levels of public spending in health and education, was a rarely questioned creed. It was largely assumed that Zimbabwe would not fall in postcolonial Africa's common predicament: political elites' predatory behavior backed by a variable degree of authoritarian rule.

If the matter was still debatable, perhaps, in the late 1990s, when corruption became ominous in several economic sectors, though not generalized to all, there must be a consensus today that the ruling ZANU-PF mafia and its crony capitalists are busy looting what is left of the national assets. Zimbabwe's ranking in the Transparency International Corruption Perception Index fell from 43rd in 1998 to 65th in 2000 and 166th in 2008. Extortion is part of everyday survival strategies, including at police roadblocks. No compelling structural factor can be blamed for the ongoing destruction of the economy. Whatever may be said about the dreadful legacy of colonialism, the confrontational apartheid era, the constraints of the Cold War until 1989, or even the structural imbalances of the international economic system, in the early 1980s Zimbabwe enjoyed one of the most promising economies in Africa with fairly good infrastructures, an efficient public administration and a well-trained manpower. By late 2003 already, what was left was the fastest-shrinking economy in the world,[4] a wrecked state ignoring the law and derelict public infrastructures. From June 2003 on there was an illegal foreign exchange (black) market and roaring inflation. Since then the economy went from bad to worse.

Was such an outcome so unexpected? Policy mistakes and bad management—which could be seen as accidental—are not convincing explanations. Rather, we focus on the behavior of the elite in the pursuit of absolute power and self-enrichment. Zimbabwe is no exception in a postcolonial Africa where the "big men"[5] logic prevailed in the context of the neopatrimonial state. However, one should not underestimate the specificities of each African country, the various mix of patrimonialization versus institutionalization, and the diversity of historical trajectories. The case of Zimbabwe is interesting inasmuch as the process was delayed by the late decolonization and the relatively high degree of institutionalization of the state, including an independent judiciary, on the eve of majority rule. The nascent but determined civic organizations and the buoyant private sector whose property rights were entrenched in the Lancaster House constitution were additional obstacles in the path of the new elite.

After independence, the top echelon of the black nationalists, as well as their dependents and clients, slowly emerged as a kind of "state bourgeoisie,"[6] taking advantage of its control of state resources, and whose greed and recklessness became more ominous in the late 1980s once the ruling party's hegemony was no longer seriously challenged. However, in the 1990s, the growing crisis of public finances and the new call for economic liberalization provoked a change in tactics: "indigenization" of the private sector became the new vehicle of this accumulation drive at a time when "straddling" positions[7] in the private sector and the government or the parastatals became more systematic. After August 1998, Zimbabwe business interests in the DRC signaled a new stage in this process with Mafia-like behavior spreading fast among ZANU-PF elites (whether in the political, economic, or military sectors). All along the monopolistic control of political power was decisive for the success of such capital accumulation.

The Patronage Benefits of the "Command Economy"

Whether or not they sincerely embraced Marxism as a creed and the building of socialism as a strategic objective most of the nationalist leaders were part of the emerging African petty bourgeoisie of the 1950s and 1960s, with a strong component comprised of former mission schoolteachers (such as Mugabe himself), nurses, and low-ranking civil servants,[8] frustrated like many other educated blacks in their aspirations to upward social mobility by the segregationist policies of white Rhodesia. Therefore, entering nationalist politics was perceived in the late 1960s as the fastest way to acquire a better social and economic status. The subsequent accumulation strategies were rooted in these early—largely legitimate—grievances. One of the many effects of the 1970s' armed struggle was to harden the determination of the nationalists to acquire wealth through the conquest of the state. The social and economic deprivation that many blacks had experienced during colonial and UDI years ostensibly justified their self-serving claim that political liberation should be followed by economic liberation.

The black nationalist elite had every reason to believe that the control of the state was crucial, since government played a strong role in the white settler society and in particular had supported the development of the farming and the industrial sectors through specific financial and structural policies. ZANU-PF's official socialist ideology conveniently justified a stronger direct and indirect control of the national economy in the 1980s. However, and in spite of the wartime rhetoric advocating state control of the means of production, Mugabe's government did not significantly alter the capitalist structure of the economy, and it tolerated a large private sector in white hands. This benevolent attitude was attributed to the widely celebrated reconciliation policy, which had earned Zimbabwe a windfall of foreign aid and was hailed as an unexpected display of "economic realism."[9] Mugabe apparently took advice from president Samora Machel of Mozambique, who had seen the disastrous results of the forced exodus of white settlers from his country in 1975, but also from transitional British governor Lord Soames.[10] Taking a long-term perspective, the preservation of a large, white-controlled private sector within Zimbabwe's mixed economy would mean that economic opportunities could be generated for the emerging black elites. As a matter of fact the socialist transformation of Zimbabwe's economy was not the new elite's primary objective, regardless of the redundant rhetoric.

A bloated public sector was, above all, a valuable resource for Mugabe's political patronage, as it offered plenty of lucrative positions for party cadres, political cronies, and family members. Through state intervention in various economic sectors, new opportunities were created for members of the ruling class to enrich themselves and position themselves for co-option. A large body of inefficient, sometimes counter-productive parastatals regulated the trade of commodities (grain, beef, dairy products, gasoline, and so on), and the ZANU-PF government seized control of various industrial and financial conglomerates at every opportunity,[11] using various techniques to persuade British or South African companies to sell their local subsidiaries to the government. Currency regulations were enforced to prevent foreign-owned companies from repatriating profits. Wage and pricing policies were used to squeeze foreign investors who could no longer run their businesses profitably. For example, Lancaster Steel, formerly a subsidiary of British Steel, relied on state-owned Zimbabwe Iron and Steel Company (ZISCO) for its supply of raw steel. The government exerted pressure by fixing the price at which Lancaster bought from ZISCO and the price at which it could sell its own products, and by enforcing workers' wage increases. Soon Lancaster Steel ran into huge losses and British Steel had no other option but to sell it at a low price to the state and Lancaster Steel was then merged with ZISCO.[12] A severe tax regime was used to dissuade foreign investors from competing with government-owned companies.[13] Some of these regulations had been introduced by Ian Smith's regime in the 1970s in the context of a wartime economy but should have been repelled in a postwar context when sustained growth—hence a high investment rate—was imperative in order for the ZANU-PF government to cope with a rapidly expanding population.

The rationale for drawing on state financial resources was the liberation war: those who had sacrificed for the struggle deserved some significant reward and should be the first to benefit from privileged access to government employment and black empowerment, not yet described as "indigenization" as it would be in the 1990s. Yet, many of those who benefited from political patronage had no war record at all. In contrast, some genuine "freedom fighters" got nothing beyond their quickly spent demobilization package in the early 1980s—until the infamous indemnities and pensions granted in 1997. Furthermore to enjoy the spoils of the struggle one had to toe the correct political line. When ZAPU's leadership was expelled from government in early 1982 and its army commanders jailed, Mugabe confiscated farms belonging to the party, bought originally to resettle ZIPRA's demobilized guerrillas. Only a few were reluctantly returned to their former owners after the so-called Unity Accord of 1987. While ZANU-PF former guerrillas tended to help each other, those who were not part of the patronage system found it difficult to survive in post-Independence Zimbabwe.

Although socialism was little more than a rhetorical objective as stated above, the nationalist elite used the Marxist-Leninist jargon to castigate the old black "petty bourgeoisie," that is, the small group of pre-Independence African entrepreneurs.[14] Although some of them had financially supported the National Democratic Party (the parent organization of ZAPU) in the early 1960s, the ZANU leaders had no sympathy for the blacks running successful businesses—however modest—while the nationalists were in exile or "in the bush." Moreover, the nationalists' aim to capture the economy through state control could only conflict with these entrepreneurs' vision of a market economy with few, if any, regulations in terms of consumer prices and workers' rights and wages. The populist-oriented labor policies of ZANU-PF in the first half of the 1980s, when the wages were raised and the Congress of Trade Unions (ZCTU) set up, made that ideological conflict more apparent. Not surprisingly, the much publicized but half-hearted promotion of small and medium-scale black businesses through the Small Enterprise Development Corporation (SEDCO) that the government ostensibly pursued during the same period produced no significant results.[15] The government did not remove all pre-existing Rhodesian limitations to the growth of African businesses and took no positive steps (in terms of tax exemptions or a better access to credit) to promote the advancement of the black entrepreneurs.[16] These entrepreneurs with an independent power base were perceived as a potential political threat to patronage-minded ZANU-PF leaders.

But the nationalist elite was not hostile to business per se, on the contrary: Eddison Zvobgo made no secret of his businesses in Masvingo; the two vice presidents Muzenda and Nkomo and the army chief Mujuru[17] were also, though more discreetly, up to their eyebrows in business ventures soon after independence. Through the years names of ministers, MPs, Central Committee members, and high-ranking civil servants would appear on lists of board members of private companies published in the press (especially in mining, tourism, and the financial sector).[18] Some of them would just eat up their share of the cake while some others were astute enough to use these lucrative positions to quick start their wealth accumulation. However, as Hevina Dashwood correctly points out, it is difficult to document this process because properties and equity owned by members of the ruling elite are most often registered under the names of friends or relatives,[19] a practice condemned by the party's Leadership Code solemnly adopted in 1984 ostensibly to prevent political corruption. Contrary to neo-Marxist authors who lament this "embourgeoisement of the ruling elite," we contend that this self-enrichment is not at variance with the actual ethos of nationalist leaders prior to independence. What is more problematic is the fact that the control of the state gave them undue advantage over potential competitors and freed them from the constraints of established rules and the observance of the law. Successive economic policies were twisted to suit these sectional interests and corrupt practices spread from the top echelon downward; these are more striking indictments of this accumulation process than the alleged betrayal of socialist ideals.

As the decade unfolded, retired civil servants and ZANU-PF politicians were recruited during the 1980s as middlemen for white-owned corporations at a time when political connections in the state apparatus had become vital to operate a business in an economic environment ridden with all kinds of regulations and state interventions. Middlemen typically would obtain an import license or a foreign currency permit in the name of some genuine entrepreneurs. Some of these politically connected middlemen were subsequently co-opted as junior partners in the same companies to help clear the way through state bureaucracy while keeping operational costs at a manageable level.

An unlikely "alliance between white settlers and the state,"[20] or, more precisely, between top echelons of the government and the ruling party and a number of white businessmen and farmers, built up during the 1980s. Despite some differences over policy issues—and sometimes public controversy—between business representatives and the government, ZANU-PF big men were willing to strike deals with big business. Numerous personal links developed between members of the embryonic black state bourgeoisie and the white corporate sector. Some white businessmen acting as intermediaries between international capital and the government collected generous kickbacks and successfully befriended ZANU-PF ministers until 2000. In discreet backrooms of exclusive clubs the members of the new political elite and some former diehard "Rhodies" (farmers, business leaders, or sanction busters) entered into deals such as political patronage in exchange for board membership or business opportunities. This situation developed to the extent that in the early 1990s a merger between white and black elites appeared as a plausible scenario for the development of a postindependence ruling class.

A special mention is required for Zidco, the holding company that operated officially as the economic arm of the ZANU-PF leadership. Formed soon after independence as a joint venture between Asian businessmen based in London and M&S Syndicate, created in 1979 to manage the assets (including about fifty real estate properties in various countries) of the Muzenda and Sumbureru families.[21] Zidco's operations are not usually publicized and the distribution of dividends remains totally unclear: as one observer noted,[22] the ruling party regularly claims to be broke and its coffers have been filled up through the years by taxpayers' money through the Ministry of Political Affairs and through the Political Party Finances Act. It is safe to assume that Zidco's dividends were not entirely lost for everybody. ZANU-PF big men packed the board of the company—in particular, Mugabe's trusted aide Emmerson Mnangagwa, chairman of M&S and Zidco holdings until 1999, and Sydney Sekeramayi, both former ministers of security in charge of the highly politicized secret service (CIO). Enos Chikowore, Didymus Mutasa, and Frederick Shava—all former or current ministers—were also listed as Zidco directors at one point.

Although Mugabe's name does not appear, it is most likely that he is on the receiving end of the dividends through M&S Syndicate. At the beginning of the 1990s, the latter holding and Zidco controlled a minimum of twelve companies and their branches in Zimbabwe provinces, with activities spreading across a wide range of economic sectors from agriculture to industry and services, employing a minimum of 10,000 people. Many of these companies had a preferential access to public tenders and posted respectable profits. During the 1990s, Zidco's conglomerate significantly expanded and diversified its activities, while acquiring minority shareholding in various more profitable local companies—about one hundred. The upward trend was sustained by the ZANU-PF big men's later business endeavors in the DRC (see below).[23] The prominent role played by Emmerson Mnangagwa in this joint effort of capital accumulation—nominally in the name of the party but in fact for the family and an array of "patrimonial servants" in Max Weber's conceptualization—underlines the pivotal role of the former head of ZANLA's intelligence in Mugabe's regime. Mnangagwa was for a long time the ruling party's treasurer. and while he was minister of justice he was appointed acting minister of finance twice (when Chidzero resigned in 1994 and when Ariston Chambati died in 1996), but not confirmed allegedly because the Bretton Woods institutions did not trust him.

Willowvale as a Turning Point

Behind legitimate business activities there was a hidden side. Civil servants in strategic positions would use their discretionary powers in exchange for money. Even minister of finance Bernard Chidzero once admitted in a press interview that the foreign exchange allocation system was corrupt. The Parliamentary Select Committee on the Allocation and Utilisation of Foreign Currency came to the same conclusion in its May 1989 report.[24] One must admit that until the late 1990s and by comparison with other African countries, Zimbabwe was largely spared of petty corruption and most corrupt low-ranking officials were brought to book.[25] Therefore, one could travel throughout the country without paying bribes to police or customs officials, although specific areas of the state administration (such as the delivery of passports, ID cards, and birth certificates) were affected by bribery. However, even during the first decade grand corruption was on the rise and ZANU-PF big men were shielded from prosecution or even public exposure as far as possible. Widespread graft in the government was better exposed in the early 1990s, when a vibrant private press investigated cases more systematically, but the practices unearthed by then had had their roots in the 1980s' opaque system of public management. Government corruption was a major theme of Edgar Tekere's and ZUM's electoral campaigns in 1990. No scandal contributed more to publicize the ZANU-PF regime's corruption than the Willowvale inquiry.

In this episode, cars produced under license by a state-owned assembly plant in a Harare suburb were appropriated irregularly by members of the ZANU-PF elite and their families and sold on the black market far above their official price.[26] This was in the context of a permanent shortage of new cars. Public outrage forced Mugabe, who claimed he knew nothing about the scam, to appoint a commission of inquiry chaired by Justice Wilson Sandura of the High Court. Five Cabinet ministers and one provincial governor were forced to resign and several were convicted, one of whom, Maurice Nyagumbo—a close associate of Mugabe since the 1970s—allegedly committed suicide in jail (according to his widow, he had threatened to tell all he knew about people at the highest level of the state who were implicated in the scandal). However, Mugabe managed to halt all investigations before the inner circle of the regime was implicated (some sources alleged that his first wife Sally benefited from the traffic) although he claimed at the same time to be supporting transparency.[27] Convicted party officials were later pardoned by the president, and former ministers Callistus Ndlovu and Frederick Shava went back to active politics in the mid-1990s.

Not only did the Willowvale inquiry demonstrate that the ruling elite totally ignored the Leadership Code, which banned self-aggrandizement through corruption and other means, but also it provided a graphic illustration of the opportunities at the heart of the state-controlled economy. Like the Lorac-Zimbank scandal, which allegedly implicated several cabinet ministers and one vice president—none of whom were prosecuted—in the mid-1980s,[28] the Willowvale scam exposed members of the ruling elite working in cahoots with unscrupulous elements of the white business elite. In the 1990s ritual denunciation of corruption in top echelons of the party and the state by some backbenchers and sometimes Mugabe himself became a regular feature of the political debate in Zimbabwe. Successive pledges to fight it more energetically appeared as mere window-dressing exercises: the party big men would never get caught unless they had fallen out with Mugabe. The Willowvale corruption scandal also signaled the limits of the 1980s accumulation model, both in terms of the relative modesty of the gains and the unsustainable character of the statist-commandist approach. A policy change was inescapable at a time when the ruling elite was hedging its bets.

Liberalization and Indigenization for Those Who "Deserve" It

By the end of the 1980s, the command economy was already paralyzed by its intrinsic weaknesses: the mismanagement of the largely inefficient parastatals with their bloated workforce and entrenched privileges for the elite, an oversize state bureaucracy with duplicate ministerial postings and a budget deficit getting out of control, an export-led commercial agriculture and mining sector strangled by the shortage of foreign exchange to buy spare parts or invest. A complex web of regulations (on consumer prices, wages, repatriation of profits, foreign exchange allocation, and so on) affected the manufacturing sector's competitiveness and discouraged private investment, which dried up when it was most needed: capital goods installed in the 1950s and 1960s were obsolete and needed replacement, and the state was not in a position to sustain public investment at the level of the early 1980s, despite a significant inflow of development aid, and the high levels of the corporate and personal income tax. As early as 1985 it was obvious that the free access to education and health provided to the poor, especially in the rural areas, was not financially sustainable given the GDP growth rate and insufficient investment in the private sector.[29] Unemployment began to rise in urban areas as the state bureaucracy could no longer absorb new generations of university graduates and school leavers and various businesses had to lay off workers. By 1987 the top ministry of finance officials were adamant that drastic economic reforms were needed.

Although it is usually portrayed in the literature as dictated by the IMF, the Economic Structural Adjustment Program (ESAP), adopted in July 1990 and implemented in 1991–95, was largely homegrown and not imposed on Zimbabwe by the Bretton Woods institutions. Although the external debt increased dramatically from 14.9 percent of the gross national product in 1980 to 48.4 percent in 1989,[30] it was manageable nevertheless by comparison with many African countries, and there was no immediate balance of payments crisis to compel the government to adopt the usual IMF package.[31] Hevina Dashwood argues convincingly that Zimbabwe's economic policy had been under review ever since 1985–86, and it had taken so long because supporters of ESAP within the government structure, the most prominent being minister of finance Chidzero, had to persuade a reluctant top leadership balking at the prospect of loosening its grip on the economy—and hiding these worries behind the usual rhetoric on socialism and anti-imperialism. Admittedly, there was also a policy debate over the need for trade liberalization and the pace at which it should be implemented. But this was at a stage when the necessity of a policy shift was no longer disputed, and, in any case, the subject had been raised before the IMF and the World Bank stepped in.[32]

However, Mugabe's hostility to market-based reforms insofar as they restrained government control over the economy might explain why substantive elements of ESAP were never implemented or only partly so, especially after a seriously ill Chidzero left the cabinet in 1994. By the end of the decade, only three loss-making parastatals had been commercialized (the Cotton Marketing Board, the Cold Storage Commission, and the Dairy Marketing Board)—and not fully privatized as the state retained a controlling share—out of more than fifty public companies. By retaining ultimate control of the market-oriented companies formed out of these parastatals, the government was still able to influence appointments to the respective boards of directors. The ESAP second-phase policy document known as Zimbabwe Programme for Economic and Social Transformation (ZIMPREST), released in 1998, listed 52 public companies to be commercialized and then privatized, with a precise timetable although leaving out some important ones like GMB or NOCZIM.[33] This renewed effort succeeded to a certain extent in seducing the IMF, and a standby credit of U.S.$193 million was approved in August 1999. However, after the IMF suspended this loan in September 1999 and in the wake of the 2000–2002 political developments, the implementation of ZIMPREST was indefinitely postponed.

On a similar line, the budget deficit never approached the original ESAP target of 5 percent of the GDP,[34] and it rose significantly again after 1997, while the internal public debt skyrocketed. When the unbudgeted payout to the war veterans in August 1997 and other political initiatives provoked on 14 November 1997 a fall of 75 percent of the Zimbabwe dollar exchange rate against the U.S. dollar, Mugabe quickly reverted to his traditional policies of controls (by the end of 2001 controls existed on foreign exchange, tariffs on imports, interest rates, consumer prices, and so on), something he had threatened to do as early as 1995 and 1996. This preference for control belongs to an authoritarian culture that ZANU-PF leaders share with the former regime of Ian Smith (since stringent foreign exchange and import controls were in force through the sanctions period before independence). It has little to do with a vestige of socialist thinking.

Mugabe and his associates eventually approved ESAP because it suited best the interests of the ruling elite as much as those of the established business class, and not because the Bretton Woods institutions managed to impose this policy on Zimbabwe.[35] The command economy had facilitated the emergence of a state bourgeoisie whose appetite for capital accumulation had been greatly enhanced by a decade of privileged access to various resources.[36] ESAP heralded the end of export licenses, a liberalized foreign exchange, liberalized imports of various commodities, and renewed capital inflows, together with the reduction of the budget deficit and the privatization of some parastatals.[37] At first glance this seemed likely to affect the privileges of the ZANU-PF elite, but the state bourgeoisie adjusted quickly to drastic economic change and espoused liberalization and privatization as means to pursue greater capital accumulation during the following decade. As Volker Wild describes it: "What is today portrayed as a break with socialism and a move towards a market economy in Zimbabwe's economic policy, proves on closer inspection to be the transition from a latent to a manifest phase of clientelistic capitalism."[38]

Contrary to the view of many analysts—including Dashwood—there was no ideological conversion to neoliberal economics on the part of the top ZANU-PF leadership. They were no more committed to liberalism than they had been to socialism. ESAP presented an opportunity to manipulate economic policy to suit their own interests. They proceeded to target the social sectors (primarily education and health) for budget cuts rather than redundant ministries including National Affairs, an unofficial channel for party funding, later renamed National Affairs, Employment Creation and Cooperatives. The bloated government structure provided numerous perks to ministers and senior bureaucrats (including luxury cars). ZANU-PF was financed de facto by the public purse. The defense budget remained the second largest allocation after education.[39] This indicates the regime's determination to preserve the core of the ZANU-PF system of domination at the expense of the larger society's welfare. As documented by Dashwood, these policy choices did not please the World Bank, which was opposed to budget cuts and cost recovery in health.[40] The World Bank was very concerned about the social dimension of ESAP, particularly its adverse impact upon the poor: drawing some lessons from the first wave of structural adjustment in Africa, the World Bank insisted upon the creation of a Social Development Fund (SDF) to cushion the poor against the worst effects of ESAP. A huge delay in setting up the SDF, an inappropriate budget allocation, and some mismanagement that landed the fund in a dire financial crisis by October 1995 (after less than two years in operation) are clear indications of the government's lack of concern for the fate of the poor.[41]

Not only was poverty alleviation a donor priority rather than that of the government but its insensibility while implementing the cost recovery measures in health and education is in stark contrast with the caution applied when dealing with parastatals' reform. The latter was an area where the ruling elite was able to withstand external pressure. The ZANU-PF big men knew on which side their bread was buttered.

Given that the "socialist" discourse and the Leadership Code were obsolete as a legitimizing ideology, a new political rhetoric was needed to allow ZANU-PF big men to take full advantage of economic liberalization and to provide a smokescreen for accumulation strategies. Hence, the "indigenization of the economy" became the dominant slogan of the 1990s, and it was used to legitimize a shameless seizure of privately owned assets by the government/party big men and their cronies, in many cases at the expense of genuine African entrepreneurs.[42] However, the primary target soon became the white business and farming interests, whose continued control of the most lucrative sectors of the economy was portrayed as the major obstacle to "black people empowerment." As early as 1995 and more consistently, during the presidential election campaign of 1996, a propaganda blitz took place with large advertisements published in the government press by "political businessmen"[43] like Roger Boka or Philip Chiyangwa, founder and leader of the Affirmative Action Group (AAG). Their propaganda with racist undertones urged Mugabe to confiscate the land without compensation and force locally established international companies to sell their assets to "indigenous" people, a discourse endorsed by ZANU-PF leaders during the presidential campaign and obviously a forewarning of what was to come after February 2000. At the time, AAG activists were often dismissed in the press as lunatics while white farmers ignored the president's vitriolic verbal attacks.

The populist theme of indigenization was from then on the backbone of Mugabe's politico-economic strategy. There has been no serious attempt on the part of Mugabe's government to formulate and implement a coherent indigenization policy framework. Policy measures suggested by the indigenization lobby earlier on were totally ignored, and the money earmarked by donors such as the African Development Bank and the World Bank was spent in a nontransparent way.[44] "Indigenization" was primarily a phony agenda to keep Mugabe in power while capital accumulation by the state bourgeoisie could be intensified. In a way this was killing two birds with one stone.

In the early 1990s, the business appetite of ZANU-PF big men within the cabinet and Politburo, their relatives and their political clients, once again pitted them against genuine black entrepreneurs, some of whom were already active before 1980 and were then sidelined. But there were also young, educated blacks who were ready to take advantage of the new, market-oriented political economy of Mugabe's regime to develop businesses. They sought fair competition and an enabling business environment that would allow market forces to prevail, and they remained apolitical. However, a confrontation was inescapable with the greedy "political businessmen" thriving in an environment of corruption, fraudulent tenders, kickbacks, and embezzlement of public funds, who saw competition from genuine entrepreneurs as a deadly threat because the latter had more business acumen and flair. A striking illustration of poor managerial skills was provided in the mid-1990s by retired general Solomon Mujuru whose businesses in Bindura went bankrupt and left him with huge debts.[45] However, one of most scandalous performances in big business was the collapse of Roger Boka's financial and industrial empire in April 1998. His commercial bank went bankrupt, and he escaped abroad in June the same year, with the complicity of segments of the state apparatus. Boka was declared a "specified person" in Zimbabwe for having traded fake commercial paper in the name of the government-owned Cold Storage Company and having illegally transferred U.S.$21 million of depositors' funds from his bank to his offshore personal accounts. But Roger Boka was never prosecuted and was allowed to return, a sick man, to die at home. The official inquiry led by the police and the Reserve Bank exposed an incredible collection of corrupt practices. In his April 1998 report, the Reserve Bank governor noted that Boka had violated all known banking regulations during the time he ran his United Merchant Bank, which had granted substantial loans to eleven other companies he himself controlled. His conglomerate was built initially on a pyramid of loans from government-owned financial institutions at low rates and with almost no collateral.[46] He had been granted a banking license in 1995 although he had no banking experience at all. He also had a license to buy gold from "indigenous" gold panners, but he was once publicly accused of buying stolen gold.

A man with a small printing business at independence but good connections that earned him the contract for printing schoolbooks for the Ministry of Education, Boka would never have built such a fortune, including his costly and controversial tobacco auction floor, without constant political protection at the highest level.[47] Indeed, his United Merchant Bank granted generous loans to many Cabinet ministers, Politburo members, and other political businessmen, although the list of these illustrious clients unfortunately disappeared during the police investigations. Boka's death was certainly a great relief for the ruling elite as he had threatened to "spill the beans" if ever arrested. He received a statesman's funeral in February 1999 with several Cabinet ministers and high-level ZANU-PF officials in attendance and has been hailed ever since as a hero of the Third Chimurenga by Mugabe's cronies—all this in spite of the crisis in which Zimbabwe's financial sector was plunged when several of his creditors went insolvent. If Boka's downfall illustrates the sheer managerial incompetence and megalomania of most political businessmen, it also points out the criminal nature of their activities and the extent of connivance they enjoyed at the highest level of the state. This does not imply that the government or state apparatus as such is "criminalized" in the sense suggested by Bayart, Ellis, and Hibou.[48]

Among the younger generation, Philip Chiyangwa is emblematic of the "political businessmen," while Strive Masiyiwa became the hero of the genuine entrepreneurs, urban public opinion, and the independent press for his courage and endurance in fighting injustice and political harassment. A distant relative of Mugabe, coming from the same home area, Philip Chiyangwa entered business in 1982 as middleman in various deals—originally in the entertainment industry—by using his good political connections and sometimes through blackmailing other businesspeople. Particularly in the late 1990s, when his reputation was well established, he used intimidation to invite himself on some companies' boards of directors[49] or to buy back companies at a bargain price. His fortunes received a major boost in the 1990s with the indigenization movement. AAG, created in July 1994, was a small but noisy lobby outflanking the older and at that times more moderate Indigenous Business Development Centre (IBDC). IBDC had been launched in 1990 by a group of black businessmen primarily interested by the expansion of the small group of black entrepreneurs through state-supported corporate investment.[50] Chiyangwa and his friends advocated a more radical policy of seizure of assets and equities in existing companies, preferably white-owned ones, and criticized IBDC's timidity.

With unlimited access to government media to spread his aggressive message and with the assent of the president himself, Chiyangwa became increasingly reckless, insulting whites and his black critics who were dubbed Uncle Toms, threatening restive corporate executives and cabinet ministers seen to be too reluctant to endorse his agenda and members of the judiciary when a court ruling went against his AAG friends' interests, staging demonstrations in the streets, and sponsoring inarticulate eccentrics like former student activist "Warlord" Lawrence Chakaredza, leader of the chauvinistic Shona "cultural association" Sangano Munhumutapa, who posed as a radical and of course hailed AAG.[51] Since nobody in government tried to stop him, Chiyangwa's capacity for stirring trouble for Mugabe's opponents or critics increased through the years, as did his wealth. Gaining the support of state-owned financial institutions and "indigenous" commercial banks, Chiyangwa became a broker in various business deals with Politburo big men—one of them being the late vice president Muzenda, it is alleged. He was also a business associate of controversial white millionaire and arms dealer John Bredenkamp, for example, in a fuel import contract in 1999–2000. About at the same time, Chiyangwa was often cited as a close associate of Mnangagwa in the DRC business ventures.

In his early climb to the top, Chiyangwa made sure he never lost the support of the president. With the late Peter Pamire, his accomplice in AAG, Chiyangwa chaired the organizing committee for Mugabe's marriage with Grace Marufu in August 1996. Chiyangwa was also a member with Pamire, Enoch Kamushinda, and Ben Mucheche (the last two from IBDC) of the fund-raising committee for the ruling party's 1995 and 1996 electoral campaigns. He then admitted entertaining political ambitions,[52] in an attempt to strengthen his economic position through the acquisition of political office. This was achieved during the parliamentary election in June 2000 when he won the seat of Chinoyi—conveniently abandoned by veteran politician Nathan Shamuyarira, a former ruling party star. Not only were rigging and intimidation rife in that election, but Chiyangwa indulged in vote-buying techniques (promising a free loan to those who voted for him) in a clear breach of the Electoral Act. It was a sign of his growing influence in the regime that the High Court judge did not dare to nullify his election, claiming that no direct link could be established between the loan offer and the actual voting behavior. Chiyangwa was also a strong supporter of the anti-white campaign, the farm invasions, and the purge of the judiciary.

Strive Masiyiwa was exactly the opposite. A telecommunication engineer by training, Masiyiwa, after working for the state-owned Posts and Telecommunications Corporation (PTC), founded an electrical construction company, Retrofit, and secured several contracts with the state and high-ranking people—including the electrical system of Mugabe's rural mansion in Zvimba. He was named Zimbabwe's "businessman of year" in 1990. Nothing in that pedigree prepared him to be haunted by the security agencies and treated like a pariah. He first attracted CIO's attention in 1990 when he got a loan from the International Finance Corporation (IFC), a subsidiary of the World Bank, on the merits of his business project instead of going through the political channels. But his real problems started in 1994 when he decided to be the first to enter the cellular phone market in Zimbabwe and obtained in December 1995 a judgment of the Supreme Court declaring the PTC monopoly on telecommunications to be ultra vires the Bill of Rights inserted in the constitution. From then on, a group of ZANU-PF big men did all they could to stop Masiyiwa by whatever means, including issuing death threats. Retrofit suddenly lost all its clients in September 1995 after its contract for sporting facilities being built for the All Africa Games was canceled on Mugabe's orders. Masiyiwa was supported only by the late vice president Joshua Nkomo, who defended him in Cabinet meetings and in the press. The young businessman fought a costly four-year battle in the courts, endured vicious attacks from partisan government ministers and civil servants, and had to move to South Africa for his safety.

What made Strive Masiyiwa so dangerous for Mugabe and his cronies? Though never a ZANU-PF card-carrying member, he was nevertheless a member of the elite and well connected with party leaders, through his parents who were both involved in the nationalist parties during the war[53] and through his personal friendship with the Mapondera family—part of Mugabe's extended family. However, he openly criticized government policy decisions in 1992–93, as a founding member and the first IBDC secretary general who drafted its manifesto.[54] When he resigned in April 1993 IBDC was deliberately subverted by Mugabe's agents.[55] A leadership struggle within the board was engineered behind the scenes and IBDC's stance was aligned to the more radical AAG. Obviously, an independent-minded IBDC claiming 3,500 members and mobilizing the urban petty bourgeoisie for indigenization was a potential source of political competition for Mugabe and his associates. Second, Masiyiwa had defied the state and, indirectly, Mugabe's authority by suing PTC over the telecommunication monopoly. Though Mugabe knew a liberalization of the sector was likely sooner or later, he hated to be forced to act when it did not suit him.

Moreover, Masiyiwa did not follow the unwritten rules like the "political" indigenous entrepreneurs. For example, in August 1994 he rejected the offer from a cabinet minister and a member of the ZANU-PF politburo to support his bid providing he paid them a bribe in addition to a substantial share of the equity of his company.[56] This incident reveals the methods routinely used by the ruling elite to accelerate accumulation, and what is described as "off track" behavior today has been going on for more than a decade. When Masiyiwa told his sinister visitors to go and buy the shares on the stock exchange when the company would be listed, the big men decided to punish such "arrogance." Besides, if Masiyiwa did not want to cooperate, it was necessary to keep him at bay to allow the "political businessmen" to rush into the space opened by the Supreme Court ruling. Some of them (in particular, individuals close to Mnangagwa) formed a joint company called Cellular Systems Technology, and got a 20 percent equity in the consortium formed by the PTC and the German company Siemens to operate the first license (Net One) granted in 1996. The second license was granted in March 1997 by order of the president, in violation of the tender specifications, to another "indigenous" company, Telecel.[57] The entire procedure was subsequently nullified by the High Court judge Wilson Sandura in December 1997, but Masiyiwa had to go once again to the Supreme Court, which ordered the Ministry of Telecommunications in early 1998 to grant him a license to operate.

By saying "No" to big men who enjoyed full support from Mugabe, Masiyiwa exposed the corrupt nature of the ZANU-PF regime and unwillingly perhaps took a political stance. Yet Masiyiwa remains, above all, an able businessman. In operation since July 1998, his cellular phone company, Econet Wireless, was introduced on the local stock exchange shortly after and had no difficulty raising money. It posted dividends after only one year in operation and quickly became the first cellular phone network in Zimbabwe and the fifth in Africa, both in terms of subscribers and equity. Since 1999 Econet has expanded its operations in other countries of the continent (Botswana, Kenya, Nigeria) and went on the London Stock Exchange. Masiyiwa, who had lost everything in 1995, is now a millionaire in U.S. dollars.[58] During the same time the rival networks led by "political businessmen" suffered from various technical and financial problems and Telecel even went bankrupt. On the political front, Masiyiwa refused to join the Constitutional Review Commission in 1999 and did not join the MDC, although he is believed to be one of its financial backers. He also led a consortium of mostly black Zimbabwean businessmen who salvaged the independent newspaper the *Daily News*. In this sense, Masiyiwa really belongs to the counter-elite formed by trade unionists, lawyers, and civic organization leaders whose natural outlet was the National Constitutional Assembly (NCA) and the MDC.[59]

Asset Grabbing by Every Possible Means

The cellular telephone saga was part of a wider picture: there was in the 1990s an organized system among members of the ruling political elite and state bourgeoisie to share significant public tenders by flouting the rules or using insider privilege. The top military hierarchy and high-ranking officials in the Ministry of Defence monopolized the lucrative arms supply deals. Deputy-minister Tony Gara, who once compared Mugabe to Jesus Christ, allegedly benefited from illicitly obtained contracts for urban public works and sewage networks. Others were after oil products or aircraft leasing contracts for Air Zimbabwe. Former minister of agriculture Kumbirai Kangai was implicated in the Grain Marketing Board scandal (see Chapter 1), with the director-general of the parastatal. Tourism was also a money-spinner, and in the mid-1990s the state bourgeoisie started to demand licenses to operate lodges in the national parks and the granting of sport hunting quotas for wildlife in designated areas; they also invested in chains of hotels. The whole sharing of spoils was under Mugabe's remote control as he could promote and demote people at will, and he was the ultimate arbitrator of intra-elite squabbles between Politburo members and their respective clientele. When Mugabe believed that one of his associates in the formally collective power structure was going too far or breaching the unwritten rules of the "belly politics," he would discipline him whoever he was. Of course, the most profitable deals went as a priority to the president's extended family and his closest aides.

As one outstanding example, the president used his discretionary powers in 1995 to reverse the Tender Board's decision to grant an international consortium led by the French company Aéroport de Paris the contract for building the new international terminal in Harare airport. He awarded the contract to Cyprus-based Air Harbour Technologies, a company with little known experience in this particular business and despite the fact that its project was seen by experts as technically faulty and more expensive. The company, owned by the son of the Saudi oil minister Sheikh Yamani, was represented in Zimbabwe by Leo Mugabe, and family members, including Mugabe, got a large share of the spoils.[60] In 1999, after a quarrel with his Zimbabwean partners, Hani Yamani wrote a letter of complaint to Mugabe, which was subsequently leaked to the press, in which he listed the commissions paid to four Cabinet ministers (including Mnangagwa), several family members (including Mugabe himself for U.S.$1 million) and Zidco, for a total of U.S.$3 million. Because donors were not happy with the violation of tender rules, none of them came forward to bankroll the project and the government had to secure a commercial loan guaranteed by the Reserve Bank. When asked to approve this loan in May 1997, ZANU-PF MPs first refused (at the time, parliamentary backbenchers' resistance was said to have been stirred up by Mujuru in retaliation for Mugabe's obstruction in the Zimbabwe Mining and Smelting Company (ZIMASCO) deal) and had to be disciplined in a party parliamentary caucus. The airport terminal was eventually built after much delay and with inflated costs and officially opened in 2000, at a time when the crisis in Zimbabwe had already damaged the country's image and Harare was no longer a major tourist destination.

A further scandal was the privatization of the Hwange power plant through a contract signed in October 1996 with YTL Corporation, one director of which was a son of Malaysian prime minister Mahathir Mohamad. The price paid by the Malaysian company to acquire a 52.5 percent equity in the joint venture African Power Ltd., formed with the Zimbabwe Electricity Supply Authority (ZESA), the parastatal enjoying a monopoly of production in Zimbabwe, was said to be far below the real value of the assets. YTL was to receive tangible assets at a bargain price against the pledge to finance the future extension of the plant. The viability of the project was also dependent on the continued supply of cheap coal by the Wankie Colliery coal mine and a substantial rise of electricity consumer prices at a time when ZESA was already burdened with a huge debt. Tender procedures and rules were obviously flouted as several bidders had offered better terms than YTL, which had little experience in electricity production, and the World Bank, again, refused to back the project. The agreement was criticized by the ZESA board, left out of the negotiations in breach of the Electricity Act. Subsequently the entire ZESA board was dismissed by Mugabe.[61] The only strong motive behind the deal was the important commissions allegedly paid to Mugabe and some family members into offshore bank accounts. The nepotistic dimension of Mugabe's economic strategy might deserve the label of crony capitalism, a concept routinely applied to the state-sponsored indigenous (Malay) business development in Malaysia that Mahathir has cunningly engineered, promoting his political clients, family members, and respective business associates at the expense of other entrepreneurs.[62] Indeed, the Malaysian model appealed strongly to Mugabe and the ruling elite in Harare in the mid-1990s not only because it seemed pretty successful but also because both leaders entertained good relations and Malaysian businessmen offered to invest in the already staggering Zimbabwe economy at the very moment Western investors dragged their feet.[63]

However the dream was short-lived with the Southeast Asia financial crisis of mid-1997. Moreover, Malaysian investors' sudden enthusiasm for Zimbabwe evaporated once the farm invasions began and the local economy crumbled, and most of the highly publicized projects (for an alleged total value of U.S.$2.5 billion),[64] such as YTL involvement in the renovation of the Hwange power plant, never materialized. Mahathir is still cited in Zimbabwe's government press as a model of Third World leadership for his rejection of the Bretton Woods institutions, which is presented as an endorsement of Mugabe's anti-West and anti-white propaganda. However, Mugabe's later behavior bears no resemblance to Mahathir's management of the 1997 economic crisis—a drastic reduction of public recurrent expenditure, the postponement of capital spending, a 10 percent symbolic cut of ministers' salaries, the rescheduling of the public debt, a strict limitation of monetary creation, and a substantial restructuring of the banking sector to discipline unscrupulous elements including some "cronies." Moreover, Mahathir encouraged the formation of a Malaysian identity across the various national communities and even allowed local businessmen of Chinese origin to buy staggering businesses held by ethnic Malays after the 1997 financial crisis. In contrast, Mugabe's interpretation of indigenization is narrowly racist rather than genuinely nationalist.

Indeed, the apparent convergence of interests between the ruling elite and white businessmen and farmers did not translate into a process of elite accommodation and the formation of an integrated capitalist dominant class. The solidarity links derived from the "old boy" network or early school relationships (the "Mafia" of the famous Kutama mission school once attended by Mugabe), wartime politics, racial prejudices, extended family networks, and patron/client relations are more potent factors than class interest. The ruling political-economic elite is structured around a core of eight to ten families who are linked through marriage.[65] When one goes through the list of powerful positions in the administration, the army, the parastatals, one can point out the in-laws and siblings of the regime's prominent figures.[66] The ultimate objective remained to wrest the control of assets and resources from the whites and humiliate them in the process. Of course Mugabe has no problem working with subservient whites in his government—such as the late Denis Norman or Timothy Stamps—or with mercenary businessmen implicated in shady deals such as Billy Rautenbach, John Bredenkamp, and Nicholas van Hoogstraten.[67]

One sector coveted by ZANU-PF big men is the mining industry that became the target of "indigenization" threats in 2000. Renewed attempts were made in 2001, through War Vets who occupied some plants to expand the expropriation of assets from farming land to the industrial and mining sectors, including subsidiaries of international companies like Lonrho and Anglo-American. A subsidiary of the latter was accused of hoarding salt, when it was actually trying to address the shortfall, and a director of the holding, Nicky Oppenheimer, was accused by the government press of plotting against Zimbabwe. The philosophy behind this policy was not new as the focus on farm invasions in the 2000–2002 period might lead many to believe. One should recall also that Mugabe had exerted strong pressure since the mid-1990s on international companies like Anglo-American to entice them to transfer their mining interests to selected indigenous businessmen at bargain prices. He eventually enacted a new law to this effect in 2008, although it is unclear how far implementation went.

To foster indigenization of the industry an ad hoc committee of five politburo members, chaired by Mnangagwa, flanked by Matumwa Mawere as a technical adviser, was formed in 1997.[68] Dumiso Dabengwa, at that time still a powerful minister of home affairs, represented the interests of the former ZAPU big men. ZAPU people also had their own channels to benefit from the patrimonialization of the state, such as the

Resources Trust of Zimbabwe, created in 1989 by the late Joshua Nkomo. In spite of the fact that several public financial institutions had been put in place through the years to support "indigenous" industrial development, such as the National Investment Trust formed in 1996, the ad hoc committee evolved into a new structure, the African Resources Trust (ART). ART was officially a hoarding mechanism for equities in various industrial companies acquired by the state and held until indigenous entrepreneurs were in position to buy them back. Typically ART did not fall under the Ministry of Finance and its operations avoided public scrutiny. Then the ad hoc committee formed the National Investment and Empowerment Company of Zimbabwe (NIECZ), appointing its members as directors of the new company and registering in its name some shares already acquired by ART, including a 19.2 percent equity in Bindura Nickel. Available information does not allow us to establish how much of taxpayers' money was used to acquire equities that were later registered with NIECZ or other screen companies. However, there has been a sustained effort by the party big men to fraudulently obtain equities and register the shares in their own names. The lack of transparency of these numerous indigenization schemes was deliberate rather than the result of careless or unprofessional behavior.

Attempts to benefit from the privatization program were thwarted however by the fact that "indigenous" businessmen had no money available to buy the shares on the stock exchange even at a discounted price. For example, shares of profit-making Delta Corporation and Astra Holdings floated on the Harare stock exchange in 1995–96 were immediately bought by financial institutions and foreign investors, bringing cash to the government. Some of the loss-making parastatals like (ZISCO) or National Railways of Zimbabwe (NRZ) had large fixed assets, which retained a significant market value. Methods had to be invented to go around this financial constraint and the major breakthrough in this respect came from a young former World Bank employee in Johannesburg and Harvard graduate, who, more important, came from the Midlands Province and was then very close to Emmerson Mnangagwa. In 1996, Mutumwa Mawere returned to Harare to create African Resources Ltd. (ARL), a holding company registered in the British Virgin Islands, which immediately bought the largest asbestos mine in Zvishavane from an international company with the full support of Mugabe's government and the Reserve Bank. This brilliant operation based on some clever but unorthodox financial engineering was then heralded as a triumph of indigenization.[69] Mawere failed to raise money from investors in South Africa but received in 1998 a loan of U.S.$60 million from a consortium of foreign banks, thanks to the guarantee offered by the Zimbabwe

Reserve Bank. Clearly, the government had then put its financial weight behind the ambitious businessman—until he fell out of favor.

After three years and with a limited initial investment, Mawere and his political sponsors who graced the boards of his various companies built a large conglomerate with subsidiaries operating in most of the economic sectors. Among them was the First Banking Corporation, an investment bank the other shareholders of which were Zidco and M&S Syndicate through its subsidiary AM Treger, but also Cellular Systems Technology. This was a clear indication of the intertwined links between political and business elites under the umbrella of ZANU-PF. The contorted privatization process of part of the National Railways of Zimbabwe was another case in point, showing how sophisticated the plundering tactics had become. It all began with the renovated Bulawayo/Beitbridge track and the new railway bridge on the Limpopo, and it enabled a private company to obtain the largest share of the freight traffic between South Africa and Zimbabwe, while the NRZ retained the deficit-making routes inside Zimbabwe—where travelers' fares are fixed by the government below cost-recovery levels.[70] The new company was supported by an alliance between ZANU's Zidco and former ZAPU's Resources Trust of Zimbabwe, in a sense the economic dimension of the Unity Accord.

The pursuit of a grand strategy did not exclude the recourse to traditional sources of money. The ruling elite and its clientele systematically abused funds set up in the 1990s to benefit specific sections of the public. Two housing schemes meant for low-level civil servants were abused by the big men and their cronies who built themselves upmarket villas in Harare's elite northern suburbs. This scam included First Lady Grace Mugabe, who built a luxury mansion dubbed "Graceland" on a piece of land bought from the government at a bargain price.[71] Once it was paid for by public funds—officially a loan, but very unlikely to be called back by the financial institutions involved—the house was sold to the Libyan Embassy in Harare for more than five times its building cost.

In this scramble for capital accumulation, the state bourgeoisie still relies on its preferential access to Mugabe and his aides. It is therefore seen as absolutely crucial for the current regime to last long enough to consolidate these economic gains, which would be threatened if a democratically elected government and an alternative political elite came into power. In this respect, it could be argued that it is not a true bourgeoisie because it does not enjoy significant autonomy from political power. Most of the "political businessmen" who are now used to easy money would be broke in few months if left outside of the president's patronage, especially if they had to compete with real entrepreneurs as demonstrated by the fate of the three cellular phone networks. They are also no true capitalists, as the risk they take as entrepreneurs is more political than economic in nature.

The pivotal role of Mugabe in the neopatrimonial system was underlined by the support of the state bourgeoisie and ZANU-PF big men to his candidacy and the rigging of the 2002 presidential election. Even former ZAPU leaders who have been mistaken for far too long as potential critical voices or moderates within the ruling party fully benefited from the plundering of national resources. The myth of a reform-minded ZANU-PF wing who could take over from Mugabe and restore Zimbabwe to its former glories ignores the strength of this web of intertwined business interests that creates a sense of solidarity between members of the political elite; a reality further solidified by Zimbabwe's involvement in the DRC.

The DRC Bonanza

Profit-making and plundering natural resources were not the initial motives for the Zimbabwe Defence Forces' intervention in the DRC in August 1998. Rather, Mugabe's personal ego and the geopolitics of SADC were at play.[72] The involvement of former South African president Nelson Mandela in the 1996 negotiations between Laurent-Désiré Kabila and Mobutu could prepare a stronger involvement of South Africa in Congo's affairs, and the arms supply contracts with Rwanda might have put Pretoria in a strong position if Kabila had been defeated and forced to flee in 1998. So Mugabe, who had supported Kabila's march to power and DRC membership in SADC, hedged his bets on Kabila's side, and he did it swiftly to save Kabila's regime.[73] However, the economic rewards of this gesture of solidarity were included in the deal from the beginning given the harsh memory of the Mozambique failure. After the end of the civil war in Mozambique in 1992, in spite of Zimbabwe's military intervention on FRELIMO's side since 1982, most business contracts went to South African companies—better positioned from a market perspective. In the Congo ZANU-PF big men were to move right from the outset to secure privileged positions.

Naturally high-ranking military personnel, including the then chief of staff General Vitalis Zvinavashe, took advantage of the war to use every occasion to make money on the supply of fuel, spare parts, and ammunition, even food rations, more than once at the expense of the troops' well being or security. An air-cargo company owned by General Zvinavashe and his family (Zvinavashe Transport), received the contract for carrying these supplies to the DRC, while one of Zvinavashe's brothers was subcontracted to provide some of the goods. None of the military contracts went through the government Tender Board. The Zimbabwe Defence Industries (ZDI), created by the government in 1984 to supply the Zimbabwe Defence Forces with weaponry, ammunition, and various items of equipment, and which provided easy entré into business for retired high-ranking officers, was contracted in the spring of 1997 to supply Kabila's army to a total value of U.S.$53 million—though the DRC government never paid the bill for the 1997–98 deliveries. ZDI board of directors included several generals like Zvinavashe and Perence Shiri and the permanent secretaries of various ministries. ZDI then formed a joint venture called Congo-Desa with its parent structure in the DRC in order to flood the Congolese market with various goods not available locally. Retired colonel Tshinga Dube, general manager of ZDI, boasted on ZTV that the Congolese imported everything, including "potatoes and cooking oil," and there was an elated feeling in Zimbabwe of an economic bonanza. Following the generals' example, many ZDF officers operating in the DRC got involved in diamond and gold smuggling and various forms of trafficking, if only by extending their protection to the smugglers for a commission.[74]

Mugabe hoped for a short war and believed that Kabila's government, having survived the first months of the rebellion, could not lose with the combined support of Zimbabwean and Angolan troops. Contracts were hastily signed with the Congolese in expectation that first comers would be the first served in the reconstruction period, if only as indispensable intermediaries between the Congolese and the international companies. Zimbabwean parastatals were encouraged to move into the DRC market. Tony Gara, Philip Chiyangwa, and some other political businessmen struck some business deals in a great variety of sectors, the implementation of which was postponed to better times. For example, the First Banking Corporation, a subsidiary of Zidco and Africa Resources Ltd., announced its intent to develop branches in the DRC and indeed opened one in Lubumbashi in mid-2000. An eventual peace agreement was likely to benefit a good number of joint projects: the renovation of the Congolese power plants by ZESA, the actual cultivation of the 500,000 hectares leased to the Zimbabwe Agriculture and Rural Development Authority (ARDA), or even the development of exports through the Zimbabwe railway.

However, the mining sector was certainly the most attractive and also the area where a quick return on investment was possible. Ridgepoint Overseas Development Ltd., registered in the British Virgin Islands and belonging to the white Zimbabwean businessman Billy Rautenbach, was granted in November 1998 a 37.5 percent equity in the Congolese mining parastatal Gécamines, which exploited cobalt and copper. Rautenbach had made some inroads in Zaire before (his transport and car dealing company Wheels of Africa had ferried processed cobalt ore for Gécamines to South African ports since the 1980s) and claimed at one time to be a friend of Mobutu. Appointed chief executive of Gécamines, Rautenbach pledged to restructure it and make it profitable.[75] Four-fifths of the cobalt-mining rights were to be transferred to a joint venture between Ridgepoint and a Congolese company controlled by a close adviser to Kabila and his minister of finances Pierre-Victor Mpoyo. In addition, 20 to 30 percent of the profits accruing to Kabila's faction was to be used to refund Zimbabwe for its war effort, following the agreement reached between Mugabe and Kabila during the latter's visit to Harare in September 1998. In January 1998, Kabila had granted Rautenbach and his associates a cobalt mine near Likasi, which produced monthly the equivalent of U.S.$6 million, providing the company repaired the road between Matadi and Kinshasa.

Emmerson Mnangagwa and an anonymous member of Mugabe's family (perhaps his cousin Philip Chiyangwa or his nephew Leo Mugabe) negotiated these deals on the Zimbabwean side, so there are strong suspicions that Mugabe himself or members of his family and Mnangagwa might be listed among the mysterious directors of Ridgepoint.[76] Rautenbach's company shared the military freight contract between Zimbabwe and the DRC with Zvinavashe's company—a typical spoils-sharing agreement. Emmerson Mnangagwa, general Vitalis Zvinavashe, air marshal Perence Shiri, brigadier general Sibusiso Busi Moyo (director general of the mining company Cosleg), colonel Tshinga Dube of ZDI, Sydney Sekeramayi, and several other prominent ZANU-PF officials were cited, along with their Congolese partners, by the UN-appointed Panel of Experts on the Illegal Exploitation of Natural Resources and Other Forms of Wealth of the Democratic Republic of the Congo, in a report that claimed Harare had become "a significant illicit diamond-trading centre."[77] The report recommended personal sanctions against them.

However, the new Gécamines boss failed to restore the parastatal to its former glory—after years of plundering and mismanagement by Mobutu—and was unable to raise the capital to pay the long-term debt and invest to replace the derelict equipment of the mines. In addition, his project to market DRC copper and cobalt by exporting it from South African ports foundered on his legal squabbles in South Africa—stemming from Rautenbach's unorthodox methods in liquidating some of his subsidiaries in that country. Early in 1999, a South African court of justice impounded some truckloads of cobalt ore carried by Ridgepoint to Durban for re-exportation overseas in order to force Rautenbach to pay his debts to the South African companies suing him. Less than impressed by Rautenbach's management performance, as the Gécamines was still accruing debts rather than profits after an initial kick start, Kabila's government seized this opportunity to cancel all contracts with Rautenbach in March 2000 and appointed George Forrest, a locally born Belgian businessman with interests in timber and mining, as the chief executive of Gécamines.[78] However, Rautenbach obtained a new mining concession in compensation, and John Bredenkamp received from Kabila's government, with the help of his ZANU-PF friends, six Gécamines concessions of copper and cobalt worth more than U.S.$1 billion exploited by the Kababankola Mining Company (KMC), in which his company Tremalt Ltd. had an 80 percent share to Gécamines' 20 percent. Tremalt remitted 34 percent of its profits to ZANU-PF big men under a profit-sharing arrangement supervised by Sekeramayi, who reported directly to Mugabe. The ultimate owners and beneficiaries of Tremalt were hidden behind a web of trusts and private holding companies registered in the British Virgin Islands and the Isle of Man.[79] According to the UN Panel of Experts, John Bredenkamp was also deeply involved in arms supply for the ZDF in contravention of an EU ban.

Zimbabwean big men looked for ways to exploit diamonds in the ZDF-held zones in the DRC. They formed a company called Osleg Ltd., whose name was derived from the official code name of the military intervention in the DRC, "Operation Sovereign Legitimacy," and whose directors were General Zvinavashe and four ZANU-PF high-ranking civil servants.[80] It was presented in the government press in Harare as the financial arm of the ZDF, with an explicit reference to the Chinese model, although Osleg is a private company with no institutional link with the Ministry of Defence or any other branch of the state. Its profits will enrich its directors or ultimate shareholders, not the Zimbabwe state. The creation of a private company by taking advantage of a public office, which is illegal and fundamentally corrupt, has become a routine modus operandi of the state bourgeoisie. This behavior entails, in one form or another, the embezzlement of public money and the use of public resources for private gains (the very definition of "patrimonialism"). It has received the blessing of the highest authorities of the state in Zimbabwe.

In July 1999, Osleg formed a joint venture called Cosleg with a company in which Kabila was the majority stakeholder, Comiex (Générale de commerce d'import/export au Congo). Cosleg was granted exclusive rights to explore for and exploit diamonds and other minerals for a period of twenty-five years, or until the reserves are exhausted, in two of the DRC's richest diamond concessions near Mbuji Mayi previously by the Congolese parastatal Minière de Bakwanga (MIBA).[81] This de facto privatization was concluded in breach of DRC laws at the expense of the Congolese state.[82] Colseg then formed another joint-venture called

Sengamines with Oryx-Zimcon, a subsidiary of Oryx Natural Resources, which was registered in the Cayman Islands and owned by the Omanese businessman Thamer al-Shanfari. Zimbabwean (ZIDCO again) and Congolese interests have some equity in Oryx-Zimcon.[83] Sengamines was in charge of mining operations while Cosleg also got involved in timber, sawmills, and manganese processing. In this complex deal, Zimbabweans provided the means to secure the mining area and protect it from a rebel attack or from banditry, Kabila sold the mining rights, while the Omanese brought their financial expertise. However, the resumption of large-scale mining operations required some serious investments and none of the partners had the necessary capital or any experience in diamond mining. So al-Shanfari created Oryx Diamonds Ltd. by buying a small South African company with a technical expertise in diamonds, Petra Diamonds Ltd., and prepared the introduction of Oryx Diamonds Ltd. on the London Stock Exchange to raise some capital. Al-Shanfari's holding company would have retained a dominant shareholding of 60 percent of Oryx Diamonds. However, a few days before this operation, the London Stock Exchange authority suspended the introduction in June 2000, at a time the British diplomatic campaign against the "diamonds of war" reached its peak. Other attempts on the Amsterdam and Dublin stock exchanges also failed, depriving Oryx and Cosleg of the capital needed to boost mining production.

It would be simplistic to suggest that Mugabe dragged his feet on the implementation of the July 1999 Lusaka ceasefire agreement out of the need to protect shady business deals in the DRC. Consolidating a friendly regime in Kinshasa was as important as a motive, and from the legalistic perspective adopted to justify the SADC intervention it was reasonable to demand that the aggressors withdraw first. War, when it lasts too long, is a risk, even for Zimbabwean companies that operated in the DRC. In addition, the cost of war was a heavy burden for the already sinking national economy. The IMF had questioned the funding of the DRC war but the minister of finance only admitted U.S.$3 million a month, when it was closer to U.S.$25 million according to most observers. On the basis of doctored documents underestimating the expected budget deficit, the IMF agreed to a stand-by credit line in August 1999. When IMF officials realized they had been duped, they suspended the agreement in September the same year—therefore it had nothing to do with the farm invasions. In September 2000, the then finance minister Simba Makoni revealed that Zimbabwe had spent U.S.$263 million on the DRC war, at the expense of health and education, a substantial amount that was unsustainable without external funding.

There is less information available on whether Joseph Kabila honored all the agreements signed by his father and inherited his business interests. However, nothing really seems to have changed if only because Mugabe swiftly moved forward to support the son as he had done with the father, by maintaining until late 2002 a significant army contingent in the DRC, which was instrumental in keeping Rwandan forces in check.[84] A close political coordination between Kinshasa and Harare was maintained through the rounds of negotiations, and Joseph Kabila paid several state visits to Zimbabwe. The fact that a Zimbabwe military unit provided the bodyguards of Joseph Kabila during his first year in office is further evidence of the strong links maintained by the two heads of state. More than the war itself, this personal relationship was crucial for the perpetuation of Zimbabwe business interests in the DRC, and Kabila remained a trusted ally of Mugabe within the SADC. During the Inter-Congolese Dialogue held in Sun City, South Africa, between February and April 2002, in order to bring about a final settlement to the civil war, all parties, including the DRC government, subscribed to a review of all commercial contracts concluded since August 1998 to establish whether they benefited the country. If implemented, such an undertaking might seriously threaten Zimbabweans' stakes in the DRC. However, according the above-mentioned UN Panel of Experts report, "six new trade and service agreements were signed between the Democratic Republic of the Congo and Zimbabwe just prior to the announced withdrawal of ZDF troops from the diamond centre of Mbuji Mayi late in August 2002."[85]

These less than transparent business deals are widely seen to typify the criminalization of the state in Zimbabwe and in the DRC. Of course, some of the business conducted by Zimbabweans in the DRC was perfectly aboveboard as far as a war situation permitted. However, the UN Panel of Experts claims that "Sengamines supplements its revenues by laundering diamonds smuggled from Angola and Sierra Leone. Sengamines also smuggles its own diamonds out of the Democratic Republic of the Congo." Diamonds are marketed by the Zimbabean-controlled Minerals Business Company (MBC), which takes advantage of its political connections in Kabila's regime to evade local tax and customs regulations. "Sengamines has also served as a front for illegal foreign exchange transactions" on which Emmerson Mnangagwa received hefty commissions. Some "criminal groups" linked to warring parties "have built up a self-financing war economy centered on mineral exploitation."[86] Avient Air, part-owned by Zidco but run by British citizens, transported Zimbabwean equipment and technicians for Sengamines to Mbuji Mayi under ZDF protection and was also involved in arms trafficking and mercenary fighting on Kabila's side.[87] Even "honest" traders used their military connections to transport their goods and shunt the DRC customs as Zimbabwean officers were "untouchable." The latter had a tendency to put themselves above the law, indulging in theft and human rights violations.[88]

From a Zimbabwean point of view the DRC endeavors represent merely the extension beyond the country's borders of the internal corrupt practices on which the accumulation project of the new political elite has been based since the early 1980s. The mining deals linked to the military intervention in the DRC are only a facet of Zimbabwean crony capitalism: for example, the Zimbabwe railway network gains a strategic dimension with the need to find a short export route for mining products from Katanga (since Lubumbashi is closer to Harare than to Kinshasa). The same techniques used in previous attempts at assets grabbing in Zimbabwe were put in practice in the DRC: joint ventures to transfer public assets into private hands, secret contracts without tender, offshore companies with secret shareholders, exclusive rights to eliminate competition, unorthodox financial arrangements, corruption, and violence when necessary. In any case, since February 2000, Mugabe and his cronies dropped the mask of respectability, morality, and legality they had assumed for so long and they seemed to believe thereafter that they enjoyed complete impunity.

These multiple business ventures, most of which, however, did not seem very profitable,[89] were made possible by the continued control, during more than two decades, of positions of power and means of coercion by members of the state bourgeoisie. Their parasitic interference with the economy is certainly as damaging as the criminal nature of many of their activities. When the economic and social crisis deepened and financial resources of the state were exhausted, the neopatrimonial state became increasingly patrimonialized as the legal institutions were undermined and elite predatory behavior became wilder and more irresistible. The above-mentioned land grabbing in the guise of agrarian reform has been a case in point. Other examples were the ruling elite's taking advantage of the unrealistic fixed exchange rate of the Zimbabwe to the U.S. dollar to make huge profits from the foreign exchange black market, something like an industry between 2004 and 2008, in spite of hypocritical police raids on the small-scale dealers in Harare and Bulawayo. Others were trafficking in scarce commodities such as oil products. For example, ZANU-PF Central Committee member and MP Saviour Kasukuwere—who had privileged access to NOCZIM's limited supplies—was involved in the illegal trading of diesel and gasoline at prices respectively 8.5 and 4 times higher than the listed prices.[90] Plunder of one form or another became a necessity for political businessmen bereft of genuine entrepreneurial skills and the overnight businessmen (including politicians and military officers) who opted for fast-track accumulation of wealth. The DRC deals also revealed the degree of integration between various segments of the ruling politico-economic elite, more specifically how the military establishment's interests were closely linked to those of the political leadership, not only in terms of political survival but also in terms of access to wealth. There was a close connection between Zimbabwean mining interests in the DRC and weapon and ammunition supply to the ZDF units in the field and the loyalty of the security forces at home.

The wrecking of Zimbabwe's economy and the entire public administration is the outcome of the ruling elite's behavior in the pursuit of the parallel goals of political hegemony and wealth accumulation. It is not a "revolution that lost its way"[91] but the outcome of a logic rooted in the core aspirations of a group of black nationalists. Mugabe's patronage facilitated the emergence of a state bourgeoisie with the addition of crony capitalists whose entrepreneurial skills are less relevant than their political connections, and who are able to take advantage of all opportunities, including the now critical condition of the economy: illegal trading in foreign currencies and other black market deals are only examples of this. Economically, plunder is not sustainable in the long term, but shadowy business deals can flourish even in war-torn countries and the ruling elite is concerned only with short-term gains. This predatory elite is highly dependent for its economic reproduction on the continuation of Mugabe's personal rule. It perceives a potential MDC government (or any other party for that matter) as a threat to its privileged access to resources. There is, therefore, more at stake than nationalist politics and ZANU-PF's exclusive claim to postcolonial legitimacy. As one businessman cum party cadre, former guerrilla, and diplomat once put it bluntly: "All we got, our jobs, cars, properties and businesses, we got it with the gun, through the liberation struggle and if the MDC wants to take it from us they will have to come with guns and we are ready to fight."[92] Genuine power sharing—forget about alternate governments—would jeopardize this hard-won, ill-acquired wealth.

Chapter 8

The International Community and the Crisis in Zimbabwe

The deepening crisis in Zimbabwe became an international issue as early as 2000, both within the region and in terms of Europe/Africa relations. Not only were some of the white farmers who were victims of violence foreigners, with their plight attracting sympathy in the Western press and chancelleries, but also the Zimbabwean internal unrest generally became the source of a major diplomatic rift between the United Kingdom, United States, and European Union on the one side, and most African countries on the other, especially in the SADC region. The parties differed strongly in their reading of the situation on the ground and on what was really at stake. As a result, the cooperation between Africa and the European Union was impeded. The Western countries took a principled stance on the violence, human rights abuses, and cynical electoral manipulation, while Mugabe's African peers opted for ostentatious solidarity and denial. If this confrontation along geopolitical fault lines was not totally unexpected, it was also stirred up by Mugabe's maneuvers, especially his recourse to anti-colonialist/anti-imperialist discourse to legitimate his abuses and portray the Western resolve as attempts at regime change.

However, the Zimbabwean saga was understandably perceived and treated, for most of the current decade, as a low-intensity crisis in comparison with other hot spots on a continent not short of crises and wars—such as the DRC, Liberia, Ivory Coast, or Darfur. Yet, many in Zimbabwean civil society and in the MDC entertained naive illusions that once Mugabe's crimes would be exposed properly global and regional powers would intervene, and these activists felt betrayed by the world leaders' complacency. While the Westerners moved toward a tougher attitude against Mugabe's regime after the 2002 presidential election, it took until March 2007, if not mid-2008, for the SADC and AU to acknowledge Mugabe's political treachery and exert significant pressure on the old autocrat. This chapter will explore the motives and consequences of the international community's delayed action in the constraining context of twenty-first-century international society.

The Western Reaction: From Mixed Messages to Ineffective Sanctions

Western powers, starting with the United Kingdom, never followed a consistent policy line on Zimbabwe as they moved back and forth from an attitude of engagement to one of withdrawal (and subcontracting to South Africa). Phases of vitriolic statements against the human rights violations and the sheer brutality alternated with unwarranted optimism on expected political reform. Such weak policies were initially rooted in a partially inaccurate assessment of the political situation in Harare: for instance, the unfounded hopes of a "reformist" or "moderate" wing within ZANU-PF imposing policy changes, or recurrent beliefs of some imminent "retirement plan" for Mugabe—as early as 1999. Indeed a consensus emerged among Western countries, following the 2002 presidential election, on the impact of Mugabe's tactics to retain power by all possible means on his country and the region at large. As the primary source of instability in the southern Africa region, he should be removed from power to allow an internal solution to emerge. However, few practical steps were taken to stop Mugabe and put sufficient pressure on his regional backers. Not only have "smart" sanctions been largely ineffective but they have also inadvertently played into Mugabe's hands and antagonized other African leaders. Eventually, unfortunately, the United States and European Union leaders put all hopes in Mbeki's alleged ability to rein in Mugabe and bring about a settlement of the crisis.

The British government reacted strongly in April 2000 against the farm occupations and denounced both the violence and the breach of legality. Tony Blair's Cabinet also criticized vehemently the electoral violence in the run-up to the parliamentary elections and all the subsequent ones. However, British minister of foreign affairs Robin Cook and his minister of state for Africa Peter Hain were heavily criticized in many quarters for their strong language. Obviously they tried to put into practice the New Labour promise of an "ethical foreign policy," to which Cook was certainly more committed than Prime Minister Blair himself. Nonetheless, their obvious disgust at Mugabe's actions played into

Mugabe's hands while his propaganda was busily portraying London's attitude as neocolonial and motivated primarily by the protection of white farmers' interests, a line of argument that proved immensely successful among African elites and public opinion. From the outset, Mugabe succeeded in casting his campaign in the perspective of the anti-imperialist struggle and the defense of African dignity. Of course, the longer the crisis lasted the more this discourse appeared dishonest, especially when Mugabe claimed there was a global plot to unseat him. Nevertheless, it left its mark on the African popular perception of what was at stake: having built Mugabe as an African icon, his colleagues later found it difficult to change tack.

Inadvertently, the British government's principled stand was confused originally by London's will to engage with Mugabe's ministers on land reform, in the vain hope of isolating the president from his more pragmatic Cabinet ministers. Blair and Cook were obviously embarrassed by Harare's claims—however hypocritical—that the British, having reneged on their initial pledge to fund Zimbabwe's land reform, had made the compulsory acquisition of white-owned farms inevitable. Agreeing to engage Harare on this terrain was a strategic mistake. The core of the issue in 2000 was not conflicting land rights and resettlement policies but violence and human rights abuses. By June 2000, it was blatant that Zimbabwe was in a governance crisis of huge proportions, one that went beyond the mere resumption of the two-decade land dispute. The British government knew better, with its deep knowledge of the local political situation, but failed to articulate this assessment forcefully and especially toward African constituencies before Mugabe had succeeded to construct it as a neocolonial issue.

The British government correctly pointed to the September 1998 conference agreement on land reform, to which the UK had pledged the largest sums—admittedly far less than would have been necessary to fund the grand program of farm acquisition proposed by Zimbabwe. Since this agreement's implementation was deliberately sabotaged, it was clear by late 1999 that the ZANU-PF leader was interested only in the political manipulation of the land issue. It was pointless therefore to try to appease Mugabe, as the British government did in April 2000 with a renewed commitment on the land policy, with a caveat that law and order should first prevail on the commercial farms. Direct talks with Zimbabwean ministers invited to London bore no fruit. Similarly the Abuja meeting in September 2001 was convened under the shared assumption that "land was at the core of the crisis." This too predictably failed to produce any lasting outcome. To be fair to the UK, it took even longer for most Western embassies and the United Nations to realize that the Zimbabwean authorities were not the least interested by the implementation of a properly planned, orderly land reform. The UNDP office in Harare was trying still to broker an agreement on land reform well into 2002.

As the crisis built up, explanations offered for the widening gap ranged from Blair's snubbing Mugabe at a Commonwealth summit in October 1997, therefore injuring his pride—a real but temporary cause for irritation—to the impact of gay activist Peter Tatchell's attempted citizen arrest of Mugabe in London in November 1999. Back in Harare the Zimbabwean president vented his fury in the government press and accused Blair of plotting against him with "gay gangsters." Following the 1995 Harare Book Fair, Mugabe had developed an obsessive homophobia, and he was outraged by the incident in London. But it was certainly not a basis for a major foreign policy change for somebody often described as one of Africa's most able statesmen.[1] However, any excuse was good enough to support his conspiracy theory and lambaste the British leaders. A few months later Mugabe accused Peter Hain of being gay and called him the "wife of Tatchell." These abusive comments were intended for Zimbabwe's domestic audience. Whether Mugabe really felt humiliated by Blair's government is of no consequence: he seized every opportunity to fuel the confrontation with abusive words as if deliberately preventing any mending of the relationship.

Some observers also point a finger at the alleged shortcomings of British development aid policy. Yet, the minister in charge at the time, Clare Short, set out perfectly legitimate preconditions in 1997 for a resumption of funding: that the land policy be directed to benefit the poor and reduce poverty. That Mugabe deliberately chose confrontation with Great Britain was made clear by the wording of the clause on land acquisition in the 1999 constitutional draft. The violation of the British diplomatic bag in March 2000—under the pretext of uncovering a plot—was part of this case building. It was Mugabe's wider survival strategy at work: his anticolonial posturing was essential in securing his African peers' support. In Mugabe's paranoid rationality—so often displayed ever since—it was worth losing a few million pounds of British aid per year.[2]

That the high-pitched British rhetoric—undoubtedly sincere—was never followed by convincing action amounted to political weakness. Besides, London's criticisms of the regime's human rights violations and later electoral rigging would have been more convincing had British policy been more consistent in the past. Far from that, the crimes against humanity perpetrated in Matabeleland during the Gukurahundi, between 1982 and 1987 attracted little public criticism from London. British reporters were hardly encouraged to investigate, and British diplomats in Harare were ordered to look the other way while the Fifth Brigade massacred villagers with impunity—as recently confirmed in the press by the British high commissioner in Zimbabwe at the time. Indeed, having escaped criticism for earlier atrocities in the 1980s, Mugabe could logically assume that once again the outside world would turn a blind eye—failing to understand how the end of the Cold War and the apartheid regime had altered the international context.

Moreover, successive Tory Cabinets were delighted by Zimbabwe's apparent conversion to economic structural adjustment in the 1990s. Mugabe became the IMF's "blue-eyed boy." London was at the time primarily concerned with advancing British business interests in Zimbabwe, where its companies could benefit from the EU development fund. Most Western powers too were satisfied with Mugabe's abandonment of his one-party state policy and overlooked the undemocratic character of the ZANU-PF regime—moderately authoritarian by "African standards." Some British diplomats claimed in 1995 that elections in Zimbabwe were as transparent as in Great Britain,[3] a self-delusive attitude common in the diplomatic community at the time. London and Washington both cultivated Mugabe until late 1997, and even in 1999 Western embassies in Harare hastened to provide funding for the ZANU-PF-packed Constitutional Review Commission in spite of an obviously biased process. Quite understandably, most Africans viewed with strong suspicion the sudden policy U-turn in London following the February 2000 massive farm invasions.

Given the failure of direct pressure and the potential discomfort of a lonely confrontation with Harare, London geared the Commonwealth to act. In order to preserve the neutrality of an organization that had suffered in the past from deep political divisions (over South Africa's apartheid and Smith's UDI in particular), secretary general Don McKinnon initially avoided attacking the Zimbabwean government and stopped short of condemning the June 2000 election outcome, although the Commonwealth Observer Group report pointed at the high level of violence and put the blame on ZANU-PF. In September 2001, Nigerian president Olusegun Obasanjo, then chairing the organization, hosted in Abuja a meeting of the Commonwealth Ministerial Action Group (CMAG) aiming at bridging the gap between London and Harare.[4] Yet the Mugabe regime's pledges to halt the invasions and restore law and order on the commercial farms were never fulfilled. Rather, the level of violence rose anew when preparations for the 2002 presidential election commenced. As a matter of fact the principles of democracy, human rights, and freedom enshrined in the Harare Declaration, adopted by the Commonwealth in 1991, were routinely violated by Mugabe's regime.

Thus, by early 2002, several Commonwealth voices—mainly the UK and the former white dominions of Canada, New Zealand and Australia—were calling for a toughening of policy ahead of the Zimbabwean presidential election. They met with strong resistance from the African members at the Commonwealth Heads of Government Meeting (CHOGM) at Coolum in Australia in March 2002. CHOGM took no action on Zimbabwe until after the election. In what Blair described as "the lowest common denominator," the troika of Thabo Mbeki, Olusegun Obasanjo, and Australian prime minister John Howard was mandated to decide on a course of action on the basis of the report from the Commonwealth Observer Group—led by Nigeria's former transitional leader general Abdulsalami Abubakar. The very critical report—unlike that of the AU Observer Mission—stated that the Zimbabwean poll was not "free and fair." This conclusion left the troika with few options, to Thabo Mbeki's great irritation (the South African observer mission delivered a "free and fair" verdict). On 19 March 2002 the troika suspended Zimbabwe from Commonwealth councils for one year, subject to review in March 2003. This largely symbolic decision was also intended to back Mbeki and Obasanjo's joint effort to broker political talks between ZANU-PF and the MDC (see below).

However, a year later no progress had been made,[5] and Mugabe shunned the invitation to dialogue with the troika at the September 2002 mid-term review, thus demonstrating his contempt for the Commonwealth. In early 2003 Mbeki and Obasanjo insisted nonetheless on the need to lift the ban to assuage Mugabe's anger, but the Australian prime minister could not agree at a time when Tsvangirai's treason trial demonstrated that Mugabe was not relenting. In mid-March 2003, Zimbabwe's suspension was extended until December.[6] Then, with Mbeki dissenting, the CHOGM in Abuja opted for full suspension from all Commonwealth organs for one year. Mugabe retaliated by scoffing at the British and "their white valets" within the organization and announced that Zimbabwe ceased forthwith to be a member of the 54-nation club. In spite of Obasanjo and Mbeki's subsequent efforts to reinstate Zimbabwe, renewed membership is precluded until Mugabe's departure from the political scene.[7] The bitter controversy deeply divided the Commonwealth—though not strictly along racial lines, since most Caribbean members supported this decision. The suspension has been as ineffective as all other international sanctions to date, including those of the EU, one of the major donors in Zimbabwe.

The original EU response to the crisis was uncoordinated. In 1999 some member states supported the NCA process, others supported the CRC, some supported both, and there was no consensus on the merits or shortcomings of the constitutional draft. The victory of the "No" vote came as a godsend, but European diplomats in Harare were taken aback by the farm invasions. However, they had dissenting views on the nature of Mugabe's regime.[8] The Swedish government—a strong supporter of the black nationalists in the 1970s and during the first decade of Mugabe's regime—reacted very strongly when a commercial farmer, a spouse of one of its citizens, was murdered. In April and May, the EU issued concerned statements on the violence and lawlessness on the commercial farms and decided to send a strong observer mission for the June 2000 elections, led by former Swedish minister Pierre Schori, but without British observers that Mugabe had vowed to ban. The EU mission's report was very clear about the intensity of violence and intimidation.

The responsibilities of ZANU-PF and Mugabe's government were highlighted, and the predictable conclusion was that such elections could not be called "free and fair." That was enough for the regime propaganda to accuse the EU of having joined the British plot. In addition, the attacks against the judiciary by late 2000—until the chief justice was forced to resign—changed the previous perception in a majority of member states that land reform and Mugabe's personal feud with the United Kingdom were at the center of the crisis. It was time to engage seriously the Zimbabwean authorities on human rights and governance issues.

According to the Cotonou Agreement, signed in June 2000 by the EU and the African, Caribbean, and Pacific (ACP) States—Zimbabwe among them—to replace the previous Lomé Convention, a good governance and human rights record were nowadays a prerequisite for EU development aid. When violations of these principles are observed, the EU can open a 75-day period of "political dialogue" with the ACP government, under the Agreement's article 96, to have the unwanted situation corrected. Such a process was begun with Zimbabwe on 29 October 2001, but it achieved nothing at all. The EU was therefore entitled under the Agreement to adopt sanctions against the rebel country. Tension rose ahead of the presidential election when Peter Schori, head of the advance party of the EU observers, was deported from the country on flimsy bureaucratic excuses, because Mugabe had not countenanced EU's damning 2000 elections report. Infuriated by the incident and convinced by several NGO reports that the legal framework and continuing violence precluded a "free and fair" election anyway, the EU Council of Ministers adopted a series of personal sanctions against ZANU-PF leaders on 18 February 2002 for a one-year period. Broad economic sanctions were rejected—contrary to Harare's subsequent lies and popular beliefs in Africa—to avoid harming the poorest Zimbabweans, in particular the many AIDS victims who benefited from a significant EU-sponsored program. New grants from the European Development Fund, however, were suspended until the government addressed the EU concerns. Humanitarian aid was not affected and funding from the European Commission Humanitarian Aid Office (ECHO) has been steady up to the time of writing.

Sanctions mattered a lot to Blair's government because they sent the right message to the British public, whose ire had been stirred up by media reports and cabinet ministers' statements. After two years of noisy rhetoric and procrastination, the personal sanctions were meant to show that the government was dealing with Mugabe in the best way it could. Not all EU member states agreed: some, like Spain, wanted to protect their business interests in Zimbabwe; others, like France, disliked the very notion of sanctions and argued that more could be achieved through political dialogue. The French maintained working relations with Mugabe for several years—the French president received him in Paris in March 2001—at a time when Zimbabwe was an important factor in the delicate political stabilization of the DRC. Traditional Anglo-French rivalry certainly played a role, as the French government for once was watching on the side as another former colonial power was being embroiled in a "neocolonial" controversy. More important, Paris was worried that sanctions might become a routine policy against uncooperative autocrats, many of whom are France's clients in West and Central Africa. France has a tradition of engagement with some of the worst African dictators and hides its preference for the status quo behind noble principles of state sovereignty and international legality.

Other critics argued that the sanctions were untimely right before the March elections. Announced earlier, for example, when the government refused to amend the election legal framework and banned postal voting, sanctions would have been more relevant. Sanctions could also have waited until after the presidential election to provide a stronger reaction to an obviously rigged ballot. With no observers on the ground, the EU could have used both the Commonwealth and the Norwegian observer mission reports as a basis for its decision. Not any more efficient post-election sanctions would have strengthened the EU case in the eyes of the African states whose leaders hurried to accuse Westerners of preconceived judgments. The European ministers did not weigh sufficiently all the strategic implications of adopting a sanctions regime.

The so-called smart sanctions targeted originally 20 members of the party and government leadership, including Mugabe, who were forbidden to travel to EU member countries and had no access to their assets registered in these countries, including banks accounts. To give this policy more credibility, on 22 July, 52 other names were added to the original list, including some army and police chiefs, deputy ministers, and ZANU-PF Politburo members. Sanctions also included an embargo on the sale of arms, ammunitions, and related training programs, and equipment that might be used for political repression in Zimbabwe. In spite of vocal criticisms from Africa, the personal sanctions were renewed in February 2003, thanks to a gentlemen's agreement between London and Paris: Mugabe was allowed to attend the Franco-African summit in the French capital city in mid-February—a standard waiver for international conferences and similar diplomatic events—in exchange for France's support of the concomitant renewal. The list was further enlarged in 2004 to include 95 names; the sanctions were renewed with little debate in February 2005 and subsequent years. Although not an EU member, Switzerland adopted the same sanctions on 9 August 2002.

However, this policy had no meaningful impact on Mugabe's behavior in the short term. Not only does the travel ban have many loopholes (Mugabe or his foreign affairs minister were able to attend several high profile UN conferences and use them to provoke the West),[9] but it can be turned into a political weapon. For example, the Harare autocrat exerted pressure on his African peers twice to have them boycott a meeting of the ACP and European parliamentary unions unless Zimbabwe ministers could attend. In April 2006 the minister of finance was allowed to take part in an ACP/EU trade meeting in Belgium within the framework of the Cotonou Agreement. In the case of the Franco-African summits, the French government was compelled to extend an invitation to Mugabe under threat of a boycott by several African heads of state, including the South African and Nigerian presidents.

The freeze of assets was potentially more biting, but there is little evidence that it has been properly enforced. Besides, Zimbabweans with ill-acquired money have long mastered the techniques of money laundering, offshore bank accounts, proxies, and straw men. European fiscal paradises like the Isle of Man and the British islands of Jersey and Guernsey were not included in the sanction regime. The Caymans and the British Virgin Islands are also often cited as safe locations for stolen money. None of the ZANU-PF ruling big men seemed the least bothered by the alleged freeze of assets. Mugabe allegedly moved some money to Malaysia, where he still enjoys VIP treatment, and has invested in real estate there. His wife was spotted in January 2004 in Pretoria's posh suburbs, scouting for some property to buy. In June 2008 she allegedly bought a £4 million residential property in Hong Kong,[10] where Mugabe's daughter was enrolled at the university. The couple also owns an expensive mansion in Harare, built in 2003 with costly imported materials, allegedly for Mugabe's retirement. More important, only a few countries joined the EU in a sanction policy that does not carry the authority of international law—unlike UN sanctions against the apartheid regime in the late 1980s.

Although the EU claimed to target individuals "engaged in activities that seriously undermine democracy, respect for human rights and the rule of law,"[11] the rationale for selection was rather simplistic and bureaucratic. The list, though further updated on 13 June 2005 (by then comprising 120 names) and again after Operation Murambatsvina (six additions including the chair of the Harare Commission), still did not include all ZANU-PF cadres who took part in the violence or benefited from the patronage system. Grace Mugabe was originally the only spouse on the list without any function either in the party or the government, whereas many others have been involved, for example, in corruption and illegal land seizure. Some targeted individuals went on with their private businesses using their spouses and offspring as fronts. The list should have included high-ranking civil servants like the chair of the Public Service Commission as well as most permanent secretaries in various ministries. There was no reason for some Central Committee members—outside the Politburo—and ZANU-PF MPs being spared, since many were elected through violence and rigging. The same logic applies to political judges such as the chief justice and the judge president; only Georges Chiweshe, head of the biased electoral court, was included in 2005. Even more puzzling was the absence up to late 2004 of "political businessmen" such as Mutama Mawere, Philip Chiyangwa, and James Makamba, who had benefited from patronage and in return had supported Mugabe and ZANU-PF financially.[12] The maverick Leo Mugabe was not included even after being elected to Parliament. As some NGO activists suggested, sanctions should have included the big men's offspring studying in Western universities. The haphazard selection betrays the lack of any thorough analysis of the nature and dynamics of Mugabe's domination.

Yet the EU personal sanctions were an important moral stand. They could have been an important policy tool also had they been combined earlier with concerted pressure on the AU and more active lobbying in international organizations such as the United Nations.

The sanctions sent a suitable message, but the momentum was lost and Mugabe's regime was quick to realize that the EU, regardless of loud barking, was toothless. Earlier differences within the EU over the suitability of sanctions might account for the lack of a proper policy rationale and insufficient explanation efforts toward the African leaders. As one French diplomat interviewed once put it, "why should we sweat to sell a decision to our friends when we do not believe it to be wise and useful in the first place?" European countries working closely with the United States to isolate Mugabe's regime—as they eventually attempted to do in mid-2008—would have carried enormous influence even on the African continent. Western aid, the fate of the New Partnership for Africa's Development (NEPAD), or the African seat in the UN Security Council could have been used successfully as bargaining chips—had the political will and clear vision existed. However, when the British government, with the support of other Western countries, tabled a discussion of the UN special envoy's report on Operation Murambatsvina[13] in the Security Council in July 2005, any further action was blocked by a coalition of China, Russia, and three African states. For EU member states, the sanction regime was only a convenient proxy for a common EU policy on Zimbabwe that was dramatically lacking: it exonerated the EU from looking for stronger policy options. It has remained a purely reactive policy without any strategic vision of Zimbabwe's future and EU capacity to influence it. Such was the case also for the U.S. policy.

The farm invasions and the rigged 2000 elections coincided with an election year in the United States, whose president-elect George W. Bush took a strong line on the erosion of the rule of law—including threats to property rights—and the violence perpetrated on the farms and against the MDC. However the emphasis of Washington's African policy was initially on the DRC crisis and the successful implementation of the 1999 Lusaka peace agreement. Neither the outgoing nor the incoming administration wanted to antagonize Mugabe. Part of the DRC war equation, he was still perceived in Washington as a rational actor, carrying some influence on his allies, including the unreliable and unpredictable Laurent-Désiré Kabila.[14] From 1991, when Zimbabwe incidentally chaired the UN Security Council that sanctioned Operation Desert Storm against Iraq, until 1997, Washington and Harare experienced a short but real honeymoon. The Democratic administration hailed ESAP, increased U.S. development aid and trade with Zimbabwe, and ranked the Zimbabwean president among the few reform-minded leaders in Africa. Mugabe had paid a successful state visit to Washington in 1994. However, relations soured considerably during President Clinton's second term, after Mugabe's disastrous policy decisions in 1997 and the 1998 food riots and subsequent general strikes. Zimbabwe's military intervention in the DRC also pitted the country against America's regional allies (Rwanda and Uganda). During his tour of African countries in 1998, Clinton pointedly avoided a stop in Harare. Renewed abuses soon attracted sterner condemnation from the White House, under Bush's administration, especially during secretary of state Colin Powell's first visit to Pretoria in spring 2001, and bilateral relations worsened steadily. Although the rhetoric grew more forceful and aggressive, little action followed until late 2001. However, the new administration excluded Zimbabwe from the list of countries eligible to the Africa's Growth Opportunities Act (AGOA)[15] in spite of South Africa's protests.

Nevertheless, there was an important shift of informed opinion in the

United States when the Congressional Black Caucus departed from its traditional stance of support for Mugabe's regime at the time the Zimbabwe Democracy and Economic Recovery Bill came before the House. Harare had cultivated the African American constituency during the Clinton administration, organizing specific investor conferences to increase their participation in Zimbabwean industry. By 2001, though, black Congress members reckoned that Mugabe harmed both his country and beyond that, Africa's image, and realized that poor black Zimbabweans were those who suffered most at the hands of his police and militias. Thus the bill was passed unanimously in December 2001 and provided for smart sanctions against the ZANU-PF leaders. From then on Washington imposed restrictions on visa deliveries for a number of Zimbabwean personalities connected to Mugabe's regime. On 6 March 2003 a freeze of the assets of Mugabe and eighty other leading ZANU-PF figures, including "indigenous businessmen" allegedly close to him, was announced; it has been renewed every year since then and slightly enlarged. Yet there are no indications to date of the effectiveness of these sanctions. It is likely that the attention of the U.S. Treasury was too firmly focused on the Al Qaeda financial networks, in the context of the "global war against terrorism," to be seriously concerned with Mugabe's cronies' bank accounts. Like Europe, however, the United States has continued to deliver food aid through the World Food Program. In July 2002 assistant secretary of state for African affairs Walter Kansteiner admitted that the U.S. government had a "strained relationship" with the government of Mugabe because the latter violated principles of "democracy, human rights, civil liberties and economic freedoms."[16]

Although Colin Powell stated that Mugabe and his regime's time had "come and gone,"[17] the mounting pressure applied by Washington on African countries to deal with Mugabe was abruptly scaled down when President Bush visited South Africa in early July 2003. Apparently bureaucratic politics nearly paralyzed the Bush administration over policy toward Zimbabwe, as Condoleezza Rice's and Powell's respective staffs clashed. Dr. Jendayi Frazer, a black American woman of radical views, was National Security Council senior director for African affairs. When a student at Stanford University—where Rice taught for twenty years—Frazer was a close friend of Jonathan Moyo, Zimbabwe minister of information from 2000 until late 2004. According to the press, Frazer disliked the (white) American undersecretary of state for African affairs, Walter Kansteiner, who advocated a tougher line.[18] During the visit in South Africa, the NSC accommodating stance prevailed over the State Department African Bureau line.

However, another reason behind the change of tone might have been the delicate negotiations on a bilateral free-trade agreement between the United States and South Africa that began in June 2003. The Bush administration was eager to promote American trade with the region (South Africa dominated the five-nation Southern African Customs Union, SACU),[19] and this was not the time to rock the boat for the sake of the less strategic Zimbabwe. Since 1994 the United States has become the largest investor in South Africa and its biggest single trade partner—although combined EU members come first—as the bilateral trade steadily increased, South Africa becoming the first destination for U.S. exports in Sub-Saharan Africa. South Africa also gets a lion's share of American development aid. The stakes were high on both sides.

Eventually, Bush declared that it was the Africans' responsibility to address the Zimbabwe crisis (an echo to Pretoria's stance of "African solutions for African problems") and stated that he regarded Mbeki as "an honest broker" and his "point man" on Zimbabwe—a view Powell and Kansteiner did not share. Bush was happy to rid himself of the trouble, and he had no reason to question the South African president's self-confidence when the latter pledged to solve the Zimbabwe crisis "within a year." However, Mbeki's claim that political talks were under way between ZANU-PF and the MDC misled Bush. Morgan Tsvangirai immediately denounced Mbeki's "false and mischievous misstatements" as an attempt to "shield Mugabe by buying him time."[20] Therefore, this high-profile visit was a lost opportunity to exert direct pressure on Mbeki, who strongly needed American economic support and investment.

As the situation worsened in Zimbabwe through 2004—a time when the Bush administration concentrated on reelection—it became obvious that Mbeki had failed to deliver. In January 2005, during a Senate hearing the new secretary of state Condoleezza Rice, reversing her hitherto moderate stance, cited Zimbabwe among the six "outposts of tyranny," together with such countries as North Korea, Cuba, Myanmar, Iran, and Belarus. While launching his party's electoral campaign in early February, Mugabe lambasted Secretary Rice: "That girl, born out of slave ancestry in the United States, should know . . . that the white man is slave master to her."[21] The newly appointed American ambassador to South Africa hinted in February 2005 that the SADC countries' apathy on the Zimbabwe crisis would put in jeopardy all American aid to southern Africa. A communiqué from the U.S. Embassy in Pretoria requested that South Africa put pressure on Mugabe to enforce the SADC principles on democratic elections. The State Department condemned the outcome of the March 2005 election process being a travesty of democracy and suggested the vote counting was heavily rigged in favor of ZANU-PF.[22]

After his early June 2005 meeting in Washington with George Bush, Mbeki said he was working to bring about dialogue, but produced no evidence of concrete steps. On the eve or the G8 summit in July the same year, Bush accused Mugabe of destroying his country. These speeches reflected Washington's growing irritation over Zimbabwe and the South African president's inability to deliver. In Washington Robert Mugabe was then seen as the epitome of a Third World brute, hostile to a free market economy and to Western democracy, and a friend of all America's foes. On 17 November 2005, President Bush signed an executive order to expand the sanctions against Zimbabwe's ruling elite to 128 people and 33 institutions, thus including the Reserve Bank of Zimbabwe's governor, some new ministers, and the wives and offspring of the prominent politicians already targeted. The relevant departments were authorized to target other individuals without the need of Bush's approval. The State Department described the Senate elections in Zimbabwe as "a non-event." Assistant secretary of state for Africa Jendayi Frazer, like her mentor Condoleezza Rice, has used increasingly strong language toward Harare and called for the African Union and the UN to act.

However, in spite of Harare's propaganda on a regime change being plotted by its Western critics, Washington never had such plans and the Zimbabwe crisis remained largely a back-burner issue.[23] Unlike the mass murders in Darfur that had become a domestic policy concern in the United States, unlike Somalia's mess linked to the global U.S. security agenda, Zimbabwe was just another failed African country at a time the military adventure in Iraq and its consequences dominated U.S. foreign policy. The low-intensity crisis was too remote to require direct and consistent policy attention from the president's office—a permanent pattern in U.S. African policy.[24] Zimbabwean civic and opposition activists resented this neglect from the West but their self-centered analysis exaggerated the importance of Zimbabwe on the world scene. A landlocked country, with no oil or any other strategic resource, and with a modest but increasingly poor population of about thirteen million—diminished by AIDS and a mass exodus of qualified people—Zimbabwe is lackluster in comparison with neighboring South Africa or resource-rich countries such as Angola or the DRC. No G8 country was prepared to jeopardize good relations with Pretoria for the sake of Zimbabwe: better to take Mbeki's word and forget about the details. In spite of NEPAD's commitments to democratic governance and economic accountability, stressed again in Tony Blair's Commission for Africa's report, the G8 summit in Gleneagles in early July 2005 did not even bother to discuss Zimbabwe. The excuse was that donor countries could not hold the whole continent "hostage" over the situation in one country, although Blair and Bush repeatedly threatened to use the Zimbabwe as a litmus test of African leaders' resolve on good governance.[25] Ahead of the summit, however, Australia and New Zealand in a joint statement announced enhanced sanctions against Harare and urged the G8 countries to further isolate Mugabe's regime, without much impact.

African politicians' and media frequent contentions that the European and U.S. sanctions punish the whole Zimbabwean people are ludicrous and baseless. EU and U.S. sanction regimes indeed prohibit bilateral development funding, but not the humanitarian assistance in health care and food aid that has been so important since 2003. The suspension of bilateral funding preceded the imposition of sanctions and is tied to Zimbabwe's deteriorating relations with Bretton Woods institutions by late 1999, and early 2000. Harare fell out with the IMF in September 1999, when a stand-by loan was suspended because the Zimbabwean government had provided misleading information. Concerns about land acquisition and other governance issues (such as rule of law and protection of property rights) came only afterward as preconditions for the Bretton Woods institutions to reengage with Harare. The country's dire economic situation has nothing to do with sanctions; it is self-inflicted misery resulting from a combination of devastating policies such as the ruin of commercial agriculture and tourism, lack of fiscal discipline, and a weird monetary policy.

Zimbabwe has been in continuous arrears with the IMF since February 2001. Although IMF's annual visits to assess the situation prompted some speculation—especially when Mugabe met the IMF's director for the Africa Department in 2004—prospects of an IMF-sponsored recovery program repeatedly faltered against Mugabe's unwillingness to shift policy. In June 2003, the IMF executive board suspended the voting and related rights of Zimbabwe and, in December the same year, decided to initiate the procedure on the compulsory withdrawal of Zimbabwe for failing to pay its debts to the fund. Once again a visiting IMF delegation in May 2005 pointed at the need for a complete overhaul of the economic policy. Rebuilding links with the international community—by implication Harare's acceptance of major political reforms—was also cited as a prerequisite. In July 2005 the IMF was taking final steps to expel Zimbabwe from the organization for its failure to pay U.S.$295 million arrears. Zimbabwe's total foreign debt at that time was about $4.5 billion (of which $900 million was owed to the IMF), and its currency reserves were reduced to nothing. A mysterious source (see below) provided Harare with the U.S.$120 million paid in early September 2005, and the arrears were fully repaid by 15 February 2006. Yet the Zimbabwe minister of finance and Reserve Bank governor returned emptyhanded from a meeting in Washington in May 2006: the IMF would not resume support without a complete revamping of the country's policies.

South Africa's Ambivalence

Among Zimbabwe's neighbors, South Africa is particularly important, not only for its economic and political power, hence its leverage in continental politics, but also for its potential capacity to exert meaningful pressure on a landlocked Zimbabwe and therefore implement a would-be SADC sanctions policy: this originally involved Harare's debt to South Africa's electricity utility (now entirely settled),[26] the control of some major trade routes to and from Durban, a significant share of Zimbabwe's oil supply (one-third of which is railed up from South Africa)—anything short of military intervention, since the Zimbabwe Defence Forces (ZDF) could prove a tough nut to crack for the South African army. However, and contrary to many Zimbabweans' expectations, President Mbeki opted from the outset for "quiet diplomacy" to persuade Mugabe to change his ways. The latter was shielded from direct criticism by the South African government although Mbeki on various occasions made some oblique remarks about the violence and the rule of law. In contrast South African government officials repeatedly criticized what they dubbed the British "megaphone diplomacy." Foreign affairs minister Nkosazana Dlamini-Zuma warned in March 2003 that condemnations of Mugabe's actions would not happen as long as the ANC was in power. Mbeki also rejected the European and American smart sanctions vehemently, and he resisted fiercely Harare's suspension from Commonwealth structures as seen above. On 26 November 2004, South Africa blocked a UN General Assembly resolution on Zimbabwe by filing a "no action motion."

In spite of ANC professed adherence to democratic values and individual rights, Western governments or various civic organizations, local and international, putting some pressure on Pretoria received some angry comments.[27] Mbeki believed that many of Mugabe's critics were racially prejudiced and overreacted because some white people had been killed. As late as May 2005, Dlamini-Zuma claimed that the "hullabaloo [on Zimbabwe] is about black people taking land from white people" and accused Mugabe's critics of racism.[28] Like most of the subregion's heads of state, the South African president shared Mugabe's anti-colonial feelings. He took it for granted that the land question was the core of the problem, and that it was largely a quarrel between Zimbabwe and its former colonial master. Therefore the ANC leaders originally downplayed governance and human rights violation issues: one of Mbeki's ministers once stated that electoral violence in Zimbabwe was nothing compared to violence during the transition period in South Africa prior to the 1994 ballot. Since the Commonwealth controversy over Harare's suspension in 2003, President Mbeki believed—and wrote it in his *ANC Today* weekly column—that Western conservative governments want to use human rights as a tool to remove Mugabe from power.

In addition, the South African leaders were structurally biased in favor of ZANU-PF and against the opposition. As a liberation front having waged a guerrilla war, the ANC has natural and also self-serving sympathies for ZANU-PF. The cadres trained in exile that took over control of the party during the South African transition deeply resent the idea of a liberation front (a "sister organization") losing power, even through democratic elections. It is hardly a surprise that leaders coming from the United Democratic Front (UDF) stable (the ANC internal wing), such as the politician turned businessman Cyril Ramaphosa, retired archbishop Desmond Tutu, or COSATU leaders have become increasingly critical of Mugabe's rule—and Mbeki's weak response—while the ANC apparatus, on the contrary, closed ranks behind the president until the development in the last two years of a leadership battle between Mbeki and Jacob Zuma. The political solidarity between the two ruling parties was born out of the common struggle against Apartheid, although ZANU was originally closer to the Pan Africanist Congress of the People of Azania (PAC), a splinter faction of the ANC created in 1959, while ZANU's rival ZAPU was ANC's traditional ally from the early years of the guerrilla war, when both were supported by the Soviet Union.[29] However, the ANC recognized Mugabe's election victory and the Zimbabwean president played a prominent role in the Front-Line States in the 1980s, paying the price with several bomb attacks in Harare and sabotages perpetrated by the Apartheid regime.[30]

Therefore, in the eyes of the former ANC leadership in exile, Mugabe was an icon of African liberation. The ANC cadres were also deeply suspicious of an opposition party, which did not fit in with their neo-Leninist political mindset, where civil society has no legitimacy of its own (being only a tool for popular mobilization during the struggle) and trade unions must uphold the workers' rights in the workplace, and otherwise follow the party line. The ZCTU-backed MDC was in the ANC's eyes reminiscent of the Zambian Movement for Multiparty Democracy (MMD) led by former trade unionist Frederick Chiluba. The MMD ended historic nationalist leader Kenneth Kaunda's one-party rule in 1991, but soon got embroiled in factionalism and corruption. By analogy—though a disputable one—Mbeki distrusted Morgan Tsvangirai and doubted the MDC's ability to survive and ultimately gain power. The late 2005 split in the opposition party did nothing to allay these suspicions.

As Tim Hughes and Greg Mills argued, "quiet diplomacy" fits neither in the realist paradigm of foreign policy analysis nor in the idealist one. "There is no convincing evidence to demonstrate that either quiet diplomacy or tacit support of the Zimbabwe government have advanced any of South Africa's vital interests. . . . The approach of quiet diplomacy is, moreover, conceptually flawed as it makes the fundamental assumption that engagement with a political leader, who has abrogated the most basic tenets of democracy and the rule of law, will be amenable to a quiet diplomatic approach to change."[31] However, the apparently ill-conceived policy of quiet diplomacy had its own rationality. Indeed the South African president never entertained any illusions about Mugabe and he did not mince his words in private,[32] but he was not prepared to shoulder the burden of a controversial and risky intervention in Zimbabwe. His purpose was not to solve the crisis but to defuse it and mitigate its potential adverse consequences for South Africa.

There have been indeed some negative impacts, such as the region's shattered image in the international markets or the influx of economic and political refugees[33]—some of whom notwithstanding were qualified black professionals much welcomed in the growing South African economy—but nothing to compare with the potential consequences of a total meltdown of the Zimbabwe economy and society.[34] A collapse of Zimbabwe or a civil war across the border would signal the end of the "African renaissance" project—the pillar of Thabo Mbeki's African policy—before it got off the ground. In other words, damage limitation is what Mbeki was up to through his strategy of engagement and his defense of Mugabe in various international forums. Undemocratic elections—as in many other SADC countries—keeping Mugabe in power for the time being seemed preferable to scenarios leading to anarchy and violent conflict—such as a military takeover following an MDC victory at the ballot box. Therefore regional stability was more important than regime change. In this perspective, not only was it necessary to oppose sanctions, but also South Africa had to keep Zimbabwe afloat, for instance, by buying grain in Harare's name, to supply the Grain Marketing Board, when Zimbabwe's creditworthiness was reduced to zero. It also supplied Harare with electricity and oil products even as its northern neighbor accumulated debts and arrears. Winning back some legitimacy for Mugabe's regime in the eyes of the international community was also crucial to seek reengagement from the international financial institutions and resumption of development aid to revive the collapsing economy. That is why it was, in mid-2005, so important in Mbeki's view to stave off Zimbabwe's expulsion from the IMF.

Whether this attitude betrayed the principles of human rights and democracy, ostensibly guiding post-apartheid South African policy,[35] and incidentally embedded in the African Union constitution, is beside the point. What really mattered was whether such a policy was sustainable. The MDC leadership and civic leaders erred in believing that the

South African president aspired to fulfill a regional moral leadership—more or less like Mandela—when in fact he was pursuing a narrower domestic and regional political agenda. Mbeki was not the least impressed by the Western countries' demands that he perform the dirty job they themselves avoided and clean the Zimbabwean stables. If Pretoria was to play the role of a regional hegemon it would be in pursuit of its own agenda. It would not act against its own best interest.[36] It would not bow to Western political pressure unless the latter was backed by some convincing threat of sanctions or loss (NEPAD, trade, AGOA)—a very unlikely prospect, as mentioned before. South Africa was primarily interested in supremacy on the continent (in NEPAD and the AU) and was seeking co-option by the world powers, through political dialogue with the G8 countries on issues such as AIDS, African development, and debt relief. Pretoria was also competing for a permanent seat on the UN Security Council. The stakes were high and Mbeki would not allow such a low-ranking issue on South Africa's agenda as the Zimbabwe crisis to impede his bid for power in world affairs.

A key element of the "quiet diplomacy" strategy was the search for political accommodation between ZANU-PF and the opposition, once Mbeki had convinced himself in 2002 that the MDC was a force to take into account, and not a mere British puppet. Right after the 2000 parliamentary elections Pretoria first floated the idea of a government of national unity in a reference to the South African transition. Predictably the MDC refused to abide by the South African model because "national unity" would remind Zimbabweans of the ill-fated 1987 National Unity Accord forced on the ZAPU leaders. MDC leaders were only prepared to accept a caretaker government to organize proper elections within an amended legal framework, and held under international supervision. In April 2002, on behalf of the Commonwealth, Mbeki and Obasanjo tried to broker a national political dialogue between the two parties right after the controversial presidential election.[37] However, after an auspicious start the political dialogue aborted in early June 2002 when Mugabe rejected the agenda previously endorsed by ZANU-PF negotiators. Some low-key discussions were held from August to October 2003, with some input from the Zimbabwean churches, and again in March 2004, when MDC and ZANU-PF delegations held separate meetings with the South African president in Pretoria.

President Mbeki revealed on television in February 2006 that these interparty talks did produce a compromise draft constitution agreed upon by ZANU-PF and MDC negotiators,[38] which was endorsed by the MDC leadership on 21 August 2004. But the delegations failed to agree on a timetable for implementation: the draft provided for joint presidential and parliamentary elections that the MDC wanted in 2005 (in line with its stance that the 2002 elections were stolen) and the ZANU-PF wanted in 2008 (a date implicitly validating the flawed presidential ballot). The agreement was shot down in a ZANU-PF Politburo meeting on 24 August 2004, and Chinamasa was rebuked by members of the Mujuru faction who believed its implementation would benefit Mnangagwa—at a time the latter was actively vying for the position of vice president. Mugabe then seized the excuse of Tsvangirai's High Court challenge to his 2002 reelection to pull out of the talks once again.

Frustrated by Mugabe's lack of cooperation, President Obasanjo threw in the towel in late 2004 and adopted a far more critical stance against Mugabe that immediately attracted some hostile propaganda from the state media in Harare. In mid-July 2005, however, as a follow-up to the AU summit in Libya, the Nigerian and South African presidents revived the idea of direct negotiations between ZANU-PF and the MDC leadership, mediated, they proposed, by a retired SADC president in order to assuage Mugabe, who rejected the offer. This new effort was probably part of a deal between Mbeki and Obasanjo and the Western countries before the Gleneagles G8 summit. The South African government attempted to hook Mugabe's regime by offering a loan to cover the IMF arrears and some urgent imports (see below), but Harare smelled the rat. In February 2006, on ZTV, Mugabe intimated that he had accepted the talks only to appease the South Africans, with no intent to reach a deal with the opposition. He sternly ordered his African colleagues to "stay away" from Zimbabwe's internal political affairs. Mbeki was no more welcome in the MDC-T: when South Africa's cabinet gave its blessing to the 2005 election results, the MDC leader declared that it no longer saw the ANC president as a neutral mediator. Tsvangirai also criticized Mbeki's attempt in October 2005 to mediate between the two MDC factions, and he claimed that Pretoria supported the Mutambara/Ncube faction. He resented Ncube's good working relationship with Mbeki.

Rather than a complete MDC electoral victory, ANC leaders wished for a reformist or moderate ZANU-PF wing taking over from Mugabe and leading the country back on the right track. The South African president increasingly saw Mugabe's retirement—or death—as the solution, to clear the way for a new leadership to emerge from within the ruling party. He cultivated Emmerson Mnangagwa when the latter seemed to be Mugabe's chosen successor. However, Mbeki prefered a younger technocrat such as Simba Makoni, who had resigned his position of minister of finance in 2002. To warn Mbeki to avoid meddling in ZANU-PF succession politics, Mugabe's secret police suddenly uncovered in December 2004 a "spying network" allegedly set up by Pretoria.[39] The identity of those arrested (including Philip Chiyangwa) and the coincidence of the revelations and the ZANU-PF congress show that the arrests and subsequent trials were part of the anti-Mnangagwa purge. The message sent to Pretoria was unmistakable, although the latter played down the issue and negotiated the discreet return of its agent.[40] South Africa's ability to influence change within ZANU-PF has been very limited until recently.

Therefore restraining the Mugabe element has always been less prominent than the protection of the Zimbabwe president from his critics. By stating beforehand that he had no reasons to doubt that the March 2005 elections would be "free and fair," in spite of overwhelming evidence to the contrary, Thabo Mbeki deliberately undercut the international pressure for a fair contest. In February 2005 his government tried to prevent the SADC secretariat from sending a team of regional legal experts to assess the preparations for the elections. Pretoria also hampered efforts by COSATU to assess the situation, and when the SADC Parliamentary Forum wanted to send its own observer mission, a foreign affairs spokesperson said it was not an official SADC organ. Instead of criticizing Mugabe's government for retaining an uneven playing field, Mbeki attacked "those who have predetermined that these elections can be nothing but illegitimate."[41] Predictably, the South African government and SADC observer mission reports endorsed the election results as "reflecting the will of the Zimbabwean people"[42]—in spite of the obvious shortcomings in the process.

South Africa's ambitions on the regional, continental, and international diplomatic scenes also shaped its Zimbabwean policy. A rampant rivalry between Harare and Pretoria for southern Africa's leadership had developed since 1994, when the new South Africa joined the SADC (as the Southern African Development Co-ordination Conference was renamed in 1992). SADCC's original mandate, when created in 1980 by the Front-Line States,[43] was to counter South Africa's economic dominance in the region—its gross domestic product being still about 75 percent of the total GDP of the other thirteen members of SADC.[44] After the dissolution of the apartheid regime ZANU-PF leaders had a hard time adapting to the new realities, Zimbabwe being the last country in the region to recognize the internally negotiated settlement in South Africa. Moreover, South Africa was admitted to the regional organization against a background of controversy over the creation of a regional free-trade zone, as most other SADC members feared it would reinforce South Africa's economic domination. The 1964 Customs Agreement[45] lapsed in 1992, at a time when trade liberalization in Zimbabwe, a component of ESAP, had exposed to competition the hitherto protected local industries. After delayed negotiations, a new agreement was signed in March 1995, which more or less restored the pre-1992 tariffs and quotas, but it was not implemented because South African companies and COSATU lobbied their government against it. Pretoria then claimed that the agreement contradicted the WTO rules, but established punitive tariffs combined with quotas for Zimbabwean industrial exports to South Africa. As predicted, the trade balance showed a huge increase for South Africa from 3 billion Rand in 1994 to 13 billion in 1999. In November 1998, Harare retaliated with a 100 percent tariff on South African commodities to protect Zimbabwe's dwindling industries, thus forcing Pretoria to seek a compromise with its primary regional trade partner. Mandela and Mbeki paid a visit to Harare in January 1999 and negotiated a system of reciprocal trade quotas with Mugabe to relieve the tension.[46] As a matter of fact, South Africa's economy needs the SADC countries: its exports to the zone are more that six times its imports and have been on the increase since 1994.

Bilateral relations were also hampered because Mandela and Mugabe never liked or trusted each other.[47] While world leaders courted the former, the hero of the struggle against apartheid, the latter's star was fast declining by the late 1990s. Zimbabwe's military intervention in Mozambique, in 1982–1993, on the side of the FRELIMO government against the RENAMO epitomized Harare's leadership role in the region, although it also underlined that such prominence was linked to a peculiar political conjuncture that had ended in 1994—the anti-apartheid struggle. Although Mandela attended Mugabe's extravagant wedding in August 1996 and paid an official visit to Harare in May 1997, the two had already differed over Zaire/DRC. Mugabe scorned Mandela's failed attempts to mediate between Kabila and Mobutu, while he himself supported the military overthrow of the old Zairian dictator.

Being the ceremonial head of the SADC Organ on Politics, Defence and Security (OPDS) since its inception in June 1996, Mugabe felt entitled to define the SADC line on Zaire, although the OPDS institutional status and authority was still to be defined and matters of regional security were handled by the troika. In a September 1997 letter to SADC leaders, Nelson Mandela made it clear that an independent OPDS (especially one headed by Mugabe was the subtext) was not acceptable for South Africa. The Zimbabwe president pushed for speeded up DRC membership in the SADC in early 1998, in the hope of forging a close alliance with Kinshasa to counterbalance Pretoria's influence. Then he sent the Zimbabwe Defence Forces to rescue Laurent-Désiré Kabila's embattled government in late August 1998 and provided close security for Joseph Kabila after his father was murdered in January 2001. Zimbabwe sought to present its intervention in the DRC as an SADC operation—part of the defense pact binding member states—with the support of Angola and Namibia. South Africa could not prevent such window-dressing at a time it maintained close ties with Rwanda and Uganda, but it backed the Zambian effort to broker peace negotiations involving all stakeholders. When the Zimbabwe internal crisis escalated, the Lusaka agreement on the DRC, signed in July 1999, was still fragile. Mbeki, who had succeeded Mandela, was careful not to be isolated within the SADC, where Mugabe could rely on Namibia, Angola, and DRC active support, notwithstanding sympathy for Mbeki among other state leaders in the region.

However, after a failed mediation by former Botswana president Ketumile Masire, Thabo Mbeki seized the opportunity of leadership failure in the SADC and Mugabe's growing troubles to sponsor the Sun City negotiations that led, in December 2002, to a power-sharing and constitutional agreement in the Congo. Mugabe's worsening international image slowly sidelined him in the regional arena: he lost the chairmanship of the SADC OPDS to Mbeki and played no significant role in the subsequent creation of the new African Union. Mbeki, lacking Mandela's charisma and eighteen years younger than his Zimbabwe counterpart, had to earn his credentials as a continental leader.[48] Hence his caution when dealing with land, elections, and human rights issues beyond the Limpopo—a far cry from his assertive attitude in other continental crises. The South African president was acutely aware of Mugabe's capital of sympathy in Africa. Under no circumstances was he willing to be seen as implementing the agenda of Western governments in Zimbabwe (Bush's "point man"). The apartheid regime's destabilization of the Front-Line States in the 1980s had left a legacy of suspicion about Pretoria's ultimate motives. Moreover its joint intervention with Botswana in the Lesotho crisis in September 1998 had been very widely criticized.[49] The astute Mugabe played on these fears, and South Africa's regional ambitions paradoxically called for a policy of accommodation with Harare that was adopted by SADC as a whole ever since the Victoria Falls April 2000 summit.

When the South Africa, SADC, and OAU/AU observer missions repeatedly endorsed Zimbabwe's fraudulent elections until 2008, the ZANU-PF leader quickly used their statements as ammunition to reject as biased the critical assessments from other quarters (the EU in 2000 and the Commonwealth in 2002). In 2002 a small SADC Parliamentary Forum observer mission produced a critical assessment of the presidential ballot, contradicting the main observer mission sent by the SADC Secretariat. Parliamentary Forum observers stressed that the conduct of the poll violated established SADC guidelines, but the heads of state did not seem to notice. Not surprisingly, the Forum was not invited to observe the March 2005 elections. The SADC protocol on the principles and guidelines for democratic elections, adopted in Mauritius in August

2004, did not make any difference. SADC leaders were easily satisfied by Mugabe's subsequent cosmetic changes to the Electoral Act to allegedly implement the protocol. They also refused to sanction Harare after the March 2005 elections for obvious violations of these guidelines. The MDC secretary general complained that the South African and SADC observers in 2005 did not bother to investigate questions of treachery that the opposition party had raised. SADC leaders sheepishly, although without enthusiasm, endorsed every fraudulent election held in Zimbabwe until 2008.

Although critical behind closed doors, SADC leaders, in their public statements, failed to condemn Mugabe's actions. This lack of courage proved to be damaging for the region: a study found that the Zimbabwe crisis has cost the SADC member countries a minimum U.S.$2.5 billion in lost investments since 2000, reducing South Africa's GDP by 1.3 percent.[50] The contrast between the SADC's limp response and the tough position of ECOWAS on the Togo crisis, which forced the son of late president Eyadema to go through elections to succeed his father, demonstrates the limits of the consensus sought by the South African government. Placing SADC unity above all other considerations guaranteed Mugabe de facto impunity, rendering the regional body powerless and irrelevant. Although the Zimbabwe crisis was discussed at all SADC heads of state summits, and South Africa, Botswana, and Mozambique voiced their criticisms, most member countries remained wary to confront Mugabe. However, the SADC summit in August 2006 did not endorse Mugabe's suggestion to appoint retired Tanzanian president Benjamin Mpaka—rather Mugabe's sycophant than a neutral figure—to mediate between Zimbabwe and Britain (!) over alleged land disputes, and the SADC leaders called for broadening the mediator's agenda.[51] Eventually in the spring of 2007 South Africa and the SADC stepped up their mediation efforts.

Africa's Tragic Procrastination

On many occasions other than the Zimbabwean crisis the Organization of African Unity (later the African Union) has failed to live up to expectations. Yet the African leaders' complacency about the level of violence and oppression in Harare has put to the test their commitment to democratic governance and their capacity to discipline Africa's rogue leaders, in the context of a revamped African Union and NEPAD, which were supposed to epitomize a new will to tackle Africa's evils. Within the SADC and the OAU/AU the response to the Zimbabwe crisis alternated between an ostrich-like attitude (let's forget the crisis next door and it might solve itself over time) and vocal public solidarity with the autocrat when he was under attack from the West. This support from his African colleagues and especially his SADC neighbors has been a crucial factor in Mugabe's ability to withstand growing international isolation and stigmatization.

Mugabe's propaganda capitalized on the prevailing anti-Western feelings in the SADC region and Africa at large. It successfully portrayed the Zimbabwe crisis as a racial confrontation (white against black), a class struggle (rich farmers against landless peasants), and a historically loaded geopolitical rift (Western neocolonialists against African nationalists). Westerners' protests over human rights were seen as hypocritical by African governments, few of which could show an acceptable record in this respect. One unsavory example is to be found in oil-rich Equatorial Guinea. Dictator Teodoro Obiang Nguema, although less bloodthirsty than his predecessor and uncle Francisco Macías Nguema, is certainly no better than Mugabe, yet Obiang does not receive the same high profile treatment, especially from the United States. Because Mugabe's political discourse fitted in the traditional ideological mold of the old OAU and pleased African leaders often inclined to place the responsibility for their troubles on others' shoulders (preferably Westerners), Mugabe's peers were eager to swallow his narrative of the crisis, or more accurately to pretend that they did.

Therefore, solidarity was the standard posture within the OAU/AU summits, and the official agenda usually made no mention of Zimbabwe. At the first African Union summit in Durban in 2002, Marc Ravalomanana's election in Madagascar was rejected ostensibly because its outcome was decided in the streets rather than in the ballot box, but the heads of state had nothing to say against the stolen Zimbabwe presidential ballot. Nkosazana Dlamini-Zuma, South Africa foreign affairs minister, even claimed, against all evidence, that the elections in Zimbabwe took place in accordance with the country's constitution.[52] At the World Conference for Sustainable Development in Johannesburg, in September 2002, a hall packed with African delegates, including some African NGOs, cheered Mugabe while Tony Blair received nasty hisses, and was attacked publicly by Namibian president Sam Nujoma. However, reform-minded African leaders interested in promoting NEPAD were appalled by developments in Zimbabwe, though only a few, such as presidents John Kuofor of Ghana, Abdulaye Wade of Senegal, and later Ian Khama of Botswana, dared speak out.

Third World countries' support ensured that the UN Economic and Social Council elected Zimbabwe twice—in 2001 and again in 2005—at the UN Human Rights Commission/Council in Geneva. It followed that resolutions condemning violence and human rights violations in Zimbabwe were defeated by a coalition of Third World countries in 2003 and 2004. Furthermore, Zimbabwe's partisan police commissioner Augustine Chihuri was reelected vice president of Interpol, showing a similar cynicism. The regular EU/Africa summits have been derailed since 2003, because African governments insisted that Mugabe's ministers should be invited, while the EU barred their participation in accordance with its sanctions against ZANU-PF leaders. The African heads of state had it their way in 2007, when they threatened again to boycott the delayed summit,[53] and Mugabe was invited to Lisbon although all European leaders snubbed him—in protest Britain was only represented by a junior cabinet minister—and the brave German prime minister openly criticized the ZANU-PF regime.

When the Operation Murambatsvina began in late May 2005, African leaders once again refused to condemn the Harare government's actions and showed some irritation at the Western stern criticisms. One AU spokesperson declared pompously that the destruction of poor people's housing was Zimbabwe's "internal affair"; some SADC governments even blindly endorsed the alleged urban planning explanation from the regime. Mugabe was welcomed, as usual, at the early July 2005 AU summit in Libya, where Zimbabwe was not an official agenda item. Nigerian president Obasanjo, then AU president, refused to voice a public condemnation of Mugabe, although the UN secretary general had urged African democratic leaders to dare criticize the continent's wrongdoers.

However, cracks appeared within the AU, when the modernizing wing of the African elites got tired of Mugabe's antics. In July 2004 the AU Commission on Human and Peoples' Rights put on the table an openly critical report on human rights abuses in Zimbabwe[54] at the AU summit in Addis Ababa, Ethiopia. The Zimbabwe government protested that it had not been allowed to comment on the Commission findings before the report was publicized. Nevertheless, the report was adopted by the Commission executive council at an AU summit in Abuja in January 2005, only to be rejected by the heads of state summit in Khartoum in 2006. Likewise, the AU 2005 election observer mission report was far more critical than the one in 2002; it cited the complaints of the MDC and asked the Zimbabwe electoral commissions to investigate them.[55] When Commission chairman Alpha Omar Konare decided to send a special envoy to investigate Operation Murambatsvina in early July 2005, Zimbabwe authorities rebuffed him on a flimsy excuse before he was recalled.[56] Because the envoy was a member of the AU Commission on Human and Peoples' Rights, the Zimbabwe government feared he would denounce the political cleansing behind the operation. The two-week mission of a UN envoy who investigated the same abuses had already annoyed Harare, as her report contradicted the government stance. Obasanjo then announced the appointment of retired Mozambican president Joaquim Chissano as an AU mediator, but Mugabe rejected him immediately.

The Mirage of the "Look East" Policy

Facing growing international isolation and scouting for resources, the Zimbabwe government had to look beyond the southern Africa region. Mugabe turned to his old allies such as Cuba, China, North Korea, Iran, and Libya. Fidel Castro delivered his usual revolutionary rhetoric and sent some Cuban doctors to Zimbabwe (about all he could offer). Muammar Qaddafi, who had driven a triumphant cavalcade into Harare after the AU summit in Durban in July 2002, financed Mugabe's presidential election campaign and provided oil products since mid-2001—though at market price—was not much help either. The Libyan loan had been secured against various stakes in the economy—including confiscated commercial farms, state-owned mines, and equity in NOCZIM. But the arrangement raised eyebrows even within the ranks of the ruling party and later collapsed. Since then Libya has ironed out its differences with the West and has cast a cold eye on Mugabe's regime. More recently Harare courted Iran's conservative leaders for oil supplies and investment (Teheran agreed to finance the extension of the Kariba power station), at a time when the two countries were targeted by American rhetoric. Malaysia's business interests, so strong in the mid-1990s when Zimbabwe's economy still looked promising, fizzled out and are unlikely to be revived. Few of the fifteen bilateral agreements signed with Malaysia have been implemented. The political connection also is weakening since Mugabe's counterpart Mahathir Mohamad retired from active politics on 31 October 2003. However, Mugabe is still welcome in Kuala Lumpur, where he spends holidays almost every year.

A major component of the "Look East" policy was the restoration of past close relations with the People's Republic of China, the only world power that did not lambaste Zimbabwe for its human rights abuses: even the Russian president had labeled Mugabe a "dictator" on the eve of the July 2005 G8 summit. Mugabe had won China's backing for his land "reform" during a high-ranking Chinese official's visit in 2004. Mugabe's Chinese connections date back to the liberation struggle in the 1970s, when China trained and armed ZANU's military wing to counter pro-Soviet ZAPU. Just before the March 2005 elections, and in spite of Zimbabwe's international pariah status—or because of it— Beijing supplied Harare with trucks, light weapons, and anti-riot gear for the police, as well as with equipment to jam an independent radio station broadcasting from Britain.[57] It was alleged in 2006 that Beijing had also shared with Harare its know-how on the monitoring and interception of Internet communications. China also sold twelve fighter aircraft to Mugabe's military and three passenger aircrafts were also purchased by the beleaguered Air Zimbabwe.[58] In the past few years China, India, and Pakistan have displaced the UK, U.S., and EU as the biggest sources of direct investment in Zimbabwe. China was the foremost in 2004 but the amount of money involved remains extremely modest.[59]

In late July 2005, Mugabe paid a six-day official visit to China—the first since 1999—and pleaded for a financial package to help Zimbabwe with IMF repayments and with essential imports in food and fuel. He offered Chinese companies stakes in the mining sector. The Asian giant is interested in chrome and platinum of which China consumes 20 percent of world's production. Zimbabwe holds the world's second largest reserves of the precious ores. Mugabe's begging bowl plays into China's strategy to extend its influence to African countries rich in oil or minerals. In spite of several investment projects announced during his last trip, which did not, however, improve the economic situation in the short term, Mugabe obtained only a paltry U.S.$6 million to buy some food and not the bailout he expected. Besides, all deals with the Chinese are valued at market prices with no preferential treatment, according to the Zimbabwe National Chamber of Commerce (ZNCC).[60] Like elsewhere in Africa, China is interested primarily in tapping the country's mineral resources and finding new markets for its products—it became Zimbabwe's second largest supplier of goods in 2006. In 2005 President Hu Jintao warmly welcomed "an old friend," yet he skipped Zimbabwe in his seven-country Africa tour in April 2006. Whatever past ideological bonds, the cold war is over and China will not bankroll Mugabe's regime. However, the main dividends of the "Look East" policy are political: Mugabe's alliance with the Chinese for the time being shields him from the wrath of the UN. Beijing has rejected all moves to censor Zimbabwe in the Security Council, including after the second run of the 2008 presidential election was marred by violence.

From "Quiet Diplomacy" to the SADC's 2007 Mediation

South Africa's "quiet diplomacy" was not rewarded with a more loyal cooperation from the Zimbabwean authorities. On several occasions since 2000 a high profile meeting between Mbeki and Mugabe, either in Harare or during an SADC summit, would lead to the announcement by Mbeki's office of a breakthrough, only to be contradicted a few days or weeks later by Harare's actions (such as a new repressive law) or Mugabe's inflammatory speeches. Instead of vilifying Mugabe's deceitful behavior, Mbeki would then castigate his critics and once again pledge to engage his Zimbabwean counterpart. The repetition of this pattern seriously dented the South African president's personal credibility. Such was the case when Mbeki promised in July 2003 that the crisis would be over "within a year" and failed to deliver. By the time of the parliamentary elections in 2005 it was clear that Pretoria's diplomacy had failed to stop Mugabe, and a growing flow of criticisms came from South Africa and the region.

The Zimbabwe crisis has had, from the outset, strong resonances in South African public opinion. The theme of land reform touches a sensitive cord among black South Africans because the pattern of land distribution inherited from the Apartheid regime is even more distorted than in Zimbabwe. The process there has been slow, and little land— much less than in Zimbabwe's first decade—has been redistributed since 1994.[61] The ANC populist wing, including Mandela's former wife Winnie, who visited invaded farms in Zimbabwe in April 2000, and other radical groups such as the PAC, hailed Mugabe's policy and called for similar methods in South Africa. On the other hand, some other voices in the ANC, such as Moeletsi Mbeki, the president's brother, have spoken out against the latter's soft approach toward the Zimbabwe crisis. Although it is hazardous to speculate on what Nelson Mandela would have done if he had completed a second term, and though he initially supported Mbeki's "quiet diplomacy," he also vilified Mugabe's actions. He called him a "tyrant" as early as May 2000. In the same year, he asked him to step down to do Africa a favor. The Democratic Party—later renamed Democratic Alliance—the main opposition in Parliament, became increasingly vocal against the government's perceived procrastination over Zimbabwe's human rights violations and violence. It voiced mostly the white South Africans' concerns and, more important, the business community's alarm, which also reverberated in the unusual political remark of Tito Mboweni, the South African Reserve Bank governor, in August 2001, who lamented that the "the wheels had come off in Zimbabwe."[62] The business community was under no illusions and had reason to fear the economic impact of the Zimbabwe crisis.[63]

However, it was far more alarming for the ruling ANC to see its traditional allies such as the Communist Party (SACP) and the trade unions (COSATU) become more and more critical of Mbeki's policy on Zimbabwe, especially after the 2002 presidential election. These organizations hailed the MDC as a labor party persecuted by an increasingly dictatorial regime, and they retain to this day close connections with the ZCTU, a brother organization deserving international working-class solidarity. When a COSATU fact-finding mission was deported from Zimbabwe at the end of October 2004, Mbeki's government defended Mugabe's decision and some voices in the ANC demanded that the secretary general of COSATU resign. Once again, in February 2005, a COSATU delegation willing to assess the suitability of the election framework and the grassroots situation in Zimbabwe was denied entry into the country, although a duly warned South African government was supposed to have negotiated a safe passage with Mugabe's police. These incidents strengthened the SACP's and COSATU's critical stance on Zimbabwe issues and these organizations pointedly contradicted the ANC by rejecting the March 2005 election results and supporting the MDC's stance. Hence, there was a widening political gap between them and the ANC, at a time when the South African government's policy for social welfare and poverty reduction was also under fire.

The Council of Churches, the Students Union, and a wide array of local NGOs, thanks to months of groundwork by Zimbabwean NGOs and churches to mobilize their South African counterparts, reinforced this protest coalition in early 2005. The South African National Editors Forum (SANEF) published a communiqué in March 2005 criticizing Mbeki for not being vocal enough about the harassment of independent media in Zimbabwe. Desmond Tutu, a Nobel Prize winner, has been increasingly critical of Mugabe's action since violence began in 2000—dubbing him a "caricature of an African dictator" (he once called him "bonkers")—and has called for full economic sanctions against Zimbabwe in 2004. In their early July 2005 joint statement to condemn Operation Murambatsvina, the South African Methodist bishops even talked of a risk of genocide. The Catholic bishops spoke out accordingly. The South African Council of Churches (SACC) urged the Zimbabwe government to stop the destruction after its fact-finding mission visit in July 2005.

These civil society protests carried some moral authority although they did not threaten ANC's political hegemony in the short term; it became increasingly difficult to ignore them. When foreign minister Dlamini-Zuma castigated the COSATU for demonstrating at the Beitbridge border post on the Zimbabwe election day, the trade union leaders retorted that the minister had forsaken her former ideals, and they likened the defense of democracy in Zimbabwe to the anti-Apartheid struggle. In addition, the growing divisions within the ANC after Vice President Zuma was sacked and fought back to regain control of the party weakened Mbeki's stance on Zimbabwe. Zuma's allies in the ANC constellation—COSATU and SACP—were critical of the government's policy, and Zuma himself became increasingly vocal by late 2007,[64] obviously using Zimbabwe's decay as an indictment of Mbeki's alleged incompetence.

However, the South African government was not yet ready to change track, as was made obvious by Mbeki's intent, in late July 2005, to bail out Mugabe's regime. This came after the release of the damning UN report on the criminal Operation Murambatsvina, and at a time the ZANU-PF-controlled Parliament debated a constitutional amendment allowing the seizure of any land without compensation. Once again Mbeki and his ministers justified their attitude by the risks of a Zimbabwean meltdown.[65] However, political strings were attached to the loan: a new constitution acceptable by the MDC, a repeal of all repressive legislation, a sound and orderly land reform, and a convincing economic recovery program. Thus Mugabe logically refused to underwrite an agreement that he said was infringing on Zimbabwe's sovereignty.[66] In an interview on ZTV in February 2006, he claimed unflinchingly that South Africa's financial arm-twisting had been part of the imperialist plot to implement regime change in Harare. The Zimbabwean government managed to pay its arrears to the IMF without Pretoria's money, by printing billions of bearer checks in Zimbabwe dollars, as its transpired later, in order to collect all foreign exchange available on the black market—a policy that stimulated hyperinflation in the following months. In November 2005, however, South Africa and Zimbabwe signed an agreement to strengthen defense and intelligence ties.[67] Zimbabwe Air Force instructors were sent to train South African fighter pilots, and the two countries intensified their cooperation in sharing political intelligence. Pretoria seemed deterred also to adopt a tougher stance by the size of growing South African private economic interests north of the Limpopo, which are exposed to retaliation as the Zimbabwean government refused to sign a bilateral agreement on the protection of investment.[68]

Zimbabwe's fast-deteriorating situation through 2006 had a growing regional impact that included reduced foreign private investment, thousands of refugees crossing the Limpopo, and fast-growing transborder crime.[69] Pretoria began to worry also about South Africa's image as the 2010 football World Cup host country. Mugabe's regime's crackdown on MDC and civic groups in March 2007 gave Thabo Mbeki an opportunity to reengage Harare. An SADC emergency summit on 28–29 March 2007 mandated the South African president to facilitate a government-opposition dialogue to overcome the deadlock. Although the dominant mood was still that Mugabe had been demonized by the West because he took white farms, and many SADC leaders remained uneasy about censuring his conduct, they were convinced by then that he should relinquish power in the best interest of the region. Unlike in previous South

African efforts since 2002, Mbeki was bound to report to the SADC heads of state and governments on the progress in the discussions.

Mbeki's objective was to create the conditions for a free and fair election in 2008 in order to restore the legitimacy of the Zimbabwean government and obtain that Western sanctions be lifted and an economic rescue package be worked out. He managed to win ZANU-PF's reluctant nod and a negotiation agenda was formally adopted on 17 June 2007. However, it became quickly obvious that Mugabe would not condone a negotiated constitutional reform. He had bowed to SADC pressure typically to buy time, but he was not prepared to let the MDC have its way. ZANU-PF leaders knew perfectly well that they would lose any election held under the draft constitution almost finalized in August 2004—before Mugabe blocked it—and amended electoral laws. Therefore, Harare responded by pushing a constitutional amendment (No. 18) through Parliament, and Mbeki pressured the MDC factions to vote for a bill that did not address their main concerns, giving them his guarantee that this goodwill gesture would be reciprocated with a new constitution before the poll. However, Mugabe never approved the draft constitution agreed upon by negotiation teams at the end of September (later referred to as the "Kariba draft"), and ZANU-PF refused to repel repressive legislation on media and public liberties. Enlarged sanctions and renewed public condemnations from Western governments and a few African voices provided Mugabe with the excuse he wanted to stifle any progress: the MDC refused to call for an unconditional lift of sanctions prior to the elections—in spite of Mbeki's pressing demands—and to give a blanket approval to ZANU-PF's land policy.[70]

Predictably, Mbeki's last chance trip to Harare on 17 January 2008 failed to convince Mugabe to adopt the new constitution—by referendum or through Parliament—ahead of the elections, although the South African president claimed his mediation to be a success when reporting to SADC heads of state in February. Once again, there was more pressure exerted on the MDC than on Mugabe who reneged on his earlier commitments, made a fool of Mbeki, and got away with it, receiving the usual ostentatious public support from fellow SADC leaders. By January 2008 Mbeki was weakened on the domestic political scene by his defeat in the ANC leadership battle, and the ascent of Zuma and his allies—supporting a tougher line on Zimbabwe—was an additional incentive for Mugabe to hurriedly call the harmonized elections on 29 March. The MDC factions, having rested all their hopes in the SADC mediation, were once again barehanded and resentful, questioning Mbeki's neutrality as a dialogue facilitator.

Thus Westerners and Africans adopted strikingly divergent approaches to resolving the Zimbabwean crisis, one of verbal confrontation and ineffective personal sanctions for the former, one of accommodation— sometimes even vindication of Mugabe's actions—and ineffective back-stage pressure for South Africa and SADC. Both approaches have failed to improve the internal political situation or restrain the Mugabe regime's most pernicious and brutal actions. After seven years of collective self-delusion, it was painfully clear at a time Zimbabwe was once again bracing itself for flawed elections that the "quiet diplomacy" achieved as little as the aggressive but largely rhetorical stances of Europe and the United States. South Africa's alleged influence behind closed doors did not stop the worst campaigns of violence whether on the farms or during the elections. It did not bring about constitutional and legal reforms significant enough to offer a more balanced electoral playing field.

In the end, Mbeki's "quiet diplomacy" was more about avoiding difficulties with an irascible neighbor rather than reining him in. Both Tony Blair and Thabo Mbeki, whose methods so sharply differed, underestimated Mugabe's cunning and cynicism. The South African president probably overstated his capacity to influence Mugabe's decisions within the SADC and AU frameworks. The old autocrat's ability to play the West against the South, a former colonial power against African solidarity, indeed prevented any efficient coordinated international action. However, by late 2007 it was also obvious that the economy was becoming increasingly unmanageable and that the state was on the verge of total collapse. No amount of cheating in the March 2008 elections could save Mugabe and his cronies from the impending chaos.

Conclusion

Chaos Averted or Merely Postponed?

Whether 2008 was a pivotal moment of change for Zimbabwe, signaling the end of the crisis opened by the February 2000 referendum, remains undecided more than one year after the coalition government between ZANU-PF and the two MDCs was sworn in.

Despite a deeply flawed process and the unending repression—in addition to the depressing rift between the two MDC factions—there was an atmosphere of desperate expectation in the country on the eve of the 29 March harmonized elections (for the first time presidential, parliamentary, and urban council elections being held the same day). The nearly complete collapse of the economy had reduced ZANU-PF's patronage money and further eroded its support—including in the rural areas, where the MDC could penetrate for the first time since 2000, and where Tsvangirai received an enthusiastic welcome from the people.

However the electoral process turned sour when it became clear in the early hours of 30 March 2008 that Mugabe had lost dismally. In the following weeks ZANU-PF resumed its violent tactics to once again steal the presidential election. But this desperate attempt to retain power at all cost created an uproar abroad not only in the West this time but also in Africa, and especially among some of Zimbabwe's SADC neighbors. Peer pressure within the AU and the SADC forced Mugabe into the reluctant acceptance of a power-sharing formula formalized in the 15 September 2008 agreement creating a tripartite government. Still, it took another six months to have the Cabinet sworn in and in the meantime the country's situation worsened dramatically.

The Electoral Holdup

Although the SADC mediation in 2007 failed to produce the overhaul of the constitutional and legal framework demanded by the two MDC factions, Mugabe needed an electoral victory seen as legitimate enough to restore his relations with the donor community (including the lifting of personal sanctions) and obtain a financial rescue package for the Zimbabwean economy. There were limited changes to the Electoral Act, a slightly improved access to state media (opposition parties' paid advertisements were aired after some legal wrangles), and the two MDC factions were allowed to campaign in the rural areas closed to them de facto since 2000, attracting huge crowds in the process.[1] Nevertheless, the state-orchestrated violent repression against the Tsvangirai-led MDC-T and civil society went on until the end of February and slowly abated closer to the election date, especially when SADC and AU observers arrived. Moreover, the playing field was still skewed in favor of the ruling party with a chaotic voters' roll, no voting rights for the diaspora, a systematic gerrymandering of constituencies, and the use of government apparatus and money to support Mugabe's campaign. ZANU-PF used its routine campaign kit: increasing the pay for traditional chiefs and headmen (yet in worthless Zimbabwean dollars), denying food aid to suspected MDC supporters (but free seeds and fertilizer for loyal supporters), in addition to intimidating the rural folk through the deployment of War Vets and "green bombers." Three weeks before the elections, Mugabe signed the controversial Indigenization and Economic Empowerment Bill requiring foreign- and white-owned firms, including banks and mining corporations, to hand over majority stakes to black businessmen in an attempt to revive the indigenization policy of the mid-1990s and placate criticism from black entrepreneurs on the government's economic mismanagement.

As in 2002 and 2005, the MDC factions fought the 2008 elections without real hope of winning the contest—"under protest" for the MDC-T, whose leaders have contemplated boycotting but yielded to calls from grass-root supporters. The division between MDC-T and MDC-M (the faction led by Mutambara and Ncube) was more entrenched than ever after renewed attempts to sign a reunification agreement formally collapsed on 3 February, when the two factions failed to agree on the mere issue of the distribution of parliamentary seats.[2] While the MDC-T was unwilling to support outgoing MDC-M MPs, not only in Harare but also in Bulawayo and Matabeleland provinces, the MDC-M leadership was reluctant to support Tsvangirai's candidacy in the presidential elections, stating in private that he was no better than Mugabe. Clashes occurred in Tsvangirai's party in November 2007 after the head of the party's women's league, trade unionist Lucia Matibenga, was sacked and replaced by the wife of Ian Makone—a member of Tsvangirai's "kitchen cabinet." This irregular and unpopular move did nothing to allay the suspicions on MDC-T's lack of internal democracy.

Although Mugabe could not be totally ignorant of the mood of the people, the president and his acolytes from the JOC were fairly complacent about ZANU-PF's chances of beating a divided opposition. They discounted both the desperation of the rural folk hit by the food crisis and the Mujuru faction's resentment for the imposition of Mugabe's candidacy without internal debate. Enraged that the "Old Man" further postponed his retirement, Mujuru supported behind the scenes Simba Makoni, a doctorate holder and former SADC chief executive who had been a loyal party technocrat until 2002, when he resigned from the Ministry of Finance over policy differences and fled to South Africa. Makoni, who enjoyed also the backing of Mbeki, declared his candidacy on 5 February 2008. The former Young Turk of the 1990s was immediately expelled from the ruling party and received the usual abuse from the state media and harassment from the police inflicted on the opposition. MDC-M leadership opted to support Makoni in the presidential ballot, while retaining separate candidates for the House and Senate elections.

Although only Dumiso Dabengwa and former Speaker Cyril Ndebele —marginalized ZANU-PF bigwigs—took the risk to campaign openly for the dissident, it was alleged in the independent press that many Mujuru faction members encouraged the electorate to vote for him.[3] Makoni hoped to divide the ZANU-PF vote and capitalize on MDC divisions, hence come second in the ballot either against Mugabe rallying the opposition for a rerun, or against Tsvangirai as the champion of a renovated ruling party. The Mujuru faction dominated the ZANU-PF caucus and the provincial party structures since 2005, and these cadres paid lip service to Mugabe's campaign. Mugabe and the Mnangagwa faction acted too late to manipulate the party primaries to exclude pro-Mujuru candidates. With only 73 independent candidates running under his colors in the parliamentary elections, but allegedly with 90 ZANU-PF candidates discreetly supporting his bid, Makoni could prevent Mugabe from obtaining a two-thirds majority in Parliament—thus preventing him a free choice of his successor.[4] A major taboo was broken in the ruling party, but in the end it did not work out as expected by Mujuru and Mbeki. Not only did Makoni's campaign kick off too late—with interference from the CIO[5]—but he was little known outside the urban middle class, and once the voters began thinking of shunting Mugabe they chose the frontrunner Tsvangirai against the eleventh hour outsider.

As in 2002 and 2005, the lesser number of polling stations allotted to the towns compared to ZANU-PF-controlled rural areas[6] and the changes in constituency boundaries were recipes for chaos and disenfranchisement of voters—mainly in the opposition camp. The ballot and the counting proceeded smoothly in most places. MDC and civil society activists were able to collate results through the night. Despite delaying tactics from the partisan Electoral Commission (ZEC) in announcing results, it became quickly obvious: ZANU-PF had lost its majority in Parliament.[7] The ruling party accused, ludicrously, government-selected returning officers in a number of polling stations of having favored the opposition in the counting and had them arrested. Then ZANU-PF demanded a recount in twenty-three constituencies, but it confirmed the MDC victories. More important, presidential election results were released on 2 May—an unprecedented five-week delay—when the ZEC announced that Tsvangirai was leading with 47.9 percent to 43.2 for Mugabe, and a runoff would be necessary.[8] According to the data collated by MDC at the polling stations, Tsvangirai obtained 50.3 percent of the vote, against 43.8 percent for Mugabe, a narrow victory avoiding a rerun.[9] Using sample survey data, the Zimbabwe Election Support Network (ZESN), a respected election monitor, published on 31 March poll projections giving Tsvangirai 49.4 percent against 41.8 percent for Mugabe.[10] Allegedly, the ZEC informed Mugabe on 1 April that he had lost decisively,[11] but was forced by the JOC to withhold results until a strategy was decided upon.[12] A significant section of the ruling party, members of the Mujuru faction close to Makoni, advised Mugabe to step down to allow a negotiated settlement leading to a unity government led by Tsvangirai as president and Makoni as a ZANU-PF prime minister; exploratory meetings were held to this end.[13] However, the Mnangagwa faction and the majority of the generals in the JOC convinced Mugabe to fight a rerun and vowed to deliver victory, suggesting he would then be in a better position to negotiate with the MDC.[14] Mugabe in his usual denial accused the people who cast a vote against him of forgetting their history and being bought by the British.[15]

The ZEC refused to declare Mugabe an outright winner, but it published figures inflating the vote for Makoni and Mugabe and lowering Tsvangirai's vote so that Mugabe's victory in the runoff remained plausible. It is estimated that out of the alleged 8.3 percent of votes obtained by Makoni, half came from MDC-M supporters—especially in the three Matabeleland provinces. Without the bitter division in the MDC, Tsvangirai would have won decisively; although it would have made no difference to the JOC. In addition, an electoral agreement between the two MDC branches would have brought them eleven more seats in the House of Assembly on the basis of the official results, offering a stronger basis for later negotiations with ZANU-PF.

Tsvangirai most certainly won in the ballot box because a majority of voters, even in some ZANU-PF rural strongholds, were affected by the economic mess and the collapse of services and now saw Mugabe as a nuisance. No amount of ZANU-PF propaganda could hide the grim reality when entire families survived on food aid and remittances from expatriate members. According to some press reports, the JOC was shocked to find out that a majority of the police officers had voted for Tsvangirai on 29 March, in spite of their involvement in political repression and successive purges of the corps through the years. It is likely that the rank and file in the army did the same. They were not allowed to repeat such folly for the runoff.

The runoff was announced for 27 June—well beyond the statutory 21 days after the announcement of first-round results—but such an inordinate delay was necessary to have the JOC's campaign strategy based on terror working. During these two months 30,000 police, army personnel,[16] and ZANU-PF militias were deployed in the countryside and in various Harare suburbs to assault, abduct, torture, and sometimes kill MDC supporters and election monitors in wards and villages having voted for Tsvangirai. They ran a network of illegal detention and torture centers. This campaign, called Operation Makavhoterapapi (meaning "Where did you put your cross on the ballot paper?"), focused primarily on former ZANU-PF strongholds that had swung toward the opposition, not only as means of retribution but with the aim of dictating the outcome of the runoff.[17] Once again, liberation war coercion techniques, such as nighttime *pungwes* and the denunciation and beating of sellouts, were revived. More than 160 MDC-T supporters were murdered, 10,000 were injured, and over 25,000 families were displaced, according to the party and civic groups. Six retired South African generals were sent on a fact-finding mission by the South African government in early May[18] and were shocked by the level of state-sponsored violence. The crackdown also targeted the MDC-T headquarters in Harare, human rights activists—also the ZESN[19]—and food relief NGOs, which were banned from the rural areas in early June,[20] a decision that significantly worsened the food and health crisis across the country.

Dozens of MPs were arrested arbitrarily, and Secretary General Tendai Biti was charged with treason and imprisoned two weeks before the runoff. Unable to campaign in the countryside, with his party's structures largely destroyed, party vehicles impounded, supporters demoralized or displaced—hence unable to vote—and his election observers scattered away, Morgan Tsvangirai—himself detained several times in June—stood no chance to be declared the winner. The election was fixed and the JOC had gone too far to accept anything other than Mugabe's re-election. The MDC candidate withdrew from the runoff five days ahead of the poll, but the ZEC claimed that it was too late to stop the electoral process. Obviously Mugabe wanted his fake election to proceed to be able to claim some legitimacy in the face of the world, and primarily his African peers. The violence during the campaign and widespread intimidation—such as rural chiefs and headmen recording the voters' ballot serial numbers—delivered Mugabe the kind of electoral victory he was used to: according to ZEC published results, he received more than twice the number of votes in the first run, but there were huge numbers of spoiled papers, many with abusive language against the ZANU-PF leader.[21]

Since March the SADC had been divided over the Zimbabwe crisis, with the leaders of Botswana, Tanzania, and Zambia advocating a tougher stance against Mugabe and supporting a broader mediation team. Significantly, a Chinese ship with a consignment of weapons and ammunitions for Harare was prevented from unloading its cargo in Durban in mid-April, and later in other harbors in the region, following a call from SADC chairman Zambian president Mwanawasa.[22] Between late March and late June, Tsvangirai canvassed support among African leaders, some of whom asked Mugabe to step down. "Only God, who appointed me, will remove me—not the MDC, not the British," indirectly replied the defiant leader.[23] A week before the runoff date Mbeki flew to Harare, with the backing of SADC and the AU Commission, to ask Mugabe to postpone the poll given the climate of violence and negotiate with Tsvangirai a government of national unity, but to no avail. In striking contrast with the 2002 election, the SADC and other African observers concurred with the verdict of the Western diplomats, NGOs, and independent press that the outcome of the presidential runoff did not reflect the free will of the Zimbabweans and violated the SADC and AU codes on free and fair elections.

For the first time Mugabe could not rely on SADC to shield him from international criticism. Western governments, especially the United States and UK, firmly criticized the violence, claimed that Tsvangirai was the true winner of the March election and should lead Zimbabwe's government, and strengthened once more their sanction regimes.[24] After the runoff results Botswana declared it would not recognize the legitimacy of the election and demanded that Zimbabwe should be expelled from the regional organization.

Unlike for the first run, Mugabe was declared elected within twenty-four hours and immediately sworn in; he then hurried to the AU summit in Egypt, on 30 June and 1 July to prevent his African colleagues from declaring his election null and void. Although receiving the usual head of state treatment[25]—to the Westerners' dismay Tsvangirai was not invited—Mugabe was told by his peers, behind closed doors, that he had no other option this time than sharing power with the opposition parties, which had won decisively the 29 March poll. He was saved the public humiliation but his rhetoric failed to change the dominant mood. He had become an international embarrassment for the continent, although he pointedly noted that some of his accusers had more blood on their hands. The AU renewed its support for the Thabo Mbeki–led SADC mediation, and the regional organization then confirmed Mbeki's facilitation mandate, although Tsvangirai had asked him in early June to step aside since the MDC-T questioned his neutrality. Indeed Mbeki had shown once again his pro-Mugabe bias before the runoff.[26] At the Lusaka summit on 12 April, SADC leaders backed Makoni's proposal to lead a government of national unity, thus further antagonizing Tsvangirai. However, the MDC leadership had no option other than resuming the talks on a power-sharing formula. Mbeki left no other avenue opened by securing a Russian and Chinese veto to a UN Security Council resolution presented on 11 July by the UK and the U.S. that sought to impose UN sanctions against Mugabe's regime. Although the U.S. ambassador to the UN harshly criticized the South African position and castigated Mbeki's mediation as "a failure,"[27] there was no other practical option on the table. The MDC expectation that the crisis would be further internationalized, and that some stronger pressure would force the stubborn autocrat out of power was doomed.

Economic Free Fall

The most spectacular sign of the collapse of Zimbabwe's economy was the highest inflation rate in the world. It reached 231 million according to official figures in July 2008, although independent economists, using black market exchange rates as a proxy, then estimated it to be in tens of billions.[28] The government then stopped publishing inflation statistics because it could not follow the pace of prices rising on an hourly basis. Besides it had no meaning, as the shelves in the shops were empty unless you could afford backdoor transactions in foreign currencies. A situation aggravated by the government siphoning the banking system of all its foreign exchange, trickling in from remaining exports (mainly mining products) and humanitarian aid transfers,[29] and imposing price controls—going as far as arresting businessmen and closing shops—that were both unrealistic and counterproductive. Inflation of course was compounded by the collapse of the productive sector and the cost of imported goods, as foreign currencies were increasingly difficult to obtain. Yet the main factor was the monetary policy of the Reserve Bank of Zimbabwe (RBZ), headed since 2003 by Gideon Gono, a close associate of Mugabe's, his personal banker, and a member of JOC.

RBZ under Gono has been printing money crazily to cater to the needs of daily operations of the state administration, for pay raises and other gratuities distributed to the military and war veterans, and to maintain the luxury lifestyle of the ZANU-PF civilian and military elite. The latter were provided loans without proper security that were seldom reimbursed, but they also had access through RBZ to scarce foreign currencies at the official exchange rate that they could sell on the black market at a huge profit.[30] Operators on this monetary black market were often straw men behind which ZANU-PF bigwigs were hiding.[31] When RBZ became short of foreign exchange, it bought it on the black market with increasingly worthless Zimbabwe dollars. Therefore, inflation was ultimately the economic manifestation of a patronage system pushed to the extreme, a budgetary profligacy (including bankrolling the dysfunctional parastatal sector outside the stated budget) and a systematic plundering of the state by the governing elite. In spite of Mugabe's regular outbursts against his greedy, self-interested ministers and party officials, the anticorruption rhetoric was essentially a weapon in the intra-ZANU-PF factional fight. The elite's predatory behavior remained a condition for its continued political support.

In a desperate attempt to curb hyperinflation and provide the economy the necessary liquidities, Gono began in late August 2006 a process of drastically devaluating the national currency and introducing a new Zimbabwe dollar (1 new Z$ = 1,000 old Z$). But inflation did not recede, as the factors fueling it had not been addressed. To cope with astronomical price increases, the RBZ introduced bigger notes, made a new drastic devaluation of the Zimbabwe dollar in 2008, and did so once again at the end of January 2009, removing twelve zeros on the currency's face value. Predictably none of these moves worked; neither had the 2006 roadblocks manned by police and youth to confiscate cash carried by ordinary citizens.[32] The Zimbabwe dollar completely lost its value in two years—de facto, it was no longer legal tender before the minister of finance announced it in spring 2009. As more and more transactions were conducted in foreign currencies (mainly SA rand and U.S. dollars), the economy fell back to informal activities and barter. Only people with access to foreign exchange could survive, while the masses were reduced to begging—and starvation. The dire situation was acknowledged by the acting minister of finance in the illegally prolonged ZANU-PF Cabinet, when, presenting the state budget for 2009, he recommended adopting the South African rand as the legal tender in Zimbabwe.

Between 2006 and early 2009 nothing had been done to reverse the dramatic trend toward the abyss in a country that was one of the most developed economies in Africa: there has been a nearly 50 percent decline in GDP since 1998, with foreign exchange reserves and capital utilization at 10 percent of what they were a decade ago, tourism at 14 percent of its 1996 rate, and agriculture at 20 percent of its pre-"land reform" level. Nearly 90 percent of the population lived under the poverty threshold. With 90 percent unemployment most people relied on the informal sector, which has been criminalized by the Murambatsvina operation (street vendors being harassed by the police). In addition, the food shortages had become recurrent; malnutrition was pervasive although the exact figures were not published. The lack of foreign currency to purchase seeds, tools, and farming inputs, and the chaos on former commercial farms, rather than irregular rainfall during the farming season led to a poor harvest by April 2008. By late January 2009, seven million Zimbabweans required food aid, according to the WFP, and the crisis was to endure in 2010. The planting season November–December 2008 was a failure with most communal farmers having eaten all the grain they usually set aside for planting and no money to buy seeds. For the third year in a row Zimbabwe has grown less than a quarter of its needs in the major staple food and will probably produce not more than 5 percent of winter crops (wheat and barley), although there were good rains in 2009. Dairy and meat production was at most at 20 percent of pre-crisis level. Only remittances from exiled family members estimated as about U.S.$1 billion annually saved many urban families from starvation and the country from total collapse.[33] However, Mugabe and ZANU-PF ministers to this day deny the failure of the so-called land reform.

Most schools closed down in 2008 (94 percent of rural schools, according to UNICEF)[34] in a country that used to have the highest literacy and school attendance rates in sub-Saharan Africa. The health care system also collapsed—few hospitals remaining open and many doctors and nurses having fled abroad—for lack of repairs, drugs, power, and running water. This was at a time when 24.6 percent of the adult population were infected by HIV and more than 3,000 people were said to be dying from AIDS-related illness every week. Decades of neglect in the maintenance of sewage and water supply systems in Harare townships and severe malnutrition were the fundamental causes of the cholera outbreak in August 2008.[35] By 7 March 2009, almost 4,809 people had died from cholera since August, and more than 88,800 had been infected, according to WHO figures,[36] while the disease was spreading countrywide through the rivers and unprotected wells. Zimbabwe's life expectancy for women at thirty-four is the lowest in the world.[37] UNICEF statistics by 2009 showed a 20 per cent increase in under five child mortality since 1990, with a 100 children dying everyday.[38] Even when pri-

mary schools were opened in the rural areas, children could no longer attend classes because of hunger and deepening poverty.

With salaries in millions of Zimbabwean dollars but with a real value of a few U.S. dollars, that could not even pay the bus fare, most civil servants failed to report to work, and the state was grinding to halt by late 2008. Foreign debt had risen to U.S.$5.7 billion by 2009 (150 percent of the GDP) with arrears of U.S.$3.7 billion, and the country lacked hard currencies to pay for imported food, fuel, and electricity, a situation resulting in severe power cuts and shortages of almost everything. In June 2006 the UN Committee on Development Policy proposed to downgrade Zimbabwe to the status "Least Developed Country" (LDC) to reflect this huge setback. For most Zimbabweans life is worse than it has ever been, even in the worst periods of the colonial time and liberation war era.

This catastrophe is the product of Mugabe's rule, including the unnecessary war in the DRC; unsustainable fiscal and monetary policies for political expediency; the destruction of agriculture for the sake of political survival; and the final plundering of all assets, including speculation against the national currency. Yet, unlike what commentators often suggested, none of this came as a surprise. As much as Mugabe's personal rule was not in essence compatible with the rule of law, democracy, justice, and the freedom of speech and media, it was not conducive to sound economic policies and a thriving private sector. Cases of corruption and misappropriation of public funds and political interference with business operations date back to the first decade of this regime. They increased over the years especially after the second phase of the structural adjustment program was dropped in 1996. Not that the first ESAP—from 1991 to 1995—had been a total success, far from it: many policy changes were needed, in particular measures aimed at shielding the poorest Zimbabweans from budget cuts and layoffs, and both the ZCTU and the Confederation of Zimbabwe Industries (CZI) had contributed interesting ideas to this debate. Nonetheless, the abandoning of economic and fiscal planning not only infuriated international donors but signaled the end of any modicum of sound management of the state's finances and of the economy.

Until 1997–98, the Western powers—especially London and Washington—overlooked ZANU-PF's wrongdoings because they wanted to preserve good political and trade relations with Harare. That they became vocal in 2000 only when white farmers were harassed, and some killed, largely impeded the building of an international consensus on the Zimbabwe crisis and was seen widely in the Third World as motivated by racial prejudice. Nevertheless the collapse of the Zimbabwe economy has nothing to do with international sanctions, which were more bark than bite. It is entirely the making of Mugabe and his retinue of patrimonial barons and their respective clientele of "political" businessmen, the ZANU-PF morally corrupt elite that preferred to take the country down rather than admit failure and relinquish power to a democratically elected government.

The Uncertain Prospects for "Power Sharing"

On 21 July 2008, as the result of several weeks of heated talks, and after the South African–led mediation was complemented by a UN and AU involvement on Tsvangirai's insistence,[39] the three main parties signed a Memorandum of Understanding (MOU) by which they agreed on negotiating further the powers and composition of a government of national unity (GNU)—leaving aside the (il)legitimacy of Mugabe's "reelection." They also committed themselves to constitutional reform, economic stabilization, and the immediate end to violence (including the disbanding of militias). Two more months were needed to reach a formal and detailed agreement, as Mugabe and Tsvangirai quarreled on the powers of the president and the prime minister and their respective positions in the future government. Mugabe wanted the MDC-T leader to recognize his authority and join the Cabinet as a junior partner, while Tsvangirai wanted to exert major executive powers and reduce Mugabe to the status of a ceremonial head of state.[40] By mid-August the cunning autocrat had succeeded in isolating Tsvangirai. Missing no opportunity to flatter the inexperienced Mutambara, Mugabe was helped by MDC-M's negotiators' profound distrust of and hostility toward their erstwhile boss. MDC-M leaders tried to capitalize on their ability to swing a majority in Parliament. Mugabe enjoyed also the support of the facilitator Mbeki who was eager to conclude to boost his political status at home, and who saw Tsvangirai's resistance to a skewed power sharing as the main obstacle to success.

Mugabe tried to bully Tsvangirai to give in by threatening to form a Cabinet without the MDC-T. He convened the Parliament—in breach of the MoU—with Mbeki's and MDC-M's tacit support, in order to elect the leaders of the two houses and establish the actual balance of power. On 21 August 2008, Mugabe also unilaterally appointed governors for eight of the country's ten provinces—another breach of the MOU—but reserved two seats for the Mutambara group in hope of securing its support in Parliament and its participation in a two-party Cabinet. To widen the breach between the two MDCs Mugabe's party announced its support for MDC-M's candidate to the position of Speaker of the House of Assembly, Paul Themba Nyathi. However, the MDC-T candidate, Lovemore Moyo, surprisingly won the secret ballot on 25 August 2008, polling 110 votes against 98. Obviously, the majority of the MDC-M MPs and perhaps a handful of their ZANU-PF colleagues—aligned to the Mujuru faction[41]—voted against their leaders' will. This implied also a rejection of a two-party agreement excluding the main opposition organization. This MDC-T success and the unprecedented scenes of opposition MPs hissing at Mugabe during the official opening of Parliament increased Tsvangirai's political leverage. However, it took another two weeks to complete the power-sharing negotiations always close to the breaking point. Cornered by the SADC leaders, who accused him of blocking an "African solution" to the crisis, Tsvangirai decided to give the GNU a try. An official signature ceremony was organized in Harare on 15 September 2008[42] and hailed in the local and regional press as "historical."

The detailed document subsequently referred to as the General Political Agreement (GPA) established a complex government structure with a dual executive. The Cabinet chaired by Mugabe with Tsvangirai as a deputy, and which included the ZANU-PF vice presidents, was in charge of adopting policies and allocating financial resources. The Council of Ministers, chaired by Tsvangirai, as prime minister, and which included his two deputies (one of whom is Mutambara), was tasked with implementing the Cabinet's decisions. ZANU-PF was entitled to 15 ministers, MDC-T 13, and MDC-M 3, but decisions were reached by consensus. Tsvangirai was deputy chairman of the Cabinet in charge of overseeing policy formulation and implementation. The head of state still appointed high-ranking civil servants and commanding officers of the armed forces, although he was to do it "in consultation" with Tsvangirai, and there are still different interpretations of what theses words mean.[43] There were 8 ZANU-PF deputy ministers against 7 for the combined opposition. Mugabe retained his right to appoint 5 senators, and 9 other appointed senators were added—3 for each party—giving ZANU-PF a short majority in the Senate. Given the last eight years' politics and the deep-seated distrust between the two leaders this arrangement was bound to lead to conflict and paralysis of government. There was no clear mechanism in the GPA to overcome a direct conflict of authority between the prime minister and the president beyond the vague formula that SADC would act as the guarantor of the agreement. The GPA did not alter the rubber-stamping status of Parliament under the current constitution. Although it was referred to as an "inclusive" government, civil society was excluded from the negotiations and the GPA was basically a deal between contending politicians. Finally, the two MDCs had to put up with some ZANU-PF-style ideological statements in the text (on colonialism, "regime change" and alleged outside interference) that could be used later to trap their ministers and curtail policy innovation. GNU members had to call for the immediate lifting of Western sanctions targeting the ruling elite and to commit themselves not to reverse the dreadful "land reform"—a bad omen for economic recovery and perhaps a testimony of MDC-T's ambiguities on the subject.

The contentious allocation of ministries between the parties was left outside the agreement on the insistence of Mbeki, who was eager to avoid further delay. Yet the bickering over cabinet portfolios, especially the control of home affairs with the authority over the police force and the administration of elections, became the major bone of contention between Tsvangirai and Mugabe during the following four months. MDC-T was vindicated in its demands by the repression against its supporters and civil society activists, about forty of whom were abducted between October and early December 2008, and repeatedly tortured by some security forces in the typical ZANU-PF style.[44] The sinister plan was to obtain false confessions of preparing a coup against Mugabe by training agents secretly in Botswana—the most outspoken critic of Mugabe within SADC—in view of implicating MDC-T leaders in another treason trial.[45] Although Mugabe and his lieutenants first denied having knowledge of these unlawful arrests, the prisoners were eventually handed over to the uniformed police and appeared in a remand court after much legal wrangling. This was an obvious breach of one of the MOU and the GPA conditions, namely the end of violence and the guarantee of free political activity. Widely seen as an attempt by the so-called hardliners in ZANU-PF to prevent the formation of the inclusive government, this provocation could very well have been part of Mugabe's tactics to force the MDC into agreeing to a Cabinet in which all important ministries would go to the ruling party. Indeed nothing was done to allay the suspicions of the opposition, quite the opposite. Mugabe unilaterally reappointed ten ZANU-PF governors in violation of the spirit of the agreement,[46] and similarly renewed in early December the mandate of the Reserve Bank governor, Gideon Gono. The President also appointed a new attorney general who hastened to claim publicly his allegiance to ZANU-PF. Another provocation was the refusal to renew Tsvangirai's passport while he was abroad, forcing him into a two-month exile in Botswana.

An extraordinary SADC summit on 9 November 2008 failed to produce a solution, as the MDC-T refused the compromise brokered by Mbeki: Home Affairs was to be shared between two ministers, while ZANU-PF controlled already the defense and state security portfolios, in addition to foreign affairs and justice. Once again the facilitator, who had lost some leverage after resigning his position as South Africa's president in late September, put more pressure on Tsvangirai than on Mugabe, condoning rather than condemning the latter's breaches of the GPA. Yet the Zimbabwean president stopped short of appointing a new Cabinet without the MDC-T, a move that would have fostered and exposed SADC's divisions, with Botswana's president becoming increasingly impatient with Mugabe. Besides, the steep decline of the economy left ZANU-PF with no other option than an inclusive government to attract donors' support. Western governments—including the usually more cautious EU Commission—had called for Mugabe's removal from power by all means; but on the other hand stood prepared to support financially a transitional government with a decent reform agenda. The cholera epidemic going out of control, worsening food shortages, and the resulting desperation of its grassroots members provided the opposition with the same compelling reasons to swallow the pill no matter how bitter this was to be. The public servants' strikes in all sectors from November to January were crushed violently, showing no intent of the ZANU-PF regime to release its grip.[47]

The MDC-T had stated its precondition for joining the Cabinet, including the immediate release of all political prisoners. Another SADC emergency summit, 26–27 January 2009, managed to squeeze a few last-minute concessions from Mugabe who knew that he would not secure a better deal once Jacob Zuma had replaced transitional South African president Kgalema Motlanthe. Although only a few of the MDC's demands were met effectively (merely a guarantee on the provincial governors and the creation of a National Security Council), Tsvangirai relented to intense political pressure from SADC leaders—especially South African—and accepted what he had refused in November.[48] This apparent surrender was criticized initially by some MDC cadres (Tendai Biti then denied in the press being against the decision but later admitted he first opposed it)[49] but was endorsed by the national executive. As a party formed to promote change by fighting elections and lacking alternate strategies, the MDC had no real choice. Besides, the GPA contained a two-year calendar for constitutional reform and democratic elections. MDC leaders hoped they could survive this transitional arrangement in spite of the conflict atmosphere, gain credibility in stabilizing the economy, and win the election eventually.

The SADC summit stated a precise timetable: first the adoption of a constitutional amendment (No. 19) to translate the GPA into law, the activation of the tripartite Joint Monitoring Implementation Committee (JOMIC) set by GPA to oversee breaches of the agreement, the adoption of a national security bill, and then the swearing in of the prime minister and later the whole Cabinet. The timetable was honored in the main as Tsvangirai became prime minister on 11 February 2009, and the Cabinet—without deputy ministers—was sworn in on 13 February. However there were signals not boding well for the success of this government.

Mugabe tried to have seven more Cabinet ministers of his party sworn in than what was allowed under the agreement, creating a hot controversy at the swearing in ceremony, which was delayed several hours. Eventually the compromise brokered by President Motlanthe gave Mugabe two additional state ministers, and four more deputy ministers than initially stipulated, bringing the total to sixty-one ministers in the largest government ever seen in the country. More important, former farmer, MP, and MDC-T treasurer Roy Bennett, named as the deputy minister of agriculture, was arrested right before the beginning of the ceremony, taken to the eastern town of Mutare, and held in custody under spurious charges. Although he was eventually released on bail after a protracted legal battle his trial was conveniently delayed until February 2010, an excuse for Mugabe not to swear him in as deputy minister.

This move put to the test the prime minister's authority and the viability of a government where ZANU-PF heavyweights, led by the powerful defense minister Mnangagwa, laid in ambush. ZANU-PF still dominated the Cabinet, and the JOC retained a de facto control over armed forces and police that Mugabe publicly praised in August 2008 for their conduct during the presidential election. ZANU-PF would not let the MDC-T take full control of the state apparatus and alter the balance of power, and they have been trying by all means to undermine Tsvangirai's credibility and ruin his future chances to unseat Mugabe. Yet, in the meantime, ZANU-PF was using Tsvangirai's aura to assuage donor countries and restore its own image in the public.

By mid-2010, in spite of Tsvangirai's cooperative attitude and some MDC ministers' dedication, there were only a few recorded successes: abandonment of the Zimbabwe dollar as legal tender immediately curbed inflation,[50] schools reopened, civil servants resumed working, and business activity kicked off again with a significant GDP growth—for the first time in a decade. Last but not least, Tsvangirai was slowly gaining statesman-like credibility both at home and internationally while Mugabe's popularity fell to the lowest.

However, the Cabinet remained deeply divided on major issues. Tendai Biti's debt reduction plans and other economic reforms were blocked by Mugabe and the ZANU-PF controlled Senate, further delaying the resumption of IMF and World Bank loans. Mugabe's attempts to appoint a partisan Media Commission and Broadcasting Authority stalled change in this area. The land audit was still to take place, while farm invasions had resumed. In the countryside violence against the opposition activists was rising again, and constitution making was marred with delays and confusion. Although claiming his commitment to the GNU, Mugabe refused to rescind the appointments of the RBZ governor—busy undermining government reforms—and of the partisan attorney general. Opposition governors and additional senators stipulated by the GPA were still to be appointed. The SADC failed to discipline the president and once again bought his line on "Western sanctions" to be lifted first. To no avail: the EU sanction list had been enlarged in 2009, and was retained for another year in February 2010, followed by a similar decision from the Obama administration as Western powers could not condone Mugabe's selective implementation of the GPA.

If the inclusive government does not collapse before its agreed term, the next elections could very well see the return of the 2008 violence and treachery, in particular if the three principals do not reach an agreement on the new constitutional and electoral framework. The defiant eighty-six-year-old leader outmaneuvered the ZANU-PF factions during the party congress in December 2009, and claimed he would stand for his party at the next presidential election. Even Mugabe's death or exile would not guarantee an end to the crisis. The mafia of lieutenants and corrupt sycophants he nurtured and relied on over thirty years have no democratic or economic credentials. They are clamping onto power and sources of wealth[51] and will hamper economic recovery long after Mugabe is gone. Potential successors such as Mnangagwa, Mujuru, or Mutasa are no lesser evils. The Makoni saga in 2008 underlined that the scenario of a takeover by some ZANU-PF reformists willing to regenerate the nationalist camp was very unlikely. The culture of violence, treachery, and recklessness that dominates the ruling party and that has permeated unfortunately the whole society, including some opposition and civil society circles, will undermine efforts to create a democratic dispensation.

Somehow and beyond the fate of Mugabe and his cronies, the Zimbabwe crisis is a distant legacy of Ian Smith's white minority regime and its obtuse repression of African nationalism. There was a defining moment in the 1950s and 1960s when a liberal colonial government could have worked toward the growing inclusion of the black majority and the building of a multiracial democratic culture—very much in the line of Garfield Todd's tenure of office.[52] But Smith's narrow-minded, white chauvinist agenda and the subsequent liberation war put Zimbabwe on a different and grimmer path. Zimbabwe's descent into the inferno today is the dreadful—but somehow logical—conclusion of the drama that unfolded in 1965 with the UDI.

Will it be possible to prevent Zimbabwe from becoming another failed state embroiled in bloody conflicts, famine, and deadly diseases? Regional and global power interference has been ineffective or inadequate to date. Indeed, the crisis underscores the failure of "preventive diplomacy" in Africa.[53] Another collateral casualty of this blunder of major proportions might be the ambitious NEPAD, meant to revive Africa's economy and fight poverty, which Mugabe quite logically dismissed as an imperialist trap. The peer review mechanism will sound hollow if the African Union remains unable to deal with Mugabe. Similarly, South Africa's "quiet diplomacy" has compromised the country's standing on the international scene at a time when the new power elite in Pretoria faced a wave of criticisms for growing corruption, increasing violence, contempt for the law, and indifference toward the destitute majority— what is already dubbed "the Zimbabwean disease." Therefore, the Zimbabwe crisis epitomizes the uncertain future of democracy and good governance in southern Africa as a whole.

Acronyms

AAG	Affirmative Action Group
ACP	African, Caribbean and Pacific Group of States
ACR	African Consolidated Resources
AGOA	Africa's Growth Opportunities Act
AIPPA	Access to Information and Protection of Privacy Act
ANC	African National Congress
ANZ	Associated Newspapers of Zimbabwe
ARDA	Agriculture and Rural Development Authority
ART	African Resources Trust
AU	African Union
AWC	Association of Women's Clubs
BBC	British Broadcasting Corporation
BSA	Broadcasting Services Act
CAZ	Conservative Alliance of Zimbabwe
CCJP	Catholic Commission for Justice and Peace
CFU	Commercial Farmers Union
CHOGM	Commonwealth Heads of Government Meeting
CHRA	Combined Harare Residents Association
CIO	Central Intelligence Organisation
CODESRIA	Council for the Development of Social Science Research in Africa
COSATU	Congress of South African Trade Unions
CRC	Constitutional Review Commission
CZG	Crisis in Zimbabwe Group
CZI	Confederation of Zimbabwe Industries
DARE	Dare re Chimurenga (exiled ZANU supreme council in 1970s)
DDF	District Development Fund

DRC	Democratic Republic of the Congo
ECHO	European Commission Humanitarian Aid Office
ECOWAS	Economic Community of West African States
ESAP	Economic Structural Adjustment Program
ESC	Electoral Supervisory Commission
EU	European Union
FAO	Food and Agriculture Organization (UN)
FLS	Front-Line State
FORUM	Forum Party of Zimbabwe (sometimes given as FPZ, also used for Federal Party of Zimbabwe)
FRELIMO	Mozambique Liberation Front
GALZ	Gays and Lesbians of Zimbabwe
GAPWUZ	General Agriculture and Plantation Workers Union of Zimbabwe
GMB	Grain Marketing Board
GNU	Government of National Unity
GPA	General Political Agreement
ICFU	Indigenous Commercial Farmers Union
ICG	International Crisis Group
IDBC	Indigenous Business Development Centre
IJAZ	Independent Journalists Association of Zimbabwe
ILO	International Labour Organization
IMC	Interministerial Committee
IMF	International Monetary Fund
IRIN	Integrated Regional Information Networks
ISO	International Socialist Organisation
JAG	Justice for Agriculture
JOC	Joint Operations Command
JSC	Judicial Service Commission
LCHR	Lawyers Committee for Human Rights
LOMA	Law and Order Maintenance Act
LRF	Legal Resources Foundation
MDC	Movement for Democratic Change
MIC	Media and Information Commission
MISA	Media Institute of Southern Africa
MMD	Movement for Multiparty Democracy
MMPZ	Media Monitoring Project of Zimbabwe
MMT	Mass Media Trust
MOU	Memorandum of Understanding
NANGO	National Association of Non-Governmental Organisations
NCA	National Constitutional Assembly
NDP	National Democratic Party

NEC	National Executive Council
NEPAD	New Partnership for Africa's Development
NGO	Nongovernmental organization
NIECZ	National Investment and Empowerment Company of Zimbabwe
NOCZIM	National Oil Company of Zimbabwe
NRZ	National Railways of Zimbabwe
OAU	Organization of African Unity
OPDS	Organ on Politics, Defence and Security
PAC	Pan Africanist Congress
PCC	People's Constitutional Convention
PF	Patriotic Front
POSA	Public Order and Security Act
PTC	Zimbabwe Posts and Telecommunications Corporation
RBZ	Reserve Bank of Zimbabwe
RENAMO	Mozambique National Resistance (Resistência Nacional Moçambicana)
RF	Rhodesian Front
SABC	South African Broadcasting Corporation
SACP	South African Communist Party
SADC	Southern African Development Community
SADCC	Southern African Development Co-ordination Conference
SAMDEF	Southern Africa Media Development Fund
SAPES	Southern Africa Political Economy Series
SAPPHO	Southern Africa Printing and Publishing House
SARIPS	Southern African Regional Institute for Policy Studies
SDF	Social Development Fund
SRC	Students' Representative Council
UANC	United African National Council
UDI	Unilateral Declaration of Independence
UN	United Nations
UNDP	United Nations Development Programme
UNESCO	United Nations Educational, Scientific and Cultural Organization
UP	United Parties
UPM	United People's Movement
UPP	United People's Party
UZ	University of Zimbabwe
VOP	Voice of the People
WFP	World Food Programme
WTO	World Trade Organization
ZANLA	Zimbabwe African National Liberation Army

ZANU	Zimbabwe African National Union
ZAPU	Zimbabwe African People's Union
ZBC	Zimbabwe Broadcasting Corporation
ZCC	Zimbabwe Council of Churches
ZCTU	Zimbabwe Congress of Trade Unions
ZDF	Zimbabwe Defence Forces
ZDI	Zimbabwe Defence Industries
ZEC	Zimbabwe Electoral Commission
ZESA	Zimbabwe Electricity Supply Authority
ZESN	Zimbabwe Election Support Network
ZFU	Zimbabwe Farmers Union
ZIANA	Zimbabwe Inter-Africa News Agency
ZIMASCO	Zimbabwe Mining and Smelting Company
ZIMPREST	Zimbabwe Programme for Economic and Social Transformation
ZIMRIGHTS	Zimbabwe Human Rights Association (sometimes ZimRights)
ZIPA	Zimbabwe People's Army
ZIPAM	Zimbabwe Institute of Public Administration and Management
ZIPRA	Zimbabwe People's Revolutionary Army
ZISCO	Zimbabwe Iron and Steel Company
ZLHR	Zimbabwe Lawyers for Human Rights
ZLP	Zimbabwe Liberators' Platform
ZNA	Zimbabwe National Army
ZNCC	Zimbabwe National Chamber of Commerce
ZNLWVA	Zimbabwe National Liberation War Veterans Association
ZRP	Zimbabwe Republic Police
ZTA	Zimbabwe Tobacco Association
ZUD	Zimbabwe Union of Democrats
ZUJ	Zimbabwe Union of Journalists
ZUM	Zimbabwe Unity Movement

Major Newspapers and Cities of Publication

Herald, Sunday Mail, Daily News, Daily Gazette, Sunday Gazette, Zimbabwe Standard, Zimbabwe Independent, Financial Gazette, Daily Mirror, Sunday Mirror Hansard (Parliamentary Gazette) in Harare

Chronicle, Sunday News in Bulawayo

Observer, Times, Daily Telegraph, Sunday Telegraph, Financial Times, in London

Guardian in Manchester
Mail & Guardian, Business Day, The Star, News 24, ZimOnline, SA *Sunday Times* in Johannesburg
New York Times in New York
Washington Post in Washington

Notes

Introduction

1. The Zimbabwe African National Union (ZANU) broke away in 1963 from the leading Zimbabwe African People's Union (ZAPU), which formed in 1961 and was led by Joshua Nkomo. The two organizations were rivals during the war of liberation and loosely united in 1979, for the Lancaster House conference, under the umbrella of the Patriotic Front, thus adding PF to the acronyms. However, they ran separately in the 1980 elections, and since then Mugabe's party, which absorbed ZAPU in 1987, has been known as ZANU-PF. Although Joshua Nkomo's party's official name between 1976 and 1987 was PF-ZAPU, it is always referred to as ZAPU in the rest of this book.

2. The Catholic Commission for Justice and Peace (CCJP)/Legal Resources Foundation (LRF) report, the most credible to date, documented 3,750 cases of murder and estimated the actual number as more than 6,000 dead. See *Breaking the Silence, Building True Peace: A Report on the Disturbances in Matabeleland and the Midlands, 1980 to 1988* (Harare: CCJP/LRF, 1997), 157. Other sources put it as high as 20,000 people, but without documented evidence.

3. It came as a shock to us to be told in 1995 by a low-ranking government employee in rural Zimbabwe: "At least in Smith's time what I earned could feed my family" (personal field notes).

4. On Matabeleland, see for example Terence O. Ranger, "Matabeleland Since the Amnesty," *African Affairs* 88, 351 (1989): 161–73. Other academics who toed the line were not ZANU-PF fellow travelers like Ranger; see John Hatchard, *Individual Freedoms and State Security in the African Context: The Case of Zimbabwe* (London: James Currey, 1993), 17–20; and David N. Beach, *The Shona and Their Neighbours* (Oxford: Blackwell, 1994), 183. Both underestimated the extent of the repression.

5. Zimbabwe-reared writer Doris Lessing, although once a communist sympathetic to Black nationalism, woke up to these grim realities. See her honest and incisive account of her successive trips to post-independence Zimbabwe in *African Laughter: Four Visits to Zimbabwe* (New York: HarperCollins, 1992). See also her charge against "political correctness" allowing African dictators such as Mugabe to get away with graft and murder; Doris Lessing, "The Jewel of Africa," *New York Review of Books*, 10 April 2003.

6. Several analysts pointed at this narrow-minded nationalist agenda; see Norbert Tengende, "Workers, Students and the Struggles for Democracy: State-Civil Society Relations in Zimbabwe," Ph.D. dissertation, Roskilde University, 1994; Lloyd Sachikonye, "The National-State Project and Conflict in Zimbabwe," in Adebayo Olukoshi and Liisa Laakso, eds., *Challenges to the Nation-State in Africa* (Uppsala: Nordiska Afrikainstitutet, 1996).

7. A Heroes' Day was instituted, and the burial or reburial in the national and provincial Heroes' Acres of deceased ex-combatants followed a ceremonial inspired by Communist countries of the Stalin era. On this cult, see Norma Kriger, "The Politics of Creating National Heroes: The Search for Political Legitimacy and National Identity," in Ngwabi Bhebe and Terence Ranger, eds., *Soldiers in Zimbabwe's Liberation War*, vol. 1 (Harare: University of Zimbabwe Publications, 1995), 139–62.

8. See the figures quoted by Hevina S. Dashwood, *Zimbabwe: The Political Economy of Transformation* (Toronto: University of Toronto Press, 2000), 41–46.

9. A point acknowledged by Brian Raftopoulos, "The Zimbabwe Crisis and the Challenges for the Left," *Journal of Southern African Studies* 32, 2 (June 2006): 203–19. However, no convincing explanation of the "Left-minded" scholarship's permanent state of denial on Mugabe's regime and ZANU-PF is offered.

10. The Unilateral Declaration of Independence in 1965, proclaimed by the Southern Rhodesian government of Ian Smith, was a rebellion against the British Crown that led to increasing international isolation and economic sanctions. It ended with the Lancaster House agreement in December 1979 and a short-term return of British authority in preparation for full independence.

11. There is a striking analogy with one of Mugabe's models, Mao Zedong; see Jung Chang and Jon Halliday, *Mao: The Unknown Story* (New York: Random House 2005).

12. Before that, the workers' strikes in 1980–81 were described in government propaganda as an unavoidable contradiction between workers' short-term interests and the country's long-term socialist project, a rhetoric eagerly swallowed by many academic sympathizers.

13. ESAP was a five-year program to cut down government spending and contain public debt with the financial support of the International Monetary Fund (IMF) and the World Bank.

14. Some radical intellectuals such as Sam Moyo still support Mugabe's land policy with the backing of African, allegedly progressive luminaries such as Mamdani; see Mahmood Mamdani, "Lessons of Zimbabwe," *London Review of Books*, 4 December 2008, and the stiff reply by thirty-four scholars, pointing at a change of mood in the small world of Zimbabwean studies, *London Review of Books*, 1 January 2009.

15. See Stephen Chan, *Robert Mugabe: A Life of Power and Violence* (London: Tauris, 2003). Chan provides no convincing explanation for the sudden turn of events. Why would an enlightened statesman, a respected Third World voice who could relish a cup of tea with the queen by Chan's own account, begin in 2000 to behave like a "madman" destroying his own country?

16. One of the early criticisms, although still in veiled terms, of ZANU-PF's domination could be found in Brian Raftopoulos, "Beyond the House of Hunger: Democratic Struggles in Zimbabwe," *Review of African Political Economy* 54 (1992): 59–74.

17. Among the best are Andrew Meldrum's touching *Where We Have Hope: A Memoir of Zimbabwe* (London: John Murray, 2004), and Martin Meredith, *Mugabe: Power and Plunder in Zimbabwe* (Oxford: Public Affairs, 2002).

18. In a large literature, see Michael Bratton and Nicholas Van de Walle, "Neopatrimonial Regimes and Political Transitions in Africa," *World Politics* 46 (1994): 453–80; Richard Sandbrook, with Judith Barker, *The Politics of Africa's Economic Stagnation* (Cambridge: Cambridge University Press, 1985); and the classic Samuel N. Eisenstadt, *Traditional Patrimonialism and Modern Neopatrimonialism*, Sage Research Papers in Social Sciences (Beverly Hills, Calif.: Sage, 1973).

19. See Robert H. Jackson and Carl G. Rosberg, *Personal Rule in Black Africa: Prince, Autocrat, Prophet, Tyrant* (Berkeley: University of California University Press, 1982). Of course "personal" qualifies a type of rulership and by no means suggests that the paramount ruler could govern without lieutenants and cronies. However, these are dispensable political clients rather than allies, let alone kingmakers.

20. See interview with Wilfred Mhanda, *Focus* (HSF), December 2000.

21. For such speculations on Mugabe's early childhood and its alleged impact on his psychology, see, for example, Heidi Holland, *Dinner with Mugabe: The Untold Story of a Freedom Fighter Who Became a Tyrant* (Johannesburg: Penguin Global, 2008).

22. For an attempt at theorizing this approach, see Samuel Decalo, *Psychoses of Power: African Personal Dictatorships* (Boulder, Colo.: Westview, 1989), chap. 1.

Chapter 1. Authoritarian Control of the Political Arena

1. The heading to this section is borrowed from Masipula Sithole, *Zimbabwe: Struggles Within the Struggle* (Salisbury: Rujeko, 1979). The young activist's book was dismissed as partisan by mainstream ZANU in the 1980s in view of Masipula's family links with Ndabaningi. A respected University of Zimbabwe professor lauded for his integrity, Masipula stood as an opposition candidate in 1990 and always supported the democratic movement. A large crowd assembled at his funeral in April 2003.

2. See David Moore, "The Contradictory Construction of Hegemony: Politics, Ideology and Class in the Formation of a New African State," Ph.D. dissertation, York University, 1990.

3. André Astrow, *Zimbabwe: A Revolution That Lost Its Way?* (London: Zed, 1983), 82–90.

4. Terence O. Ranger, "Missionaries, Migrants and the Manyika: The Invention of Ethnicity in Zimbabwe," in Leroy Vail, ed., *The Creation of Tribalism in Southern Africa* (London: James Currey, 1989), 118–50.

5. For an early example of such literature, see John Day, "The Insignificance of Tribe in the African Politics of Zimbabwe, Rhodesia," *Journal of Commonwealth and Comparative Politics* 18 (1980): 85–109.

6. The Zimbabwe People's Army supposedly combined ZANLA and ZIPRA (respective guerrillas of ZANU and ZAPU) into one army in November 1975, as demanded by heads of the Front-Line States (Angola, Botswana, Mozambique, Tanzania, Zambia), but collapsed in June 1976 due to serious infighting in training camps.

7. See Moore, "Contradictory Construction of Hegemony," chap. 4. The rift between the James Chikerema and Jason Moyo factions in ZAPU contributed heavily to the subsequent alignment of Shona guerrillas with ZANU, leaving ZAPU as a predominantly Ndebele organization.

8. Norma Kriger, *Guerrilla Veterans in Post-War Zimbabwe: Symbolic and Violent Politics, 1980–1987* (Cambridge: Cambridge University Press, 2003), 28.

9. Trevor Grundy, "Chitepo's Death Still Haunts Mugabe," *Zimbabwean*, 25 March 2005. Edgar Tekere also said it was an inside job, but he claimed Tongogara had been framed. See "Chitepo Murdered by ZANU-PF: Tekere," *Harare Financial Gazette*, 28 August 1997.

10. John Mataure was killed on the spot. More than one hundred Manyikas were subsequently murdered in Zambia and Mozambique in retribution and as a follow-up to Chitepo's assassination.

11. David Smith, Colin Simpson, and Ian Davies, *Mugabe* (London: Sphere, 1981), 76–77; Sithole, *Zimbabwe*, 61–62.

12. Rugare Gumbo, Henry Hamadziripi, Kumbirai Kangai, and Mukudzei Mudzi were also implicated in Chitepo's death by in the OAU report. See *Report of the Special International Commission on the Assassination of Herbert Wiltshire Chitepo* (Lusaka: Government Printer, March 1976). Other sources also implicate Rex Nhongo and Robson Manyika for carrying the bomb from Tanzania; see *Zimbabwean Standard*, 30 September 2005, 14 October 2001.

13. See David Martin and Phyllis Johnson, *The Chitepo Assassination* (Harare: Zimbabwe Publishing House, 1985). They rely on confessions by former white police special branch operatives who claimed to have organized the bomb blast. However, many of these operatives worked for state security after independence, when Security Minister Mnangagwa wanted to benefit from their experience to build his own apparatus. Therefore their testimonies could be part of a deception operation. The same can be said of Ken Flower, since he remained head of Zimbabwe's CIO until his retirement in the mid-1980s.

14. Sithole, *Zimbabwe*, 47.

15. A process that began much earlier while Mugabe and fellow prisoners were in detention at Wha Wha security prison. See Robert Cary and Diana Mitchell, *African Nationalist Leaders in Rhodesia Who's Who* (Bulawayo: Books of Rhodesia, 1977).

16. Sithole, *Zimbabwe*, 64, 70, 75

17. Kriger, *Guerrilla Veterans*, 26.

18. See interview with Wilfred Mhanda, *Focus* (HSF), December 2000; also R. W. Johnson, "Wilfred Mhanda," *London Review of Books*, 23 February 2001.

19. Sithole, *Zimbabwe*, 120. According to Masipula's account, the ZANU camp commanders' support for Mugabe's leadership bid in late 1975/early 1976 was made conditional on Mugabe's obtaining the release of Tongogara and his group from Zambian prisons.

20. First attempt at direct negotiations between Ian Smith's regime and the coalition of black nationalists—excluding the 1975 Victoria Falls meeting between Smith and Nkomo—the conference organized by the British government with the support of both South Africa and the Front-Line States, on the basis of U.S. secretary of state Henry Kissinger's peace plan, opened on 28 October 1976 and closed on 14 December without significant result. See Martin Meredith, *The Past Is Another Country: Rhodesia UDI to Zimbabwe* (London: Pan Books, 1980), 242–93.

21. Smith, Simpson, and Davies, *Mugabe*, 93.

22. Although a former ZANLA High Command member under Tongogara, subsequently working with Nhongo in the ZIPA High Command, Dzinashe Machingura had nothing to do with Chitepo's assassination, according to Sithole, *Zimbabwe*, 125.

23. See Moore's thesis and his letter to *London Review of Books*, 5 April 2001.

24. See interview with Wilfred Mhanda, in *Focus*; see also *Daily News*, 1 January

2001. According to Mhanda, Tongogara offered him the chance to come to his side and topple Mugabe and Nhongo. Mhanda refused and was jailed with his junior officers (interview with Wilfred Mhanda, Harare, 13 August 2001). This supports the latter's contention that Tongogara would not have been any better than Mugabe. It also provides a strong potential motive for Tongogara's alleged assassination by Mugabe's henchmen after the Lancaster House agreement.

25. Smith, Simpson, and Davies, *Mugabe*, 107.

26. Smith, Simpson, and Davies, *Mugabe*, 170.

27. Some were later offered a job in the Zimbabwe Broadcasting Corporation to use their ideological training.

28. Interview with Wilfred Mhanda, Harare, 13 August 2001.

29. See the intelligence reports at the time cited by Mark Olden, "This Man Has Been Called Zimbabwe's Che Guevara: Did Mugabe Have Him Murdered?" *New Statesman*, 8 April 2004. Ian Smith got similar information from the Rhodesian special branch; see Ian D. Smith, *The Great Betrayal: The Memoirs of Africa's Most Controversial Leader* (London: Blake, 1997), 335.

30. See *Report of the Special International Commission*, 51, quoted in Sithole, *Zimbabwe*, 63.

31. This was anathema to Mugabe, as Wilfred Mhanda puts it: Mugabe "referred to unity with Zapu as sharing the spoils with those who had not shouldered the burden of fighting," *New Statesman*, 8 April 2004.

32. Smith, Simpson, and Davies, *Mugabe*, 156. Apparently Tongogara and Nkomo got on very well and had several private conversations during the conference. Nkomo allegedly offered Tongogara a top job in a future united Cabinet or at the head of the national army.

33. ZANU released an undertaker's statement saying Tongogara's injuries were consistent with a road accident, but no autopsy results or pictures were ever released. According to Margaret Dongo, one of the last people to see him alive, the accident was not genuine (interview, Harare, 1996). Among the people who must have known the truth were Solomon Mujuru (Rex Nhongo), Simon Muzenda, and those allegedly on the scene, including Oppah Rushesha/Muchinguri and Josiah Tungamirai, some of whom were likely to have been involved.

34. See the chapter "Elections Within the Elections" in John W. Makumbe and Daniel Compagnon, *Behind the Smokescreen: The Politics of Zimbabwe's 1995 General Elections* (Harare: University of Zimbabwe Publications, 2000).

35. A former protégé of Mugabe and his first wife, Sally, Dongo was elected in the Third Parliament, where she criticized the party heavyweights on governance issues. Margaret Dongo and Patrick Marime (also victimized in the 1994 primaries) sat on the Parliamentary Committee on Public Accounts when it was chaired by the late Sydney Malunga, and investigated widespread corruption in the government. She clashed publicly with the then minister of commerce and industry, Nathan Shamuyarira, over the fate of destitute war veterans and Shamuyarira's own war record. She also castigated the older politicians clinging to power. Several Cabinet ministers colluded with the provincial executive of the Harare province to try to get rid of her. See Makumbe and Compagnon, *Behind the Smokescreen*, 123–26.

36. His sister Sabina Mugabe and his cousin Ignatius Chombo retained their seats. Sabina's sons Leo Mugabe (a successful "political businessman"—see Chapter 7) and Patrick Zhuwawo were newly elected; in April 2005 the latter was appointed deputy minister for science and technology. Mugabe also appointed his uncle Nelson Samkange, Mashonaland West governor, to Parliament.

37. The electorate in the Makokoba constituency was not deceived by this maneuver: in the by-election following his death only 6 percent of voters went to the polls.

38. Interview with Wilfred Mhanda, Harare, August 2001. Chris's brother Herbert Ushewokunze alluded to the assassination in his obituary in Shona at Heroes' Acre: "if you kill all your children, who will bury you?" he rhetorically asked Mugabe, although he was familiar with political violence himself, having threatened people with a gun during at least one election campaign. In and out of the Cabinet, his insubordination was tolerated and he amassed significant wealth before dying of illness in 1995.

39. For an elaboration on political factions, see Frederick G. Bailey, *Stratagems and Spoils: A Social Anthropology of Politics* (Oxford: Blackwell, 1969).

40. Kumbirai Kangai, a former Dare re Chimurenga founding member and then minister of land and agriculture, was accused by an anticorruption task force created by Mugabe and headed by his relative Philip Chiyangwa. Kangai was eventually cleared of these accusations and bounced back after the 2005 elections as a deputy speaker of Parliament and party secretary for external affairs—if only to keep Mutasa in check.

41. See Geoffrey Nyarota's account of Chiwenga's career, "Why Chiwenga Would Die for Mugabe," 23 June 2008, http://www.thezimbabwetimes.com/. According to this senior journalist and political observer since the 1980s, Chiwenga was retained in the army at independence on Mugabe's orders despite failing the exams to become an officer. Shiri got promoted because he is from the same village as Mugabe. Chihuri was rehabilitated in 1980 after a long period of incarceration in Mozambican prisons during the liberation war.

42. A minister of state for political affairs in the late 1980s, Shava was forced to resign over the Willowvale corruption scandal, duly convicted, and then pardoned by Mugabe. He resumed his career in Midlands in the shadow of Mnangagwa.

43. By mid-2005 Mawere was fighting a rearguard legal battle in Johannesburg against the Mugabe regime and claimed that the U.S.$120 million arrears paid to the IMF by the Reserve Bank of Zimbabwe were snatched from his frozen bank accounts. He broke his association with Mnangagwa and sided with Simba Makoni in the 2008 presidential election.

44. Joyce Mujuru, a party stalwart, is lacking statesmanship qualities, according to insiders. For instance, at the beginning of the farm invasions, then a second rank Cabinet minister, she urged land occupiers to return with T-shirts soaked with the blood of white farmers; see Trevor Grundy, "Bloody Pledge of Mugabe's Protégé," *Scotsman*, 5 December 2004.

45. Claiming to embody the "third way" between ZANU-PF and MDC, Jonathan Moyo announced by late July 2005 the launch of the United People's Movement (UPM). He was joined by Pearson Mbalekwa, a former ZANU-PF MP for Zvishavane (Midlands Province) and by a central committee member who quit the ruling party in protest against Operation Murambatsvina. Mnangagwa hastened to distance himself from Moyo's initiative.

46. The former chairman for Masvingo province, Daniel Shumba, founded the United People's Party (UPP) in January 2006, attracting a number of disenchanted ZANU-PF middle-level cadres, mainly from Masvingo. He attended the Christian Coalition conference with other opposition parties in late July 2006 but failed dismally in subsequent elections.

47. For example, President Banana's claim in early 1981, "in unity we fought

for independence and in unity we must now strive to consolidate it," *Herald*, 3 January 1981.

48. See Victor de Waal, *The Politics of Reconciliation* (London: Hurst, 1990).

49. Interview with Ian Smith (Harare, 1995); see also his memoirs, *The Great Betrayal*, 361–72. Obviously Mugabe pretended to observe Westminster-style parliamentary customs.

50. Formed in December 1971, as ZANU and ZAPU were banned and their leaders in jail, the African National Council led by Methodist bishop Abel Muzorewa was the black nationalists' legal façade. It organized the successful protests against the agreement signed by Smith and the British Conservative government during the Pearce Commission visit in 1972. Demanding overall leadership of the nationalist movement—but rejected by the guerrillas—until the 1976 Geneva conference, Muzorewa enjoyed significant support inside Rhodesia. However, he compromised his integrity by signing the 1979 Internal Settlement with Ian Smith, becoming a nominal prime minister of Zimbabwe-Rhodesia, and leading the government delegation at the Lancaster House negotiations. The revived United African National Council (UANC) secretly supported by the Rhodesian intelligence was trounced in the 1980 elections.

51. Yet, Mugabe detained Muzorewa under spurious charges in 1982–83, if only to dissuade him from siding with ZAPU. In 1995 again he became the target of vicious propaganda ahead of general elections.

52. This was achieved through Constitutional Amendment No. 6 adopted with the support of the five independent white MPs. Yet ZANU-PF made no distinction between "moderate" white MPs and CAZ because it was more convenient for propaganda's sake to vilify all whites.

53. The first serious fighting, in the Entumbane suburb of Bulawayo in November 1980, was sparked by Enos Nkala's vitriolic speech calling ZAPU "the enemy." Fighting resumed in Entumbane in February 1981, and spread to neighboring areas and the Midlands. The report of the Commission of Enquiry on these incidents (in which more than 300 people were killed), chaired by justice Enoch Dumbutshena, was never made public but is said to have pointed at ZANLA.

54. The best account of this strenuous process can be found in Kriger, *Guerrilla Veterans*.

55. See Jocelyn Alexander, "Dissident Perspectives on Zimbabwe's Post-Independence War," *Africa* 68, 2 (1998); also the testimonies collected by Katri Yap in "Voices from the Matabeleland Conflict: Perceptions of Violence, Ethnicity, and the Disruption of National Integration," paper presented at Britain/Zimbabwe Research Day conference, St. Anthony's College, Oxford University, 8 June 1996; Diana Auret, *Reaching for Justice: The Catholic Commission for Justice and Peace, 1972–1992* (Harare: Mambo Press/CCJP, 1992), 153; CCJP/LRF, *Breaking the Silence, Building True Peace: A Report on the Disturbances in Matabeleland and the Midlands, 1980 to 1988* (Harare: CCJP/LRF, 1997), 32–34; Kriger, *Guerrilla Veterans*, 133–38.

56. CCJP/LRF, *Breaking the Silence*, 41. It was suggested that a white CIO officer—Matt Calloway, allegedly a covert South African agent—deliberately misled the Zimbabwean government into believing ZAPU was engineering a coup; see John Hanlon, *Beggar Your Neighbours: Apartheid Power in Southern Africa* (Bloomington: Indiana University Press, 1986), 183. Even if true, this story does not exonerate Mugabe for the subsequent bloody repression. Besides, all other evidence suggests Mugabe knew perfectly well what he was doing. See for confirmation, Judith Garfield Todd, *Through the Darkness: A Life in Zimbabwe* (Cape Town: Zebra Press, 2007).

57. They had been acquitted in 1983, after a lengthy treason trial, but were kept in extrajudicial detention under the state of emergency powers. Masuku was ill and died in April 1986.

58. Meredith, *Mugabe. Power and Plunder in Zimbabwe*, 63.

59. Even a decade later, Dyke did not understand that he had been used by the regime and fully supported government terror in Matabeleland; see Yap, "Voices from the Matabeleland Conflict."

60. Africa Watch, *Zimbabwe: A Break with the Past? Human Rights and Political Unity* (London: Africa Watch, 1989), 16.

61. See CCJP/LRF, *Breaking the Silence*, 48–50. The balanced report also covers atrocities allegedly committed by "dissidents" (38–39). About 600 civilians lost their lives at their hands. However, this unjustifiable violence was at the time grossly exaggerated by Mugabe's propaganda, which blamed the "dissidents" for some state agencies' crimes.

62. Masipula Sithole, "The General Elections: 1979–1985," in Ibbo Mandaza, ed., *Zimbabwe: The Political Economy of Transition, 1980–1986* (Dakar: CODESRIA, 1986), 73–97; and Per Nordlund, *Organising the Political Agora: Domination and Democratisation in Zambia and Zimbabwe* (Uppsala: Uppsala University Press, 1996), 147–48.

63. Hanlon, *Beggar Your Neighbours*, 175–77.

64. See CCJP/LRF, *Breaking the Silence*, 30, 34–35.

65. See CCJP/LRF, *Breaking the Silence*, 58

66. On 13 September 1982, all areas where a curfew was in force in Matabeland were closed to the press, and foreign correspondents had to seek authorization from the Ministry of Information to travel outside a 40 km perimeter around Harare and Bulawayo; Auret, *Reaching for Justice*, 149.

67. See Peter Godwin, *Mukiwa: A White Boy in Africa* (London: Macmillan, 1996), 342–85. Godwin managed to enter the closed area to report on the war crimes in articles published in the *Observer*. Tiny Rowland, a friend of Mugabe (and previously a supporter of Nkomo) and owner of the newspaper, banned his articles. Godwin was then expelled from Zimbabwe along with *Guardian*'s correspondent Nick Worrall who first reported the atrocities.

68. See Welshman Ncube, "Constitutionalism, Democracy and Political Practice in Zimbabwe," in Ibbo Mandaza and Lloyd M. Sachikonye, eds., *The One-Party State and Democracy: The Zimbabwe Debate* (Harare: SAPES Trust, 1991), 165.

69. On the negotiations leading to the Unity Accord, see Willard A. Chiwewe, "Unity Negotiations," in Canaan S. Banana, ed., *Turmoil and Tenacity: Zimbabwe, 1890–1990* (Harare: College Press, 1989), 242–87.

70. See however Welshman Ncube, "The Post-Unity Period: Developments, Benefits and Problems," in Banana, *Turmoil and Tenacity*, 306–9; Ncube, "Constitutionalism, Democracy and Political Practice," 161–66. This brave attitude is perfectly in line with his later MDC involvement.

71. MP for Mutare Central, Daniel Sithole, made sexist comments on women in Parliament; *Herald*, 9 March 1995.

72. Government propaganda promptly labeled it a "whites' party" although white members were only a handful and the leadership was all black. The same trick has been used ad nauseam against the MDC.

73. The merger attempt predictably collapsed when Tekere and Muzorewa quarreled over the top leadership position. At that time both were aging, discredited politicians.

74. For example, the FORUM gathered evidence of rigging in several constit-

uencies in Harare and Bulawayo in the 1995 elections but was unable to challenge the results in court because the electoral campaign had exhausted its limited financial resources.

75. For example, in the run-up to the 1995 elections the government media lambasted Muzorewa for the bombing of ZANU-PF guerrilla camps in Mozambique by the Rhodesian air force when he was prime minister of Zimbabwe-Rhodesia.

76. See Lloyd Sachikonye, "The 1990 Zimbabwe Elections: A Post-Mortem," 99.

77. This controversy was discussed in detail in Makumbe and Compagnon, *Behind the Smokescreen*, 91–95.

78. On ZANU-PF's political culture, see Makumbe and Compagnon, *Behind the Smokescreen*, chap. 9, "Towards an Entrenched Authoritarianism?"

79. Liisa Laakso makes a similar point in "When Elections Are Just a Formality: Rural-Urban Dynamics in the Dominant-Party System of Zimbabwe," in Michael Cowen and Liisa Laakso, eds., *Multi-Party Elections in Africa* (London: James Currey, 2000).

80. After his defeat in Harare Central in March 1995, he lost his farm in the outskirts of Harare when the government-owned Zimbank demanded repayment of past loans. Most of his properties were auctioned to settle his debts (interview with Dumbutshena, Harare, August 1999). The first black chief justice in Zimbabwe history died almost a pauper.

81. See *Sunday Gazette*, 3 December 1995. In the run-up to the Masvingo mayoral election in April 2001, Hungwe harangued the audience in a meeting with these words: "If you do not vote for ZANU-PF in the coming mayoral election, people are going to be killed. I want to tell you, someone is going to die," *Daily News*, 4 April 2001.

82. See *Herald*, 1 April 1995, and for another presidential statement of this kind, *Herald*, 5 April 1995.

83. Heroes' Day speech, 12 August 2002 (*Guardian*, 13 August 2002).

84. Interview with ZUD leader Margaret Dongo, Harare, August 1999.

85. See Washington Sansole's comments quoted in Andrew Meldrum, "Zimbabwe: Rubber-Stamp Parliament," *Africa Report* 40 (May–June 1995): 62–63. In 1995 Sansole was FORUM's national chairman and a candidate in Bulawayo South.

86. Interviews with Margaret Dongo, Harare, August 1999 and April 2000. Besides, parliamentary rules forbade MPs to cross the floor without going for a by-election.

87. See International Crisis Group, *Zimbabwe: An Opposition Strategy*, ICG Africa Report 117, 24 August 2006, 9.

88. A farm in the outskirts of Harare that Sithole used to resettle members of his party/tribe was deemed a health hazard by government and forcibly evacuated by the police after months of public controversy.

89. Nhamakonda's trial was held in camera, raising heavy suspicion about the methods used to extort his admission of guilt, and Sithole has never been publicly cross-examined in the presence of his accusers.

90. See John Hatchard, *Individual Freedoms and State Security in the African Context: The Case of Zimbabwe* (London: James Currey, 1993).

91. In the political culture of the ruling party ever since the guerilla camps, "chef" borrowed from the French points at those who make decisions, the powerful, in opposition to the "povos," a Portuguese word meaning the people, the powerless commoners.

92. See Jonathan N. Moyo, *Voting for Democracy: A Study of Electoral Politics in Zimbabwe* (Harare: University of Zimbabwe Publications, 1992), 19–21. These anti-Smith white MPs believing in a true multiracial democracy and trusting Mugabe's "reconciliation" policy, genuinely wanted to remove the political privileges of the white minority.

93. Luc Mhlaba, "Le retour du Pangolin," *Année Africaine 1987–88* (Bordeaux: CEAN, 1989), 225–38.

94. Ironically Zvobgo later supported constitutional reform, and in a speech delivered in early 1996 he almost proposed to undo what he had done in 1987.

95. See *Sunday Gazette*, 19 March 1995.

96. See Greg Linington, "Can the President Be Constitutionally Removed from Office?" *Legal Forum* (Harare, Legal Resources Foundation) 7, 1 (1995): 52.

97. In principle these regulations had limited time validity and had to be consolidated through proper parliamentary Acts. In most cases the ZANU-PF caucus did not dare to challenge the president's authority. Sometimes the backbenchers registered their concerns by dragging their feet, such as was the case with the passing of the Urban Councils Act (1995).

98. See Welshman Ncube, "The Concept of Separation of Powers in Zimbabwe: Constitutional Myth or Reality?" paper presented at the Zimbabwe Institute of Public Administration and Management (ZIPAM) Seminar for Senior Diplomatic Staff and Aid Agencies, Holiday Inn, Harare, 14–18 October 1996.

99. See the pioneer work, Aristide R. Zolberg, *Creating Political Order: The Party-States of West Africa* (Chicago: Rand McNally, 1966).

100. Ncube, "Constitutionalism, Democracy and Political Practice," 171.

101. For a more detailed account of the election of chiefs to Parliament, see Welshman Ncube, "Review of Electoral Laws and Institutions in Zimbabwe," *Legal Forum* 6, 3 (1994): 17.

102. With 16 appointed senators, Mugabe needs only 6 elected senators to avoid a no confidence motion. With the hegemonic control of the three Mashonaland provinces that ZANU-PF has maintained since 2000 this was easily achieved. Even a coalition of a rebel ZANU-PF faction and the MDC, however unlikely, would hardly defeat the government in Parliament.

103. See *Strengthening Parliamentary Democracy in Zimbabwe, Final Report of the Parliamentary Reform Committee*, 2 vols. (Harare: Parliament of Zimbabwe, May 1998, May 1999).

104. Such an example was the dreadful Operation Murambatsvina in 2005, decided and planned outside the Cabinet and the ruling party's organs, to the extent that most ZANU-PF ministers and party cadres were caught unaware as much as other Zimbabweans; ICG, *Zimbabwe's Operation Murambatsvina: The Tipping Point?* ICG Africa Report 97, 17 August 2005, 6.

105. The Office was for 23 years headed by Charles Utete, secretary to the president and the Cabinet, sometimes nicknamed "Prime Minister" since he was more powerful than Cabinet members. Utete retired in April 2003 but remained influential behind the scenes. He is said to be related to Grace, Mugabe's second wife.

106. This technique was used from the very beginning of the new regime. See Ian Smith's account of his frustration with Mugabe on the issue of community schools in 1980–81, when Mugabe, feigning ignorance, blamed the minister of education for his own decision; Smith, *The Great Betrayal*, 367–98.

107. See Makumbe and Compagnon, *Behind the Smokescreen*, 281–86.

108. Zimbabwe Human Rights NGO Forum, *Of Stuffed Ballots and Empty Stomachs: Reviewing Zimbabwe's 2005 Parliamentary Election and Post-Election Period* (Harare: Zimbabwe Human Rights NGO Forum, 2005), 7. The MDC lost two urban constituencies as a direct result of this gerrymandering. See also ICG, *Post-Election Zimbabwe: What Next?* ICG Africa Report 93, 7 June 2005, 5.

109. See ZESN, *Report on Zimbabwe's 2005 General Election* (Harare: ZESN, April 2005), 21.

110. ICG, *Post-Election Zimbabwe,* 4.

111. ZESN, "The Senate and Gutu North Parliamentary By-Election: Preliminary Election Report," ZESN, 23 November 2005, 6.

112. For an analysis of POSA see Derek Matyszak, "Democratic Space and State Security: Zimbabwe's Public Order and Security Act," *Zimbabwe Human Rights Bulletin* (Zimbabwe Lawyers for Human Rights, Harare) 11 (September 2004): 80.

113. These headmen and chiefs played a crucial role in 2005, according to Zimbabwe Human Rights NGO Forum, *Of Stuffed Ballots and Empty Stomachs,* 20.

114. According to Dr. Daniel Shumba—a retired army officer and former ZANU-PF provincial chairman and central committee member—this trick was used to rig the presidential election in 2002 in particular; see *Mail and Guardian,* 18 July 2006. However, in the 2005 election the numbers were insufficient to affect the results; see Zimbabwe Human Rights NGO Forum, *Of Stuffed Ballots and Empty Stomachs,* 24–25.

115. Prior to 2002, the Election Directorate, made up of trusted high-ranking civil servants, did it; in 2005 it was the preserve of the National Logistics Committee, staffed with army officers and ZANU-PF stalwarts.

116. The total vote announced on radio did not tally with the number of votes finally attributed to the contending parties. See the NGO Sokwanele's detailed report, "'What Happened on Thursday Night': An Account of How ZANU PF Rigged the Parliamentary Elections," 5 April 2005, http://www.sokwanele.com/articles/sokwanele/whathappenedonthursnight_5april2005.html (accessed August 2006). See also Zimbabwe Lawyers for Human Rights, *Report on the March 2005 Parliamentary Elections* and articles in the Zimbabwean *Standard,* 3 April 2005; *Zimbabwe Independent,* 8 April 2005.

117. ZESN, *Report on Zimbabwe's 2005 General Election,* 47.

118. The MDC challenged the results in only fourteen constituencies, and its petitions presented procedural complaints rather than any clear evidence of rigging. According to the Zimbabwe Human Rights NGO Forum, it was an admission that it did not lose through ballot stuffing; see *Of Stuffed Ballots and Empty Stomachs,* 27.

119. Zimbabwe Human Rights NGO Forum, *Of Stuffed Ballots and Empty Stomachs,* 28.

120. The latter, like suppression of mobile polling stations, was meant to limit the risk of ballot box stuffing, but the results could still be manipulated at the polling station level, especially in remote rural areas where MDC polling agents and ZESN observers might not be deployed.

121. For a detailed analysis of the Act showing how ZEC is government-controlled, see Zimbabwe Human Rights NGO Forum, *Of Stuffed Ballots and Empty Stomachs,* 10, 15, where the influence of the ruling party at all stages is underlined. Polling-station presiding officers often behave in a partisan way (19).

122. Chiweshe oversaw the highly controversial 2008 elections and remained

at the head of the ZEC until January 2010, when the retired High Court judge Simpson Mtambanengwe was appointed to the job by the transitional government.

123. Daniel Compagnon, "Zimbabwe: Life After ZANU-PF," *African Affairs* 99 (2000): 449–53.

124. On these attempts and Minister Chombo's arm-twisting tactics, see Amin Y. Kamete, "The Return of the Jettisoned: ZANU-PF's Crack at 'Re-Urbanising' in Harare," *Journal of Southern African Studies* 32, 2 (June 2006): 255–71.

125. Figures from Electoral Supervisory Commission, "Report on the March 2002 Presidential, Mayoral and Council Elections, 2002. The remainder went to minor candidates.

126. See *Tsvangirai v. Mugabe*, Election Petition HC 3616/2002, 12 April 2002.

127. Some 150,000 people were deprived of their right to vote in the Senate and subsequent elections when the government declared all descendants of migrant workers and Zimbabweans of European descent non citizens.

128. "A storm is on the horizon. The dictator must brace himself for a long, bustling winter across the country." ICG, *Zimbabwe's Continuing Self-Destruction*, Crisis Group Africa Briefing 38, 6 June 2006, 7.

129. "Zimbabwe: ZANU-PF, MDC Sign New Constitution," *Zimbabwe Independent*, 19 October 2007.

Chapter 2. Violence as the Cornerstone

1. R. W. Johnson, *Zimbabwe: The Hard Road to Democracy: Survey Analysis and the Parliamentary Election of June 24–25, 2000* (Parklands, S.A.: Helen Suzman Foundation, 2000), 15–17.

2. Rival nationalist factions settled their scores with extreme violence in African townships in the early 1960s; see Timothy Scarnecchia, *The Urban Roots of Democracy and Political Violence in Zimbabwe: Harare and Highfield, 1940–1964* (Rochester, N.Y.: University of Rochester Press, 2008).

3. See Norma Kriger, "Zanu (PF) Strategies in General Elections, 1980–2000: Discourse and Coercion," *African Affairs* 104, 414 (2005): 1–34.

4. *Harare Herald*, 2 October 2000.

5. Kriger, *Guerrilla Veterans in Post-War Zimbabwe*, 47. Some of the ZANLA troops in the assembly camps were hastily armed civilians and young auxiliaries (*mujibas*) to boost the numbers, while the most experienced cadres remained in the bush. Several hundred more infiltrated from Mozambique until the late February 1980 elections; see Martin Meredith, *The Past Is Another Country: Rhodesia, 1890–1979* (London: A. Deutsch, 1979), 395, 400.

6. David Smith, Colin Simpson, and Ian Davies, *Mugabe* (London: Sphere, 1981), 185. Nkala, then the party treasurer and a Mugabe loyalist, became minister of finance in the first cabinet. He was later involved in the killings in Matabeleland and lost his cabinet position after the Willowvale corruption scandal.

7. Smith, Simpson, and Davies, *Mugabe*, 180–81. See also lengthy quotes from the British Election Observers Report in Norma Kriger, *Guerrilla Veterans in Post-War Zimbabwe*, 48–50. The role of the black UNAC auxiliaries of the security forces in the Tribal Areas remains also controversial; see Meredith, *The Past Is Another Country*, 396. However, British and Commonwealth reports deny widespread auxiliary intimidation of voters.

8. Report of the Election Commissioner, Sir John Boynton, MC, *Southern Rho-*

desia Independence Elections 1980 (London: Her Majesty's Stationery Office, 1980), 19; see also Meredith, *The Past Is Another Country*, 401–3.

9. Smith, Simpson, and Davies, *Mugabe*, 182.

10. This does not legitimate his claim that the ballot was deliberately rigged; see Joshua Nkomo, *Nkomo: The Story of My Life* (London: Methuen, 1984), 206–210.

11. Masipula Sithole, "General Elections: 1979–1985," in Ibbo Mandaza, ed., *Zimbabwe: The Political Economy of Transition 1980–1986* (Dakar: CODESRIA, 1986), 84.

12. See B. H. Mashonganyika's testimony in a letter published in the independent press in defense of Muzorewa: "The brutality committed on peasants by 'comrades' was no better than that by the Rhodesian forces. . . . In brutality ZANLA forces were the worst"; see *Sunday Gazette*, 2 April 1999.

13. Norma J. Kriger, *Zimbabwe's Guerrilla War: Peasant Voices* (Cambridge: Cambridge University Press, 1992), 154, 152–57. What makes Kriger's essay so convincing and useful is her reliance on extensive interviews with ordinary people who suffered from all sides during the war.

14. To a large extent, the same violence occurred in ZAPU areas of operation; see Richard Werbner, *Tears of the Dead: The Social Biography of an African Family* (London: Edinburgh University Press/International African Institute, 1991), 149–51; see also Jocelyn Alexander, JoAnn McGregor, and Terence Ranger, *Violence and Memory: One Hundred Years in the "Dark Forests" of Matabeleland* (Oxford: James Currey; Portsmouth, N.H.: Heinemann, 2000), 152–79.

15. There are eyewitness testimonies of villagers burned alive in their huts by guerrillas; see, for example, Peter Godwin, *Mukiwa: A White Boy in Africa* (London: Macmillan, 1996).

16. Cf. Moto, March 1995, 1, 5–7; Diana Auret, Reaching for Justice: The Catholic Commission for Justice and Peace, 1972–1992 (Harare: Mambo Press/CCJP, 1992), 147–66; Lawyers Committee for Human Rights, Zimbabwe: Wages of War: A Report on Human Rights (New York: LCHR, 1986); also the letter to the editor from B. H. Mashonganyika, Sunday Gazette, 2 April 1995. The most complete source is now CCJP/LHF, *Breaking the Silence*, Building True Peace: A Report on the Disturbances in Matabeleland and the Midlands, 1980 to 1988 (Harare: CCJP/LRF, 1997), especially the case studies, 77–139.

17. Welshman Ncube, "Constitutionalism, Democracy and Political Practice in Zimbabwe," in Ibbo Mandaza and Lloyd M. Sachikonye, eds., *The One-Party State and Democracy: The Zimbabwe Debate* (Harare: SAPES Trust, 1991), 162. Some local elders said that the Fifth Brigade atrocities surpassed those of the Rhodesian army; Werbner, *Tears of the Dead*, 157, 166–67.

18. See Emmerson Mnangagwa's statements in the *Chronicle*, 5 April 1983. The minister of state security compared the Matabeles to cockroaches that should be crushed.

19. Private conversation in 1995 with a high-ranking ZANU-PF official, later appointed ambassador to an Asian country.

20. Amnesty International, *Zimbabwe: The Toll of Impunity* (London: AI, June 2002), 9.

21. *Daily Gazette*, 6 January 1994.

22. On "Super-ZAPU," see John Hanlon, *Beggar Your Neighbours: Apartheid Power in Southern Africa* (Bloomington: Indiana University Press, 1986), 178–81.

23. *Sunday Times* (UK), 11 August 2002, quoting the Zimbabwean independent press.

24. CCJP/LRF, *Breaking the Silence*, 56–57.

25. For an account of the assassination attempt, see CCJP, Fourth Report to the Electoral Supervisory Commission, 1990.

26. See R. W. Johnson, *Political Opinion in Zimbabwe 2000* (Parklands, S.A.: Helen Suzman Foundation, 2000).

27. *Financial Gazette*, 14 December 2000; *Zimbabwe Independent*, 15 December 2000.

28. First applied to the Ndebele and Shona uprisings against white settlers in 1896 and 1897, the Shona word *chimurenga* (rebellion) was adopted by the ZANU propaganda machine to label the guerrilla war of the 1970s "Second Chimurenga." The use of this label again is supposed to legitimize the state-sponsored violence and lawlessness from 2000 onward through a claim of historical filiations.

29. *Daily News*, 17 March 2000.

30. Zimbabwe Human Rights NGO Forum, "Who Was Responsible? Alleged Perpetrators and Their Crimes During the 2000 Parliamentary Elections Period" (Harare, July 2001), 1, 33.

31. Commonwealth Secretariat, "The Parliamentary Elections in Zimbabwe, 24–25 June 2000: The Report of the Commonwealth Observer Group," 2000; European Union, "Report of the EU Election Observation Mission on the Parliamentary Elections which took place in Zimbabwe on 24th and 25th June 2000," 4 July 2000, Harare and Strasbourg.

32. Amnesty International, *Zimbabwe: The Toll of Impunity*, 10.

33. Amnesty International, *Zimbabwe: The Toll of Impunity*, 25–26.

34. The most important cases are recounted in detail in Solidarity Peace Trust, *Subverting Justice: The Role of the Judiciary in Denying the Will of the Zimbabwean Electorate Since 2000* (Johannesburg: SPT, 2005), 18–21. The SPT is a church-sponsored NGO reporting on the Zimbabwe crisis. http://www.solidaritypeace trust.org/index.php?page=reports.

35. Zimbabwe Human Rights NGO Forum, "Politically Motivated Violence in Zimbabwe, 2000–2001: A Report on the Campaign of Political Repression Conducted by the Zimbabwean Government Under the Guise of Carrying Out Land Reform" (Harare, August 2001), http://www.hrforumzim.com/frames/inside_frame_reps.htm (accessed February 2010).

36. See the interview with a senior war veteran in Amnesty International, *Zimbabwe: The Toll of Impunity*, 19.

37. Amnesty International, *Zimbabwe: The Toll of Impunity*, 1.

38. Amnesty (General Pardon) Ordinance 12 of 198 granted a blanket amnesty to all perpetrators of human rights violations on both sides during the war and set a terrible precedent.

39. Clemency Order 1 of 18 April 1988 granted a general amnesty to the state security forces and the so-called dissidents for all violations of human rights committed between 1982 and the end of 1987. There was also an amnesty for the politically motivated violence during the 1995 elections. See AMANI Trust and Redress, *Torture in Zimbabwe, Past and Present: Prevention, Punishment, Reparation? A Survey of Law and Practice* (London: Redress, June 2005), 15–17.

40. Section 31(1) of the Zimbabwe Constitution gives the president unlimited power to grant pardon, amnesty, or clemency to criminals (another legacy of the Rhodesian constitution). According to Per Nordlund, the frequent use of the presidential pardon is a deliberate encouragement to the CIO and ZANU-PF thugs to perpetrate such violence; see Nordlund, *Organising the Political Agora:*

Domination and Democratisation in Zambia and Zimbabwe (Uppsala: Uppsala University Press, 1996), 207.

41. See evidence produced in court by the victims, reported in the *Daily News*, 10 July 2001. These court proceedings were linked to MDC's electoral challenge against the election of Joram Gumbo in Mberengwa West, not the trial of Chitoro for murder.

42. See Amnesty International, *Zimbabwe: The Toll of Impunity*, 24.

43. See Solidarity Peace Trust, *Subverting Justice*, 7, 22.

44. By 2005 "90% of MDC MPs [reported] having suffered human rights violations at the hands of the State, including assassination attempts, torture, assaults, illegal detention." None of the perpetrators have been prosecuted. See Solidarity Peace Trust, *Subverting Justice*, 8.

45. Amnesty International, *Zimbabwe: The Toll of Impunity*, 15.

46. *Daily News*, 6, 12 July 2001.

47. *Daily News*, 16 October 2001; 3 November 2001.

48. *Daily News*, 18 July 2001. Border Gezi made the same threats as early as September 2000, to justify a political purge of the civil service; *Herald*, 12 April 2001.

49. In the Honde Valley on 13 January 1995, ZANU-PF chairman for Manicaland and minister of agriculture Kumbirai Kangai, uttered public threats against civil servants supporting an opposition party, stating that the state and the ruling party were the same: "No one should say: I work for the government and not for the party. If you hear any civil servant saying that in this area, please let me know so that I may approach the ministry he works for so that he is removed from Manicaland," *Herald*, 14 January 1995. Although Kangai's statements were then disowned by other ministers, they betrayed ZANU-PF's true line of thinking.

50. Nordlund, *Organising the Political Agora*, 180.

51. Zimbabwe Human Rights NGO Forum, *Political Violence Report* (Harare, March 2002), and *Are They Accountable? Examining Alleged Violators and Their Violations, Pre and Post the Presidential Election March 2002* (Harare, December 2002).

52. Amnesty International, *Zimbabwe: The Toll of Impunity*, 31. On the use of torture in the run-up to the presidential elections, see also AMANI Trust, *Beating Your Opposition: Torture During the 2002 Presidential Campaign in Zimbabwe* (Harare, 25 June 2002).

53. Although MDC supporters resorted to violence occasionally, most of it was defensive in nature; see Zimbabwe Human Rights NGO Forum, *Politically Motivated Violence*, 11.

54. From July 2001 to November 2004 one human rights coalition reported 2,742 allegations of torture in a total of 11,456 gross human rights violations; see Redress and AMANI Trust, *Zimbabwe: The Face of Torture and Organised Violence (Torture and Organised Violence in the Run-up to the 31 March 2005 General Parliamentary Election)* (Harare, March 2005), http://www.redress.org/publications/ZimbabweReportMar2005.PDF.

55. AMANI Trust and Redress, *Torture in Zimbabwe*, 28.

56. Solidarity Peace Trust, *Subverting Justice*, 35.

57. Solidarity Peace Trust, *Subverting Justice*, 8.

58. See Amnesty International, "Unfair Trial of Roy Bennett, MP," statement released 24 December 2004.

59. Arms were "discovered" by the CIO at the Mutare home of Peter Michael

Hitschmann, a white professional hunter and former policeman, who was detained and later convicted, although all the weapons found in his premises were fully licensed and he denied any link with the alleged plot.

60. For evidence of such retribution in April–May 2005, see Zimbabwe Human Rights NGO Forum, *Of Stuffed Ballots and Empty Stomachs*, 28–41. Denial of food aid to alleged MDC supporters was one of the most common forms of punishment.

61. The Shona code name is said to mean "drive out trash or filth," but the government provided the press and outside world with the more innocuous, misleading label "Restore Order" (significant differences often exist between the vernacular languages and the English versions of ZANU-PF leaders' speeches). Murambatsvina started in the capital, Harare, but quickly was extended to most urban centers, including Bulawayo, Chinhoyi, Gweru, Kadoma, Kwekwe, Marondera, and Mutare. The UN special envoy, Anna Kajumulo Tibaijuka, produced a damning report that assessed the consequences of this brutal policy; see *Report of the Fact-Finding Mission to Zimbabwe to Assess the Scope and Impact of Operation Murambatsvina, by the UN Special Envoy on Human Settlements Issues in Zimbabwe, Mrs. Anna Kajumulo Tibaijuka*, United Nations, 18 July 2005. See also ICG, *Zimbabwe's Operation Murambatsvina: The Tipping Point?* Africa Report 97, 17 August 2005; Solidarity Peace Trust, *Discarding the Filth*, released in June 2005, and *Crime of Poverty*, released October 2005. For a useful academic assessment also underlining the complex urban situation before Murambatsvina, see Deborah Potts, "'Restoring Order'? Operation Murambatsvina and the Urban Crisis in Zimbabwe," *Journal of Southern African Studies* 32, 2 (June 2006): 273–91.

62. Tibaijuka's report rebuts convincingly the government's excuses and legal arguments; see *Report of the Fact-Finding Mission*, 56–63.

63. NGOs estimate that 75 percent came back to the urban areas after a few weeks as they had no means to make a living in the rural areas.

64. ICG, Zimbabwe's Operation Murambatsvina, 7.

65. Solidarity Peace Trust, *"Meltdown": Murambatsvina One Year On*, 30 August 2006, http://solidaritypeacetrust.org/reports/meltdown.pdf.

66. ICG, *Zimbabwe: A Regional Solution?* Crisis Group Africa Report 132, 18 September 2007, 2, http://www.crisisgroup.org/home/index.cfm?id = 3535 (all Zimbabwe reports). See also various NGO reports: Human Rights Watch, *Bashing Dissent: Escalating Violence and State Repression in Zimbabwe*, May 2007 (all Zimbabwe reports, http://www.hrw.org/en/publications/reports?filter0 = **ALL** &filter1 = 129); Zimbabwe Human Rights NGO Forum, *Political Violence Report*, June 2007; *At Best a Falsehood, at Worst a Lie: Comments on the Zimbabwe Republic Police (ZRP) Report "Opposition Forces in Zimbabwe: A Trail of Violence"*, special report, August 2007; and Amnesty International, *Zimbabwe: Between a Rock and a Hard Place—Women Human Rights Defenders at Risk*, July 2007, http://www.amnesty.org/en/library/info/AFR46/020/2007/en.

67. On 19 June 1994, a ZANU (Ndonga) meeting in Chitungwiza ended up with 26 people injured (but only two treated in a hospital) and 18 arrested by the police. On these clashes, see *Daily Gazette*, 19 and 21 June 1994; *Herald*, 21 June 1994.

68. *Herald*, 25 June 1994. Dumbutshena, when asked by his supporters what they could do when faced with the guns owned by some ZANU-PF supporters, replied they would, in that case, have to use "spears and arrows."

69. *Daily Gazette*, 25 June 1994. Interestingly, this part of the Zimbabwe Inter-

Africa News Agency (ZIANA) dispatch was scrapped in the *Herald* report on the same day.

70. Although these are informal, they involve a certain organization, hierarchy, and military discipline, as well as national coordination, warranting the use of the word "militia"; for a similar approach, see Amnesty International, *Zimbabwe: The Toll of Impunity*, 1.

71. The War Victims (Compensation) Act of 1980 provided for disability pensions for civilians and guerrillas *injured* in the war, pensions for the surviving spouses and dependents of the war dead, and medical and vocational rehabilitation for the war-disabled; see Norma Kriger, "War Victims Compensation: Collusion Between Zimbabwean Ex-Combatants and Government," *Journal of African Conflict and Development* 1, 1 (2000): 35–45; and Norma Kriger, "Transitional Justice as Socioeconomic Rights," *Peace Review* 12, 1 (2000): 59–65.

72. See Norma Kriger, "Epilogue: The Past in the Present," in Kriger, *Guerrilla Veterans in Post-War Zimbabwe: Symbolic and Violent Politics, 1980–1987* (Cambridge: Cambridge University Press, 2003).

73. War Veterans Act (1992), Section 2, defines war veterans as "any person who underwent military training and participated, consistently and persistently, in the liberation struggle which occurred in Zimbabwe and in neighboring countries between the 1st January, 1962, and the 29th February, 1980, in connection with the bringing about of Zimbabwe's independence on the 18th April, 1980." In the course of 1981 demobilized guerrillas received a gratuity equivalent to two years of a private's monthly salary (on the African pay scale) plus the estimated value of military rations, seen at the time as attractive payments. However, demands for financial compensation of war services kept bouncing back in the public debate during the last two decades.

74. See Kriger, *Guerrilla Veterans*, 132–39.

75. Zimbabwe Government, *Report of the Commission of Inquiry into the Administration of the War Victims Compensation Act* (Harare: Government Printers, May 1998), 30–33, annex 1. The Commission, presided over by a High Court judge personally loyal to Mugabe, was appointed to appease the war veterans. It interviewed 79 prominent ZANU-PF, government, and army officials who received undue compensation, but the hearings exposed how the association's own leadership took part in the scam.

76. See Zimbabwe Human Rights NGO Forum, *Who Was Responsible?* 22–23.

77. A repentant militiaman confided: "We called ourselves 'the Taliban.' Our doctrine was to be against the white man, he was our worst enemy, and our hero was bin Laden because of the way he stood up against the West." See *Sunday Telegraph*, 25 August 2002.

78. Commonwealth Secretariat, *The Zimbabwe Presidential Election, 9–11 March 2002: The Report of the Commonwealth Observer Group* (London: Commonwealth Secretariat, 2003), 32

79. Amnesty International, *Zimbabwe: The Toll of Impunity*, 31; also the testimonies presented in the *Sunday Telegraph*, 25 August 2002.

80. Amnesty International, *Zimbabwe: The Toll of Impunity*, 26.

81. For example, the chairman of Zimbabwe Lawyers for Human Rights was beaten by the militias and then by police officers at Sadza police station in April 2001; see Zimbabwe Human Rights NGO Forum, *Zimbabwe Parliamentary Election Challenges Newsletter*, 16 April 2001.

82. See the case of Mataga police station in Mberengwa district, *Financial Times*, 21 June 2000.

83. *Sunday Mail,* 7 June 2001.

84. Amnesty International, *Zimbabwe: The Toll of Impunity,* 20.

85. Andrew Ndlovu is a former ZAPU dissident allegedly involved in kidnapping, murder, and rape between 1982 and 1987, who benefited from the amnesty; Zimbabwe Human Rights NGO Forum, *Politically Motivated Violence,* 26. Dissident activities took a distinctive criminal character after 1983 and often targeted white farmers and Christian priests.

86. Jocelyn Alexander and JoAnn McGregor, "Les élections, la terre et l'émergence de l'opposition dans le Matabeleland," *Politique Africaine* (March 2001), republished as "Elections, Land and the Politics of Opposition in Matabeleland," *Journal of Agrarian Change* 1, 4 (October 2001): 510–33.

87. Zimbabwe Human Rights NGO Forum, *Political Violence Report,* July 2000.

88. According to Amnesty interviews with former militia, about half the "green bombers" were under age eighteen; see Amnesty International, *Zimbabwe: The Toll of Impunity,* 38.

89. Besides Hunzvi and Ndlovu already mentioned, Joseph Chinotimba, who played a central role in Harare Province (see Chapters 3 and 5), is facing murder attempt charges for shooting an MDC supporter but never faced trial. He is accused of sponsoring the murder of another one in 2008. Twice a ZANU-PF candidate in parliamentary elections he became a businessman and the chairman of his party in Harare Province. See Geoffrey Nyarota, "Joseph Chinotimba—Profile of a War Veteran," *Zimbabwe Times,* 14 June 1 2008, http://www.thezim babwetimes.com/?p = 439 (accessed February 2010).

90. See interview with Wilfred Mhanda, in *Focus* (Helen Suzman Foundation), December 2000; *Daily News,* 1 January 2001.

91. Zimbabwe Human Rights NGO Forum, *Who Was Responsible?* 16–17.

92. Norma Kriger, "Zimbabwe's War Veterans and the Ruling Party: Continuities in Political Dynamics," in Staffan Darnolf and Liisa Laakso, eds., *Twenty Years of Independence in Zimbabwe: From Liberation to Authoritarianism* (Houndmills and New York: Palgrave Macmillan, 2003), 104–21. Creation of a politically loyal army was perhaps one of the prominent motives behind the treatment of the alleged "dissident" problem.

93. *Daily News,* 16 March 2000.

94. However, an implausible military coup by junior soldiers was exposed in July 2007 and immediately used by the Mujuru faction against Mnangagwa; see ICG, *Zimbabwe: A Regional Solution?* 7.

95. The army rank and file always received good salaries, about twice the average salary in the mid-1990s; see "Zimbabwe: Training the Guns," *Africa Confidential,* 12 August 1994.

96. See "Security Officers Resort to Crime," *Zimbabwe Standard,* 30 October 2005; "Mass Desertion to South Africa," *Zimbabwean,* 30 October 2005.

97. "Mugabe Pampers Security Forces Amid Rising Public Discontent," *ZimOnLine* (S.A.), 14 August 2006; *Herald,* 25 August 2006.

98. "Mugabe Beefs Up His Security Forces," *ZimOnLine* (S.A.), 11 April 2006.

99. Knox Chitiyo and Martin Rupiya, "Tracking Zimbabwe's Political History: The Zimbabwe Defence Force from 1980–2005," in Martin Rupiya, ed., *Evolutions and Revolutions: A Contemporary History of Militaries in Southern Africa* (Pretoria: Institute for Security Studies, 2005), 359.

100. See ICG, *Zimbabwe's Continuing Self-Destruction,* Crisis Group Africa Briefing 38, 6 June 2006, 10. See also "Operation Maguta Soldiers Terrorise Villagers in Lupane," *Zimbabwe Standard,* 20 August 2006.

101. ICG, *Zimbabwe: A Regional Solution?* 7. See also *Business Day*, 11 April 2007.

102. See Geoffrey Nyarota, "Shiri's Assassination Attempt Was a Hoax," 6 January 2009, http://www.thezimbabwetimes.com: "By 2002 Chiwenga was the proud owner of eight houses and mansions in Harare and Marondera; that was apart from commercial farms. A company belonging to Chiwenga's wife, the controversial Jocelyn Chiwenga, has been awarded contracts, going back to the 1990s to supply protective clothing to the army, the police and the Air Force and many government departments."

103. Redress and Amani Trust, *Torture in Zimbabwe*, 8.

104. Peta Thornycroft makes this point convincingly in "The Never-Ending War of Robert Gabriel Mugabe,"*eAfrica* 2 (May 2004), South African Institute of International Affairs (SAIIA).

105. Cited in Meredith, *Mugabe*, front page.

106. Symptomatically the Zimbabwean government refused to sign and ratify the 1984 UN Convention Against Torture and Other Cruel, Inhuman or Degrading Treatment or Punishment.

Chapter 3. Militant Civil Society

1. Brian Raftopoulos, "The Labour Movement and the Emergence of Opposition Politics in Zimbabwe," in Brian Raftopoulos and Lloyd Sachikonye, eds., *Striking Back: The Labour Movement and the Post-Colonial State in Zimbabwe, 1980–2000* (Harare: Weaver Press, 2001), 1.

2. See, for example, Christine Sylvester, "Whither Opposition in Zimbabwe?" *Journal of Modern African Studies* 33, 3 (1995): 403–23.

3. See, for example, Patrick Chabal and Jean-Pascal Daloz, *Africa Works: Disorder as Political Instrument* (London: James Currey, 1999), chap. 2; Mahmood Mamdani, *Citizen and Subject: Contemporary Africa and the Legacy of Late Colonialism* (Princeton, N.J.: Princeton University Press, 1996).

4. See for example, Richard Saunders, "Association and Civil Society in Zimbabwe," paper presented at the Conference on the Historical Dimensions of Democracy and Human Rights in Zimbabwe, University of Zimbabwe, September 1996; also Rene Loewenson, Richard Saunders, and Niki Jazdowska, "Civic Organisations in Zimbabwe," Report for the African Network on Economic Policy, Equity and Health, Harare, June 1995.

5. For a typology of Zimbabwe NGOs and an analysis of their perennial problems, see Sam Moyo, John Makumbe, and Brian Raftopoulos, eds., *NGOs, the State and Politics in Zimbabwe* (Harare: SAPES Books, 2000); for more details on Zimbabwean NGOs, see Adrienne LeBas, "From Protest to Parties: Explaining Effective Opposition in Democratizing Africa," Ph.D. dissertation, Columbia University, 2006, 181–92.

6. The Zimbabwe Council of Churches (ZCC), the main interdenominational Protestant organization, followed a similar line; on the relations between the churches and the state in the postindependence period, see Sara Rich Dorman, "'Rocking the Boat?' Church NGOs and Democratization in Zimbabwe," *African Affairs* 101 (2002): 75–92.

7. Per Nordlund, *Organising the Political Agora: Domination and Democratisation in Zambia and Zimbabwe* (Uppsala: Uppsala University Press, 1996), 172.

8. Speech by Sydney Sekeramayi, minister of state security, *Legal Forum*, March 1993, 36.

9. The ZCTU shared a building with ZANU-PF headquarters until 1988 and its first secretary general was Mugabe's half brother Albert Mugabe.

10. Nordlund, *Organising the Political Agora*, 150–51.

11. Raftopoulos, "The Labour Movement and the Emergence of Opposition Politics," 6–7.

12. Vice-chancellor Professor Walter Kamba resigned over the new legislation. See Nordlund, *Organising the Political Agora*, 167–69. See also the excellent analysis in Angela P. Cheater, "The University of Zimbabwe: University, National University, State University or Party University?" *African Affairs* 90 (1991): 189–205.

13. Nordlund, *Organising the Political Agora*, 175.

14. As quoted in the ZCTU magazine *The Worker*, 4 June 1993.

15. Nordlund, *Organising the Political Agora*, 189–90. The SCR "military wing" led by "Warlord" Lawrence Chakaredza, an activist with ZANU-PF/CIO connections, alienated many students and members of the public.

16. Some student leaders continued to work with the ZCTU. Tendai Biti, secretary general of the University of Zimbabwe SRC in 1987–88, became a legal practitioner and represented the unions in various court cases. He was Dongo's lawyer in the Harare South court case and later an active member of the new opposition.

17. See Michael Bratton, "Micro-Democracy? The Merger of Farmer Unions in Zimbabwe," *African Studies Review* 37, 1 (1994): 9–38.

18. Brian Raftopoulos, "The State, NGOs and Democratisation," in Moyo, Makumbe, and Raftopoulos, *NGOs, the State and Politics*, 21–46.

19. For a summary of the events, see Economist Intelligence Unit, *Country Report: Zimbabwe, Fourth Quarter, 1995* (London: EIU, 1995), 8; and *Country Report: Zimbabwe, Fourth Quarter, 1996* (London: EIU, 1996), 9.

20. This was when one of the abused shot at a fellow military personal who had called him "Banana's whore" and brought up the issue at his own trail.

21. Canaan Banana was sentenced in 1998 to ten years jail, nine of them suspended. He died of illness in November 2003.

22. See Private Voluntary Organisations Act, Parliament of Zimbabwe, downloadable as pdf, http://www.parlzim.gov.zw/inside.aspx?mpgid=14&spid=49, and comments of the Act in NGO Briefing Paper: The Private Voluntary Organisations Act; a Widening Rift Between Civil Society and the State in Zimbabwe," anonymous mimeo, no date; also Nordlund, *Organising the Political Agora*, 202.

23. See Diana Mitchell, "Gongos on the March in Zimbabwe," *Frontiers of Freedom*, South Africa Institute of Race Relations 11 (1997): 4–5; also the articles she signed in *Zimbabwe Independent*, 12 July, 11 October 1996.

24. See *Herald*, 12 February 1997.

25. Before three fellow FORUM members (including Diana Mitchell), Nick Ndebele claimed in 1996 having been "framed" and intimidated by the CIO to work for the agency.

26. Interview with Mike Auret, 9 August 1999.

27. Raftopoulos, "The Labour Movement and the Emergence of Opposition Politics"; Peter Alexander, "Zimbabwean Workers, the MDC and the 2000 Election," *Review of African Political Economy* 27, 85 (2000): 385–406. However, where Alexander sees a workers' party, Raftopoulos correctly emphasizes the NCA component of the new party.

28. An odd name for an organization whose members were not popularly elected and had no legal mandate to write a constitution. It was rather the

broad-based alliance for constitutional reform that was so patently necessary as early as 1996, as argued in John W. Makumbe and Daniel Compagnon, *Behind the Smokescreen: The Politics of Zimbabwe's 1995 General Elections* (Harare: University of Zimbabwe Publications, 2000), 310–11. However the ZANU-PF government, by then seen as retaining some democratic legitimacy, was unlikely to surrender the whole constitution-making process to a self-proclaimed constitutional assembly (interview with Ben Hlatshwayo, Secretariat of the CRC, 16 August 1999). According to one founding member, the NCA was originally a civil society task force to push for the election of a people-based constitutional assembly in the place of the ZANU-PF controlled Parliament. However, the government rejected that option on the pretext that there was no time to do so before the 2000 parliamentary elections (interview with Welshman Ncube, NCA spokesman, Harare, 5 August 1999). See also Adrienne LeBas, *From Protest to Parties*, 209–226.

29. See *Financial Gazette*, 26 February 1998.

30. Constitutional reform was debated in the Bulawayo ZANU-PF conference in 1996, again in Mutare in 1997, and finally a motion was passed in Gweru in 1998. It was therefore on the ZANU-PF agenda long before the NCA campaign, but Mugabe was reluctant to address it (interview with Mike Mataure, then reformist ZANU-PF MP for Chimanimani, Harare, 17 August 1999).

31. Interview with Ncube, 5 August 1999.

32. See Commissions of Inquiry Act, Chapter 10:07, Sections 2, and 3(2). Parliament of Zimbabwe, downloadable as pdf, http://www.parlzim.gov.zw/inside.aspx?mpgid=14&spid=49.

33. Some like Eric Bloch, chairman of the thematic committee on public finance, claimed they had obtained guarantees from Zvogbo, namely a right to resign and publicize the reasons, a referendum on the CRC draft, and the inclusion of minority views in the report (interview, Bulawayo, 19 August 1999). Subsequent events showed what these guarantees were worth.

34. See Dorman, " 'Rocking the Boat?' "

35. Interview with ZUJ secretary general and independent journalist Basildon Peta, 6 August 1999. Basildon Peta had taken a high profile in the case of the *Zimbabwe Standard*'s tortured journalists in the previous months and had been harassed by the CIO.

36. Rita Makarau was careful not to attack Mugabe directly. A lawyer by training, she was appointed in mid-2000 as a judge in the High Court, and to the surprise of many she initially delivered some fairly independent-minded judgments.

37. Interview with Ben Hlatshwayo, Secretariat of the CRC, 16 August 1999.

38. Interviews with independent members of the CRC (John Deary, Tony Hawkins, Basildon Peta, and Greg Linington) in August 1999 and April 2000, Harare.

39. A former associate professor at the University of Zimbabwe and author in 1992 of a vibrant criticism of the ZANU-PF regime (*Voting for Democracy*), Jonathan Moyo began to sneer at some opponents and civil society activists in the press in early 1995. His turnaround was allegedly part of a deal with justice minister Emmerson Mnangagwa. In return for the state dropping criminal charges—for the abduction of his children after he divorced his first wife—in order to allow him back in Zimbabwe, he was to work covertly for the ruling party. His reputation was further damaged by his alleged involvement in two corruption cases, in Nairobi with the Ford Foundation and in Johannesburg with Witwatersrand University.

40. The prominent CRC figures were later rewarded. Godfrey Chidyausiku became chief justice in 2001. Moyo was made a cabinet minister after the 2000 elections and a Politburo member in following December until the Tsholotsho saga (see Chapter 1). Patrick Chinamasa became minister of justice and later a close adviser to the president, and Ben Hlatshwayo, previously a university lecturer, was appointed judge in the High Court.

41. For example, when CRC members were sworn in, the November deadline was not known and some heard the president mentioning a minimum one-year time frame (interview with John Deary, Harare, 11 August 1999); the deadline was suddenly imposed in June and by then it was already clear that the CRC could not complete its task properly before the set date.

42. See Geoff Feltoe, Charles Goredema, and Greg Linington, "The Constitutional Reform Process and the Constitutional Commission's Draft Constitution for Zimbabwe," part 1, *Legal Forum* 12, 1 (2000): 31.

43. See "Draft Constitution of Zimbabwe: Corrections and Clarifications," *Government Gazette*, 19 January 2000. The amendment was formally endorsed by the CRC executive committee whose mandate had been conveniently prolonged beyond the commission's life. Previously, Mnangagwa had stated that the president wanted no compensation to be paid to the white farmers but was then outvoted in the CRC coordinating committee, which opted for a compromise between the need to acquire land and the need for compensation.

44. See Feltoe, Goredema, and Linington, "The Constitutional Reform Process," 34–40, also the chart in Appendix 1, part 2 of the article, *Legal Forum* 12, 2 (2000): 87–89.

45. Brian Raftopoulos, "Whither the NCA?" *Agenda* 3, 1 (February 2000): 8–10.

46. A former Public Service Commission member, then close to Nathan Shamuyarira, Ibbo Mandaza posed as a radical intellectual in Pan-African circles such as the African Political Science Association and CODESRIA. He succeeded in attracting Scandinavian donor funding for his expanding SAPES publications group and training institute SARIPS (however the donors withdrew in 2002 because of the lack of financial transparency in SAPES/SARIPS). Mandaza, sometimes portrayed as the "technocratic wing of ZANU-PF" (Chan, *Robert Mugabe: A Life of Power and Violence*, 125, 140), benefited from the privatization of the Rainbow Tourism group and was named owner of multiple farms in various reports on the landgrab. The *Daily News* once published a long list of his alleged assets.

47. See ZCTU, "Beyond ESAP: Framework for a Long-term Development Strategy in Zimbabwe Beyond the Economic Structural Adjustment Programme," Harare, 1996.

48. Raftopoulos, "The Labour Movement and the Emergence of Opposition Politics," 10–11.

49. The police docket was closed in March 1998. However, independent investigations carried out on behalf of the ZCTU identified three of the assailants, partly on the basis of an army ID card found on the premises.

50. Zimbabwe Human Rights NGO Forum, *Human Rights in Troubled Times: An Initial Report on Human Rights Abuses During and After Food Riots in January 1998* (Harare: the Forum, March 1998).

51. Interview with Morgan Tsvangirai, Harare, August 1999.

52. ZCTU, "Declaration of the National Working People's Convention," Harare, February 1999. On the MDC formation see also LeBas, *From Protest to Parties*, 295–303.

53. According to Peter Alexander, up to 25 percent of the ZCTU membership—probably leaning to ZANU-PF—opposed the launch of the party but did not dare to openly challenge Tsvangirai. See Alexander, "Zimbabwean Workers, the MDC and the 2000 Election".

54. Raftopoulos, "The Labour Movement and the Emergence of Opposition Politics," 22.

55. Jocelyn Alexander and JoAnn McGregor, "Les élections, la terre et l'émergence de l'opposition dans le Matabeleland," *Politique Africaine* (March 2001), republished as "Elections, Land and the Politics of Opposition in Matabeleland," *Journal of Agrarian Change* 1, 4 (October 2001): 510–33.

56. Alexander and McGregor, "Les élections, la terre et l'émergence de l'opposition," 69.

57. See Makumbe and Compagnon, *Behind the Smokescreen*, 246–53. Without ZANU-PF rigging, FORUM candidate Washington Sansole would have been elected in Bulawayo South in 1995. Mugabe received only 13 percent of the vote in the 1996 presidential election in that city.

58. Interview with Cont Mhlanga, Bulawayo, 19 August 1999.

59. In the Nguni tradition, the Imbovane was a special regiment of men aged between twenty-five and forty, who did not marry or consort with women, and who formed the trusted king's guard. Interview with founding member Lovemore Moyo, Bulawayo, 25 August 1999.

60. See Brian Hungwe, "Zimbabwe's Speaker Makes History," BBC News, 26 August 2008, http://news.bbc.co.uk/go/pr/fr/-/2/hi/africa/7582119.stm.

61. See Alexander, "Zimbabwean Workers, the MDC and the 2000 Election"; Patrick Bond, "Radical Rhetoric and the Working Class During Zimbabwean Nationalism's Dying Days," in Raftopoulos and Sachikonye, *Striking Back*, 40–43. According to Bond, Eddie Cross represented "the MDC conservative flank pulling the MDC to the right," whereas Tsvangirai backed the "left," which had organized the National Working People's Convention (33–34). Bond's fanciful interpretation sheds no light on subsequent squabbles within the MDC, as Cross, who lives in Bulawayo, remained loyal to Tsvangirai after the party split.

62. See, for example, Job Sikhala's remarks in "Kitchen Cabinet Destroyed MDC: Sikhala," *Herald*, 7 January 2006.

63. "The MDC will establish an economic and development policy framework that is geared for stable and equitable growth in the economy and the provision of basic needs. . . . Savings will be realized through debt reduction measures, the privatization of parastatals and the restructuring of government budgetary framework. The MDC will move away from the current regime of high spending that drives high taxation and high inflation." Movement for Democratic Change, *Manifesto* (Harare: mimeo, August 1999), 18–19.

64. Movement for Democratic Change, "Economic Policy Statement," mimeo (Harare, 5 April 2000).

65. Interview with Tsvangirai, Harare, April 2000.

66. See Tsvangirai interview in *Southern Africa Report*, 3 June 2000.

67. Unlike what Chan suggests, there was no "turbulence" since the succession had been prepared for months; see Chan, *Robert Mugabe*, 142. However, smaller political parties' leaders in the task force were unhappy with the perceived MDC dictate.

68. As reflected in its board, ZESN includes roughly the same civic organizations as the NCA; *Ballot News, Official Newsletter of the ZESN,* June 2001, 3–5. The first chairman of ZESN, Dr. Reginald Matchaba-Hove, was chairman of ZIM-

RIGHTS from 1992 to 1998 and had represented the human rights body in the NCA task force.

69. Some suspected him of having masterminded the witch hunt against Thoko Matshe in the NCA in early 2001. The accusations of corruption proffered against her were cleared after a proper internal investigation.

70. The Crisis in Zimbabwe conference was convened in Harare on 3–4 August 2002 and brought together 1,200 participants from 250 organizations; the total membership was estimated to be one million although many individuals had multiple affiliations.

71. Zimbabwe *Standard*, 28 May 2006.

72. Arnold Tsunga and Tafadzwa Mugabe, "Zim NGO Bill: Dangerous for Human Rights Defenders," Zimbabwe Lawyers for Human Rights, 28 July 2004.

73. Zindoga and two other ZCTU leaders have been criticized for signing a declaration of intent on the government's proposed "social contract" without permission from the general council, and they were subsequently disciplined by this body, which rejected the proposal. Zindoga, acting secretary general of the ZCTU, also accepted Mugabe's invitation to join the Zimbabwe delegation to the Lankawi meeting in Malaysia in November 2000.

74. "ZANU-PF Fails in Bid to 'Hijack' Zim's Unions," *Cape Argus* (S.A.), 26 February 2001.

75. The Friedrich Ebert Stiftung, a German foundation supporting the NCA and ZCTU, was invaded and the German ambassador personally had to beg ministers to intervene. The Canadian high commissioner was manhandled when he tried to stop War Vets from tackling the Canadian manager of an aid NGO. War Vets threatened to invade "hostile" Western embassies.

76. See Brian Raftopoulos, "Reflections on Opposition Politics in Zimbabwe: The Politics of the Movement for Democratic Change," in Chuma Wallace, Brian Raftopoulos, and Karin Alexander, *Reflections on Democratic Politics in Zimbabwe* (Cape Town: Institute for Justice and Reconciliation, 2006), 10–12.

77. On this episode, see Amin Y. Kamete, "The Return of the Jettisoned: ZANU-PF's Crack at 'Re-Urbanising' in Harare," *Journal of Southern African Studies* 32, 2 (June 2006): 255–71.

78. Cf. *Daily News*, 25 August 2000.

79. "MDC Criticises Gwisai," *Daily News*, 26 February 2001. Tsvangirai's initial patience probably stemmed from the fact that Gwisai had been a leader of the University of Zimbabwe SRC in 1989–90, when Tsvangirai supported the student movement. The influential Tendai Biti was also a close friend of Gwisai.

80. Interview with an MDC activist and CHRA member who wants to remain anonymous. However, once Mayor Mudzuri bravely refused to bow down to bullying ZANU-PF minister of local government Ignatius Chombo, the latter arbitrarily suspended him and appointed another commission to run the city.

81. Interview with Morgan Tsvangirai, Harare, April 2000.

82. Raftopoulos, "Reflections on Opposition Politics in Zimbabwe," 12.

83. ICG, *Zimbabwe's Continuing Self-Destruction*, Crisis Group Africa Briefing 38, 6 June 2006, 4.

84. Raftopoulos, "Reflections on Opposition Politics in Zimbabwe," 24.

85. LeBas, *From Protest to Parties*, 334–336.

86. See excerpts of Commission of Inquiry into Disturbances at Party Headquarters (Draft Report), December 2004, quoted in Raftopoulos, "Reflections on Opposition Politics in Zimbabwe," 14. The report was never finalized as the commission of inquiry itself was affected by factionalism.

87. See Raftopoulos, "Reflections on Opposition Politics in Zimbabwe," 16.

88. Raftopoulos, "Reflections on Opposition Politics in Zimbabwe," 20–21.

89. Raftopoulos, "Reflections on Opposition Politics in Zimbabwe," 21. The Tsvangirai faction subsequently claimed that these papers in its favor were not counted unfairly, but in her account of the NEC meeting, Trudy Stevenson corrected the facts: "There were two spoilt papers—one had a big star in the 'yes' box, the other had a very small cross in one corner of the 'yes' box, so in fact they were both 'yes' votes but we ruled them spoilt." See Trudy Stevenson, "MDC's October 12 Meeting—The Facts," *Zimbabwe Independent*, 13 January 2006.

90. See Stevenson, "MDC's October 12 Meeting-the facts".

91. See "Tsvangirai Says Faction Working with ZANU PF," *Daily Mirror*, 31 October 2005.

92. That Tsvangirai readmitted to his party the youth excluded in May 2005 and reemployed the two officials suspended in June the same year is worrying evidence of his condoning his supporters' violence, in spite of public reassurances. However, there are also a few violent people in the Mutambara faction, such as the young activists who assaulted Bekithemba Nyathi during one of Tsvangirai's Senate boycott rallies.

93. See report from SW Radio Africa, ZWNEWS, 4 July 2006; see ZWNEWS, 11, 13 July 2006 and "Report of the Commission of Inquiry into the Assaults Perpetrated on Honourable Trudy Stevenson, Mrs Simangele Manyere, Mr Linos Mushonga, Mr Luxton Sibanda and Mr Tawanda Mudzerema on Sunday, 2 July 2006," presented to MDC on 11 September 2006. In 2001 already the provincial leadership elections in Harare were marred by violence and those responsible were later involved in further intraparty violence; see Report of the Commission of Inquiry.

Chapter 4. The Media Battlefield

1. Nathan Shamuyarira, Foreword to Elaine Windrich, *The Mass Media in the Struggle for Zimbabwe* (Gweru: Mambo Press, 1981).

2. On the structure of MMT and Zimpapers and the evolution of Zimbabwean print media in the 1980s, see Richard Saunders, "Information in the Interregnum: The Press, State and Civil Society in Struggles for Hegemony, Zimbabwe 1980–1990," Ph.D. dissertation, Carleton University, 1992.

3. Shamuyarira, Foreword.

4. Interview of Elias Rusike in *Moto*, July 1991; see also Elias Rusike, *The Politics of the Mass Media: A Personal Experience* (Harare: Roblaw, 1990), 86–88.

5. Richard Saunders, "The Press, Civil Society and Democratic Struggles in Zimbabwe," paper presented at the Conference on National Identity and Democracy, Cape Town, March 1997, co-sponsored by Mayibuye Centre of the University of the Western Cape, Bellville, South Africa, and Nordic Africa Institute (NAI), Uppsala, Sweden, 6.

6. See Judith Todd, "Nothing Personal: My Time with Zimpapers," *Sunday Gazette*, 26 September 1993. The Todd family's impeccable political record against Smith after UDI provided some credibility and an appearance of pluralism to such media boards.

7. Saunders, "The Press, Civil Society and Democratic Struggles." The two editors of the *Sunday Mail*, Willie Musarurwa and Henry Muradzikwa, were dismissed in 1985 and 1987 respectively; Geoff Nyarota, editor of the *Chronicle*, was

sacked in 1989. For a detailed account of this period see Richard Saunders, *Information in the Interregnum: The Press, State and Civil Society in Struggles for Hegemony, Zimbabwe, 1980–1990* (Ottawa: National Library of Canada, 1992), chap. 4.

8. According to the director of information; see Todd, "Nothing Personal."

9. See Todd, "Nothing Personal," and *Herald*, 2 June 1994. See also Geoffrey Nyarota, *Against the Grain: Memoirs of a Zimbabwean Newsman* (Cape Town: Zebra, 2006).

10. See Saunders, Information in the Interregnum, chap. 5.

11. See Helge Rønning, "The Media in Zimbabwe: The Struggle Between State and Civil Society," in Staffan Darnolf and Liisa Laakso, eds., *Twenty Years of Independence in Zimbabwe: From Liberation to Authoritarianism* (Basingstoke: Palgrave Macmillan, 2003), 202.

12. See for example, ZimRights, "The Eight Minimum Conditions for Free and Fair Elections," *ZimRights Bulletin*, Harare, December 1994, 35.

13. See Media Monitoring Project of Zimbabwe, *A Question of Balance: The Zimbabwe Media and Constitutional Referendum* (Harare: MMPZ, 2000). The MMPZ is a joint initiative of the Media Institute of Southern Africa (MISA) and local NGOs.

14. See Rønning, "The Media in Zimbabwe," 216.

15. Rønning, "The Media in Zimbabwe," 204–5.

16. For more on this story, see John W. Makumbe and Daniel Compagnon, *Behind the Smokescreen: The Politics of Zimbabwe's 1995 General Elections* (Harare: University of Zimbabwe Publications, 2000), 208–10.

17. Already in 1991, a modest grant from the Swedish International Development Agency (SIDA) to start the magazine *Horizon* had caused some uproar in government circles and Parliament. See Rønning, "The Media in Zimbabwe," 212.

18. Two opinion polls by the Afrobarometer, in 1999 and 2004, established that the people placed little trust in the government media: in 2004, only 41 percent trusted ZBC and 32 percent Zimpapers' titles. The independent media were not in a better position. See Annie Chikwanha, Tulani Sithole, and Michael Bratton, *The Power of Propaganda: Public Opinion in Zimbabwe, 2004*, Working Paper 42, Afrobarometer, August 2004, http://www.afrobarometer.org/abseries.html.

19. See Rønning, "The Media in Zimbabwe," 209.

20. See *Zimbabwe Independent*, 12 August 2008. Mandaza was kicked out the following December after losing his case in the High Court. According to press reports, the same strategy was used to silence the *Financial Gazette*.

21. There has been a steady flow of new periodicals, especially regional newspapers such as the *Masvingo Mirror, Telegraph, Sun*, and *Midlands Observer*. It is difficult to assess their independence and financial viability. Some of their journalists were harassed when publishing information embarrassing the government or ZANU-PF.

22. For instance, in his comments on foreign press correspondents and local independent journalists, *Sunday Mail*, 2 February 2003, Moyo parroted Mugabe's extraordinary ranting against British homosexuals.

23. See Media Monitoring Project of Zimbabwe, Special Report on Quality of Access to National Public Broadcasting Stations Between ZANU-PF and MDC: February 26–March 17, 2005 (Harare: MMPZ, 2005).

24. Established by two Acts of Parliament, the Broadcasting Services Act (Chapter 12:06), and the Zimbabwe Broadcasting Corporation (Commercializa-

tion) Act (Chapter 12:01); the latter split the former state monopoly into two companies, ZBC proper and Transmedia, a provider of signal transmission services.

25. Parliament of Zimbabwe, *Second Report: Portfolio Committee on Transport and Communications on Zimbabwe Holdings (ZBH)*, Fourth Session, Fifth Parliament, Harare, 2004.

26. ZUJ representatives sat in the CRC to take part in the debate on this media council and protect members' interests. Interview with Basildon Peta, 6 August 1999.

27. See Parliament of Zimbabwe, Zimbabwe Parliamentary Debates, Vol. 28, no. 46, starting at col. 4166, cited in MISA-Zimbabwe, "The Access to Information and Protection of Privacy Act, Five Years On: A Trail of Destruction" (Harare: MISA-Zimbabwe 2007), 6. MISA-Zimbabwe website http://www.misa zim.co.zw, last accessed in 2007, is no longer working.

28. The IJAZ, led by Abel Mutsakani, then news editor of the *Financial Gazette*, was formed in 2000 by private media journalists accusing the ZUJ of failing to defend independent journalists attacked by the militias and CIO. It underlined the deepening polarization of the media profession.

29. In early 2002, prior to the enactment of AIPPA, several foreign journalists willing to cover the March presidential elections were denied accreditation, as were British journalists who wanted to cover cricket matches in 2003.

30. Dr. Mahoso was also appointed by Jonathan Moyo to head a mysterious "Media Ethics Committee," a position he immediately began to exploit to criticize the independent press.

31. See *Daily Mirror*, 9 December 2003; *Sunday Independent* (S.A.), 14 December 2003.

32. See Amnesty International, "Zimbabwe—Rights Under Siege," 2 May 2003. For a detailed critical analysis of the BSA, see MISA-Zimbabwe, *Broadcasting Services Act Analysis*, briefing paper, 2002.

33. This ban is hardly enforceable because shortwave radio receivers can tune in to foreign transmission stations.

34. For some examples, see Amnesty International, "Zimbabwe—Rights Under Siege."

35. Amnesty International, *Zimbabwe: The Toll of Impunity* (London: AI, 2002) 32.

36. See MISA-Zimbabwe, "State of the Media Report," December 2002. See other reports at http://www.misa.org/.

37. At least 21 journalists from independent media have been arrested and charged under AIPPA, many more than once; see Amnesty International, "Zimbabwe—Rights Under Siege."

38. Ironically Bornwell Chakaodza was director of information in the mid-1990s, toeing the ruling party line and vilifying the independent press. Appointed editor of the *Herald* in May 1998, he was sacked in September 2000 by Jonathan Moyo, who demanded total obedience.

39. This incredible saga is chronicled in detail in MISA-Zimbabwe, "The Access to Information and Protection of Privacy Act."

40. See *Mail and Guardian* (S.A.), 21 July 2004.

41. The Criminal Law (Codification and Reform) Act in June 2005 introduced harsher penalties to punish independent reporting than those provided for under POSA and AIPPA.

42. See *Washington Post*, 23 July 2004. Wetherell is now in management of the Mail and Guardian media group in Johannesburg.

43. Committee to Protect Journalists, "Attacks on the Press, 2003: Zimbabwe," http://cpj.org/2004/03/attacks-on-the-press-2003-zimbabwe.php (last accessed 2005).

44. Chikwanha, Sithole, and Bratton, *The Power of Propaganda.*

Chapter 5. The Judiciary

1. On the evolution of the judicial system in Zimbabwe, see Karla Saller, *The Judicial Institution in Zimbabwe* (Cape Town: University of Cape Town, Faculty of Law, May 2004). We had access to this report after the completion of this chapter.

2. There are magistrate courts for lesser offenses, customary courts held by traditional chiefs and headmen, and several other specialized courts not dealt with here. The High Court is also an appeals court for magistrate court rulings.

3. For all quotes from the 1980 constitution, see *Southern Rhodesia: Report of the Constitutional Conference, Lancaster House, London, September–December 1979* (London: Her Majesty's Stationery Office, January 1980).

4. In the Lancaster House constitution, the highest court of the land was the High Court, which included a general and an appellate division. The latter became the Supreme Court with Amendment No. 2 (Act 25 of 1981).

5. Interview with Enoch Dumbutshena, Harare, 5 August 1999.

6. Interview with David Coltart, Bulawayo, 18 August 1999.

7. Quoted in Legal Resources Foundation, *Justice in Zimbabwe*, 30 September 2002, 8.

8. Cf. Welshman Ncube, "The Concept of Separation of Powers in Zimbabwe: Constitutional Myth or Reality?" paper presented at a ZIPAM seminar for members of the diplomatic corps and international agencies personnel, Holiday Inn, Harare, 14–18 October 1996.

9. Dumbutshena retired in 1990 but accomplished some missions for the OAU, the Commonwealth, and the International Commission of Lawyers. His unsuccessful foray into active politics in 1993–95 was born out of a sincere worry about the state of the country and he was appalled by the 1999–2000 events.

10. ZLHR's central objective stated in its February 1996 constitution was as "to foster a culture of human rights in Zimbabwe and to encourage the growth and strengthening of human rights at all levels of Zimbabwean society" through various means, including supporting litigators in human rights cases.

11. However the LRF, sponsoring test cases such as Chavunduka's application to the Supreme Court, complained that even members of ZLHR demanded extravagant fees when they should have argued these cases free of charge (conversation with LRF officials, 21 August 1999). NGOs and opposition also complained about litigation costs.

12. See John Makumbe and Daniel Compagnon, *Behind the Smokescreen: The Politics of Zimbabwe's 1995 General Elections* (Harare: University of Zimbabwe Publications, 2000).

13. *Financial Gazette*, 14 December 2000; *Zimbabwe Independent*, 15 December 2000.

14. International Bar Association, *Report of the Zimbabwe Mission, 2001* (London: International Bar Association, 2001), 94. The International Bar Association and the United Nations special rapporteur on the independence of judges and lawyers both sternly condemned these attacks.

15. Judgment No. SC 132/2000 of 21 December 2000, *Commercial Farmers Union v. President of Zimbabwe and Others.*

16. See *Movement for Democratic Change v. Chinamasa*, 2001 (1) ZLR 69 (S), at 70.

17. Of the original 39 petitions, 10 were withdrawn, 5 never set down for hearing by the High Court, 2 were dismissed by the High Court on procedural grounds, 7 were ruled in favor of MDC, 9 in favor of ZANU-PF. Of these 16 rulings, the MDC candidates appealed 6 and the ZANU-PF MPs appealed all rulings against them. Of these 13 appeals to the Supreme Court, only 3 had been heard by the 2005 general elections; no judgment was ever delivered. See Solidarity Peace Trust, *Subverting Justice: The Role of the Judiciary in Denying the Will of the Zimbabwean Electorate Since 2000* (Johannesburg: SPT, March 2005), 5–6.

18. Quoted respectively in *Daily News*, 14 April 2000, and *Herald*, 15 April 2000. For more statements of this kind, see Legal Resources Foundation, *Justice in Zimbabwe*, 10.

19. Amnesty International, *Zimbabwe: The Toll of Impunity* (London: AI, 2002), 49–50.

20. In an open letter to the Judicial Service Commission and before Justice Chidyausiku's appointment became permanent, the Zimbabwe Law Society questioned his legal acumen and personal integrity in very strong terms; see *Zimbabwe Standard*, 20 May 2001. Many of his previous rulings in the High Court were overturned by the Supreme Court.

21. See his speech for the opening of the judicial year, *The Star*, 9 January 2001.

22. She ruled in favor of the MDC in Chiredzi North but dismissed its election petitions in Chiredzi South and Zvishavane for lack of evidence—through an excessively restrictive interpretation of the Electoral Act. She also nullified the election of the MDC MP in Seke, when the ZANU-PF candidate claimed that chaotic voters' rolls prevented his supporters from voting, accusing Mudede of incompetence, a strange line of argument given the registrar general's bias toward the ruling party. See *Financial Gazette*, 21 June 2001; *Daily News*, 24 January 2002.

23. Interview with Geoff Feltoe, University of Zimbabwe law professor, Harare, August 2001.

24. Judith Todd was denied a passport and the right to vote by the registrar general on the excuse that she had never renounced a New Zealand citizenship that she was erroneously assumed to have inherited from her New Zealand-born father, Sir Garfield Todd. She was a Zimbabwean by birth and most lawyers argue that the Citizenship Act (2001) is in breach of the constitution.

25. See Solidarity Peace Trust, *Subverting Justice*, 23–24.

26. *State v. Humbarume*, HH 148–2001, at 5 (issued 26 September 2001).

27. See *ZimOnline* (S.A.), 6, 14 October 2005.

28. He never delivered the written judgment on Goromonzi, preventing the MDC from appealing to the Supreme Court; see Solidarity Peace Trust, *Subverting Justice*, 27. Several other of his rulings were controversial. He convicted for "murder with constructive intent" in September 2002 a white farmer who accidentally ran over a squatter with his truck (while none of the murderers of 13 white farmers and more than 200 black opposition supporters over the previous two years were ever convicted). Hlatshwayo also refused to order the immediate release of Blackie illegally detained by the police in September 2002.

29. Allegedly, ten other Supreme Court and High Court judges received farms from the government.

30. In the ZANU-PF fashion Hlatshwayo grabbed Gwina farm near Banket in 2002. In June 2003 he forced his way into the homestead in violation of a High Court order and tried to evict the farmer from his property. See *Daily Telegraph*, 17 June 2003. Ironically, he was himself evicted from the property in 2008 by Gushungo Holdings, a company belonging to Grace Mugabe, which he sued in the High Court for "unlawful conduct"; see CNN, online edition, 4 February 2009; "Ben Hlatshwayo's mistake was not in using his power as a Zimbabwe high court judge to steal a farm from one of his white compatriots. His error was in proving to be a decent enough farmer to catch the rapacious eye of the president's wife," Chris McGreal, "Judge's Stolen Land Taken Back from Him—by Mugabe's Wife," *Guardian*, online edition, 6 March 2009.

31. A technique denounced by Justice Gillespie before he resigned; see AMANI Trust, *Neither Free Nor Fair: High Court Decisions on the Petitions on the June 2000 General Election* (Harare: AMANI, 3 March 2002). Justice Garwe did nullify the Makoni East election, but only in October 2003, two years after hearing the MDC petition (Solidarity Peace Trust, *Subverting Justice*, 25).

32. Solidarity Peace Trust, *Subverting Justice*, 29.

33. Solidarity Peace Trust, *Subverting Justice*, 33–34.

34. This appeal was dismissed by the Supreme Court in February 2006.

35. See *ZimOnline* (S.A.), 18 October 2005.

36. Other striking examples are Justice Anele Matika and Justice Charles Hungwe on Andrew Meldrum's deportation case in 2002, and Yunus Omarjee on an ANZ case in 2003 and on Masiyiwa's ECONET in 2004.

37. See the Law Society chairperson's response, "Beatrice Mtetwa Responds to Makarau," *Zimbabwe Independent* (online), 16 January 2009. Yet this controversy suggests that the legal culture of the 1980s and 1990s survived to a certain extent the politicization of the judiciary.

38. See *ZimOnline* (S.A.), 27 August 2004. Supreme Court Justice Luke Malaba reversed the acquittal a year later; see *Herald*, 2 August 2005.

39. Whatever the source of the quarrel, Makamba had to leave the country and lost his properties in Zimbabwe. His shares in Telecel, for example, went to Leo Mugabe; see ICG, *Zimbabwe: A Regional Solution?* Crisis Group Africa Report 132, 18 September 2007, 9.

40. This was deliberate cruelty. Other MDC activists died, such as Vusumuzi Mukwedi, detained without charge in Gokwe Remand Prison; see *Daily News*, 15 August 2001.

41. See ANAMI Trust and Redress, *Torture in Zimbabwe, Past and Present: Prevention, Punishment, Reparation? A Survey of Law and Practice* (London: Redress, 2005), 26–27. Unfortunately the brave judge died of cancer in October 2005; see SW Radio Africa, 1 November 2005.

42. The attorney general's office admitted being outwitted in January 2001 when requesting the postponement of an important hearing in the Supreme Court to hire a South African lawyer who could "argue the matter in the manner the [MDC lawyers] can do" (*Daily News*, 4 January 2001). The attorney general has been criticized within ZANU-PF for going to trial insufficiently prepared. In May 2003 Andrew Chigovera, attorney general appointed in July 2000 when his predecessor became minister of justice, was forced to resign for alleged secret sympathies for the MDC.

43. Held in Pretoria from October 1963 to June 1964, this trial, named after the hiding place of the ANC-banned leadership, ended with Nelson Mandela's conviction and sentence to life imprisonment on Robben Island with seven others.

44. Born in Tehran to Iraqi-Jewish parents, he emigrated to Israel and then to Canada.

45. *Zimbabwe Independent*, 23 August 2004; *Cape Argus*, 28 August 2004.

46. See Legal Resources Foundation, *Justice in Zimbabwe*, 14–18. One senior magistrate in Gokwe had to flee for his life in November 2001. Another was beaten in Chipinge in August 2002 in full view of the police. Judge Majuru from the administrative court had to flee the country when his 2003 rulings in favor of ANZ publishers annoyed the ministers of information and justice; see Majuru's confession, *Daily News* (online edition), 22 August 2004. Intimidation was directed sometimes toward court officials such as the court messenger or the sheriff.

47. Legal Resources Foundation, *Justice in Zimbabwe*, 7.

Chapter 6. The Land "Reform" Charade

1. One early publication emphasizing the land issue, though with a pro-ZANU bias, is Terence O. Ranger, *Peasant Consciousness and Guerrilla War in Zimbabwe* (London: James Currey, 1985).

2. In the extensive literature, see T. A. S. Bowyer-Bower and Colin Stoneman, eds., *Land Reform in Zimbabwe: Constraints and Prospects* (Aldershot: Ashgate/ SOAS, 2000); also Lloyd M. Sachikonye, "From 'Growth with Equity' to 'Fast-Track' Reform: Zimbabwe's Land Question," *Review of African Political Economy* 96 (2003): 227–40; Sam Moyo, "The Political Economy of Land Acquisition and Redistribution in Zimbabwe, 1990–1999," *Journal of Modern African Studies* 26, 1 (2000).

3. The colonial land grab was a key factor in the rebellions by the Ndebele in 1893 and the Shona and Ndebele in 1896–97.

4. The indigenous population was recorded as 881,000 in 1920. See David Beach, *The Shona and Their Neighbours* (Oxford: Blackwell, 1994), 171.

5. With a fast-growing African population after World War II, communal areas were overpopulated, and the overexploited farmland in drought-prone areas produced declining household income for African farmers and an increase in landless families by the late 1970s.

6. See Roger C. Riddell, *The Land Problem in Rhodesia: Alternatives for the Future* (Salisbury [Harare]: Mambo Press, 1978); also Robert Palmer, *Land and Racial Domination in Rhodesia* (London: Heinemann, 1977).

7. However, William H. Shaw disputes its economic rationality and equity; see his "'They Stole Our Land': Debating the Expropriation of White Farms in Zimbabwe," *Journal of Modern African Studies* 41, 1 (2003): 75–89.

8. The urban-based petite bourgeoisie and the labor movement contributed decisively toward shaping the nationalist discourse and agenda, in what was primarily a fight for majority rule and human dignity; see Timothy Scarnecchia, *The Urban Roots of Democracy and Political Violence in Zimbabwe: Harare and Highfield, 1940–1964* (Rochester, N.Y.: University of Rochester Press, 2008).

9. It came to an end officially in August 2004, according to a statement by President Mugabe, but illegal farm appropriations went on until the 2008 presidential election and even after the swearing in of the tripartite government in February 2009.

10. See Peter Godwin and Ian Hancock, *"Rhodesians Never Die": The Impact of War and Political Change on White Rhodesia c. 1970–1980* (Oxford: Oxford University Press, 1993).

11. At the Lancaster House conference, the dominant concern of the Patriotic Front was the security arrangements and guarantees for democratic elections; see Jeffrey Davidow, *A Peace in Southern Africa: The Lancaster House Conference on Rhodesia, 1979* (Boulder, Colo.: Westview, 1979); also *Southern Rhodesia: Report of the Constitutional Conference, Lancaster House, London, September–December 1979* (London: Her Majesty's Stationery Office, January 1980).

12. Quoted in Martin Meredith, *Mugabe: Power and Plunder in Zimbabwe* (Oxford: Public Affairs, 2002), 184–85.

13. Subsection 3, allowing citizens and residents to claim payment in foreign currencies outside Zimbabwe, made land acquisitions costly for the treasury. However, most farmers accepted Zimbabwe dollars in the 1980s, as the exchange rate to the U.S. dollar and pound was still good.

14. According to CFU, between 1985 and 1997 nearly 5 million hectares of land were put on sale while the government had the first option to purchase; see Angus Selby, "Commercial Farmers and the State: Interest Group Politics and Land Reform in Zimbabwe," Ph.D. dissertation, University of Oxford, 2006), 144, http://www.zwnews.com/issuefull.cfm?ArticleID=14982.

15. Other figures give 54,000 families on three million hectares by 1990; see Jocelyn Alexander, "State, Peasantry and Resettlement in Zimbabwe," *Review of African Political Economy* 61 (1994): 325–45. This was a far cry from the 1982 government target of 162,000 families to be resettled.

16. See Bill H. Kinsey, "Land Reform, Growth and Equity: Emerging Evidence from Zimbabwe's Resettlement Programme," *Journal of Southern African Studies* 25, 2 (June 1999); and "Zimbabwe's Land Reform Program: Underinvestment in Post-Conflict Transformation," *World Development* 32, 10 (2004): 1669–96; also John Cusworth, "A Review of the UK ODA Evaluation of the Land Resettlement Programme in 1988 and the Land Appraisal Mission in 1996," in Bowyer-Bower and Stoneman, *Land Reform in Zimbabwe*, 25–34.

17. See Hevina S. Dashwood, *Zimbabwe: The Political Economy of Transformation* (Toronto: University of Toronto Press, 2000), 162–65, 180–87.

18. "Zimbabwe: Back to the Land," *Africa Confidential*, 22 September 1989, 5.

19. Such was the case of Churu farm belonging to ZANU (Ndonga) leader Ndabaningi Sithole. The government designated the farm in 1993 and ignored a High Court injunction suspending its decision. The riot police subsequently evicted some 20,000 people in 1994.

20. Many agreed within ZANU-PF, and in the party's internal meetings abusive language against white farmers was routine; see Mugabe's speech in the Central Committee in 1993, quoted in Selby, "Commercial Farmers and the State," 228.

21. Some sources suggest that £75 million was pledged by the UK during the Lancaster House agreement; see Bertus de Villiers, *Land Reform: Issues and Challenges* (Johannesburg: Konrad Adenauer Stiftung, 2003), 7. Others suggest that Lord Carrington and the American administration made some vague promises to fund resettlement and agricultural development at Lancaster House to break a negotiation deadlock over the constitution in mid-October, without specifying a sum; see Martin Meredith, *The Past Is Another Country: Rhodesia UDI to Zimbabwe* (London: Pan Books, 1980), 381. For sure the British government spent far less on Zimbabwe's land reform than on the Kenyan Million Acre Scheme, but as Selby points out the Zimbabwe government chose to spend far more on defense than on land reform, sowing doubts about its policy priorities. Besides farmland was far cheaper in Zimbabwe than in postcolonial Kenya; see Selby, "Commercial Farmers and the State," 141–43.

22. However, a 1996 study commissioned by the British Overseas Development Administration (ODA) recommended funding a five-year program to resettle 25,000 households on land acquired on a "willing seller, willing buyer" basis.

23. The approximately U.S.$100 million looted in the War Victims Compensation Fund scandal (see Chapter 7) and the U.S.$200 million or so squandered in gratuities for the war veterans amounted to nearly twice the total funding spent by government on land reform since 1980; see *Financial Gazette*, 5 November 1997.

24. Selby, "Commercial Farmers and the State," 247.

25. Interview with a French agricultural expert assigned to this UNDP unit, Harare, April 2000.

26. Less than 5 percent of the white farmers in the late 1990s were descendants of nineteenth-century settlers, and less than 10 percent belonged to pre-World War II settler families; see Selby, quoting CFU statistics, "Commercial Farmers and the State," 334.

27. According to Selby, "Commercial Farmers and the State," 277, most white farmers did campaign for the "No" vote and mobilized their farm workers, but this does not account for the massive rejection of the constitutional draft in urban black-only townships where the turnout was higher than in the rural areas. The NCA, which led the "No" campaign, was not a white-dominated organization.

28. Angus Selby even calls it an "alliance" between the ZANU-PF government and the white farmers' associations, the CFU and the ZTA, between 1980 and 1990; see Selby, "Commercial Farmers and the State," chap. 3.

29. Per Nordlund, *Organising the Political Agora: Domination and Democratisation in Zambia and Zimbabwe* (Uppsala: Uppsala University Press, 1996), 177.

30. Quoted by Michael Hartnack, "The Real Positive News," comment on ZWNEWS, 12 September 2003.

31. Yothan farm in Masvingo Province was the first occupied on 16 February 2000. Acquired by the government in 1987, it was abandoned in the 1990s after a resettlement project's failure.

32. For example see Sam Moyo, "The Land Occupation Movement and Democratisation in Zimbabwe: Contradictions of Neoliberalism," *Millennium* 30, 2 (2001): 311–30.

33. Yet there was a disturbing trend of High Court orders being ignored by the police as early as the mid-1980s; see Selby, "Commercial Farmers and the State," 168.

34. However, in two areas of Chiredzi District—Fair Range Ranch and Gonarezhou National Park—there have been land invasions fairly more spontaneous and orderly—even "technocratic"—than what was usually reported; see Joseph Chaumba, Ian Scoones, and William Wolmer, "New Politics, New Livelihoods: Agrarian Change in Zimbabwe," *Review of African Political Economy* 98 (2003): 585–608; also Joseph Chaumba, Ian Scoones, and William Wolmer, "From *Jambanja* to Planning: The Reassertion of Technocracy in Land Reform in South-Eastern Zimbabwe?" *Journal of Modern African Studies* 41, 4 (2003): 533–54.

35. This was noted in various CFU, press, and human rights group reports and is confirmed by Selby's field research; see Selby, "Commercial Farmers and the State," 287.

36. Border Gezi was the first to spill the beans in the government press; see

Herald, 5 April 2000. However, other ministers denied it for several months in order to blur the picture further.

37. See Selby, "Commercial Farmers and the State," 298–99.

38. For example Kombo Moyana, governor of the Reserve Bank, was implicated in such a scandal for his Olympia Farm; see *Parade*, April 1992.

39. *Commercial Farmers' Union v. Commissioner of Police and Others*, HH-3544–2000.

40. *Commissioner of Police v. Commercial Farmers' Union*, HH-84–2000.

41. Made as early as 1993; see Selby, "Commercial Farmers and the State," 238.

42. R. W. Johnson, *Political Opinion in Zimbabwe 2000* (Parklands, S.A.: Helen Suzman Foundation, 2000), 41.

43. T. A. S. Bowyer-Bower, "Implications for Poverty of Land Reform in Zimbabwe: Insights from the Findings of the 1995 Poverty Assessment Survey Study," in Bowyer-Bower and Stoneman, *Land Reform in Zimbabwe*, 83–101.

44. One farmer, Philip Buzuidenhout, was arrested and convicted for running down a settler with his truck although some witnesses said it was a traffic accident rather than a murder. Yet it provided a convenient excuse to seize his farm.

45. Tim Henwood, who had taken a firm stance against the farm invasions, had his farm seized in 2001 when he stepped down from the CFU executive to avoid a split in the organization; see *Independent*, 16 March 2001.

46. Interview with Colin Cloete, Harare, August 2001. He and CFU director David Hasluck supported continued cooperation with the government.

47. See CFU, "Zimbabwe Joint Resettlement Initiative," press release, 24 May 2001.

48. On the split and the subsequent fate of the CFU and JAG, and also the secession of the Matabeleland CFU branch in 2004, see Selby, "Commercial Farmers and the State," 310ff.

49. One case is documented for the 2005 parliamentary elections in Chegutu West; see *Zimbabwe Independent*, 29 July 2005. The group of farmers alleged to have contributed U.S.$44 million to ZANU-PF's campaign included Colin Cloete and his father, as well as former president of the Zimbabwe Tobacco Association (ZTA) Kobus Joubert, his son, and the then vice-chairman of the ZTA.

50. For such examples and their ultimate fate, see Selby, "Commercial Farmers and the State," 301–2.

51. See *Zimbabwe Independent*, 23 August 2002.

52. In Selby's survey area, half the farms designated went to army, police, or CIO personnel; see Selby, "Commercial Farmers and the State," 329.

53. When presenting the 99-year lease scheme on 9 November 2006, Mugabe assessed the results of the land reform as follows: 6,517 farms measuring over 10 million hectares listed for resettlement, of which 2,740 farms measuring 4,137,085 hectares were used to resettle 140,698 A1 families, while 2,280 farms measuring 2,681,642 hectares were divided among 14,856 A2 beneficiaries; see *Daily Mirror Reporter*, 10 November 2006. A2 farms are not subdivided and are devoted to commercial farming.

54. Quoted in *Guardian*, 8 August 2002.

55. See *Daily News*, 18, 20 August 2003.

56. The tax on underutilized land was a recommendation of the Rukuni Commission; see Dashwood, *Zimbabwe: The Political Economy of Transformation*,

184. Contrary to Dashwood's conclusion, however, the ZANU-PF big men did not seek elite accommodation but moved to destroy and replace the white agrarian class.

57. See Zimbabwe Independent, 2 May 2003.

58. See *Sunday Times*, 9 March 2003, *Sunday Mirror* (Zimbabwe), 2, 16 March 2003.

59. See Shamuyarira's statement after a Politburo meeting, quoted in *Herald*, 31 July 2003.

60. See *Financial Gazette*, 11 September 2003. There were more than 50 people listed for Matabeleland North alone.

61. See *Zimbabwe Independent*, 27 February 2004.

62. This provision was included in Constitution Amendment No. 17, but the government had no money to compensate even the farmers who lost their farms after August 2005.

63. Conflicting exact figures have been published ranging from 322,000 to 460,000.

64. Estimates by mid-2002 varied from 100,000 to 270,000. Taking into account workers' families, about one million people were pushed out of their homes. See Norwegian Refugee Council, "Displaced and Forgotten: Internally Displaced Persons (IDPs) in Zimbabwe," Global IPD Project (Oslo: Norwegian Refugee Council, 2003), 6.

65. Selby, "Commercial Farmers and the State," 307–8.

66. Zimbabwe Independent, 9 August 2002.

67. *Zimbabwe Standard*, 3, 10 August 2003.

68. *Zimbabwe Independent*, 12 September 2003. Only 93,000 in the first category and 7,500 in the second had taken up the offer to effectively move onto the farms, according to Utete. See Charles Utete, *Report of the Presidential Land Review Committee into the Implementation of the Fast-Track Land Reform Program, 2000–2002* (Harare: Government Printers, 2003).

69. See Jeffrey Herbst, *State Politics in Zimbabwe* (Harare: University of Zimbabwe Publications, 1990), 89–92, 96–98.

70. For the above figures, see International Labour Organization, *Structural Change and Adjustment in Zimbabwe* (Geneva: ILO, 1993), 45–63.

71. Cited in Norwegian Refugee Council, "Displaced and Forgotten," 4. In the district surveyed by Selby, about 20 percent of the arable land cultivated in 2000 was being cropped in 2003 with three-fourths less irrigated areas; see Selby, "Commercial Farmers and the State," 315.

72. *Zimbabwe Independent*, 21 February 2003.

73. IRIN, "Zimbabwe: Man-Made Element to Crisis," Johannesburg, 30 July 2003.

74. "No One Will Starve—President," *Herald*, 18 March 2005.

75. See *ZimOnline*, 24 August 2006.

76. For empirical evidence, see Selby, "Commercial Farmers and the State," 318.

77. Zimbabwe Independent, 1 August 2003.

78. *Daily News*, 7 August 2002.

79. *Mail and Guardian*, 24 February 2004.

80. In Southern Africa, corn is commonly referred to as "mielie" or "mealie," from the Portuguese "milho." Mealie-meal is a relatively coarse white corn flour that is cooked into a kind of polenta called "sadza" in Zimbabwe.

81. *News 24*, 18 February 2003.

82. *Financial Gazette*, 8 August 2002.

83. *Washington Post*, 10 August 2002.

84. See Physicians for Human Rights Denmark, "Vote ZANU-PF or Starve, Zimbabwe: August to October 2002," 20 November 2002, http://www.phrusa.org/healthrights/phr_denmark.html.

85. *Daily News*, 14 August 2002.

86. In Binga, after the presidential elections, donor food was stopped by war veterans for six weeks. In early October, the government suspended all donor food to starving schoolchildren in Binga as the Catholic Church, Save the Children Fund, and Oxfam Great Britain were ordered to stop their feeding schemes. In both cases it was retaliation for the district's strong MDC vote.

87. However, in most other instances WFP officials were deceived by ZANU-PF and did not know how the lists were manipulated.

88. ZANU-PF rural district councillors played a strategic role in the sale and distribution of GMB food and controlled who was eligible for "Money/Food for Work" schemes.

89. *Daily Telegraph*, 9 August 2002. From August to November 2002, there were almost daily reports in the local independent and international press about the politicization of food aid by the ruling party.

90. *Mail and Guardian*, 18 March 2005; *ZimOnline*, 11 March 2005.

91. According to Selby, the government spent only U.S.$170 million to purchase farming land in two decades, an average of 0.5 percent of total government expenditure every year, and far less than the taxes accruing from the agricultural sector. Therefore, "the consistency and magnitude of these major budgetary decisions suggest that land reform was never as high on the real agenda as the ruling party has claimed"; see Selby, "Commercial Farmers and the State," 340–41.

92. See Selby, "Commercial Farmers and the State," 324ff.

93. *Zimbabwe Standard*, 29 November 2008. See full SADC Tribunal ruling, Case No. 2/2007, posted on the website "The Zimbabwe Situation," http://www.zimbabwesituation.com/dec1a_2008.html.

94. On farm workers, rural women, and children, see Anne Hellum and Bill Derman, "Land Reform and Human Rights in Contemporary Zimbabwe: Balancing Individual and Social Justice Through an Integrated Human Rights Framework," *World Development* 32, 10 (2004): 1785–1805.

Chapter 7. The State Bourgeoisie and the Plunder of the Economy

1. Stephen Chan, *Robert Mugabe: A Life of Power and Violence* (London: Tauris, 2003), 18. Teurai Ropa and Rex Nhongo were guerrilla nicknames. Most guerrillas adopted such names during the liberation war for security reasons and were known only under those names when they took over the government in 1980. War nicknames had a distinctive flavor as a symbol of belonging to the new elite of genuine "freedom fighters" free from tribal allegiance.

2. See the story on Joyce Mujuru's evading personal sanctions and dealing with gold from war-torn DRC, Grant Ferrett, "Zimbabwe Elite Seeks to Evade Sanctions," BBC News Africa, http://www.zwnews.com, 24 February 2009.

3. As reflected in the well-known policy document, Government of Zimbabwe, *Growth with Equity* (Harare: Government Printers, 1981).

4. It was estimated by local economists in late 2003 that the GDP had decreased by 30 percent at least since 2000, an average of 10 percent per year.

About 800,000 formal jobs were lost since 2000 in agriculture and manufacturing, and the unemployment rate was above 75 percent, with 80 percent of Zimbabweans living below the poverty line. IRIN, various reports.

5. Jean-Pascal Daloz, "'Big Men' in Sub-Saharan Africa: How Elites Accumulate Positions and Resources," in Mattei Dogan, ed., *Elite Configurations at the Apex of Power* (Leiden: Brill, 2003), 271–85.

6. Sandbrook provides a convenient definition: "We are designating as the ruling class a political elite which aspires to become a bourgeoisie. But this aspiration itself connotes little more than an opportunistic exploitation of 'insider' privileges . . . not the development of the classic risk-taking entrepreneurial behavior"; Richard Sandbrook with Judith Barker, *The Politics of Africa's Economic Stagnation* (Cambridge: Cambridge University Press, 1985), 72. Fauré and Médard use the concept "state bourgeoisie" as opposed to a true capitalist entrepreneurial class that would be independent of the state; Yves-A. Fauré and Jean François Médard, eds., *État et bourgeoisie en Côte-d'Ivoire* (Paris: Karthala, 1982).

7. On this notion of "straddling," see Michael Cowen and Kibaru Kinyanjui, *Some Problems of Capital and Class in Kenya*, Occasional Paper 26 (Nairobi: Institute for Development Studies, University of Nairobi, 1977); Jean-François Bayart, *L'état en Afrique: la politique du ventre* (Paris: Fayard, 1989), chap. 3, "L'illusion bourgeoise"; Yves-A. Fauré and Jean-François Médard, "L'état-business et les politiciens entrepreneurs: néo-patrimonialisme et 'Big Men' (économie et politique)," in Stephen Ellis and Yves-A. Fauré, eds., *Entreprises et entrepreneurs africains* (Paris: Karthala-Orstom, 1995), 289–309.

8. For a preliminary analysis see Patrick Quantin, "Portrait d'une élite au pouvoir (1980–1990)," in Jean-Louis Balans and Michel Lafon, eds., *Le Zimbabwe contemporain* (Paris: Karthala, 1995), 181–99. Important biodata on Zimbabwean political elite were published in Diana Mitchell, *Who's Who, 1981–1982: Nationalist Leaders in Zimbabwe* (Harare: author, 1981); Robert Cary and Diana Mitchell, *African Nationalist Leaders in Rhodesia Who's Who* (Bulawayo: Books of Rhodesia, 1980).

9. Mugabe's choice was effectively constrained by the 1979 Lancaster House agreement's clauses entrenching the white minority's property rights, especially on farming land. But no such provisions existed for banking or manufacturing, for example.

10. See David Smith, Colin Simpson, and Ian Davies, *Mugabe* (London: Sphere, 1981), 168–69, 204–5.

11. For a (probably incomplete) list of government-owned companies, see Eric Bloch, "Indigenisation—Is It Failing?" *Financial Gazette*, 15 September 1994.

12. Interview with independent economist John Robertson, Harare, 23 August 1999.

13. John Robertson, "The Economy: A Sectoral Overview," in Simon Baynham, ed., *Zimbabwe in Transition* (Stockholm: Almqvist & Wicksell, 1992), 71–72; Volker Wild, *Profit Not for Profit's Sake: History and Business Culture of African Entrepreneurs in Zimbabwe* (Harare: Baobab Books, 1997), 260.

14. For an estimate of the size of this group, see Hevina S. Dashwood, *Zimbabwe: The Political Economy of Transformation* (Toronto: University of Toronto Press, 2000), 93.

15. Wild, *Profit Not for Profit's Sake*, 258–59.

16. See Dashwood, *Zimbabwe*, 94.

17. See "How Mujuru Made His Millions," *Horizon*, February 1993.

18. For some examples of civil servants moving to the private sector, see Dashwood, *Zimbabwe*, 100.

19. Dashwood, *Zimbabwe*, 96.

20. Scott D. Taylor, "Race, Class, and Neopatrimonialism in Zimbabwe," in Richard Joseph, ed., *State, Conflict, and Democracy in Africa* (Boulder, Colo.: Lynne Rienner, 1999), 244.

21. See "How ZANU (PF) Built a Capitalist Empire," *Horizon*, April 1992.

22. I. Wetherell, "ZANU (PF)'s Zidco a Model for Thebe," *Weekly Mail*, 30 July 1993.

23. See "Directors flee as ZANU PF Probes Own Companies," *Sunday Mirror*, 4 April 2004.

24. See Dashwood, *Zimbabwe*, 126–27, 220 n. 45.

25. Carolyn Jenkins, "The Politics of Economic Policy-Making in Zimbabwe," *Journal of Modern African Studies* 35, 4 (1997): 594–95. She relies heavily on EIU reports, yet many cases unveiled by the press were ditched and never led to actual conviction. Lost dockets between police and magistrate courts and interference in the judicial process were quite frequent.

26. Reginald Austin, "Néo-colonialisme et corruption: le scandale 'Cressida' au Zimbabwe," *Politique Africaine* 36 (December 1989): 119–24.

27. Apparently, another inquiry into a similar, much larger scam involving Leyland transporters was stopped because more top men and women in government were implicated (source: Simome Mubi's conversation with Diana Mitchell).

28. See Dashwood, *Zimbabwe*, 102.

29. Dashwood, *Zimbabwe*, 35, 49. The achievements of the first decade of independence should not be overstated: "GDP grew at 3.4 per cent, not much faster than the estimated population growth rate. The real per capita income of Z\$471 in 1990 [was] thus only slightly higher than the 1980 level of Z\$454, and has since plummeted below the 1980 level" (23). Workers' real earnings began to decline as early as 1983 as wages did not catch up with inflation, and the formal employment ratio fell from 18.4 percent of the total population in 1974 to 11.8 in 1991, all this before ESAP was implemented (47).

30. World Bank, quoted in Dashwood, *Zimbabwe*, 64.

31. See Jenkins, "Politics of Economic Policy-Making," 597.

32. ESAP was launched in July and the government approached the World Bank only in October 1990. An agreement with the IMF was signed in October 1991. "Pressure from the World Bank (and from 1991 on, the IMF) was more on the lines of pushing the government to go farther and faster with reforms, rather than forcing it to change policy direction" (Dashwood, *Zimbabwe*, 80–81, 114–30). In particular, the Bretton Woods institutions demanded a stronger commitment on the budget deficit and parastatal reform. For a converging viewpoint, see Jenkins, "Politics of Economic Policy-Making," 598.

33. See Dashwood, *Zimbabwe*, 157–58.

34. In fiscal year 1994/5 the budget deficit was 13.5 percent of GDP; Government of Zimbabwe, *ZIMPREST: Zimbabwe Programme for Economic and Social Transformation, 1996–2000* (Harare: Government Printer, 1998), 3. Throughout the 1980s the deficit ranged between 10.6 to 13.3 percent of GDP.

35. The fact that white businessmen and farmers were able to lobby the government for policy change does not imply that they played a decisive role in the decision-making process as suggested by Jenkins, "Politics of Economic Policy-Making," 588–91.

36. In Africa this scenario is not peculiar to Zimbabwe; see Sandbrook, *Politics of Africa's Economic Stagnation*, chap. 4.

37. Parastatals said to be playing a strategic or social role were to be kept in the public sector, although these constituted about three-fourths of the parastatals' total losses; see Dashwood, *Zimbabwe*, 157.

38. See Wild, *Profit Not for Profit's Sake*, 262.

39. Although the SADC region's security situation improved significantly throughout the decade, with the transition to majority rule in Namibia and South Africa, democratization in Zambia and Malawi, and the peace agreement in Mozambique, the share of defense in the state budget was higher in fiscal year 1996/7 than in 1993/4 (8.9 vs. 8.5 percent) and continued to rise dramatically with Zimbabwe's military operation in the DRC. Figures quoted in Dashwood, *Zimbabwe*, 151–52.

40. See Dashwood, *Zimbabwe*, 165.

41. Dashwood, *Zimbabwe*, 5, 77, 172, 174, 178. Dashwood's quotes from World Bank documents are very telling.

42. For a more detailed analysis, see Brian Raftopoulos and Daniel Compagnon "Indigenization, the State Bourgeoisie and Neo-Authoritarian Politics," in Staffan Darnolf and Liisa Laakso, eds., *Twenty Years of Independence in Zimbabwe: From Liberation to Authoritarianism* (Basingstoke: Macmillan/Palgrave, 2003), 15–33.

43. A prominent independent black entrepreneur dubs "political businessmen" those black businessmen who rely on their connections with ZANU-PF big men to obtain a preferential or even exclusive access to resources and markets and outflank competitors; interview with Strive Masiyiwa, Harare, 24 August 1999. Not all political businessmen take political stances, although they are all on ZANU-PF's side.

44. Raftopoulos and Compagnon, "Indigenization, the State Bourgeoisie and Neo-Authoritarian Politics."

45. See *Horizon*, February 1993 and various issues in 1995 and 1996.

46. *Financial Gazette*, 19 November 1998.

47. Boka was a Zezuru from Mashonaland East, like Charles Utete (the former powerful director of the president's office) and Solomon Mujuru and Sydney Sekeramayi.

48. See Jean-François Bayart, Stephen Ellis, and Béatrice Hibou, *The Criminalization of the State in Africa* (London: James Currey, 1999).

49. In 1999, in connivance with the government, Chiyangwa agitated with a group of policy-holders to destabilize the white management of First Mutual Life Assurance Society by accusing them of insider trading; see *Zimbabwe Independent*, 15 October 1999. However, another group of policyholders led by black businessman Dillion Mvuri denounced these "shallow and myopic race politics calculated to cause a corporate boardroom coup at FMLS" and encouraged the management to sue Chiyangwa for damages done to the company's public image; see *Financial Gazette*, 5 August 1999.

50. On these two organizations, see Brian Raftopoulos, "Fighting for Control: The Indigenization Debate in Zimbabwe," *Southern Africa Report* 11, 4 (1996): 3–7; and "The State, Politics and the Indigenization Process in Zimbabwe: Class Formation Behind Closed Doors: 1990–1996," Harare, Institute of Development Studies, University of Zimbabwe, unpublished mimeo, March 1999; see also Taylor, "Race, Class, and Neopatrimonialism."

51. Chakaredza was involved in the rioting that followed a demonstration

organized by ZimRights in November 1995. His alleged connections with the CIO—see Per Nordlund, *Organising the Political Agora: Domination and Democratisation in Zambia and Zimbabwe* (Uppsala: Uppsala University Press, 1996), 193—led to suspicions that the violence was a staged provocation to discredit the human rights group at a time when it was targeted by CIO's destabilization maneuvers. Chakaredza once boasted some links with the ZANU-PF hierarchy. Indeed, the day after the riots, Philip Chiyangwa complained in anger to the government paper the *Herald* that his car, unfortunately parked in the vicinity, had been burned by the very people on his payroll. Among the fifteen rioters arrested by the police, only one could possibly be linked to ZIMRIGHTS.

52. *Zimbabwe Independent*, 28 June 1996.

53. The late vice president and former high-ranking ZAPU official Joseph Msika was Masiyiwa's maternal uncle and his parents supported ZAPU when they were in exile in Zambia. Other members of his family were ZANU and some were involved in the famous raid on Chinoyi in April 1966; interview with Strive Masiyiwa, Harare, 24 August 1999.

54. In this early document the emphasis was put on government support to small and medium-scale black entrepreneurs in the informal sector, not on the acquisition of equities in white-owned big companies; see IBDC, "Background Paper," unpublished mimeo, Harare, December 1993.

55. New secretary general Enoch Kamushinda had close links with Mugabe and his lieutenants. Mugabe often used divide-and-rule tactics to quell opposition from within the ruling party or in civil society. IBDC was no exception.

56. See *Mail and Guardian*, 11–17 April 1997. Even in a confidential interview, Masiyiwa refused for his own safety to name the Politburo members who attempted to blackmail him.

57. Telecel was a joint venture between DRC, American, and Zimbabwean businessmen and included among its prominent shareholders Philip Chiyangwa, Leo Mugabe, the president's nephew, and James Makamba, in his own capacity and in the name of the Mujuru family. At that time Joyce Mujuru, the wife of the general, was minister of telecommunications, and the conflict of interest was blatant.

58. *Zimbabwe Independent*, 2 February 2001.

59. Daniel Compagnon, "Le rôle de la société civile dans l'émergence d'une opposition démocratique: le cas du Zimbabwe," *Revue Internationale de Politique Comparée* 9, 2 (2002): 261–75.

60. See *Financial Gazette*, 19, 26 October 1995.

61. On the Hwange saga, see *Zimbabwe Independent*, 4, 11, 18 October 1996; *Financial Gazette*, 10, 17 October 1996; *Financial Times*, 15 October 1996.

62. Cf. Peter Searle, *The Riddle of Malaysian Capitalism: Rent-Seekers or Real Capitalists?* (Honolulu: University of Hawai'i Press, 1999).

63. Daniel Compagnon, "Discours et pratiques de 'l'indigènisation' de l'économie: une comparaison Zimbabwe—Malaisie," *Revue Internationale de Politique Comparée* 6, 3 (1999): 751–76.

64. *Herald*, 19 September 1996.

65. Interview with Margaret Dongo, Harare, August 1999.

66. To provide a complete list would require an intimate knowledge of these family connections that most ordinary Zimbabweans do not even suspect. Some examples are sometimes mentioned in the local press: Sidney Gata, chairman of the board and executive manager of the power utility ZESA was Mugabe's brother-in-law (now divorced, he was married to Regina, Mugabe's half sister),

and Gideon Gono, director of the Jewel Bank, is also related to Mugabe; Tizirai Gwata is Charles Utete's brother-in-law.

67. Nicholas van Hoogstraten, known for his brutality and absence of scruple, was convicted of manslaughter in 2002 by a London court and sentenced to ten years, but released from jail in December 2003 when the verdict was overturned on appeal on largely technical grounds. Hoogstraten is Zimbabwe's largest private landowner—600,000 acres of farmland, including profitable ostrich farms—and one of the Mugabe regime's financial backers. He owned 30,000 head of cattle before the farm invasions and was the largest shareholder of Wankie Colliery, the main coal mines. He vocally supported the land reform, although some of his farms have been invaded by the War Vets. See *Sunday Times* (UK), 25 January 2003.

68. *Herald,* 8 August 1997.

69. Details of this story can be found on the Internet in the anonymous (but allegedly authored by a USAID official), well-researched document "The New Scramble for Africa," http://www.zwnews.com.

70. See "The New Scramble for Africa." On par with other public tenders the railway routes exploitation rights were attributed in violation of the Tender Board rules, now a kind of routine pattern of the government's behavior in Zimbabwe.

71. See *Financial Gazette,* 1 April 1998.

72. Michael Nest, "Ambitions, Profits and Loss: Zimbabwean Economic Involvement in the Democratic Republic of the Congo," *African Affairs* 100 (2001): 469–90; with the same line of argument, Daniel Compagnon, "Le Zimbabwe: l'alternance et le chaos," introduction to special issue on Zimbabwe, *Politique Africaine* (March 2001).

73. See *Wall Street Journal,* 9 October 1998. Zimbabwe is alleged to have supplied Kabila with ammunition as early as 1996, to have paid U.S.$5 million to help finance his war against Mobutu and to have deployed military intelligence on the ground to help coordinate his offensive. The 1998 intervention is in line with this early investment.

74. For an example, see Nest, "Ambitions, Profits and Loss," 478.

75. *Africa Confidential,* 23 October 1998, 14 May 1999, 5 November 1999; *Wall Street Journal,* 9 October 1998.

76. Billy Rautenbach was a longtime business partner of ZANU-PF, in particular Emmerson Mnangagwa, and his company Wheels of Africa imported Japanese cars and controlled 75 percent of the haulage market in Zimbabwe.

77. See "Final Report of the Panel of Experts on the Illegal Exploitation of Natural Resources and Other Forms of Wealth of the Democratic Republic of the Congo," presented to UN Secretary General on 15 October 2002, S/2002/1146, 8.

78. See *Africa Confidential,* 31 March 2000. Forrest, who was chairman of the company since November 1999, was apparently instrumental in getting rid of Rautenbach, see Nest, "Ambitions, Profits and Loss," 489–90. In addition to his DRC businesses, Forrest owned a company manufacturing ammunitions and light weapons in Belgium. Head of Gécamines until August 2001, he engaged in assets-stripping on a large scale, according to the UN Panel of Experts.

79. See "Final Report of the Panel of Experts," 10.

80. See *Zimbabwe Standard,* 26 September 1999.

81. One estimate of the deal's value was U.S.$208 million—political risk and production costs deducted; see "New Scramble for Africa." According to the

UN Panel of Experts report, the 800-square-kilometer concession would be worth at least U.S.$2 billion once in full production. A total U.S.$5 billion worth of assets were transferred from the state mining sector to private companies from mid-1999 to mid-2002; see "Final Report of the Panel of Experts," 7, 9.

82. The operation is clouded in mystery. Sengamines statutes have not been published and the company is not affiliated with the Fédération des Entreprises du Congo (FEC), a usual legal requirement in the DRC. Sengamines also enjoys a complete tax exemption for at least six years. See Amnesty International, "Democratic Republic of Congo: Making a Killing, the Diamond Trade in Government-Controlled DRC," AI Report 62/017/2002, 22 October 2002. Since August 2000, Osleg has controlled 49 percent of the shares in Sengamines (35 percent for Comiex-Congo, 16 percent for MIBA), but uses Oryx as a front to deceive the international community; see "Final Report of the Panel of Experts," 10.

83. The Asian businessman Kamal Khalfan, Oman's honorary consul in Harare and a longtime business associate of the ZANU-PF leaders in Catercraft, a subsidiary of Zidco, introduced the dynamic al-Shanfari to Mugabe sometime in 1999. Al-Shanfari supported financially ZANU-PF's electoral campaign in 2000.

84. Following peace accords signed by the Congolese government with Rwanda on 30 July 2002 and with Uganda on 6 September 2002, foreign troops on both sides have begun to withdraw from the DRC.

85. "Final Report of the Panel of Experts," 6–7. Apparently, Zimbabwe's defense minister Sekeramayi suggested to Mugabe to hide Zimbabwe's mining interest in a holding company based in Mauritius and to form a private Zimbabwe military company out of ZDF units to guard the mining concessions.

86. See "Final Report of the Panel of Experts," 5, 12–13. The fact that Rwandan and Ugandan forces behave in the same fashion—as documented by the same report—provides no excuse.

87. "Final Report of the Panel of Experts," 5, 12.

88. Zimbabwean soldiers guarding the mining concessions in Mbuji Mayi are reliably accused of extrajudicial killings and unlawful arrests and detentions; see Amnesty International, "Democratic Republic of Congo," Report 62/017/2002. They are also involved in large-scale theft of diamonds at the expense of the MIBA, literally fighting with the local police over the bounty; see "Final Report of the Panel of Experts," 11.

89. One should not be deluded by official balance sheets. Huge Sengamines and KMC losses were not deemed credible by industry specialists, but much of the revenue derived from these joint ventures came from overpriced subcontracting and procurement arrangements with companies and individuals linked to the big men; see "Final Report of the Panel of Experts," 10–11.

90. Reported by News24 (S.A.) and displayed on ZWNEWS on 28 August 2003.

91. André Astrow, *Zimbabwe: A Revolution That Lost Its Way?* (London: Zed Press, 1983).

92. Conversation with the author in Harare, 15 August 2001.

Chapter 8. The International Community and the Crisis

1. See Stephen Chan, *Robert Mugabe: A Life of Power and Violence* (London: I.B. Tauris, 2003), chaps. 5, 6.

2. Britain placed an embargo on delivery of weapons, ammunition, and spare

parts in 2000, but maintained its humanitarian aid, being one of the three top EU member states for its contributions to the European Commission Humanitarian Aid Office, or the World Food Program for food aid.

3. In informal conversation with a British deputy high commissioner in Harare in the mid-1990s the author questioned the transparency and fairness of the electoral process in Zimbabwe.

4. The CMAG is the enforcement mechanism of the Millbrook Commonwealth Action Program adopted in New Zealand in 1995, as a follow-up to the Harare Declaration. Comprising foreign affairs ministers from eight member countries, it is charge do deal with "serious or persistent violations of principles contained in the Harare Declaration . . . and recommend measures for collective Commonwealth action aimed at the speedy restoration of democracy and constitutional rule." See Commonwealth Secretariat, http://www.thecommonwealth.org/Internal/38125/cmag/, accessed March 2010.

Foreign affairs ministers or representatives from Australia, Canada, Jamaica, Kenya, South Africa, Zimbabwe, and the UK, as well as the Commonwealth secretary general, attended this Abuja meeting. The agreement signed on 6 September 2001 acknowledged the need for land redistribution, but only through a return of law and order, and committed the Zimbabwe government to ending state-sponsored violence. However, the focus was on land, helping a disingenuous Mugabe to disregard the respect of human rights.

5. See Zimbabwe Human Rights NGO Forum, "Zimbabwe, the Abuja Agreement and the Commonwealth Principles: Compliance or Disregard?" 8 September 2003.

6. It is worth noting that the secretary general's statement on 17 March 2003 reiterated the organization's commitment to "transparent, equitable and sustainable measures for land reform, as agreed at Abuja in September 2001."

7. Mugabe's spokesman George Charamba said Zimbabwe would not seek readmission to the Commonwealth: "We have had a very bad and unfair experience with this effete club. . . . Zimbabwe left the Commonwealth and did so for good." *Herald*, 12 July 2005, quoted by Reuters.

8. The French ambassador who befriended Mugabe's ministers compared the constitutional draft to the French Fifth Republic constitution and held the NCA and the MDC responsible for the subsequent upheaval. He prophesied also a return to normality after the June 2000 elections (interview, August 1999), not really understanding what Mugabe was up to.

9. On 8 April 2005 Mugabe attended the funeral of Pope John Paul II. The Vatican is not a member of the EU, and the Italian government had to grant him a transit visa under the concordat governing the relations between the Catholic Church and the Italian Republic. Mugabe then managed to shake hands with a confused Prince Charles in full view of the international press.

10. See "Found: Robert Mugabe's Secret Bolthole in the Far East", *Sunday Times*, 15 February 2009.

11. EU Council Common Position 2004/161/CFSP of 19 February 2004, article 4.

12. Such a sanction list would have required frequent updates. These three businessmen fell victim to intra-ZANU-PF feuds, and only Chiyangwa bounced back as a member of the ruling mafia.

13. The report on the humanitarian disaster was an indictment of Harare's actions as violations of human rights and international law reminiscent of colonial oppression; see *Report of the Fact-Finding Mission to Zimbabwe to Assess the Scope*

and Impact of Operation Murambatsvina, by the UN Special Envoy on Human Settlements Issues in Zimbabwe, Mrs. Anna Kajumulo Tibaijuka, United Nations, 18 July 2005.

14. Interview with an American diplomat, American embassy, Harare, April 2000.

15. The AGOA was signed into law by former president Bill Clinton in May 2000 and was a major component of his strategy "trade not aid." The AGOA allows duty- and quota-free entry for a range of African goods into the wide U.S. market. However, African governments have to meet standards on democracy, human rights, the rule of law and a market-based economy set by the Act, for their country to be eligible.

16. "Former White House Official Slams Mugabe for Perfect Crime'," Washington File (US State Department), 2 August 2002, published on line by *The Zimbabwe Situation*, archive, http://www.zimbabwesituation.com/ aug4_2002.html#link19, accessed March 2010.

17. Colin Powell, "Freeing a Nation from a Tyrant's Grip," *New York Times*, 24 June 2003.

18. See *Sunday Times* (UK), 13 July 2003.

19. However, the all-encompassing free trade agreement proved to be unattainable, and the negotiations switched in 2006 to the more limited Trade Investment and Development Cooperation Agreement, eventually signed in July 2008.

20. "The Zimbabwe Crisis: The Correct Position, Statement by Mr. Morgan Tsvangirai, MDC President," Press release, Harare, 9 July 2003, published on line by *The Zimbabwe Situation*, archive, http://www.zimbabwesituation.com/ jul10_2003.html,accessed March 2010.

21. "Mugabe Changes Aid Stance," *Times*, 12 February 2005, published on line by *The Zimbabwe Situation*, archive, http://www.zimbabwesituation.com/ feb13_2005.html, accessed March 2010.

22. "US Planning Tougher Sanctions Sgainst Mugabe," *Daily News* online edition, 22 April 2005, *The Zimbabwe Situation*, archive, http://www.zimbabwesituation.com/apr23a_2005.html, accessed March 2010.

23. Calling Mugabe a tyrant does not necessarily trigger direct intervention; the examples of Belarus, Cuba, and Myanmar are there to remind us that Bush's administration rhetoric and its strategic decisions were two different things.

24. See Peter J. Schraeder, *United States Foreign Policy Toward Africa: Incrementalism, Crisis and Change* (Cambridge: Cambridge University Press, 1994).

25. See Chris Alden and Garth le Pere, *South Africa's Post-Apartheid Foreign Policy: From Reconciliation to Revival?* IISS Adelphi Paper 362 (Oxford: Oxford University Press, 2003), 50–51.

26. According to the *Financial Mail* (S.A.), 10 June 2005, Zimbabwe has paid off its long-term R100 million debt to the South African company Eskom. In 2005 Zimbabwe imported 30 percent of its power needs, about 4 percent from Eskom (versus 55 percent at the beginning of the crisis). The bulk of the electricity came from Mozambique's Cahora Bassa and the DRC Inga project. This underlines that any effective sanction policy requires participation of all SADC member states.

27. For instance, Thabo Mbeki invited "white supremacists" to leave the Commonwealth in early March 2002 after Tony Blair had criticized the weak Commonwealth Heads of Government Meeting (CHOGM) statement on Zimbabwe and claimed that African countries' ambivalence over good governance could jeopardize the NEPAD.

28. See "Zim: Hints of Racism," *News24*, 11 May 2005.

29. See Scott Thomas, *The Diplomacy of Liberation: The Foreign Relations of the African National Congress Since 1960* (London: Tauris Academic, 1996), 146–47.

30. See John Dzimba, *South Africa's Destabilization of Zimbabwe, 1980–89* (New York: St. Martin's, 1998).

31. Tim Hughes and Greg Mills, "Time to Jettison Quiet Diplomacy," *Focus* (Helen Suzman Foundation), March 2003, http://zimbabwe.ms.dk/themes/zimupdate/timetojettison.htm.

32. Separate interviews with MDC leaders Welshman Ncube, David Coltart, and Paul Themba Nyathi, Harare, August 2001. In spite of the SADC leaders' public support for Mugabe, in mid-2001 the MDC leaders who would later form the MDC-M entertained good relations with South Africa and claimed President Mbeki consulted with them frequently, as did the Botswana and Mozambique presidents.

33. Zimbabwean illegal residents in South Africa are estimated as 3–4 million; 25,000–30,000 are allegedly crossing the border every month to flee poverty and food shortages in most cases.

34. This factor was particularly important for South Africa's decision makers; see, for example, the deputy minister for foreign affairs Azid Pahad's statements, in the *Star* (S.A.), 5 February 2001.

35. In 1993, a year before assuming presidential office, Mandela stated that "Human rights will be the light that guides our foreign affairs"; see Nelson Mandela, "South Africa's Future Foreign Policy," *Foreign Affairs* 72, 5 (November–December 1993): 86–97.

36. See Z. Pallo Jordan, "Much Ado About Zimbabwe," *ANC Today*, 6–12 April 2001.

37. Special envoys Professor Adebayo Adedeji (Nigeria) and Kgalema Motlanthe (South Africa) presided over these initial efforts in April and May 2002.

38. On the ZANU-PF side, justice, legal, and parliamentary affairs minister Patrick Chinamasa and then state security minister Nicholas Goche, supported by Zimbabwe's Pretoria high commissioner, Simon Moyo; in the MDC delegation, Welshman Ncube and Gibson Sibanda. Mbeki personally facilitated the talks; see International Crisis Group, *Zimbabwe's Continuing Self-Destruction*, Africa Briefing 38, 6 June 2006, 3–4.

39. On 18 December 2004, a South African agent was arrested by the CIO at Victoria Falls, and he allegedly implicated several ZANU-PF cadres: MP Phillip Chiyangwa, the ruling party's provincial chairman of Mashonaland West; external affairs director Itai Marchi; security director Kennedy Karidza; the ambassador designate to Mozambique and former consul general in South Africa Godfrey Dzvairo; and former banker Tendai Matambanadzo. See "How SA Spied on Mugabe," *Mail and Guardian*, 20 January 2005. Most of the accused were later convicted, but Chiyangwa was released on bail pending his trial and later left alone. Other accused were tortured: Karidza could hardly walk and talk when brought to trial, more than a month after his arrest.

40. Deputy foreign affairs minister Aziz Pahad remarked: "That's the world of intelligence. Everyone expects that every country has declared and nondeclared agents in operation but we [South Africa and Zimbabwe] are not enemies"; *Sunday Times* (S.A.), 23 January 2005. After the March 2005 elections, Harare stated that the South African agent was only held as a witness for the trials.

41. Thabo Mbeki, "Zimbabwe Elections: Let the Voice of the People Be Heard," *ANC Today*, 1–7 April 2005.

42. Statement by the leader of the South African observer mission, labor minister Membathisi Mdladlana, 2 April 2005. It congratulated the government for the "peaceful, transparent, credible, well-mannered elections, which reflects the will of the people." Cf. Phumzile Mlambo Ngcuka's preliminary statement, 3 April 2005. The South African energy and minerals minister was the chair of the SADC mission.

43. Zimbabwe has played a major role in the SADCC/SADC. It provided the first two executive secretaries and fulfilled the important regional food security portfolio.

44. Le Pere, *South Africa's Post-Apartheid Foreign Policy*, 56.

45. This preferential tariff agreement enabled Rhodesia to export goods such as gold, ferroalloys, chrome, asbestos, tobacco, beef, cotton/textiles, and even low-grade sun-dried Virginia tobacco to the South African market duty free. This became vital to Rhodesia's economy when the UN adopted economic sanctions against Ian Smith's regime in 1967.

46. See Colin Stoneman, "Lessons Unlearned: South Africa's One-way Relationship with Zimbabwe," in David Simon, ed., *South Africa in Southern Africa: Reconfiguring the Region* (Oxford: James Currey, 1998), 89–102.

47. When the ANC won the 1994 elections, Mugabe favored the PAC, which got only a tiny share of the vote, and he befriended Mangosuthu Buthelezi, leader of the Inkatha Freedom Party (IFP), the ANC's archrival in Kwazulu-Natal. These moves irritated the ANC leadership.

48. According to ANC insiders, Mbeki bitterly remembered being sent back home with disdain by Nigerian general Sani Abacha, in 1995, when he pleaded for mercy for the Ogoni activists. Disciplining an African dictator required strong support from other African countries. Going it alone was a recipe for disaster.

49. Although ostensibly an SADC operation to restore the legal government and quell a military coup, the intervention was widely perceived as South Africa's protection of its traditional strategic interest, especially the security of the Lesotho Highlands Water Project, which is crucial for the Pretoria-Johannesburg area water supply.

50. "More Zimbabweans Seek Asylum," IRIN, 21 June 2006.

51. ICG, *Zimbabwe: An Opposition Strategy*, Africa Report 117, 24 August 2006, p. 17.

52. See SABC News, 1 August 2002, released the day after on ZWNEWS.

53. The EU mellowed its stance in that case, because the summit was supposed to assess the important trade negotiations on Economic Partnership Agreements started in 2002 and to be concluded by the end in 2007. The EU had signed a Trade and Development Cooperation Agreement with South Africa in October 1999 that entered into force on 1 May 2004, but the regional EPA was negotiated with SADC countries.

54. The AU Commission on Human and Peoples' Rights compiled its report after a fact-finding mission to Zimbabwe, 24–28 June 2002.

55. "AU Observers Call for Probe into Poll Results," *Daily News*, 5 April 2005.

56. Bahama Tom Nyandunga was a member of the AU Commission on Human and Peoples' Rights and a special rapporteur for refugees, asylum-seekers, and the displaced. Harare claimed protocol was not observed and refused to give him proper accreditation.

57. See also ICG, *Zimbabwe's Operation Murambatsvina: The Tipping Point?* ICG Africa Report 97 (Brussels: ICG, 17 August 2005), 5.

58. According to press reports this military equipment was delivered against advance sales of one-year's crop of tobacco and production of gold; see *The Age* (Australia), 30 July 2005, *Business Day* (S.A.), 24 August 2006. Other contracts signed with the Chinese involved electricity generators, commuter buses, and farming. Zimbabwean authorities claimed in early 2005 that the trade with China was fast expanding as cheap Chinese goods, derisively called "zhing zhong," flooded Zimbabwean shops. However, a significant part of this trade was through barter arrangements, as Harare could not pay for its imports in hard currency. Zimbabwe's exports to China were limited to U.S.$264 million in 2004.

59. According to the Zimbabwe Investment Centre, China invested Z$123 billion in the manufacturing industry and Z$3 billion in tourism and services. At the central bank foreign exchange auction rate of Z$9,016 to U.S.$1, this in mid-2005 made approximately U.S.$14 million, and at the black market rate of Z$25,000 to U.S.$1, which reflected more correctly the real value of local currency, this amounted to a paltry U.S.$5 million. See *Business Report* (S.A.), 28 June 2005.

60. See interview of ZNCC chief executive in "'Look East' Policy Staves Off Collapse with Grants and Deals," IRIN, 29 July 2005.

61. By mid-2003 South African land reform efforts had transferred 2.3 million hectares—about 2.8 percent of all agricultural land, a far cry from the official targets; ICG, *Blood and Soil: Land, Politics and Conflict Prevention in Zimbabwe and South Africa*, ICG Africa Report 85 (Brussels: ICG, 2004), 166.

62. See "Mugabe Dangerous Dictator," *Zimbabwe Independent*, 24 August 2001.

63. The International Crisis Group estimated in 2003 the loss of potential investment to Southern Africa as some U.S.$36 billion. The American Chamber of Commerce has estimated that for the financial year ending in mid-2001 South Africa had lost U.S.$3 billion in potential investment because of developments north of the Limpopo. South Africa's investment risk rating was affected, although other factors may have played a role.

64. Since he was elected South Africa's president Zuma's policy on Zimbabwe did not differ radically from Mbeki's. Zuma resents Western interference as much as Mbeki does and his primary concern is still the stability of Zimbabwe. However, since summer 2009 he has exerted a stronger pressure on Mugabe to fully implement the September 2008 "general political agreement," the basis of the current power-sharing formula.

65. "We don't want Zimbabwe collapsing here next door," Mbeki is quoted as saying; "South Africa Would Inherit All of the Consequences," BuaNews Online, 24 July 2005, http://www.buanews.gov.za/index.html. See also *Business Day*, 25 July 2005. His finance minister added that South Africa did not want a "failed, rogue state next door." Yet by 2005 Zimbabwe was already a failed state with only a façade of normality.

66. ICG, *Zimbabwe's Continuing Self-Destruction*, 15.

67. The agreement provides for a joint permanent commission on defense and security, boosting military, police, and intelligence cooperation. It will also tackle specific areas of concern, such as cross-border crime and illegal immigration. See *News24* (S.A.), 17 November 2005.

68. ICG, *Zimbabwe's Continuing Self-Destruction*, 16.

69. See "Cross-Border Crime Rising as Economy Sinks," IRIN, 7 April 2006; "Zimbabwe Meltdown Is Concern to SA—Pahad," *Business Day*, 18 May 2006.

70. ICG, *Zimbabwe: Prospects from a Flawed Election,* Crisis Group Africa Report 138, 20 March 2008, 5–7.

Conclusion

1. In comparison with previous elections, the MDC adopted a positive campaign discourse, emphasizing political change, economic recovery, and promises of compensation and truth-telling about past state atrocities, in a far more convincing way than the rival Makoni campaign.

2. ICG, *Zimbabwe: Prospects from a Flawed Election,* ICG Africa Report 138 (Brussels: ICG, 20 March 2008), 15. According to various testimonies, the MDC-M National Council adopted the agreement while the MDC-T produced last-minute new demands showing little goodwill toward unity. At the end two Matabeleland seats only were in the balance. See also "The MDC Unity Agreement Tsvangirai Refused to Sign," NewZimbabwe.com, posted 8 February 2008.

3. His campaign team was led by disenchanted ruling elite members such as Ibbo Mandaza, the former owner of the SAPES group and editor of the *Daily Mirror* who fell out with the government and was outmaneuvered by the CIO. The spokesperson was former Mugabe press secretary turned businessman Godfrey Chanetsa. It is said also that Makoni received significant financial support from various businessmen.

4. ICG, *Zimbabwe: Prospects from a Flawed Election,* 14.

5. See "CIO Disrupt Makoni Plan," *Zimbabwe Independent,* 29 February 2008.

6. Average numbers of registered voters per polling station were, in Harare and Bulawayo, between three and four times the numbers in rural areas.

7. According to the ZEC, MDC-T won 99 seats, against ZANU-PF 97, MDC-M 10 and 1 for an independent (Jonathan Moyo voting alongside ZANU-PF most of the time). Three seats were not filled because the candidates died close to election date. The Senate results, released on 6 April, gave 30 seats to the MDC-T 24 to ZANU-PF, and 6 to the MDC-M, notwithstanding the fact that following Amendment No. 18, Mugabe still appoints 5 senators and 10 governors sitting in the Senate, in addition to 18 elected chiefs (a pro-ZANU-PF constituency). Therefore the higher house remained in firm ZANU-PF control.

8. In the previous presidential elections (1990, 1996, 2002), a candidate with the highest number of votes, even if below 50 percent of the electorate, was elected. The 29 March 2008 election required a stipulated 50 percent + 1 vote to be elected. Otherwise the Act provided for a runoff.

9. Patricia Mpofu, "MDC Declares Victory in Zimbabwe Elections," *ZimOnline,* 2 April 2008. However, it is alleged that Tsvangirai could not substantiate that figure when requested to do so by the ZEC; see Peter Kagwanja, *Saving Zimbabwe: An Agenda for Democratic Peace* (Pretoria: Human Sciences Research Council and Africa Policy Institute, 2008), 9.

10. The 95 percent confidence interval—linked to the size of the sample—was 47.0 to 51.8 for Morgan Tsvangirai. This meant that the MDC figure based on more polling stations but with less stringent statistical methods could very well be true. See "ZESN Poll Projections on March 29 Presidential Election," ZESN, 31 March 2008.

11. See ICG, *Negotiating Zimbabwe Transition,* Africa Briefing 51 (Pretoria/Brussels: ICG, 21 May 2008). There were several press reports suggesting the same drama behind closed doors.

12. According to ZESN's election report, the electoral watchdog "could not

verify the presidential results that were announced by ZEC on 2 May 2008 as the ZEC National Command Center was closed on the 6th of April and only opened on the 1st of May for tabulation of Presidential results. . . . ZESN was not aware of the chain of custody of the ballot materials during the aforementioned period. . . . Transparency in the verification, collation and tabulation of Presidential results was highly suspect as party agents who are required by the law to be present were not invited to witness the process"; Zimbabwe Election Support Network, *Report on the Zimbabwe 29 March Harmonized Election and 27 June Presidential Run-off*, Harare, August 2008, 40.

13. See Morgan Tsvangirai interview on BBC *Hardtalk*, 17 April 2008.

14. See ICG, *Negotiating Zimbabwe Transition*, 4–5.

15. See his Independence Day speech, "Mugabe Denounces Britain in Post-Poll Speech," Reuters, Friday, 18 April 2008.

16. The extent of the involvement of the army, CIO, and uniformed police in the JOC-led violence is precisely documented in Solidarity Peace Trust, *Punishing Dissent, Silencing Citizens: The Zimbabwe Elections 2008*, Johannesburg, 21 May 2008.

17. Solidarity Peace Trust, *Desperately Seeking Sanity: What Prospects for a New Beginning in Zimbabwe?* Durban, 29 July 2008, 28–29. One of the most disturbing trends was the use of family members (including women and children) as surrogates when MDC officials or electoral agents could not be found. The violence was extensively chronicled in SADC and AU election observer mission reports as well as by various NGOs such as Solidarity Peace Trust and Human Rights Watch.

18. Dumisani Muleya, "Zimbabwe Violence 'Shocks' SA Generals," *Business Day*, 14 May 2008.

19. Its election observers were beaten up, its offices raided on 25 April 2008, its officials harassed by the police, and the organization was accused by Chinamasa and Mnangagwa of being pro-MDC and bent on bribing ZEC members to declare Tsvangirai the winner; see ZESN, *Report on the Zimbabwe 29 March Harmonized Election*, 50.

20. This ban coincided with the worst incidents of violence in the rural areas, and it was largely seen as means to prevent NGOs from witnessing and reporting these abuses. The ban was officially lifted in September, but it took several more weeks for the humanitarian agencies to work effectively in these areas.

21. See ZESN, *Report on the Zimbabwe 29 March Harmonized Election*, 58–59. Neither the opposition parties nor the ZESN were able to monitor polling stations in the way they did in March. The ZEC figures are not credible: the voter turnout is recorded at 42.37 percent compared to 42.7 percent in March, although eyewitnesses saw many fewer people voting at least in the urban areas, where voters were aware of Tsvangirai's withdrawal. Indeed many opposition supporters chose to spoil papers out of frustration when intimidated into voting by militias in the rural areas and popular townships. Moreover, it is impossible that Mugabe received as much as the sum of his and Tsvangirai's votes in first run; this is a symbolic figure to demonstrate the annihilation of Mugabe's rival.

22. See ICG, *Negotiating Zimbabwe Transition*, 10–11.

23. See "Only God Will Remove Me!" SA *Sunday Times*, 22 June 2008.

24. The EU added thirty-seven individuals and four companies to its list for targeted sanctions in July 2008, and a further eleven persons in early December. The United States expanded its list in November.

25. Only Botswana's vice president and Kenya's prime minister called for Zimbabwe's suspension from the African Union.

26. Mbeki refused to condemn Mugabe for the violence against the opposition and went as far as saying on 12 April that there was "no crisis in Zimbabwe but a normal electoral process." South Africa, then a member of the UN Security Council, maneuvered to tone down a U.S.- and UK-sponsored resolution adopted on 24 June, preventing it from declaring Mugabe's reelection illegitimate.

27. See "UN Zim Vote Sours US-SA Relations," *Sunday Independent*, 13 July 2008. However, such strong words allow Mbeki to rally Pan-African solidarity against Western interference. He exploited this polarization as much as Mugabe did.

28. Steve Hanke, professor of applied economics at the Johns Hopkins University, Baltimore, and a hyperinflation specialist, estimated inflation in Zimbabwe at 89.7 sextillion percent in November 2008; see IRIN, "Remittances Saved the Country from Collapse,", 20 February 2009.

29. Both proceeds from private companies' operations and money transfers from humanitarian agencies and NGOs had to go through the central bank and be exchanged at a punishing official exchange rate—from a fifth to less than a tenth of the black market rate. This explains why remittances from Zimbabweans abroad went though private transfer systems. These shortsighted policies not only increased the cost of humanitarian assistance to the poorest and the sick, but made conducting business increasingly difficult for private companies in Zimbabwe.

30. ICG, *Zimbabwe: A Regional Solution*, 8.

31. See "New Currency Already Working Overtime," *Zimbabwean*, 7 September 2006.

32. See Solidarity Peace Trust, *"Meltdown": Murambatsvina One Year On*, 30 August 2006, http://solidaritypeacetrust.org/reports/meltdown.pdf. The official rationale for this racket was to forcibly reduce the monetary mass when in fact the RBZ was the main cause of monetary creation.

33. See IRIN, "Remittances Saved the Country from Collapse", 20 February 2009.

34. Cited in "Zimbabwe Gets Back on Track with Education Goals," *Media Global* (United Nations), 2 March 2009, online, http://www.mediaglobal.org/article/2009-03-02/zimbabwe-gets-back-on-track-with-education-goals (accessed March 2010).

35. It is worth noting that a better run Bulawayo under its MDC mayor was spared by the epidemic except for four imported cases.

36. See WHO, "Cholera in Zimbabwe: Epidemiological Bulletin Number 13 Week 10 (1–7 March 2009)," published online by the UN Office for the Coordination of Humanitarian Affairs (OCHA), http://ochaonline.un.org/Cholera Situation/CholeraSituation/tabid/5399/language/en-US/Default.aspx (accessed March 2010).

37. ICG, *Zimbabwe: An Opposition Strategy*, Africa Report 117 (Brussels: ICG, 24 August 2006), 1–2.

38. See "UNICEF and Government of Zimbabwe Release New Social Sectors Data," 24 November 2009, online, http://www.unicef.org/infobycountry/media_51917.html (accessed March 2010).

39. A "reference group" was set up to assist the mediation that included AU Commission chair Jean Ping, UN Zimbabwe envoy Haile Menkerios, and SADC emissary George Chikoti. However, this group played no significant role in subsequent negotiations.

40. In a radio interview, Welshman Ncube, MDC-M secretary general and lead negotiator, acidly summed up the then stalemate by stating that Tsvangirai demanded a transitional government transferring effective power to his party instead of a government of national unity based on genuine power sharing. Ncube argued that Tsvangirai's demands were illegitimate because his party did not have an absolute majority in the House of Assembly and the only solution was the "Kenyan model"—rival president and prime minister sharing executive powers—in spite of the many differences between the two crises; see "Ncube: ZANU-PF Power-Sharing Offer 'Practicable,'" *ZimOnline* and NewZimbabwe.com, 22 August 2008. Despite Ncube's denial, the MDC-M effectively toed the ZANU-PF line.

41. Or perhaps for tribal reasons; see "Blow for Robert Mugabe as Morgan Tsvangirai's Man Elected Speaker," *Daily Telegraph* (UK), 26 August 2008.

42. The draft document, signed 11 September 2008, was apparently tampered with by Chinamasa, one of the ZANU-PF negotiators, and Mbeki refused to allow the final version, signed 15 September 2008, to be corrected when the MDC noticed the differences; see "Ncube Explains Altering of Document," *Zimbabwe Times*, 23 February 2009, http://www.thezimbabwetimes.com/.

43. Whether this means that the president must decide in accordance with the prime minister as suggested by the MDC-T or not is immaterial. Tsvangirai does not have the practical means to force Mugabe to follow this line.

44. See Human Rights Watch, *Crisis Without Limits: Human Rights and Humanitarian Consequences of Political Repression in Zimbabwe* (New York: HRW, 2009), 27–30.

45. See the testimony of the MDC counselor in Kadoma Bothwell Pasipamire on his arrest by CIO, torture, and escape, http://www.zwnews.com/issuefull.cfm?ArticleID = 20036.

46. The MDC-T claimed that it was agreed on 11 September, when the draft was finalized, that the three parties to would nominate the provincial governors according to the proportion of their respective representation in Parliament. However, this clause does not appear in the written agreement signed by the three leaders and Mbeki on 15 September. MDC-T negotiators claimed foul play and delayed the signature for several hours but Mugabe refused bulk.

47. For example, 70 union members were arrested at a demonstration that police violently dispersed on 3 December 2008.

48. There are indications, however, that Tsvangirai accepted the sharing of Home Affairs in early November in a face-to-face meeting with Mugabe but later backtracked when confronted with criticisms from his party's national executive; see ICG, *Ending Zimbabwe's Nightmare: A Possible Way Forward*, Africa Briefing 56 (Pretoria/Brussels: ICG, 16 December 2008), 5.

49. A press statement released in Harare 7 January 2009 by the MDC information department criticized the SADC summit resolution.

50. From January 2009 to January 2010, the consumer price index declined by 4.8 percent against a projected 7 percent, although inflation will rise again and is projected to increase by 5.1 percent in 2010. See "Zimbabwe Inflation Rising as Disinflationary Effect of Hard-Currency Move Fades," *VOA News.com*, 24 March 2010, http://www1.voanews.com/zimbabwe/news/economy/Zimbabwe-Consumer-Prices-Rises-IMF-Weighs-Restoring-Voting-Rights-18Feb10-84724062.html (accessed March 2010).

51. A good example is the Marange diamond field near Mutare, belonging to UK-based African Consolidated Resources (ACR) and seized by the govern-

ment in 2006, then invaded by squatters mining illegally until it was taken over by the army in 2008 with brutal force and several hundred civilians killed. Army generals conscripted neighboring villagers to dig the mines and the diamonds ended on the black market. ZANU-PF factions fought over control of the mining rights, but eventually all party big men—including Mugabe—got their share. See "Zimbabwe's Great Diamond Rush Brutally Suppressed by Robert Mugabe's Regime," *Telegraph* online, 26 March 2009, http://www.telegraph.co.uk; also "Mutare's diamond trail", *New Zimbabwe.com*, 11 December 2009, http://www .newzimbabwe.com (both accessed March 2010).

52. See Ruth Weiss, *Sir Garfield Todd and the Making of Zimbabwe* (London: Tauris, 1998); Judith Garfield Todd, *Through the Darkness: A Life in Zimbabwe* (Cape Town: Zebra Press, 2007); Timothy Scarnecchia, *The Urban Roots of Democracy and Political Violence in Zimbabwe: Harare and Highfield, 1940–1964* (Rochester, N.Y.: University of Rochester Press, 2008).

53. "Preventive diplomacy" is at the heart of the new African Union and its strategy to deal with conflicts on the continent, allegedly in sharp contrast with past OAU inaction. "Preventive diplomacy" is mentioned in sections 3 and 6 of the protocol establishing the African Peace and Security Council.

Index

Acknowledgments

This book would never had been written without Diana Mitchell's friendship and support to my research activities in Zimbabwe, her and Brian's wonderful hospitality, and her careful editing of the draft at various stages of completion. Although I bear responsibility for the ideas and analyses in this book, and all the mistakes they might include, Diana shared with me her intimate knowledge of Zimbabwean (and Rhodesian) politics, and she helped shape the contents of the manuscript. Therefore I remain indebted and grateful to her.

I wish to thank also Michael Dwyer, who originally sponsored the project, and the Université Antilles Guyane (CAGI), which funded my research trips to Zimbabwe. I lived in Zimbabwe from July 1994 to June 1997, and have visited the country several times since then. I wish to thank the Zimbabweans who helped me in my research, whether they are cited in this book or remain anonymous, as they are ultimately my best source of information. Many of them are dedicated activists fighting dictatorship, corruption, and violence, sometimes for several decades—some died for this ideal. It is to them and to the people of Zimbabwe that this book is dedicated.

Stephen Ellis read parts of the manuscript and made some useful comments. Norma Kriger carefully read it throughout and contributed valuable detailed corrections and additions far beyond the usual reviewer's brief. Another anonymous reviewer was also very constructive in commenting on the manuscript. However, I was not able to implement all the reviewers' wonderful suggestions, and the defects that remain are mine entirely.

Last but not least, Bill Finan and Alison Anderson did a very fine job at the University of Pennsylvania Press in editing the manuscript for publication—my broken English being an additional complication. I am grateful for their enthusiasm and professionalism.